Advance praise for

Teaching Green: The High Sch...

"*Teaching Green: The High School Years* is a treasure trove for environmental educators who want to engage teens in developing skills and abilities to understand and constructively address today's complex issues. Every educator of secondary students will find useful ideas here."

— KAREN HOLLWEG, 2008 President of the
North American Association for Environmental Education

"As a teacher educator, I am always on the lookout for resources to recommend, particularly secondary-level materials. For those teaching in schools or non-formal settings, this jam-packed book is filled with practical and innovative activities and ideas. I highly recommend it."

— CONSTANCE RUSSELL, Co-Editor, *Canadian Journal of Environmental Education*, and Professor, Faculty of Education, Lakehead University

"*Teaching Green: The High School Years* completes a valuable series of environmental education resources. This practical resource presents stories from educators in the field in a way that enables others to embark on similar journeys. It is especially useful to find many of my favorite *Green Teacher* articles included in one high school-focused collection."

— PETA WHITE, President, Saskatchewan Outdoor and
Environmental Education Association

"For those willing to engage students directly in authentic learning experiences, *Teaching Green: The High School Years* is the most stimulating, useful book that I have seen in the past 50 years. It is a 'must have' guide for any educator who wants to grow their teaching beyond teacher-centered traditions to powerful student-centered learning within an authentic context of environment and sustainability applications. The entire text is filled with useful practical exemplars that 'teach' the academics in an applied, timely and critical life context."

— WILLIAM "BILL" HAMMOND, Professor Emeritus,
Florida Gulf Coast University

Teaching Green
The High School Years

Hands-on Learning
in Grades 9-12

Edited by Tim Grant and Gail Littlejohn

NEW SOCIETY PUBLISHERS

Cataloging in Publication Data:

A catalog record for this publication is available from the National Library of Canada.

Cover design by Diane McIntosh.

Printed in Canada.

Green Teacher acknowledges the support of The Ontario Trillium Foundation, an agency of the Ontario Ministry of Culture.

THE ONTARIO TRILLIUM FOUNDATION

LA FONDATION TRILLIUM DE L'ONTARIO

New Society Publishers acknowledges the support of the Government of Canada through the Book Publishing Industry Development Program (BPIDP) for our publishing activities.

Paperback ISBN: 978-0-86571-648-3

To order directly from the publishers, please contact:

GREEN TEACHER
95 Robert Street, Toronto, ON M5S 2K5, Canada
P.O. Box 452, Niagara Falls, NY 14304-0452, USA
Toll-free (North America): 1-888-804-1486
Outside North America: 1-416-960-1244
www.greenteacher.com

or

NEW SOCIETY PUBLISHERS
P.O. Box 189, Gabriola Island, BC V0R 1X0, Canada
1-800-567-6772
www.newsociety.com

New Society Publishers' mission is to publish books that contribute in fundamental ways to building an ecologically sustainable and just society, and to do so with the least possible impact on the environment, in a manner that models this vision. Green Teacher's mission is to publish resources that help educators to foster young people's appreciation of the natural environment, understanding of the Earth's systems, and desire and ability to apply their knowledge in solving environmental problems. Both organizations are acting on their environmental commitments by phasing out paper supplies from ancient forests worldwide. This book is one step towards ending global deforestation and climate change. It is printed on acid-free paper that is **100% old growth forest-free** (100% post-consumer recycled), processed chlorine-free, and printed with vegetable-based, low-VOC inks.

FSC
Recycled
Supporting responsible use of forest resources
www.fsc.org Cert no. SW-COC-1271
© 1996 Forest Stewardship Council

NEW SOCIETY PUBLISHERS
www.newsociety.com

Table of Contents

Acknowledgments vii

Introduction ix

Approaches to Learning

Teaching for the Future: Systems Thinking and Sustainability *by John Goekler* (L, S, SS) 2

From Learners to Leaders: Using Creative Problem Solving in Environmental Projects
by David Bauer, David Hetherly and Susan Keller-Mathers (S) 10

Teaching Controversial Issues *by Pat Clarke* (L, SS) 18

Integrated Studies in Systems *by Pam Russell* (L, S, SS) 22

Tamarack: Responsibility, Community and Authenticity *by Bill Patterson* (L, O, S, SS) 28

The Small School: Human-scale Education *by Satish Kumar* (All) 31

Environmental Industries Co-op Education *by John Perry* (L, M, S) 36

Education for Sustainability: An Ecological Approach *by Marc Companion* (All) 40

Learning About Ecosystems

Discovering Lake Management *by Matthew R. Opdyke* (S) 46

The Tantramar Wetlands Centre Project *by Chris Porter* (A, S, T) 53

Using Epiphytic Lichens as Bio-indicators of Air Pollution *by Andrew Kett, Sonia Dong,*
Heather Andrachuk and Brian Craig (A, M, S, SS) 58

Carbon Cycle: Measuring CO_2 Flux from Soil *by Robert Lessard, L. Dennis Gignac*
and Philippe Rochette (M, S) 64

Tank Tips: A Freshwater Aquarium in the Classroom *by Rebecca Holcombe* (L, M, S, SS) 70

Nitrogen Pollution: Too Much of a Good Thing *by David A. Bainbridge* (M, S, SS) 75

Living Systems in the Classroom *by Mark Keffer* (S) 82

RiverWatch: Science on the River *by Cal Kullman* (S) 91

Living Sustainably

Eco-economics in the Classroom *by Susan Santone* (B, SS) 96

Measuring Your School's Ecological Footprint *by Julie Sawchuk and Tim Cameron* (S, SS, M) 103

Choosing Our Future *by Jan Cincera* (S, SS) 110

Linking Trade, Human Rights and the Environment *by Tricia Jane Edgar* (B, SS) 114

The subject codes shown in brackets are as follows:
A=Art; All=cross-curricular; B=Business Studies; H=Home Economics; L=Language Arts; M=Math;
O=Outdoor Education; S=Science; SS=Social Studies; T=Technology

Planet Transit: Profit or Survival? *by Georgi Marshall* (B, SS) 121

Global Morning: A Consumer Awareness Activity *by Mary Gale Smith* (B, H, SS, L) 127

The Debate About Hemp: A Role Play *by Sara Francis* (SS) 133

Teaching About Biodiesel *by Richard Lawrence* (S, T) 139

Making Biodiesel from Waste Vegetable Oil *by Alison K. Varty and Shane C. Lishawa* (S) 141

Small-scale Science *by Alan Slater* (S) 146

Green Driving Lessons: Oxymoron or Opportunity? *by Tim Altieri* (M, SS) 150

Making Interdisciplinary Connections

Green Mapmaking *by Robert Zuber and Wendy E. Brawer* (L, S, SS, T) 156

Connecting Students with Special Needs to the Environment *by Lynn Dominguez
   and Mary Lou Schilling* (O, S) 161

Exploring the Earth Charter *by Linda Hill* (SS) 165

Walking into Wonder *by Cynthia Macleod* (A, L, S) 173

Building Green *by Jennifer Wolf* (T) 177

Ancestral Arts *by Elizabeth Lorentzen* (A, S, SS) 183

GIS in the Classroom *by Marsha Alibrandi* (S, SS, T) 187

Voices of the Land: A Course in Environmental Literature *by Emma Wood Rous* (L) 191

Social Justice and Language Arts *by Christopher Greenslate* (L) 197

Designing a Green City *by Iori Miller and Susan Sheard* (L, S, SS) 202

Exemplary Models and Programs

Global Field Trip *by Rosemary Ganley* (SS) 208

Tips for Successful Overseas Projects *by Alana Robb* (SS) 211

The Earth Community School *by Frans C. Verhagen* (All) 212

Soy-powered Learning *by Gail Littlejohn* (S, T) 216

The Steveston Fish Hatchery *by Bob Carkner and Barry Barnes* (S) 218

The Living Machine at Darrow School *by Lisa Riker* (S, T) 221

The subject codes shown in brackets are as follows:

A=Art; All=cross-curricular; B=Business Studies; H=Home Economics; L=Language Arts; M=Math;

O=Outdoor Education; S=Science; SS=Social Studies; T=Technology

Acknowledgments

More than 200 individuals have contributed their time and expertise to the publication of this third "best of *Green Teacher*" book in our *Teaching Green* series. In particular, we thank the dozens of contributing authors who have shared their wide-ranging knowledge, their diverse experience and their passion for a new model of education. Most of them volunteered their time to revise articles they had previously contributed to *Green Teacher* magazine, in most cases updating teaching strategies and activities to reflect current practices and further developing their ideas in response to the comments of reviewers.

We also owe an enormous debt to a group of educators who gave their time to review and critique the proposed contents of the book. Their detailed and thoughtful comments showed us where improvements were needed and helped to guide authors in their revisions. They also suggested many additional topics, some of which we incorporated in order to make the book a more complete and helpful resource. We thank the following reviewers:

AUSTRALIA

Tasmania – Nel Smit

CANADA

Alberta – David Gue, David Lunn, Marie Meeres, Julia Millen

British Columbia – Liza Ireland, Del Morgan, Mary Gale Smith, Sue Staniforth

Manitoba – Brock Brown, Heidi Holst, Barbara A. McMillan, John Perry

New Brunswick – Katherine Bunker-Popma, Trevor Gallant

Newfoundland – Grant A. Gardner, Jean Harding, Joanne McGrath Power

Northwest Territories – Mike Mitchel

Nova Scotia – Janet Barlow, Susan Dean, Daisy Kidston, Sylvia Moore, Stephanie Sodero, Airin Stephens, Heather Taylor, Alan Warner, Tracy Webb

Ontario – Judy Arai, Heather Arnold, Melanie Climenhage, Christopher J. Clovis, Joan Cornfield, Ian Crawford, Katie Gad, Gordon Lewer, Stana Luxford, Amanda MacIvor, Mark Mitchell, Tim Murphy, Julia Nicholson, Niki Popper, Constance Russell, Laurie Schutt, Elizabeth Straszynski

Québec – Loyola Leroux

Saskatchewan – Ken Boyd, Rhonda Phillips

Yukon – David Benton, Gregory Heming, Lina Radziunas

NEW ZEALAND

Lynette Brown

UNITED STATES

Alabama – Shawn A. Bivens, Francine Hutchinson

Arizona – Edward Franklin, Jo Miller, Christine L. Newell, Monica Pastor, Tonya Randolph

California – Rob Ewing, Dave Ficke, Kathe Poteet, Scott C. Silverman

Colorado – Sue Kenney, Betsy A. Leonard, Camille Schiraldi, Beth Simmons

Connecticut – Kristen Allore, Laura Castro-Rogers, Heidi A. Rerecich, Ellen Turner

District of Columbia – Karen Heys

Florida – Laura O'Brien

Georgia – Deb Goldberg

Illinois – Peter Berg, Cathy Bartlow, Sabiha S. Daudi, Laura Kiedaisch, Cliff Knapp, Mark Spreyer

Indiana – Sam Carman, Lenore P. Tedesco

Maine – Bridget Butler

Massachusetts – Marsha Alibrandi

Michigan – David J. Wilson

Minnesota – Nalani McCutcheon, Nate Meyer

Mississippi – John Guyton

Missouri – Dan Lane, Janice Schnake Greene

Montana – Bernie Smith

Nebraska – Marian Langan

New Hampshire – Pamela Caswell

New Jersey – Scott Bortnick, Patricia Camp, Mary Jane Davis, Oresta M Ferrito, Dave Grant, Jessica Kratz, John Michalski, Michelle Painter, Laurie Pappas, Nancy Sklavos

New York – April Anderson, Karin Badey, Carmela M. Federico, Andrea Hines, David Kowalewski

North Carolina – Heather Lannon

Oklahoma – David Holder

Pennsylvania – Theresa Alberici

South Carolina – Leslie Hill

Tennessee – Maurice Houston Field, Tom Howick, Julia Sherman

Vermont – Jimmy Karlan

Virginia – Charles K. Jervis, Mary Lynn Everhart, Lee Teevan

Washington – David Greenwood

Wisconsin – Greg Bisbee, Jennifer Kobylecky, Kristen Mueller, Dan Sivek, Lynn Terrien

Finally, we offer our heartfelt appreciation for those who worked behind the scenes to make this book a reality: a group of Ontario educators whose letters of support helped us obtain funding from a competitive grants program; the editorial staff at New Society Publishers; Lisa Rebnord, who produced the attractive layout; and last but not least, our editorial assistants, Lisa Newman and Pamela Clark, whose months of patient fact-checking, research and assembly work were critical to the creation of this book.

Tim Grant and Gail Littlejohn
Toronto

Introduction

by Tim Grant and Gail Littlejohn

Since 1991, we have had the pleasure of working with a great many inspired educators who have shared their innovative environmental education programs, strategies and activities in the pages of *Green Teacher* magazine. This book is a selection of the best of those "green" teaching ideas for educators who work with young people of high school age. Virtually all of the 55 contributors have revised and updated their articles based on the comments and suggestions of reviewers. The result is a wide variety of up-to-date activities and teaching strategies designed to engage adolescents in learning the fundamentals of environmental citizenship in the 21st century. Some are strategies for teaching about local ecosystems and what is needed to protect them. Others explore lifestyle changes that may be required if we are to lessen our environmental impact and live more sustainably on the planet. Still others help students recognize global disparities in resource use and our connections with other peoples and other species. Perhaps most important, many of the activities provide opportunities for young people to develop and reflect on their values and to consider how they might take an active role in solving environmental problems, both locally and globally.

But what exactly does it mean to "teach green"? While definitions and frameworks abound among environmental, global and outdoor educators, most agree on a few fundamental principles.

Students should have opportunities to develop a personal connection with nature.

We protect what we care about, and we care about what we know well. If teenagers are encouraged to explore the natural world — to learn about local plants and animals, to get their feet wet in local rivers — they are more likely to develop a lifelong love of nature that will translate into a lifelong commitment to environmental stewardship.

Education should emphasize our connections with other peoples and other species, and between human activities and planetary systems.

We are connected to other peoples, other species and other lands though the food we eat, the clothes we wear, the items and materials we use every day, and our common reliance on a healthy environment. If young people understand these global interdependencies, they are more likely to take steps to reduce inequalities, preserve biodiversity, and work together to find ways of lessening our impact on the Earth's life support systems.

Education should help students move from awareness to knowledge to action.

Awareness of environmental issues does not necessarily lead to action. When students have opportunities to act on environmental problems, they begin to understand the complexity of those problems, to learn the critical thinking and negotiating skills needed to solve them, and to develop the practical competence that democratic societies require of their citizens.

Learning should extend into the community.

Community partnerships and service learning projects provide authentic "real-world" reference points for classroom studies and help students develop a sense of place and identity while learning the values and skills of responsible citizenship.

Learning should be hands-on.

The benefits of hands-on learning are widely acknowledged among educators and supported by findings in brain research. Learning is a function of experience, and the best education is one that is sensory-rich, emotionally engaging and linked to the real world.

Education should be future-oriented.

In order to solve environmental problems we need to think about the future, or what British educator David Hicks has called "that part of history that we can change." Teenagers should have opportunities to explore alternatives to our current paths of development, to consider the kind of world they would like to live in, and to think realistically about incremental steps that might be taken to achieve it.

Education should include media literacy.

With constant exposure to mass media, our mental environments can become just as polluted as the natural environment. Media studies can help students learn to distinguish between fact and fiction in advertising, to recognize racial and gender stereotypes and to consider the difference between needs and wants.

Education should include traditional knowledge.

It is important that young people become aware that our dominant scientific, social and economic models represent a worldview that is not held by everyone. Native elders can share aboriginal perspectives on nature and ecology, exposing students to a worldview that recognizes the intrinsic value and interdependence of all living things. Further, the stories of grandparents and other elders in our communities can help young people realize that the consumer society is a very recent development and that many people in the past enjoyed satisfying lives with fewer material possessions and less strain on the Earth's resources.

Teachers should be facilitators and co-learners.

An educator's role is to facilitate inquiry and provide opportunities for learning, not to provide the "answers." Teachers do not need to be experts to teach about the environment. The natural world is an open book that invites endless discovery for all. As co-learners alongside their students, teachers both model and share in the joy of learning.

Education should integrate subject disciplines.

The division of high school education into separate subjects reflects the Western philosophical tradition of dissecting knowledge into discrete branches and is maintained in large part to meet the entrance requirements of colleges and universities. The emergence of global environmental problems exposes the weaknesses of this subject-based learning. Environmental issues are complex, and addressing them requires holistic perspectives and knowledge and skills from all disciplines. Students need to be able to grasp the "big picture" of environmental problems if they are to find ways to effect change. Integrated learning programs in which students apply expertise from all of their subjects, often through field studies and community projects on issues of importance, offer one way to help students develop that big-picture understanding and provide opportunities for authentic learning.

Whether you are just beginning or are an old hand at environmental education, we hope you will find many ideas in this book to enrich your teaching. The Table of Contents indicates the subject areas with which each article is most closely aligned; and on the first page of each article is a handy summary that indicates the subject connections, key concepts, skills to be developed and, if appropriate, the time and materials needed to carry out activities. With more than 50 individual contributors, the book presents a diverse mix of approaches and styles and a wide spectrum of environmental topics. It only tangentially addresses climate change, a topic now central to many environmental education programs. In response to the anticipated impact of climate change in the coming decades, we have published a separate book, *Teaching About Climate Change* (2001), which is a collection of some of the best articles and activities on the topic from *Green Teacher* magazine.

The environmental and social problems bedeviling humankind will not be solved by the same kind of education that helped create these problems. It is our hope that this book — and the companion books for the elementary and middle school levels — will inspire educators to take a leading role in helping the next generation to develop the knowledge, skills and values that will enable them to enjoy and share the Earth's bounty while living within its means.

Approaches to Learning

John Steer

❀ **Teaching for the Future** by John Goekler

❀ **From Learners to Leaders: Creative Problem Solving** by David Bauer, David Hetherly and Susan Keller-Mathers

❀ **Teaching Controversial Issues** by Pat Clarke

❀ **Integrated Studies in Systems** by Pam Russell

❀ **TAMARACK: Responsibility, Community and Authenticity** by Bill Patterson

❀ **The Small School: Human-scale Education** by Satish Kumar

❀ **Environmental Industries Co-op Education** by John Perry

❀ **Education for Sustainability: An Ecological Approach** by Marc Companion

Teaching for the Future:
Systems Thinking and Sustainability

*To create a greener, more peaceful future,
we need a shared vision based on a new worldview*

by John Goekler

Subject areas: environmental science, physical science, social studies, language arts

Key concepts: systems thinking, mental models and worldviews, the process of change, visioning

Skills: observation, critical and conceptual thinking, visioning, diagramming

Location: classroom

Time: one class period for introductory concepts and terminology; one additional period for each activity selected

Materials: chart paper, markers or crayons

To anyone who has been involved in environmental education for a while, it's clear that the serious problems facing the human community haven't changed much over the past few decades. Far from abating, critical issues such as deforestation, extinction of species and atmospheric pollution — to name a few — are accelerating. In the social arena, war, poverty, disease and the unraveling of civil society are today as prevalent, or more so, as they were ten, twenty or thirty years ago. Most of these problems have not only persisted, but intensified, despite — and sometimes because of — innumerable policies and programs intended to resolve them. We've written thousands of laws and allocated trillions of dollars to prevention, intervention and remediation, and yet we are no closer to world peace, a sustainable economy and a cleaner global environment.

Why is this so? Quite simply, I would argue, because these problems are caused by the ways we think, learn and communicate. Our thinking determines the kind of political, economic and social structures we build; and those, in turn, create the patterns of events we see in the world and study in our classrooms. If we want to change those events, we must change the structures that create them, which means we must learn to change the way we think and to communicate that learning effectively.

In the course of my work, I have led workshops for educators, students and community activists across North America. In the beginning, I emphasized facts, figures and trends, assuming that telling people enough bad news would somehow motivate them to change. But most already knew the bad news. And if they didn't, the announcement of potential calamity not only failed to motivate them, but often drove them into denial or despair. One of the most difficult things about being an educator, I learned, is that we know too much about the state of the world. And we are working with young people who also know too much and are fearful of their future. Sobered by this, I began to emphasize personal and structural solutions and the actions each of us can take to implement those.

I learned something else, too — that most of us are already aware of the solutions. For instance, I often give workshop participants the following exercise, based on a simulation developed by ecologist Paul Hawken:

The Earth has been severely degraded, to the point that it will no longer support our population. You and your team must design a spaceship capable of making a 6,000-year voyage, carrying everyone that you care about, and bringing their descendants back to Earth safe and happy. Propulsion and construction are already taken care of, so you don't have to figure out how to move the vessel or construct the hull. What you do have to deal with are the life support systems (oxygen, food, water, energy and waste) and the social systems (governance, recreation and entertainment). The ship can be as large as you want. The only thing you can take in is sunlight, and the only thing you can

exhaust is heat. Everything must be done using existing technology.

What's interesting about this exercise is that the participants typically succeed. They come up with clean, renewable power, sustainable agriculture, natural hydrologic cycles, oxygen-generating forests and oceans, and closed-loop systems in which everything is recycled and reused. They also mandate a stable population, social and gender equity (because anything else is an invitation to mutiny), a crew that includes not only engineers, scientists, healers and teachers, but also artists, musicians, dancers and storytellers. And they tend to choose a meritocracy in command. In short, they design a sustainable system aimed at maximizing not only security, but also happiness. Sometimes it takes a bit of prompting, but most also make the connection between this Star Trek scenario and the big blue-green spaceship we're currently flying through the galaxy.

Which brings us to a hard question: If we recognize not only the problems, but also the solutions, why don't we create a just, secure and sustainable world? The easy answer is to blame someone else — often government or corporations — or to put it down to political, structural or economic roadblocks. But the real roadblocks are not material. They are mental, cultural and educational. Belief underlies behavior, and all of the things we do or don't do are shaped by the ideas we hold about how the world works — in other words, by our worldview.

Windows on our worldview

What is a worldview? It is a collection of assumptions, which we believe are self-evident truths, that both interpret our past and to a great extent determine our future. Since our worldview is our built-in "operating system," we are not even aware that our ideas and actions are filtered through it. In fact, a worldview could be described as a mental environment that is to humans what water is to a fish — the stuff we swim around in every day and do not even recognize.

If we explore the dominant worldview (which might once have been called the "western" worldview, but which has now spread across virtually all borders and cultures with the adoption of western economic models) we encounter certain key assumptions:

- Constant and unlimited growth is not only possible, but essential.

- Humans have dominion over the Earth.

- Nature is income — resources are free because we "found" them.

- If we destroy our environment, we can simply move west or invent some new technology to save us.

- We can understand the natural world through reductionism: that is, by breaking it down into small parts.

It is helpful to explore these assumptions with students. Ask them to look closely to see if (or how) they are manifested in the curriculum they study, particularly in history, science, global studies or contemporary world issues. For example, how are our scientific models reductionist in their worldview? Is "smart growth" a component of local land use planning? How do accounting practices discount or ignore ("externalize") environmental impacts? How do we attempt to manifest our "dominion" over the Earth, such as in efforts to "control" or "defeat" nature through interruption of natural processes? And how often do we speak of dealing with such issues as population growth and resource depletion by saying we will "just" colonize space?

As we examine the assumptions of the dominant worldview, we see that it is an open-system view. It assumes a world without limits — a world of unlimited land, unlimited resources, and unlimited human knowledge and wisdom. To be fair, it has served us reasonably well for several centuries. Today, however, it is clearly false and increasingly dangerous. The only biological model for unlimited growth, after all, is a cancer cell, which ultimately kills its host. Humans are only a small part of the Earth, entirely dependent upon it, and most certainly not in control of it.

Creating a Vision and Acting from It
An exercise for implementing and managing change

This exercise teaches critical thinking and can serve as a template for solving problems and implementing change in your classroom, school or community. It can be used at a very local level, such as in creating the best learning environment in your classroom, or can be applied to tackling global challenges such as creating a safe, sustainable energy future.

Introduction
1. If applying this exercise to global challenges, begin by asking students to describe briefly what the world will look like in 20 years. Then ask them what they want the world to look like in 20 years, especially as they begin to raise their own children. Students may either brainstorm collaboratively in small groups or complete individual free-writing assignments outlining their vision of the future. To help them imagine their ideal future, suggest that they address specific human needs and quality-of-life issues, such as food, water, energy, housing, work, transportation, education, peace, the environment, security and governance. Encourage them to focus on what they want rather than on what they don't want. For example, instead of saying, "We won't use polluting fossil fuels," say, "In the future, we'll use only clean, renewable energy."

Observe
Orient
Decide
Act

To apply the exercise at a local level, break it down into much smaller pieces and shorter timeframes that students will be able to imagine and monitor more easily. As an example, ask them to visualize how they would like their school to work in order to maximize learning, safety and happiness, and to minimize environmental impacts. Components might be scheduling, classroom management, recycling, food systems and energy use.

2. Have the students share the most important elements of their visions and make a class list of these elements. Then divide the class into groups and assign each group one topic from the list. Ask students to use the planning sequence below to develop an action plan for creating the future they envision. As they work, circulate among the groups to facilitate and keep them thinking in positive terms.

Action planning sequence
1. Visualize your desired outcome: Brainstorm, discuss, and write a summary of your desired outcome for your specific topic (e.g., school energy efficiency, waste reduction, or a safe and supportive classroom and school environment). Define as clearly as possible "How things will be."

Nature is an endowment — a savings account, if you will — and when it is gone, so are we. We have now grown to the western edge of an entire civilization of western expansion and are, as the old seafarers would say, "beached" on planet Earth. And while reduction-ism can lead to some valuable insights, it cannot explain how a spider knows geometry or a microscopic seed carries within it both the genetic blueprint for and the commitment to create a new life.

Yet we continue to cling to our worldview, and we continue to act out of it. When things don't work, we do them harder, we do them longer, we throw more money at them. We're like the fabled tourist abroad, who, upon discovering that the natives don't speak his language, simply repeats himself at higher and higher volume. We are not doing this because we are evil, excessively greedy or terminally stupid. We're doing it because we are loyal to our culture and because our culture rewards and reinforces this behavior. We are also acting out of our own evolutionary mandate. For almost all of human history, we lived in small groups in local ecosystems and had to think only in very short time frames ("We need to find some food" or "Watch out for that cave bear!"). Thus we evolved to relate to and care about small numbers of people, to pay atten-tion only to our immediate surroundings, and to be concerned only about short-term events and trends. All of this made sense for the first two or three million years of human existence, but it has become a tremen-dous handicap in today's world of six-plus billion people, climate change, bio-terrorism, and toxic wastes that have half-lives measured in millennia.

The game has changed — in large part because of our own success as a species — and we must learn to change with it. We must not only change our actions; we must change our ways of thinking, because, as Einstein observed, "We can't solve problems by using the same kind of thinking we used when we created them."

2. Gather companions: A vision must be shared to unleash its power. Brainstorm, discuss, and list people and groups that share a similar vision and are stakeholders or poten-tial allies in this work. Plan how to invite those people into the process.

3. Identify and prioritize objectives: Brainstorm, discuss, list and prioritize two or three key steps or components necessary to achieve your vision. In other words, what are some specific things you will need to accomplish in order to reach your goal?

4. Identify the obstacles (including your own ways of thinking!) that might get in the way of realizing your vision. List a number of these and include ways to address them that are compatible with the values of your vision. (This means, for example, that you cannot bomb people in order to achieve peace.)

5. Identify resources, information and assistance avail-able to help achieve your vision.

6. Implement your plan.

Change management model

Once your plan is implemented, a change management model will help you monitor how you are doing and make corrections to keep on track:

Observe: What are we doing? What are the current con-ditions? What resources are being depleted and what new ones have become available? (In an energy audit, for example, current electric bills are necessary, as are technologies for reducing them, such as compact fluores-cent bulbs, insulation and appliance timers.)

Orient: What trends are developing? How is our plan working? Are we making progress toward our goals? What new obstacles or allies have emerged?

Decide: In light of those changing conditions — and in concert with our vision — what new plan or action do we need to undertake?

Act: And then do it again — observe, orient, decide, act — and keep doing it.

You must do this continuously, because working towards a vision is a dynamic, evolving process in which conditions continuously change. It is very important to remember that success changes the game, so that doing what you did before will not give you the same result. The hardest thing of all — because we all get tunnel vision under stress — is deciding what to do when things are not work-ing. Stop what you're doing! Don't do it harder. Don't do it longer. Don't throw more resources at it. Instead, back off, regroup, and work through the change management model to resolve the problem.

Any process of change is a complex system. It is goal-driven, interactive, and has both positive and negative feedback loops built in. But it won't operate in a vacuum. It needs a vision to drive it.

— by **John Goekler**, based on the exercise "Creating Our Future" by Facing the Future.

Teaching for the future

If the ways of thinking that got us to this point are inadequate for the future, how do we consciously learn to think in new ways? And how do we communicate or teach that learning? It begins with understanding the nature of the problem. Systems thinkers sometimes use an "iceberg" model, so named because its shape is much like the natural object. At the tip of the iceberg — the ten percent we see above the surface — are events such as we see on the news or read about in the newspaper. But if we look beneath the surface, we can see that these events are part of larger patterns. If we look further below the surface, we see that structures — political, economic and social — create these patterns. And if we look all the way down to the base of the iceberg — to the great mass upon which the currents push to determine the berg's movement — we see paradigms. These are the beliefs we hold about how the world works, and these beliefs generate the structures that create the patterns of events we so often find appalling.

Paradigms, also called mental models, are not only assumptions about how things are. They are also a commitment to making things that way. They lead us to treat our assumptions as facts, and since they profoundly influence the results we get from our actions, they are self-reinforcing.

We do not have to look very far for an example of how our mental models generate unintended negative outcomes. Brain research tells us that adolescents do not learn very well early in the day. But we persist in scheduling early classes because we hold the mental model that we need to maximize bus efficiency to save money, and (less often acknowledged) that we must warehouse children during parents' working hours. If instead we held the model that schools are to maximize learning and fulfillment for our children, we would organize them quite differently and solve transport and babysitting issues in new and more creative ways.

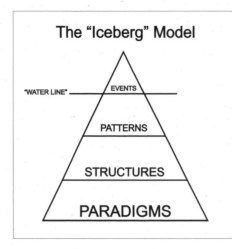

The "Iceberg" Model

"WATER LINE"

EVENTS

PATTERNS

STRUCTURES

PARADIGMS

Change Factors 2003

Mental models in the classroom

There are simple and non-threatening ways to challenge our own mental models and those of our students. One of my favorite ways is using the exercises in *The Systems Thinking Playbook* by Dennis Meadows and Linda Booth Sweeney.[1] The book offers a number of quick little exercises called "Mind Grooving" that can help us see how our own mental models operate. Here are a few to try:

Word Association: In this exercise, words are spoken in sequence and students write down the first word that pops into their minds. The sequence is as follows: a color, a piece of furniture, a flower. Ask students to write down their words and then ask for a show of hands. How many people said "red"? How many said "chair"? How many said "rose"? How many people said "blue"? "couch"? "daisy"? How many said some combination of the above: red or blue, chair or couch, rose or daisy?

I've done this with groups ranging from fewer than a dozen students to hundreds of teachers, and typically three quarters or more of the participants say "red, chair, rose" or "blue, couch, daisy," or some combination of these. How could this happen? After all, we North Americans like to think we're the most individualistic people on the planet. This exercise is a simple demonstration of how strong our socialization and enculturation are. A biologist would say our neural networks are operating — that we have learned to think in particular ways and, like wagon wheels in a rut, we follow those tracks. In short, we can see only what our mental models allow us to see. If some students say something completely different — "purple, table, lupine," for example — grab them. They see the world differently. They're not constrained by our mental models, and they can help us see differently, too. On the other hand, it's easy to beat this game by second-guessing — "He thinks I'll say X, so I'll say Y" — but coach students to try to respond naturally.

Oak, Joke, Croak: Ask in sequence: "What is the tree that grows from an acorn?" *(oak)*; "What do you call a funny story with a punch line?" *(joke)*; "What is the sound a frog makes?" *(croak)*; "What do you call the white of an egg?" Most people will respond "yolk." Of course, that's not right, but we are lulled by the pattern and answer automatically.

Thumb Wrestling: This is a simple game in which the instructor pairs off the participants and has them lock their right hands together with thumbs up. On the command "Go!" each player attempts to pin the other's thumb with his or her own. Offer a prize for the most pins, and then time a 60-second bout and ask how many pins were achieved. Typical responses are two, three or four. But someone is likely to have 50 or more. When we explore how this could be, we find that the opponents agreed to become partners to achieve the goal of winning the prize. One pinned the other repeatedly to collect the most pins, and then shared the prize. In this case, the mental model of competition (win-lose) guarantees failure, while the new model of collaboration (win-win) assures success.

Leverage for change

While mental models can trap us in dangerous ways (consider that there are over 25,000 nuclear weapons in the world, based on the "peace through strength" paradigm), they can also be very powerful agents for positive change. Remember the iceberg? Since it tells us where the most powerful leverage points are, we can turn it upside down to create a "ladder of influence" which looks like this:

Paradigm or Shared Vision (Generative Mode): The paradigmatic or shared vision level is the most powerful leverage point for change. When we hold a vision of the results we desire, that vision shapes everything else.

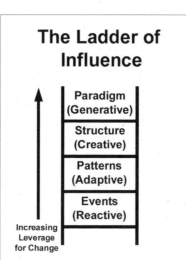

The Ladder of Influence

Paradigm (Generative)

Structure (Creative)

Patterns (Adaptive)

Events (Reactive)

Increasing Leverage for Change

Change must begin at the level of paradigm, or shared vision, which gives rise to the structures, patterns and events we observe.

Change Factors 2003

Systemic Structure (Creative Mode): We generate structures in response to our shared visions and paradigms. They are the means to the end we envision, and they in turn create the patterns of events we see.

Patterns of Events (Adaptive Mode): At this level, we can see the behavior that our systems create over time, which can help us break out of our short-term thinking. This is a learning level.

Events (Reactive Mode): The event level is purely a reactive one. At this level, all we can do is act in response to events, not change the pattern of events, much less the structure that spawns them.

We can see that if we want to create or manage change, we have to do so at a generative level, not a reactive one. If the goal of a system (the vision) changes, the results it generates will change, too. If we want different outcomes, we have to hold different visions. We also have to remember that, as Zen teaches, no action is an action. The lack of a positive vision engenders a chaotic or opportunistic system that can spiral off and create severely negative outcomes. Or, as songwriter Bruce Cockburn put it, "in the absence of a vision there are nightmares."

One powerful foil to random and opportunistic systems is the art and practice of systems thinking. It could well be the single most effective tool currently available to better understand the world we live in and to create a sustainable future.

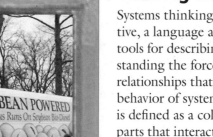

Thinking in systems

Systems thinking is a perspective, a language and a set of tools for describing and understanding the forces and interrelationships that shape the behavior of systems. A system is defined as a collection of parts that interact to function as a whole and continually affect each other over time. The parts of systems are not only interconnected, they are coherently organized around some purpose. Some examples of systems are a family, a soccer team and an airplane. Systems also have emergent properties not found in their separate parts. When the parts are organized into a system, they create new properties, characteristics and behaviors.

Systems thinkers can be identified by certain characteristics that they share. They:

- think long term
- see the big picture
- focus on structure, not on blame
- look for interdependencies and cause-and-effect relationships
- change perspectives to see new leverage points
- consider how mental models determine our future
- hold the tension of paradox and controversy without feeling the need to resolve them quickly

Comparing traditional mechanistic thinking to systems thinking, we see very significant differences.

Mechanistic thinking sees:	Systems thinking sees:
Parts	Wholes
Objects	Relationships
Events	Structures
Isolation	Interdependence
Specificity	Generality
Statics	Dynamics
Simplicity	Complexity

Watch Where You Step activity: A good way to get students thinking in a systems way is through an exercise called "Watch Where You Step."[2] This exercise asks students to work in groups of four to seven to brainstorm and diagram all the products, processes and impacts associated with seemingly simple things in their daily lives: their houses, their transportation to school, and their favorite food, possession and article of clothing. The exercise reveals interconnections and offers an expanding systems perspective as students see parts as components of larger wholes, objects within larger relationships, and the complexity that underlies seeming simplicity.

Exploring a favorite food — a hamburger, for example — spirals off into farmland,

grain production, irrigation (and potential water scarcity), pesticides and fertilizers (and potential pollution), soil erosion, tractors, trucks, fuel (and resulting emissions and contributions to global warming), packaging, the restaurant that served the burger, and on and on. I have students extend a roll of paper across the room as they trace the connections and impacts. When each group is finished, they explain their work and the most surprising thing they learned, and then place their diagrams side by side and brainstorm the interconnections between them. Because this new awareness of their impacts can be staggering, the follow-up is a brainstorming session to determine at least three things students can do as individuals or a group to lessen those impacts.

Creating the vision

There is a science fiction story about a man who builds a time machine to visit the future. When he comes back to the present, he tells people what he saw there. "It's beautiful," he says. "People are peaceful, healthy, creative and fulfilled. The Earth is pristine, poverty and disease have been defeated, art and music flourish."

Inspired by this vision of the future, people set off to create it, and they succeed. On his deathbed, the time traveler makes a confession. He never built a time machine and never visited the future. It was simply a vision of the future he hoped for. And it inspired and empowered people to create that future.

If shared vision is the most powerful leverage point for change, how do we go about forging it? Visioning is not something that comes easily to most of us. Perhaps because of that evolutionary upbringing mentioned earlier, many of us initially find it almost impossible to do. The good news is that visioning can be learned. And it can then be taught. Here's an easy exercise to begin practicing it.

It is 2050, and you're still here. Close your eyes, breathe deeply for a moment, and imagine what the world looks like and how it got that way. Is it ugly or scary? For those of us in environmental education, it often is. Because we simply know too much about current trends, our first responses are often negative. ("All the trees are gone. You can't breathe the air. Everything is radioactive. The animals are all extinct.") Many times, these negative visions express our deepest fears for the future. So we have to turn them gently toward the positive — to express not what we fear the future will be like, but what we want it to be like, what we wish for our own children some day, and for their children. Things begin to change when we do this. If we can express our greatest hopes, our deepest faith, our most powerful desires for the Earth, our compassion, courage and love, a picture of a very different, very positive and very possible future emerges.

Holding a positive vision of the future is much like planting a tree that takes many years to bear fruit. When you plant the seedling, you are undertaking an act of faith. You are believing that there will be a future. You are consciously choosing to do something, not for yourself, but for your grandchildren. You have to have a vision of that child sitting in the shade eating that fruit. You have to have the courage to believe in the future, the clarity to see that long view, and the commitment to see it through — not to cut it down for firewood to stay warm one night.

How do we instill that in our students? By becoming visionaries ourselves: by creating and sharing and calling into being visions of a just, humane and beautiful world. By stimulating imagination, because we must be able to imagine all these things are possible before they can be. By challenging and inspiring and fostering the best in ourselves and in our students. By building community and engaging with others in creative and constructive actions to move toward that shared vision. By modeling the skills we want to see in our students, by demonstrating courage, clarity, truthtelling, commitment and adaptability in our classrooms, in our schools and in our lives. And by being storytellers. For almost all of human history, stories were the way we learned, shared experience, transmitted wisdom and built community.

Today, our worldview — our story — no longer tells us of our place in the world or provides a context in which to root our communities. In short, it is inadequate to explain the times in which we live. Perhaps this is why so many people seem lost, why they pursue addictions or material gluttony, join cults or become survivalists. And why, most tragically of all, our young people are increasingly killing themselves and each other. As the wise old badger says in Barry Lopez's fable "Crow and Weasel," telling stories is how people care for each other. "Sometimes," the badger says, "a person needs a story more than food to stay alive."

Teaching for the future is really about changing the way we think, learn and communicate. It is about creating, telling and teaching new stories. These must be stories of compassion and community, faith and spirit, celebration and love. Stories of a just, sustainable and joyous future. And stories not only of, but in concert with, the beauty and wonder of the Earth.

John Goekler *is the principal of Change Factors, former executive director of Facing the Future: People and the Planet, author of* Population Issues, Impacts, and Solutions *and co-author of* Facing the Future: Population, Poverty, Consumption, and the Environment. *He lives in Santa Fe, New Mexico.*

Notes

1. Dennis Meadows and Linda Booth Sweeney, *The Systems Thinking Playbook: Exercises to Stretch and Build Learning and Systems Thinking Capabilities*, The Institute for Policy and Social Science Research, 2001.

2. "Watch Where You Step," in *Engaging Students Through Global Issues: Activity-based Lessons and Action Projects*, Facing the Future: People and the Planet, 2000, downloadable at <www.teacherscorner.org/activities.html>.

Resources

Hutchens, David. "Outlearning the Wolves," "The Lemming Dilemma" and "Shadows of the Neanderthal" in *Learning Fables*. Pegasus Communications, 2000.

Kim, Daniel. *Systems Thinking Tools: A User's Reference Guide*. Pegasus Communications, 2000.

Meadows, Donella H. *The Global Citizen*. Island Press, 1991. A collection of essays on systems thinking, sustainability and community.

Meadows, Donella H. "Places to Intervene in a System," *Whole Earth*, Winter 1997.

Meadows, Donella H. "Dancing With Systems," *Whole Earth*, Winter 2001.

Meadows, Donella H., Dennis L. Meadows and Jørgen Randers. *Beyond the Limits*. Chelsea Green Publishing, 1992.

Richmond, Barry. *The "Thinking" in Systems Thinking: Seven Essential Skills*. Pegasus Communications, 2000.

Walljasper, Jay and Jon Spayde. *Visionaries: People and Ideas to Change Your Life*. Utne Reader Books, 2001.

From Learners to Leaders:
Using Creative Problem Solving in Environmental Projects

Students brainstorming "obstacles to be overcome." Using Post-its allows the ideas to be easily grouped and arranged.

Photographs by David Bauer

**by David Bauer, David Hetherly and
Susan Keller-Mathers**

Subject areas: science, environmental science, student clubs and leadership organizations

Key concepts: divergent and convergent thinking, developing a plan of action, students as teachers, creative problem solving

Skills: problem solving, group leadership, project facilitation

Time: 45 minutes for practicing creative thinking tools; from three class periods to several weeks for project implementation

Materials: flipchart paper, colored adhesive dots, Post-it pads (3" x 3"), fine-point water-based colored markers

A s educators, we want our students to become independent thinkers, prepared for meeting life's challenges when they leave our classrooms. We take pride in helping them develop into leaders who are able to apply their knowledge and skills to improving society and the environment. This process requires time and energy. If students are to become leaders, they must have learning experiences that fill them with passion and purpose, and develop skills and attitudes for creative thinking and problem solving. Educators, in turn, must transform their teaching methods to reflect and support students' growth from learners to leaders. Creative problem solving is an excellent way to do this.

Creative problem solving is a process that can be used to guide groups and individuals in generating ideas, building on those ideas, and then putting them into action in order to create change. The guidelines for creative problem solving were mapped out in the 1950s by Alex Osborn, best known as the originator of the technique of brainstorming. Osborn's framework, later refined in collaboration with educator Sidney Parnes, has become the basis of many problem-solving approaches. It is a multi-step process in which participants move between divergence and convergence, or between the generation of ideas and the critical assessment and selection of those ideas. It is a means of looking at problems in new ways so that they become easier to solve. The model is flexible and easily adapted to the specific needs of the people involved and the problem they wish to solve.

Brainstorming issues related to the project's budget.

We have found creative problem solving to be particularly helpful in developing and implementing environmental projects with students. Following the model of Osborn and Parnes, we have developed an eight-step process that teachers and students can use to investigate any environmental topic, select a related problem that is of concern to them, and then develop and implement an action plan for creating change. Each step moves students closer to the role of leaders who are capable of taking action to address environmental problems. Because responsibility is gradually shifted from teacher to students, the role of the educator also changes throughout the eight steps. The teacher becomes a change leader, one who creates avenues for role reversal by removing barriers that inhibit students' growth; by cultivating students' knowledge, understanding and skills; and by exploring, critically evaluating and infusing novel ideas and methods into the learning.

In what follows, we outline the process of creative problem solving. As an example, we describe an environmental project that illustrates how the process can help students develop leadership through environmental action. We encourage teachers, club advisors and student leaders to adapt the process to their specific needs. One need not follow the entire process: any of the techniques can be used in any situation that calls for novel thinking and skillful decision making.

Pond Project: a case study

The construction in 2003 of a pond in the courtyard of Alden High School in Alden, New York, provides a good example of creative problem solving. This project was formulated by two student environmental groups, Friends of the Planet and ECO-COM, with their teacher, David Bauer. Bauer and the students began by investigating the topics of ponds and pond life. They then targeted issues of importance to them, brainstormed to generate ideas, and formulated and executed a successful action plan for constructing and operating a pond ecosystem. The resulting 3.5 x 6-meter structure contains two ponds connected by a small stream and fed by a cascading waterfall. The ponds beautify the courtyard, provide habitat for native plants and animals, and are used for aquatic studies by students throughout the school district. The project has heightened environmental awareness within the school and community and given students a passion for this environmental topic that is now self-sustaining.

The roles of Bauer and his students changed as the project progressed. The students began the learning experience as listeners, intent on grasping the information presented to them. Bauer, as their teacher, began as the conveyor of knowledge. As techniques of creative problem solving were integrated into the learning, Bauer moved into the facilitator role, guiding the process and allowing students to formulate and develop their own ideas. Eventually, the students began to put their ideas into action and thus became "doers." As the students became more competent and confident in their ability to work creatively, develop plans and seek solutions, Bauer moved into a consultative role, shifting more responsibility for the learning to the students. Ultimately, the students were able to implement their plans for the aquatic ecosystem with confidence and independence, and subsequently move into the teacher role, ready to ignite passion in others. At that stage, Bauer provided support as an adviser to the students, but was no longer central to creating change because the students had taken on that role.

This teacher-student role reversal is an important aspect of the creative problem-solving process — and of our goal as educators.

Students as ➡ Listeners ➡ Doers ➡ Teachers

➡ Students' increasing competence and confidence in their ability to work creatively, develop plans and seek solutions ➡

Teacher as ➡ Leader ➡ Facilitator ➡ Consultant

Left: Provide as many information-gathering opportunities as possible, including sharing prior knowledge. Right: Preparing water-testing kits for use in student-led workshops.

Eight-step process to creating environmental projects

Step 1: Introduce creative problem-solving concepts and tools

Before a project can begin, students must understand the concepts, rules and tools of creative problem solving. The two important concepts are divergence and convergence.

Divergence

Diverging means to branch out, to open up thinking in order to explore the topic or task at hand in new and exciting ways. Divergence is used when students want to generate new ideas, options and possibilities. The rules of divergence are:

1. Don't judge the ideas.

2. Generate a lot of ideas.

3. Generate wild and crazy ideas.

4. Build and improve on ideas.

In practice, this means using tools such as the following.

Brainstorming: Brainstorming is a well-known diverging tool used to generate ideas. In brainstorming, the facilitator writes the topic at the top of large chart paper, reviews the diverging rules with the group and then writes down the ideas of the group members as they are generated. The facilitator leads and guides the brainstorming process, but does not contribute ideas. A variation of this tool is called "Brainstorming with Post-its." As the students generate ideas, they quickly jot each idea on a Post-it note, raise their hand and then state their idea out loud as they hand their Post-it to the facilitator to stick on the chart paper. Using Post-its makes it easy for the group to arrange and sort ideas after the brainstorming session.

Forced Connections: This simple diverging tool is useful when students are having difficulty thinking of new

Rules of diverging and converging

Diverging

- Don't judge the ideas (wait until you are finished generating them).
- Generate a lot of ideas (at least 25 to start).
- Generate wild and crazy ideas (stretch your thinking).
- Build and improve on ideas (get ideas from other ideas; slight adaptations can be very useful).

Converging

- Be positive (focus on affirmative judgment).
- Have a goal (keep in mind the outcome that you want to achieve).
- Pay special attention to new ideas (particularly consider unusual or unique ideas).

—from *Big Tools for Young Thinkers*, Keller-Mathers and Puccio, 2000

Approaches to Learning

ideas while brainstorming. If a session begins to slow down, students are shown a toy, picture or other object that is unrelated to the topic, and asked, "What ideas can you get from this?" Forcing a relationship between the topic and an unrelated object can get their thinking "unstuck" and guide it in different and unusual directions.

Convergence

Converging involves bringing together divergent ideas, analyzing those ideas, and selecting the "hits," or those that look most promising. The rules of convergence are:

1. Be positive.

2. Have a goal.

3. Pay special attention to new ideas.

A simple converging tool for selecting key information or ideas is to hand out five colored adhesive dots to each student, allow them to review the information or ideas gathered, and ask them to place their dots next to the statements that they feel are most interesting, spark an idea or are particularly promising. When all of the dots have been placed, identify the statements that have gotten the most dots, or "hits." Selecting "hits" is a great tool to use in groups as it allows students to have equal input in selecting information or ideas.

Diverging (exploring a topic) and converging (selecting ideas) work together and are the heartbeat of the creative process. Use visuals to help students better understand and remember these concepts, and post the rules of diverging and converging around the classroom. Review them before every creative problem-solving exercise.

Have students practice these concepts and rules of creative problem solving in large groups, and then in smaller groups. Start slowly with practice problems that are simple and fun, avoiding any sensitive or highly controversial topics. For example, Bauer and his students practiced divergence by brainstorming ways in which a home aquarium functions as a pond. Then they converged by selecting the five most important ideas they had generated. This was a fun topic that allowed the students to concentrate on practicing the tools. Once students know how to use these tools and techniques well, they can apply them to a range of real-life challenges.

Step 2: Investigate the topic

Gather information on the environmental topic or problem by as many means and from as many sources as possible.

First, provide an opportunity for students to share what they already know about the topic. A simple way to do this is to ask students, individually or in small groups, to compile a list of ten things they know about the topic and then take turns presenting their lists to the class. An interview is another way for students to share their prior knowledge. Working in pairs, students interview one another, record their partners' responses, and then share the information with the class. Use the following data-gathering questions:

- What do you know about the topic or problem? (Who? What? Where? When? Why? How?)

- What are some of your impressions of this topic or problem? What have you observed?

- What do you think is key to this topic or problem?

Regardless of the technique used to draw out students' prior knowledge, the aim should be to fill the room with information. Show students that together they possess a wealth of information and that working as a team is the best way to investigate a topic and begin a project.

Once you have reviewed with students their prior knowledge, ask them to compile a list of things they would like to know by the time they are finished with the topic. Give them an opportunity to share their responses, and allow their interests to guide the next phase of information gathering. In addition to giving class lectures on the topic, encourage students to explore other sources of information, such as the Internet, journal and newspaper articles, books, case studies of others already working on the subject, guest speakers, information provided by businesses and corporations, and the expertise of parents and other teachers. If the project is school-wide, teachers from different subjects or grade levels may wish to collaborate on this step, having their classes gather and share information collectively.

When investigating a topic, students are essentially involved as listeners. Whether searching a site on the Internet, asking questions or participating in a discussion with a guest speaker, they are actively creating a foundation of information on the topic. It is important to allow students as many opportunities as possible to explore the topic. For example, as a creative way to gather information on ponds and pond life, the students at Alden High School visited a store that sells materials for constructing and maintaining ponds. They saw many examples of ponds and the equipment and materials needed to build them, learned how ponds are constructed, and interviewed a pond expert about pond life. This investigation gave the students a thorough base of information that enabled them to move on to the next step of the project.

At the end of each data-gathering experience, creative problem solvers use a technique called "debriefing" to assess understanding. Teachers should use this technique after any new learning experience to assess how students are doing. Debriefing is a way for students and teachers to share information and celebrate breakthroughs, as well as a guide to the direction of future learning. To debrief, ask your students:

- What did you experience? How did it go? What did you notice?

- What does this tell you about _____?

- How might you use this? What can you apply from today?

Putting the plan into action, a student arranges plants on the underwater shelves of the newly dug pond.

Step 3: Target the goal or challenge

Having gathered information on a broad, general topic of interest, students are now ready to select a specific environmental goal or challenge associated with their topic. This step has three stages: identifying the challenge, gathering information and clarifying the challenge.

Identifying the challenge

To help students find the goal or challenge associated with their topic, use a diverging technique called "Wouldn't it be great if...." Review the rules for divergent thinking and then ask students to list on chart paper all of their goals or wishes related to the topic. Have them phrase their ideas by beginning with "Wouldn't it be great if...." Phrasing statements in a positive, inquisitive manner opens a topic to possibilities. Here are some questions to get students started:

- What ideas have been on your mind since we first began learning about this topic?

- Why have they been on your mind?

- What could be done better in regard to this topic?

- What do you wish would happen as we learn about this topic?

- What do you see as the issues or challenges surrounding this topic?

After students list their wish statements, have them converge and select the most appropriate goal or challenge for the project. This should be a goal that students are motivated to pursue and one that will enable them to have some influence and to learn and experience new things. For example, Bauer and the students at Alden High School came up with the statement "Wouldn't it be great to have a pond to use for studying ponds and pond life?"

Gathering information related to the challenge

The next stage is to diverge in order to gather information specifically related to the goal or challenge that has been selected. Ask students to form small groups and use the same data-gathering questions that were used in the interview technique described in Step 2. For example, Bauer and his students used these questions: What do you know about pond life? What do you see when you look into a pond? What personal experiences have you had with ponds?

Have each group write their responses on chart paper and then share this information with the class. Then ask students to review the information on the charts and converge by marking the key information or "hits." Give each student five colored dots and remind them that they are to place the dots next to the statements that are most interesting, spark an idea or are particularly promising. Once they return to their groups, discuss the statements that have gathered the most interest. Those are the ideas that should help guide the project.

Clarifying the challenge

Stage three requires students to look at situations or problems in different ways, which is the basic premise of the creative problem-solving process. Have students diverge by restating, in as many different ways and from as many perspectives as possible, the goal or challenge they selected for the project. Start each statement with "Wouldn't it be great if..." or "How to?" For example, "Wouldn't it be great to have a pond to use for studying ponds and pond life" might now get restated as "How to get a pond on the school grounds for studying pond ecology?" and "How to raise environmental awareness?" and so on. If students get stuck, have them review the key data to get new ideas and perspectives.

Try to generate at least 25 different restatements of the challenge. Then have students mark the key ones. Discuss the statements that receive the most "hits," and have students select one of them for their project. At Alden High School, students selected the following clear and concise problem statement for their project: "How to build a pond ecosystem in the courtyard?"

Alden High School students take charge of cleaning and maintaining the pond year round.

Step 4: Generate ideas

Now you are ready to start generating ideas that move you toward finding solutions to your problem statement. Write the problem statement at the top of the board or on chart paper and review the rules for diverging. Then have students, in small groups or as a class, brainstorm ideas for addressing the goal of the project. When enough ideas have been generated, converge and select those that are most interesting or promising.

Step 5: Formulate an action plan

Now it is time to transform these ideas into a plan of action. First, review the most promising ideas from Step 4 and try to blend them together in the form of a written "idea phrase." Start your idea phrase with "What we see ourselves doing now is...." The idea phrase can be as long as you like — a paragraph is good — but should include as much detail as possible.

Second, start developing a plan of action. Ask, "What steps might you take to put your idea phrase into action?" List these steps in as much detail as much as possible. If students get stuck, ask some guiding questions, such as "Who or what might assist us?" and "Who or what might resist us?" Once you have listed all the actions that might be taken, mark the ones that

are essential to achieving your project goal. Next, make a chart with three headings: Action Step, Timeframe, and Who is Responsible. Select the action that must be accomplished first and enter it in the table. Have students decide, "Who is responsible?" and "By when?" Continue to enter each of the actions and the accompanying information.

Step 6: Execute the plan

Now that students have selected the challenge, generated ideas, and are prepared for action, it is time to execute the plan. At this stage, it will be helpful to follow these guidelines:

• Have your students execute one of the first steps of the plan within the next 24 hours. This is the period when creative juices are actively flowing and enthusiasm and energy are high.

• Be sure that the first steps of the plan can be accomplished easily so that students have a chance to succeed right from the start. Environmental projects often present many challenges, and an early experience of success will help carry students through the difficult times.

• Make the time to address and eliminate any obstacles to the action steps in your plan. Obstacles not only make projects more difficult, but also can cause them to fizzle out! Spending the necessary time to eliminate them will clear a path toward success and keep the project moving forward. The students at Alden High School identified three obstacles, all of which are common to environmental projects: insufficient funding, too little time, and a shortage of experts to help with the advanced and technical work. Funding may be found by applying for grants and holding fundraising events. In regard to time, take a look at the size of the project and determine whether it can be accomplished in phases, with students in each semester or school year working on one phase, or different classes contributing to the project. To find technical assistance, invite the participation of supportive groups or individuals who may have an interest in your project. Students at Alden were able to develop a network of organizations and local businesses that would provide assistance.

Note that while students begin the project as "listeners," throughout Steps 3–6 they are actively involved as "doers," using tools of creative problem solving to determine the actions needed to address their challenge and reach their goal. The teacher must allow students greater independence as they progress through these steps, giving them increasingly more responsibility for the project and project learning. Teachers can appoint student team-leaders to carry out action steps, ask individual students to take charge of equipment needs, and increase opportunities for students to stand in the front of the class and direct the learning. Ask, "Who would like to present tomorrow's activity?" and then meet with these students ahead of time to help them plan.

The execution of the plan is an exciting stage of the process for both students and educators. Having developed the necessary knowledge, skills and attitudes, students should now be completely responsible for the project and project learning. One of the action steps in the Alden High School project was to draw up a technical design plan that included the structure and workings of the pond, stream and waterfall. Students made drawings and met with a local environmental architect who helped them develop their ideas. Another action step was to gain approval for the project from the board of education. The students took charge of the presentation to the board, which included videotaped conversations with the pond expert that demonstrated the students' knowledge and level of involvement in and commitment to the project. When they reached the action step of digging the pond, the

Setting up Earth Day lab stations to teach others about the plants, animals and microorganisms in the pond.

students helped a pond builder with the digging. Such opportunities ensure the success of projects, but also the success of students — our goal as educators.

Step 7: Sustain students' passion and purpose

Passion and a sense of purpose grow naturally out of hard work and the experience of making positive changes in the environment. When students find passion and purpose in their project, it becomes a more sustainable effort, one in which they take the lead and continue to develop. Educators can encourage this by providing ongoing opportunities for students to apply their work and knowledge. Educators at this point must act as consultants to the project and allow students to be teachers, leading environmental change and teaching others about the goals they have reached and the solutions they have created. For example, the environmental students at Alden High School are not only in charge of the pond, but also have become the teachers. Every April during Earth Week, lab stations are set up and students throughout the district come to learn about the plants, animals and microorganisms in the pond. Follow-up environmental workshops are conducted throughout the year.

Step 8: Celebrate successes

It is important for students to experience and share the feeling of success throughout an environmental project, not only at its completion. The celebration of students' successes moves the project forward. Further, it builds the confidence that students need to take their work into the community and create real change. There are many ways to celebrate success. For example, the Alden High School students celebrated their project by going out to dinner, with the environmental clubs covering the cost. In addition, newspaper articles were written about their efforts on the project.

Exciting possibilities await students and educators when they use creative problem solving to guide their passion for making a difference in the environment. We have found that students who engage in such efforts are much more likely to view obstacles as challenges to be overcome than to see them as rigid barriers. By learning the tools and techniques of creative problem solving, becoming proficient in the project process, and developing a sense of passion and purpose, these students can venture out into the world and continue to create solutions that heal the Earth.

Dave Bauer is the president of Sustainable Earth Solutions, having retired from 32 years of teaching science in Alden, New York. David Hetherly is a science educator in Buffalo Public Schools who holds a Certificate of Advanced Studies in Educational Leadership. Susan Keller-Mathers is an Associate Professor at the International Center for Studies in Creativity at Buffalo State College in Buffalo, New York, and the author of two books on creative problem solving.

Eight Steps to Environmental Projects

1. Introduce Creative Problem-solving Concepts and Tools
2. Investigate the Topic
3. Target the Goal or Challenge
4. Generate Ideas
5. Formulate an Action Plan
6. Execute the Plan
7. Sustain Students' Passion and Purpose
8. Celebrate Successes

References

Keller-Mathers, Susan and Kristin Puccio. *Big Tools for Young Thinkers: Facilitating CPS for Primary Students.* Prufrock Press, 2000.

Keller-Mathers, Susan, Kristin Puccio and Donald Treffinger. *Adventures in Real Problem Solving: Facilitating Creative Problem Solving with Primary Students.* Prufrock Press, 2000.

Resources

Basadur, M., P. Pringle, G. Speranzini and M. Bacot. "Collaborative Problem Solving through Creativity in Problem Definition: Expanding the Pie," *Creativity and Innovation Management,* 9:1, 2000, pp. 54–76.

Basadur, M., S. Taggar and P. Pringle. "Improving the Measurement of Divergent Thinking Attitudes in Organizations," *Journal of Creative Behavior,* 33:2, 1999, pp. 75–111.

Davis, G. A. *Creativity is Forever.* Kendall/Hunt Publishing, 1998.

Firestien, Roger L. *Leading on the Creative Edge: Gaining Competitive Advantage Through the Power of Creative Problem Solving.* Pinon Press, 1996.

Fox, J. M. and R. Fox. *Exploring the Nature of Creativity.* Kendall/Hunt Publishing, 2000.

Isaksen, Scott G., Mary C. Murdock, Roger L. Firestien and Donald J. Treffinger, eds. *The Emergence of a Discipline: Nurturing and Developing Creativity.* Ablex Publishing, 1993.

Miller, B., J. Vehar and R. Firestien. *CPS Facilitation: A Door to Creative Leadership.* Innovation Systems Group, 2001.

Osborn, Alex F. *Applied Imagination: Principles and Procedures of Creative Problem-solving.* Scribner, 1963.

Parnes, Sidney J. *Optimize the Magic of Your Mind.* Bearly Limited, 1997.

Parnes, Sidney J. *Source Book for Creative Problem Solving: A Fifty Year Digest of Proven Innovation Processes.* Creative Education Foundation Press, 1992.

Puccio, Gerard J. "Creative Problem Solving Preferences: Their Identification and Implications," *Creativity and Innovation Management,* 8:3, 1999, pp. 171–178.

Vehar, J.R., R.L. Firestien and B. Miller. *Creativity Unbound: An Introduction to Creative Problem Solving.* Innovation Systems Group, 1997.

Teaching Controversial Issues

A four-step classroom strategy for clear thinking on controversial issues

Illustrations by Paul Papin

by Pat Clarke

Key concepts: critical thinking, ethical judgment, media literacy, argument analysis

Skills: analysis and evaluation of issues and the arguments relating to them

Time: approximately 2–3 hours; varies with the issue being discussed

Materials: background readings on issues (stories, articles, reports)

For the past decade, one of the most popular workshops offered by the British Columbia Teachers' Federation has been one titled "Teaching Controversial Issues — Without Becoming Part of the Controversy." The popularity of the workshop reflects a growing awareness of the need to teach social issues. Yet the motivation for teaching about such topics as environmental sustainability, animal rights or euthanasia is tempered by an understandable wariness of controversy. So while our workshop on teaching controversial issues is well subscribed, we know that many teachers avoid the pedagogical danger zone that social issues represent.

Teachers may be uncomfortable tackling controversial topics if they do not feel "expert" or at least well versed on the issues. Furthermore, teachers may be concerned that complex issues will take too long to cover and that mandated curriculum will be neglected as a result. With increasing standardization and calls for "accountability," many teachers are not inclined to venture down the sideroads of learning where social issues can so often lead. Teachers may also be disinclined to take on "hot" topics for fear that classroom chaos might ensue. We live in a time of general decline in the protocols of civil discourse: television talk shows bristle with outrageous behavior, which teachers are understandably reluctant to see reproduced in their classrooms. And, too, teachers sense that we are living in particularly cantankerous times when their actions as teachers are under close and often uninformed scrutiny. If we teach about an issue, we can easily find ourselves accused of bias or ulterior political motives. In other words, in teaching about a controversy, we become the controversy. Teachers in one British Columbia community experienced this when they attempted to have their students consider multiple perspectives on the first Gulf War in 1990. Some parents and students expressed the view that there were no "perspectives;" there was only the right side and the wrong side, and they didn't see any merit in spending time talking about the wrong side!

In spite of these impediments to addressing controversial issues, the fact remains that contemporary teaching presents certain challenges, not the least of which is relevance. The value of a formal education is increasingly measured according to the degree that it is future-oriented and helps students think critically about and act upon social issues and problems. Further, there is a growing belief that a good contemporary education is a "global education" — that is, an education that helps students develop an awareness of the planetary condition, understand connections and interdependence, and take action as responsible citizens in a complex world. In that context, the relationship between education and contemporary issues is apparent. We could well ask, what are our chances of providing our students with a global education if we remain averse to taking on controversial public issues as part of our teaching practice?

What is needed is an approach to teaching issues that overcomes these obstacles — specifically, concern for the influence of a teacher's own biases, fear of becoming a lightning rod for controversy oneself simply because a controversial issue is discussed in a class, and lack of confidence because of unfamiliarity with an issue. The approach to teaching about issues that is put forward here tries to answer these concerns at least partially. It does not deal directly with the role of issues in prescribed curricula because the possibilities for teaching issues as permitted or encouraged by curricula vary from place to place. However, it would not be extreme to suggest that any teacher who wants to can find a way to integrate consideration of issues into regular course work.

I sometimes refer to this approach to teaching issues as a demystification strategy. It is a way of teaching that is helpful for students because it offers them a way of making sense of a complex and confusing world. It is a method of analyzing an issue, considering the merits of an argument and forming an opinion on the basis of critical analysis. As an essentially inductive process, it is student-centered, and the teacher's role is primarily that of a monitor or resource person. In this way, the teacher's bias is less of a concern. The risk of public concern over teaching a controversial issue is addressed because the strategy is itself a demonstration of fair consideration. As an inquiry method, it provides teachers a framework for classroom activity that discourages one-sided argument or ill-informed opinion.

The Demystification Strategy: A framework for teaching controversial public issues

This strategy for teaching controversial public issues has four steps or elements. Each step provides a set of questions that give students a number of ways of looking at an issue, as well as a sound basis for making a judgment. In the following, the controversial issue of keeping large mammals in captivity is used as an example for demonstrating how the strategy and related questions work.

1. What is the issue about?

Where controversy is concerned, the question of what the issue is about is not as simple or obvious as it may appear. The task here is to identify the key question over which there is a controversy. Virtually every controversy turns around three types of questions: those relating to values — what should be? what is best?; those relating to information — what is the truth? what is the case?; and those relating to concepts — what does this mean? how should this be defined? In short, what is this controversy about: values, information or concepts?

By responding to these questions, students begin an analysis of an issue that identifies the nature of the controversy. In doing this, they can fairly quickly determine the heart of the issue. The primary value of this element of the strategy is that it helps students get past some of the frustration that can be experienced in trying to understand an issue. It also gives them a chance to analyze an issue dispassionately before any consideration of the merits of a case.

Example: An inquiry into the issue of keeping mammals in captivity would start by determining if this is a values issue. Is it a controversy over what should be — that is, whether animals should be in captivity or should be free? Or is it an information issue — that is, is it a controversy about what information is to be believed regarding the harm or lack of it that is caused to animals in captivity. Lastly, could it be a question of what we mean by the concept of captivity? Students would likely conclude that keeping mammals in captivity is mostly a values issue, with information and concepts related but not central to the main question of "Is it right to keep mammals in captivity?"

2. What are the arguments?

Once students have determined what the issue is about or the nature of the controversy, the second element of analysis considers the arguments supporting the various positions on the issue. The key concern here is determining just what is being said and whether there is adequate support for the claims being made.

This step is largely analytical in that it calls for some determination of the content of an argument. It is also judgmental to a degree. It is at this step that students can begin judging the validity of a position on a controversial issue. If students have determined that the controversy surrounding an issue involves information, then they should ask questions about the information available or provided. Is it adequate? Are the claims in the information accurate? Is the information appropriate to the issue? Are the sources primary or secondary? In general, are the conclusions presented in the argument reasonable, given the information?

Most controversial issues are about values, and there are critical questions that students can ask about the values stated or employed in an argument. Specifically, what criteria are being used in making a judgment? In general, there are two criteria, moral and prudential. Moral criteria for judgment are based on a concern for how all people will be affected. Prudential criteria are those concerned mainly with how I or my group will be affected.

Other questions students can use to test the acceptability of values claims are well known and quite universal in application. They are: How would you like that done to you? What if everybody did that? Are there any situations in which you would feel different or disagree with this value? These questions give students a set of criteria for making judgments that can take them beyond relativism and, because of their universal application, can help them to reflect on the validity of dogmatic positions.

If the controversy is one that seems to involve issues of definition, meaning or concepts, students should try to determine if the arguments presented use meanings or definitions that are clear. They should also test to see if meanings are used consistently and if they are appropriate and used in a proper context.

Example: If students have decided that the question of keeping mammals in captivity is about values, they will have to respond to a moral question and then decide if it has a universal application. They may decide that it is acceptable to keep mammals in captivity because it has prudential value, that of helping humans to understand mammals. Having decided that, however, they will need to consider the limits of that value, such as how many in captivity is enough? Likewise, if they decide on the moral imperative "I wouldn't want this for me," then they also have to ask in what instances that value not would apply, such as with animals that are habituated to captivity.

3. What is assumed?

Once students have considered the arguments in an issue, the critical question becomes what are the assumptions, or what is taken as self-evident in the presentation of arguments? It is at this stage that crucial matters of principle are employed to determine the validity of a position.

This framework or process has at its heart the fundamentally important aspect that there is no values

Common Strategies for Manipulating Arguments

Scapegoating: Assigning blame.

Polarized Thinking: Us/them, weak/strong, rich/poor, good/bad; encourages distrust, suspicion; presents limited and false choices.

Ad Hominem Strategy: Judgment based on who said something rather than on the merit of the statement.

Straw Person: Creating a caricature of a person or group.

Irrelevant Appeals: Appeals to emotion, patriotism, tradition.

Either-Or Tactic: Forcing a choice by presenting only two possibilities when there may be others.

Leading Statements, Slogans: Designed to damage credibility, encourage hostility, create a false impression.

False Analogies: An analogy that makes an inappropriate connection or comparison.

Extreme Examples: Used to prove a point, to slant an argument, to support a prejudice.

relativity. It is not true that any opinion, position or point of view is acceptable or legitimate. If the assumptions that justify an argument are based in prejudice, if the attitudes behind an argument are ethnocentric, racist or parochial, then these assumptions are grounds for criticism and reduce the legitimacy of the argument. The question for students to pose is, what are the assumptions behind the argument? Is it based on a prejudice or some other attitude that is contrary to universally held human values, such as those set out in the United Nations Declaration of Human Rights?

A second element that students can use to evaluate assumptions, or what is "behind" an argument, is the voice of the argument. Who is saying this? Are they "insiders" or "outsiders"? Insiders may have particular information and interests that could give an argument a certain shape or orientation. If the voice is that of an outsider, does the outsider know the issue, or is being an outsider an advantage in this case since outsiders have no special interest? Often the assumptions behind an argument can best be tested by hearing views of both insiders and outsiders.

Example: The United Nations Declaration is not applicable to the question of keeping mammals in captivity, but the question can be analyzed from the "who is saying this?" perspective. Are the people who make a case for captivity mostly those who receive some financial benefit from doing so, such as zoo owners? Are those on the other side of the argument experts on animal behavior or is their advocacy based more on sensitivities and anthropomorphism than on facts? Once the arguments have been analyzed and the assumptions scrutinized, the final step is to consider how the issue or the arguments pertaining to it are presented or manipulated. The final question in the process then tries to help students judge the quality of the information they are receiving.

4. How are the arguments manipulated?

This is the stage of the process when questions are asked on the politics of the issue. This step is particularly important for students because it can help them understand how information can be used to influence opinion.

To determine how an argument is being manipulated, students must first determine who is involved and what their particular interests are in the issue. What is the rationalization for their position? What are their reasons for taking the position they advance? By considering these questions, students begin to see how information can be selected, emphasized or ignored according to its value in supporting various positions on an issue. The degree to which the parties involved are acting in self-interest and use information only to

support that interest could affect the legitimacy of a position. On the other hand, a strongly supported position or one with strong moral reasons could add credibility to an argument.

A growing contemporary concern is the role of media in controversial issues, specifically how media can engage in argument manipulation. The question for students to address is, how can the media both reflect and create reality? To what extent on any given controversial issue is the media either creating the issue or manipulating the arguments? Argument manipulation is usually accomplished through such strategies as scapegoating, making false analogies and providing extreme examples, to name a few. The degree to which media or advocates of a position rely on such strategies is an indication to students of the validity of an argument. Detecting such tactics gives students a useful tool for assessing an argument and making a judgment on an issue.

Example: In examining the question of keeping mammals in captivity, students may find a great deal of argument manipulation. In the end, it may not lead to a conclusion, only to an awareness that manipulation happens, which in itself is a worthy learning outcome. Nevertheless, for this issue it is evident that looking at statements on either side should allow an informed opinion on where the manipulation is found and whether one side is more prone to it than the other.

At the end of such an inquiry, or demystification process, students may well be less certain of their position than when they began. That is a legitimate outcome of having more information and going through a process that requires critical reflection and open-mindedness. Most important, they will have arrived at their conclusions through their own deliberation, and we teachers will have provided the lamp of learning, not the pointer and the answer book.

Now retired, **Pat Clarke** *is a former social studies teacher and former director of professional development for the British Columbia Teachers' Federation in Vancouver.*

This article and the BCTF workshop "Teaching Controversial Issues" were based on *The Media and Public Issues: A Guide for Teaching Critical Mindedness* by Walter Werner and Kenneth Nixon, Althouse Press, 1990.

Integrated Studies in Systems

Using the characteristics of ecosystems as a framework for learning

Photographs by Pam Russell

by Pam Russell

Subject areas: science, social science, language arts

Key concepts: systems thinking, environmental literacy

Skills: report writing, public presentation

Location: classroom, community

Time: one semester to two years

"Break the pattern which connects the items of learning and you necessarily destroy all quality." — Gregory Bateson, *Mind and Nature: A Necessary Unity*

Few adults, when asked to talk about a powerful learning experience, mention diagramming sentences or learning the periodic table by heart. Rather, most wax nostalgic in recounting the time Uncle Henry or Aunt Em taught them to fly fish on the Big Hole River in Montana. They talk about

how they learned to tie the fly and swing the rod, and they reminisce about their relationship with Henry or George, their relationship with the fly, the ripple and flow of the river. In other words, they not only describe what they learned but also detail the rich context in which the event transpired. Most of these learning experiences have taken place in a natural, out-of-doors setting that was somehow related to the learning event.

The belief that most powerful learning experiences — those that stay with the learner — take place in the rich context of the natural environment was at the heart of Integrated Studies in Systems (ISIS) at Lincoln High School in Stockton, California. ISIS was a two-year interdisciplinary program in which Grade 9 and 10 students earned credits in Science, Social Science and Language Arts. Three teachers, three classrooms, three disciplines, three periods each day, 90 to 100 students — these human and logistical components of the program were similar to those of many other interdisciplinary programs. What made ISIS unique was that the program used the characteristics of ecosystems as a framework for inquiry and learning, and as a model for the biological, social, political, historical and cultural systems that made up the content of the Grades 9 and 10 curricula. While not able to access the natural world for all learning experiences, we believed that through a systems approach we could bring to the learner some of the elements of non-formal education in natural environments.

The framework

The ISIS framework began with the notion that the study of an ecosystem reveals at least six characteristics that can be identified in all systems, whether they be biological processes or social and cultural systems. ISIS students learned to recognize these six characteristics in the natural environment, to find their correspondences in other systems, and ultimately, to apply them to their own relationships with the natural world. These ecosystem characteristics are:

Networks: Interdependency, Diversity and Complexity — The components of an ecosystem are interconnected in a vast network of relationships in which all life processes are interdependent and achieve stability through a diversity of linkages.

Boundaries: Scales and Limits — At all scales of nature (atom, molecule, organelle, cell, organ and so on), living systems nest within other living systems, each with its own boundary and limits.

Cycles: Recycling of Resources and Partnership — The interactions among members of an ecological community involve the exchange of resources in continuous cycles so that all waste is recycled through pervasive cooperation and countless forms of partnership. On the planetary scale, each of the elements vital for life goes through a closed loop of cyclic changes.

Flow-through: Energy and Resources — The constant flow of solar energy sustains life and drives ecological cycles: all organisms feed on flows of energy and resources, each species producing output that is food for other organisms.

Development: Succession and Co-evolution — The unfolding of life, manifested as development and

learning at the individual level and as evolution at the species level, involves an interplay of creativity and mutual adaptation in which organisms and environment co-evolve.

Dynamic Balance: Self-Organization, Flexibility, Stability and Sustainability — All ecological cycles act as feedback loops so the ecological community regulates and organizes itself, maintaining a state of dynamic balance characterized by continual fluctuation.

The process

Early in the school year, students became accustomed to the six characteristics of systems through discovering the characteristics of an ecosystem. One activity that worked well was what we called the Mobile Metaphor. This is a permutation of an old back-to-school lesson that asks students to make a personal mobile representing themselves. Our twist was to ask them to show themselves in relation to the six characteristics of systems: Networks, Boundaries, Cycles, Flow-through, Development and Dynamic Balance. In other words, how could they demonstrate their relationship to the context in which they live? How were they part of a system? The students defined the system they wished their mobiles to symbolize, such as their family or group of friends or even the band they played in. Then, to add another twist, one that forced them into the environment, we asked that they find and construct their mobiles of natural materials that corresponded metaphorically with aspects of themselves as part of a system. We knew this was a stretch, and they knew it was a stretch, but those stretches started the year with interest.

An example was a mobile containing a blown egg, a colorful leaf, a shell, a feather and an acorn, all balanced on twigs. The student explained that the egg represented herself as an individual with a boundary of skin, but who was once part of her parents, demonstrating a relationship to others, in this case, her family or first network. The colorful leaf represented her development: as the seasons change, so does she. The leaf required the flow-through of energy from the sun just as she required energy from food. The feather of a bird represented her first love, music. Songs usually have repeats, or cycles: she was part of the cycle of life. Her whole mobile was suspended in dynamic balance, adjusting itself with changes in the environment just as she must adjust to heat, cold, hunger, emotions and so on. We then took this activity a bit further by asking groups of students to combine their mobiles into community mobiles. They made their own individual mobiles at home and we took a class period to assemble the finished products into communities. We spent another part of a period talking about them. These mobiles were suspended from our classroom ceilings all year as reminders of ways in which we could describe our personal contexts using the language of ecosystems.

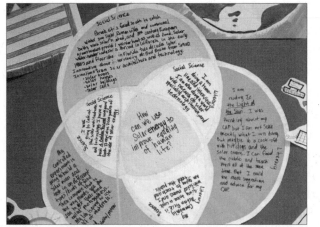

Venn diagram highlighting the interdisciplinary links in a student's research to answer the question "How can we use solar energy to improve the quality of human life."

Once students became fluent in the language used to describe the characteristics and relationships evident in ecosystems, we began to use this language to draw analogies between the natural environment and other systems. Like the Okanagan people of the Pacific Northwest, who gain meaning from the landscape, our goal was to teach the traditional curriculum in such a way that students' learning was connected to the environment. We did this in two ways: first, through an interdisciplinary curriculum that helped students to identify how the characteristics of ecosystems are manifested in all systems; and second, through a process of inquiry that used these systems characteristics as a framework.

The Physical and Philosophical Bases

ISIS began as part of a community-wide response to the demands of education in a changing culture. The success of ISIS may be related in part to the elements of infrastructure, or the physical and philosophical underpinnings that permitted the program to work. These elements are:

1. The teachers selected each other and worked together because they chose to.

2. Time and money were committed to the program. In the beginning, teachers were given time to develop strategies and lessons plans.

3. Students chose to be part of the program. Students in the eighth grade heard about ISIS from former students and siblings, from staff at parent-student information nights, and through an outreach program during which ISIS students shared information with eighth graders from feeder schools.

4. The student population was ethnically, racially and intellectually diverse. It was our belief that ISIS should reflect the diversity of the school and the community.

5. ISIS courses met the standards for application to the state university system, but some students lacked the ability or motivation to meet the university standard. Teachers were permitted to differentiate the credit: that is, we could give credits toward high school graduation rather than university- or college-prep credit. This allowed us to recognize the efforts of students whose talents were not demonstrable in the traditional formats of student assessment. We typically had special education students and others who had not personally developed to the point of being able to produce the assignments required.

6. Students typically remained in the program for two years. This greatly increased the potential for developing relationships within the learning community of ISIS.

7. The three classrooms were physically close, and one of the rooms was large enough to allow all of the ISIS students to meet together.

8. The classrooms opened onto an oak grove teeming with squirrels, insects, woodpeckers, scrub jays, robins and migrating birds. This setting provided a readily available example of a natural ecosystem.

9. The program was scheduled for the first three of seven class periods, a time of day when we were fresh, as were our students. We often had potluck breakfasts where we learned the civility of breaking bread and talking.

10. Teachers shared a common prep period that most years backed up to lunch.

—by *Pam Russell*

Integrated curriculum

The traditional disciplines of English, social science and science were taught in an interconnected, interrelated fashion using the characteristics of systems as a common language. As students in science class discovered food webs, surface-area-to-unit-volume ratios, energy pyramids, insect life cycles, cloud patterns, and ambient and substrate temperatures, they were asked to look for similar relationships in history, economics or literature. For example, what are the differences between natural boundaries and geopolitical ones or the ones created by the protagonists and antag-onists in literature? How are they alike? What is the role of DNA in the story of Romeo and Juliet? What was the role of DNA in the conflict in Yugoslavia? How are events in Romeo and Juliet analogous to what happened in Nazi Germany?

As the "science piece" of their projects, students investigate bacterial growth on lunch boxes.

Interdisciplinary inquiry projects

ISIS students completed two interdisciplinary inquiry projects each year, during which they strove, among other things, to answer an essential question by examining the evolution of issues surrounding the topic over time and how the topic has been related to the environment and to human culture. Each step in the process was intentionally linked to the characteristics and processes of ecosystems. For example, one of our students was interested in alternative energy. Her first assignment was to formulate the essential question that would guide her research, and she decided on "How can we use solar energy/devices to help improve the quality of human life?" This was the initial boundary of research, the determination of the project's scale or limit.

Planning activities: In addition to the definition of the essential question, phase one of the inquiry included the following planning and rudimentary research activities:

• Brainstorm: As an exercise in diversity of thought, students wrote down any and all notions that came to mind about their topic.

• Preliminary Venn Diagram: An exercise in pondering interrelationships among the three ISIS disciplines as they related to the topic.

• KWL: Addressing the questions "What do you Know?" "What do you Want to know about?" and "What have you Learned?" students developed a key word list for finding information.

• Systems Thinking Map Notes: A challenging exercise that demonstrated how all things have an impact on the environment, human culture and history.

• Preliminary Annotated List of Works Cited: Students found out what information was available to help answer their essential question and learned the proper format for citing sources.

Community and research activities: The next phases of research involved interactions with the community and continued research and development. The main assignments were:

• Interview: A chance to interact with an expert (usually) and gain intergenerational experience.

• Off-Campus Experience: A direct experience that would help answer the essential question. Students' off-campus activities took them to organic farms, natural spawning areas and fish hatcheries, the human genome project at Lawrence Livermore National Lab, a homeless shelter school, the port of Stockton, a cloning lab at the University of California at Davis, the mayor's office, the delta with a local water pollution watchdog, the FBI headquarters in San Francisco, and the virtual reality facilities at the University of California at Berkeley.

Conceptual Integrated Curricular Matrix

Essential Questions	Science	Social Science	Language Arts	Homeroom
How have our large population, intolerance of diversity, and technological development affected natural cycles locally and globally? Human activities that interrupt natural cycles include destruction of vast forests, war, combustion of fossil fuels, production of synthetic chemicals and disposal of wastes that do not readily decompose.	How do biological systems sustain themselves? Analysis of complex biogeochemical cycles with particular emphasis on the carbon cycle. What sustains plant and animal populations in the environment? How are the processes of photosynthesis and respiration connected? How does the structure of a plant or animal enable the organism to function and maintain its population as part of an ecosystem?	What are the social, political, cultural and historical cycles that include war? What were the causes and consequences of World War I? What factors contributed to the rise of totalitarianism in Nazi Germany and Stalinist Russia? Readings from *Darkness at Noon* by Arthur Koestler. Comparison of anthropocentric and biocentric views of war. What effect does war have on population?	In *All Quiet on the Western Front*, the ecological principle of cycles is encountered in relationships that entail the exchange of resources, including survival strategies such as camaraderie, tolerance and resilience. Characters begin to realize that the war is a result of human systems in industrialized society, characterized by struggle for control of resources. Students study current sociopolitical struggles over resources and make predictions about the future. (How has the struggle over fossil fuels thwarted public awareness of alternative energy sources?)	Town meetings Most environmental problems arise when only short-term or parochial interests are considered. Investigate real environmental problems and facilitate students' development as citizens who can negotiate to help ensure that decisions that affect natural resources serve longer term and wider interests. Problem-solving skills related to dealing with conflict, change and diversity within the ISIS community; coping with an era marked by the explosive growth of information; taking action in solving current environmental problems and preventing new ones from developing.

Above: A sample curricular matrix: such concepts as resource cycling, exchange and competition are used to draw analogies between ecosystems and social, political and historical systems and events.

• Science Piece: A chance to complete a controlled experiment, create a model, or teach a concept that would help answer the essential question.

• Time Line: A chance to observe the temporal context or evolution of a problem or an issue.

• Literary Piece: A chance to respond to the findings in a creative way.

• Outline: An organization plan that laid the foundation for a 1500-word paper on the topic.

• Community Action Piece: A chance to give back to the community that provided the student with experiences that helped answer the essential question.

Students' research itself had a pattern that demonstrated elements of a system. For example, in the assignment called "Systems Thinking Map Notes" students related their topic to systems characteristics by answering the following:

1. Networks: What impact does the problem addressed by your question have on the environment? What are the social, cultural, scientific/technological and natural interconnections?

2. Boundaries: Beyond your own personal interest, why is the local and global impact of your topic important now and for the future?

3. Development: How does getting a historical perspective on your topic help you to understand the answer to your essential question? Who are significant people connected to your topic and question? What is the historical, scientific and technological background?

4. Cycles: What has been the human relationship to the question you are investigating? Have the human responses to the problem or issue you are investigating created a situation in which you might say that history is repeating itself? For example, how have wars compromised or degraded the environment? How has reconstruction after a war helped or hindered the situation?

5. Flow-through: Using the transfer of energy

through a system as a metaphor, how has your science research enhanced your understanding of the question you are trying to answer?

6. Dynamic Balance: What do you think will result if there is continued lack of awareness and action on this problem? What further impact will it have on our local and global ecosystem?

During the second phase of the inquiry, we scheduled several days for Assessment, Clarification and Extension, or "ACE." On ACE days, all three ISIS periods were used by students and teachers to assess progress, clarify issues, and take individual and small-group field trips for interviews, off-campus experiences, library visits, science research and so forth. Students made their own arrangements for these trips, following the guidelines used for whole-class trips.

ACE days provided students opportunities for self-organization, both as individual researchers and as a community of learners. We began with a Town Meeting during which we discussed the "rules" or organization of the day. On some ACE days, one room was designated as a quiet area and one for working on specific problems of the inquiry, such as the science piece. Often teachers arranged to meet with students individually. As these matters were discussed, students prepared a personal agenda and checklist. Often questions arose that were important for whole-group discussion. The Town Meeting was therefore a time for community consideration of community issues. As students developed in their ability to research, and toward the final weeks of the inquiry, more and more ACE days were made available.

During the final phase, emphasis was placed on presentation to the community from which students had gathered the information they needed to answer their essential questions. The presentation phase began with a week-long dress rehearsal held in an amphitheater that accommodated all of the ISIS students, the three teachers, and guests such as counselors and members of the administration. By the end of the week, all students had presented their essential questions and the key findings that supported their conclusions, and all three teachers had evaluated all students' papers. This

Images painted on the classroom door by a student to represent the nature of systems.

process was the ultimate feedback loop before the final presentation, which took place during the evening and was open to the entire community.

The presentation to the community at large became a celebration of knowledge. In order to accommodate roughly 90 presentations within a two-hour time frame, students were grouped into venues — typically various adjacent classrooms — according to their audio-visual equipment needs and complementary topics. A program listing students' essential questions and venues was distributed along with invitations and a reminder to students that they would be prudent to ensure their own audiences. During their research, we had encouraged students to stretch to develop the weaker of their multiple intelligences, but for their presentations we encouraged them to use their strengths. As a result, the presentation styles exhibited by students varied widely. There was a formal reception following the presentations at which students were available to defend their papers, which were on display, share refreshments and receive accolades. The audience was invited to critique the works on formal feedback forms. Finally, students wrote a reflective essay, and evidence of their work was placed in their permanent portfolios.

Although elements of the interdisciplinary inquiry project are familiar to all teachers, we believe that the framing of the process as a system was the key to teaching habits that promote environmental literacy. Even the doors to the classrooms were painted with images that represented and served as constant reminders of the nature of systems. With its emphasis on systems thinking and inquiry, it was our hope that the ISIS program would nurture a diverse community of learners able to consider both the short-term and the long-term outcomes of what they do — citizens who will be mindful of the environmental impact of their behavior.

Pam Russell taught Biology/Chemistry in ISIS, ESL Science and Advanced Placement Environmental Science at Lincoln High School in Stockton, California. She is currently retired and lives in Port Angeles, Washington.

TAMARACK:
Responsibility, Community and Authenticity

by Bill Patterson

Subject areas: Earth science, geography, English, physical education

Key concepts: integrated learning, problem solving

Skills: outdoor recreational skills, such as canoeing, snowshoeing, rock climbing; communication skills, including interviewing, writing, magazine production and marketing, oral presentations, literature study; word processing and desktop publishing; field study skills, such as mapping, water testing, organism identification and data recording

Location: classroom, natural wilderness area, seniors' homes for interviews

Time: one semester

Materials: camping and outdoor gear, computers, word processors, desktop publishing software, tape recorders, digital camera, soil and water testing equipment

Historically, education was a community responsibility: children learned from the adults and the other children they came in contact with. This was the core of schooling for most people until the development of public school systems at the end of the 19th century. It was then that the "business" of education began. Education (learning) would take place in a learning center (school) under the direction of a professional educator (teacher). Subject matter would be organized into independent, fragmented packages called disciplines. The result has been that schools are frequently worlds unto themselves and isolated from their communities and the resources that are available in them. Students — and some teachers too — regard schools as the only place where "real" education occurs. At the same time, however, they often see school as having little to do with the real world. And they are right! Schools do a good job of preparing students for more schooling; they frequently do not do as good a job of educating kids for living.

One of the major reasons for the isolation of schools from their communities is the typical structure of the institution: four 75-minute periods and four separate subjects per day. Field trips, or even study projects in the community, disturb the smooth running of the institution. The result is that the institutional structure discourages interaction with the community outside school and frequently gets in the way of worthwhile, relevant learning.

After running an extensive "outers" program for over 20 years and involving my students in an exchange program and other out-of-school activities, I came to the conclusion that these activities were frequently more relevant and valuable than much of the curriculum. However, they also disrupted the smooth operation of the school, in spite of our having the cooperation and support of other teachers. As a solution to the dilemma of institutional constraint, in 1989 I suggested a program within which I would teach several course credits. My principal and I discussed the idea with an official from the provincial ministry of education and selected a group of three course credits for the program. This multiple-credit program of study was named TAMARACK.

Today, TAMARACK is a four-course program offered as an integrated package to 20 students in Grades 11 and 12 at Mackenzie High School in Deep River, Ontario. The package comprises the students' entire program for one semester and makes up one teacher's full teaching assignment. This allows for the students and teacher to become a more or less independent unit that can function with flexibility both in the classroom and outside of the school. The school serves as a base of operation, but field trips, extended outdoor activities and community activities can take place without interfering with other programs in the school.

Students who complete the TAMARACK Program receive credits in Earth Science, Physical Education, English and Geography. While these subject credits are given individually, the program is operated on an integrated basis. For example, when students plan and participate in an eight-day wilderness canoe trip, they keep journals, read and write about wilderness, analyze water and air quality, paddle and portage a canoe, and work together as a group.

After a volunteer firefighter presented a course on fire prevention and suppression, several students went on to summer jobs with firefighting crews.

The TAMARACK Program emphasizes active participation in a variety of learning experiences beyond the school. It is anticipated that these experiences will help students to better appreciate their community and the wilderness, as well as foster lifelong learning. Students have extensive opportunities to write; to read and produce media; to learn, organize and practice outdoor recreational skills; and to develop a healthy environmental ethic and an interest in fitness. Field and lab studies permit the investigation of a wide range of environmental phenomena. Major outdoor outings include a five-day winter snowshoeing trip, a five-day backpacking expedition in Algonquin Park, a five-day cycling and rock-climbing outing and an eight-day wilderness canoe trip.

Of central importance in the program is that students have opportunities to interact with adults in the community in new and different ways. Students gain some appreciation of the history of the Ottawa Valley by interviewing and recording the life stories of the "old timers" who have lived their lives there. They publish these oral histories in a magazine called *TAMARACK*, which they write, produce and market. It is a project that permits them to develop meaningful relationships in the community while making a significant contribution to the written history of the Ottawa Valley. Over the years, a variety of other community activities have evolved. Participation in an archeological dig is being explored, as well as helping out with research in a local ecological preserve.

While a program like TAMARACK has considerable costs associated with it, the actual direct cost to students is $500; this represents approximately 40 percent of the funding required. As there is virtually no school budget for the program, the rest of the funding comes from fundraising and magazine sales and from various organizations, businesses and individuals who support the program. Most of the transportation is provided by parents, and this helps to keep the cost of the program very low. Regular meetings, which all parents attend, have been very helpful in building strong support. Frequently, parents participate in the outings as staff members, and many people in the community wish to help with the program — in fact, often more than can be accommodated. Strong parental and community support are absolutely essential for the successful implementation and operation of the program.

TAMARACK is an enriching experience, giving students a variety of life skills, increased confidence in talking to older people and a greatly expanded awareness of their community. Through contact between students and old-timers, the program bridges the gap between school and community with real-life experiences that are highly valued by both. The wilderness outings provide opportunities to study environmental phenomena, to experience nature first hand by doing hard physical work, and to discuss literature and ideas in a natural setting. Most important, students who participate in the TAMARACK program demonstrate an environmental awareness and sensitivity to nature that are considerably beyond that of most high school students.

Bill Patterson *is the former Science Head of Mackenzie High School in Deep River, Ontario, and founder of TAMARACK <www.tamarackprogram.com>.*

The Integral Ingredients of TAMARACK

Bert Horwood, retired professor of Education at Queen's University in Kingston, Ontario, interviewed students who had been in the TAMARACK Program in an effort to determine factors crucial to its success. His study, published in the *McGill Journal of Education*,[1] identified four factors which, by students' own evaluation, contributed most to the experience of integrated learning. These he termed complete process, authenticity, community and responsibility.

Complete process: Complete process refers to seeing a project through from conception to finished product. It is, notes Horwood, "a hallmark of virtually every element of the program... [and] possibly the single most important feature underlying the students' perception of integration." Students are responsible for every aspect of producing *TAMARACK* magazine. They arrange and conduct interviews, write and edit stories and participate in layout, cover design, financing, printing and sales. Similarly, their scientific work begins with problems, and moves through experimental design, experiment, observation, analysis and report writing. In preparing for a wilderness outing, students even designed and made their own pack baskets from black ash trees, stripping the bark and pounding the wood into long flexible strips.

Authenticity: Authenticity refers to students' sense that their work is both real and valuable because it is done in and for the community. Students work as lab assistants alongside scientists, and they frequently speak to school and community groups and write for publications.

Horwood's study revealed that "Students were sensitive to the isolation of the world of school and to the relative inconsequence of school work. For them, work outside school or with school outsiders counted; it made a difference in the world."

Community: The strong sense of community that develops among students in the TAMARACK program does not occur accidentally but is the result of students' continually finding themselves in situations where mutual tolerance, respect and helpfulness, along with the giving and taking of constructive criticism, are essential to getting the job done. Noting the high value that students placed on the communal good, Horwood suggests that community "promotes integration because it provides a safe but stimulating climate within which students can begin to push back their unexplored limits and horizons."

Responsibility: TAMARACK students reported feeling a responsibility that was greater, both quantitatively and qualitatively, than in regular school programs. They were in charge of critical elements of every undertaking and were responsible not just to themselves but to the teacher, the group and the wider community. Responsibility is a key factor in integrated learning, concludes Horwood, "because it ensures that students are fully committed to the processes... leads to a pride in the entire enterprise and a feeling that they are in charge of what is going on."

1. Bert Horwood, "Integration and Experience in the Secondary Curriculum," *McGill Journal of Education*, 29:1, 1994, pp. 89-102.

The Small School:
Human-scale Education

A popular event during Music Week is drumming on steel band instruments made from discarded agricultural equipment.

by Satish Kumar

Subject areas: science, mathematics, language arts, art, music, home economics

Key concepts: human scale, biomimicry

Skills: cooking, sewing, cleaning, fundraising

Location: classroom, kitchen and community

Time: four-year program

In 1982, my son was ten years old and nearing secondary school age. The prospect was that he would have a journey of more than one hour each morning and evening to and from a state secondary school 15 miles away from our village of Hartford in Devon, England. The thought of his two hours of travel time every day — a commuter's life at the age of eleven — led me to think that this was not the kind of education I wanted my son to have.

Secondly, I had left an urban community in order to live in a rural community, and sending my child out of this community and back into urban culture was not what I wanted. And once he arrived at that urban school, my son would have faced an education that was very academic and intellectual, very exam-oriented and job-oriented — whereas I wanted education to be a kind of discovery, a discovery of the particular, unique gift of each individual child. So for all these reasons, I thought that I would like to educate my child near, around and in the community where I lived.

I called a meeting in the village, and about 30 people came to my house. We sat down and talked about the state of education in general and about the state secondary school in particular. That school had 2,000 children, and each class had a minimum of 30 students. A child is just a number in a school of that size, and there was a lot of bullying and smoking at the school. By the end of our discussion, the parents of nine children were courageous enough to take the plunge and say that if a new school were started in the village they would send their children to it. So there we were: with nine children, we had enough to start a school. At that time, there was a Methodist chapel for sale in the village. Even though I had no money, I went along to the auction. Putting my faith in the project, I bid for the chapel and got it for £20,000 — which was not too expensive — and within the next six weeks, I raised the £20,000. Seven months later, in September 1982, we opened the smallest school in the U.K. with nine children.

When we started The Small School, we asked ourselves, what kind of school do we want? We decided to design our curriculum in three parts. One third would be academic and intellectual, including science, mathematics, English, French — all the things one needs for a normal education. Another third would focus on imaginative themes and subjects, such as art, culture, music and painting. But one third would be more practical and ecological. It would include physical training, environmental education, and manual work such as gardening, cooking and woodwork.

We also decided that we would like our school to teach about three basic things that every person needs. One of these needs is food, but hardly any school teaches you how to grow, cook or serve food, or how to do the dishes. A school that does not teach children

Top: At least one afternoon is set aside each week for physical activities. Bottom: During Clothes Week, every student must make an item of clothing. Opposite: Daily lunch preparation begins with a visit to the village greengrocer.

how to do dishes is not a good school in my view. If children can cook and serve food and do dishes with respect, love and care, they can look after trees and animals with love and care, they can look after their parents with love and care, they can treat their neighbors with love and care. So to ensure that every child would learn about food, our teachers and children worked together to turn a kitchen into a classroom.

Secondly, we all need clothing. But no school teaches every student how to mend clothes, how to design clothes, how to spin, how to weave, how to sew. When buttons are broken, mothers hear, "Mum, my button is broken, please sew it." But we should be replying, "Why don't you sew it?" So we decided to teach children the practical skills of spinning, weaving, mending, designing and making clothes. A number of our children have since turned out to be great dressmakers and designers.

The third thing we need is housing. Yet today hardly any schools teach children how to make a foundation, how to build a roof, how to install plumbing and electrical wiring. At The Small School, our children learn these practical hands-on skills. Many of the ideas that we implemented I learned from Mahatma Gandhi, who started the movement for basic education that introduced cleaning, gardening and cooking as part of the curriculum in India.

We were also concerned that mainstream education at that time was based almost entirely on classroom learning, which made it difficult to learn about the natural world. It was important to us that children learn not only *about* but *from* nature. To learn *from* nature, one must be *in* nature. Too often, education is anthropocentric. It teaches us about nature only in order to manipulate it or control it, assuming that nature is "out there" for us. We felt that nature should be as important a teacher as the classroom teacher. So we decided that at least once a week our classroom would be the outdoors. The nearby river, woodlands and birds would be our teachers as we learned how nature

does things. In her book *Biomimicry*, Janine Benyus explores how this approach to learning has spawned a whole new scientific field. She describes, for example, how scientists are creating innovative materials and agriculturists are studying prairie ecosystems in order to grow food more sustainably. What these farsighted initiatives have in common is that people are studying closely how nature works. So we decided that at least one day a week the children would go out, often with a picnic lunch, and learn from nature. We soon realized that when you learn from nature, you can learn anything. You can learn music by listening to birds singing — birds that didn't go to any music school. You can learn how to paint by studying the colors of butterflies. Georgia O'Keeffe learned to paint by closely observing flowers.

For me, it is important that education be of a human scale. A school should be a community and not just a knowledge factory — a community of children, parents and teachers who all know each other and who work, celebrate and develop ideas together. But for that to happen, the size of the school must be modest. From nine children in the beginning, we grew to 15, 20 and then to 40, the maximum number of students that we could accommodate with our limited space and resources. For every eight children, we have one full-time teacher, so that when we have 40 children we have the equivalent of five full-time staff at the school. In addition, we have many local people — experienced craftsmen, musicians, artists, writers, poets, painters and gardeners — who come, most on a volunteer basis,

to teach a class that might last from two hours to a full day each week. If they can't afford to come as a volunteer, then we pay them an hourly rate.

To cover the cost of tuition, we charge parents a small donation rather than a fee, but it is not compulsory. If you can't afford it, you don't have to pay. But if a farmer wants to contribute produce, such as potatoes or firewood, instead of making a financial donation, that's fine. If someone has the time to do volunteer work at the school, such as decorate the building, repair the roof or do some gardening, that, too, is an acceptable fee. Since not all parents can afford to contribute in these ways, we try to raise funds from non-profit organizations and charitable foundations. Finally, we organize dinner parties on Saturdays and prepare and serve lunches or dinners for 200 to 300 people at public events such as the Schumacher College lectures. This is how we raise the monies we need.

After more that two decades, the school is going from strength to strength and we are now finding that lots of other people are trying to start similar schools. At the moment, there are six or seven schools that are part of our Movement for Education on a Human Scale. We have an umbrella organization that holds alternative education fairs and annual conferences and publishes a newsletter. We are now trying to persuade the government to give grants and financial support to small schools, because most people don't have enough money to start them. While we have managed to run our school without state funding, we recognize that many people cannot do that.

We find that the children who have gone through our school are very self-confident and have many practical skills. For my son and daughter, it is no sweat to cook a meal for 10 or 20 people, because they have learned it at school. It is no sweat for them to mind the house, tend the garden and manage the compost heap because they have learned it. Our aim has been to equip children not only intellectually, but also spiritually, physically, emotionally and practically.

Our children have no problem in getting into universities — they can handle exams as well as other

Day to Day at The Small School

Located in the village of Hartford in Devon, England, The Small School has had an enrolment of between 16 and 38 students over the past five years. The current staff includes two full-time and five part-time teachers (some of whom teach only one subject). They are assisted by numerous parents and other skilled volunteers who teach classes in such topics as woodworking, blacksmithing, rock climbing, building maintenance and stained glass.

Unlike most other small "human scale" schools in the U.K., The Small School is in a poor, rural area. Approximately 35 percent of The Small School's funding comes from fees paid by parents who can afford to pay them. About 40 percent comes from private foundations or from "guardians" who make individual donations to the school. The other 25 percent is raised through special events organized by students and parents. They host special dinners at the school and organize village fairs at Christmas and Easter. They cater larger events such as the lectures at nearby Schumacher College or annual general meetings of various organizations. The school's maintenance is mostly undertaken by parent volunteers.

The Small School does not follow the U.K. National Curriculum rigidly, except in the fifth, senior year, when all students must take the national exams. In the academic classes, students are divided into two groups according to their skill levels, such as their proficiency in French, rather than by their grade level or age. Mornings are typically devoted to academic subjects, whereas afternoons are spent on topics and activities of personal interest to students. One afternoon each week is set aside for physical activities undertaken in small groups, such as ball games in the village hall, swimming or rock climbing, or simply going for walks.

In the warmer months, much of the learning occurs outdoors, where students tend a vegetable garden, compost lunch wastes, take bike rides and nature walks, and visit a graveyard to study local history. Although environmental education is not a deliberate focus of the school, learning about the environment is reinforced by presentations given by parents on topics such as fair trade coffee and organic agriculture, and by visits to local experts such as noted scientist and author James Lovelock, the creator of the Gaia hypothesis. In addition, lessons in photography and sculpture make use of the natural world and the natural materials in the area around the school. Next year, the school will have a writer-in-residence, one of whose aims will be to help students develop a sense of place through observing, reflecting on and writing about their natural and cultural surroundings.

Each year, six special theme weeks are designated. During Music Week, local musicians or a steel band from a nearby city come to the school to teach students how to make and play instruments. During Clothes Week, which was originally developed to break down gender roles, every teenaged girl and boy produces a piece of clothing. Other special weeks focus on academic subjects that need particular attention, such as writing, science or statistics. Some, like Sculpture Week or Circus Week, are oriented to practical skills. Still others combine both, such as when students learn French while bicycling through northern France. Throughout the year, the school tries to ensure a balance in the special weeks between academic, artistic and physical themes.

What particularly sets The Small School apart from conventional schools is that students are actively involved in daily activities such as cooking and cleaning. Each morning on a rotational basis, one or two students miss their morning classes and head out to a local green grocer to purchase the fresh foods needed for that day's lunch. Returning to the school, they prepare lunch for all students and staff, working under the supervision of one of several parents who have taken a one-day government course in food hygiene. Once the students have some experience, they are also involved in planning the meals. Perhaps not surprisingly, cleaning the school at the end of the day is a much less popular activity. Each student typically spends about 15 minutes to clean a portion of the school, again on a rotational basis.

In all of these activities, students must cooperate with one another and take considerable responsibility for themselves and those around them. With no more than eight students per class, students at The Small School can never become quietly "invisible," as often happens in the much larger classes of public high schools. Teachers get to know each of them as an individual, and are able to adapt their teaching to each student's particular needs.

— by **Tim Grant**, with thanks to Julia Mickeljohn, former head teacher of The Small School, Hartford, England.

For more information about The Small School, contact:

The Small School
Fore Street
Hartland, Bideford
Devon, UK EX39 5EA

(continued from page 33)

students. My daughter got a degree in philosophy at the University of Durham in North England, and after finishing university she worked and saved money and then traveled in India for 18 months, completely on her own. Her self-sufficiency was a result of the self-confidence that The Small School provided. Now she's in Spain, where she is teaching English and translating Spanish literature, poetry and philosophy. My son went to university in London, where he earned a degree in communication studies. Afterwards, he wanted to travel the world. But having learned about greenhouse gases and climate change as part of his environmental learning at The Small School, he said, "I don't want to fly in planes." So he got a job on a yacht and sailed to the Caribbean, hitchhiked all around Central and South America, and later sailed up to New York City and back home. He then decided to build a boat and he built it. The Small School equipped him with that confidence and many of those skills. Those are but two examples of successful graduates.

Many other children who went through The Small School are doing similar things. They work in organic farming, woodland management or dress designing. They work for non-profit organizations or they work overseas on sustainable development projects. There are lots of green jobs out there, so our students don't have to worry, "If I go to The Small School and learn about the environment, what am I going to do?" You don't have to work for Coca-Cola or McDonald's or Mitsubishi or other big companies. You can work for the United Nations. You can work for non-governmental organizations. You can create your own non-profit group or start your own business. Green job opportunities are emerging in the renewable energy field, in organic farming and eco-design. There are many ecology fields into which children can go. I think we need to overcome this fear — which many parents have — that if we send our children into environmental alternative education, they are going to lose out. They are not! They will be happier and more fulfilled.

For us, education is not about receiving information. It is about participating in the process of life.

Conventional education assumes that children start with a certain ignorance, not knowing anything, and that we must use books filled with knowledge to put information into the child. Our view is that a child is like an acorn. Just as an acorn is capable of becoming an oak tree, a child is very capable of becoming a fully developed human being. We don't have to teach an acorn how to become an oak tree. It knows how. In the same way, a child knows how to be a human being. The job of a teacher and parent is like that of a forester or gardener — to support, encourage, protect, inspire and provide. In the case of the acorn, you provide water and some shelter. You provide a little support so the wind doesn't blow away the little seedling. In the same way, the school, the community and the parents provide children with support.

In The Small School, we try to find what is the unique gift of each particular child and then help the child develop that uniqueness. Instead of saying, "You are no good in this and therefore you are no good," we say, "You are good at something: try to develop that." It is education from the inside out, rather than from the outside in. It's *educatis*, to lead out what is inside, as the oak comes out from the acorn. An oak is not put inside the acorn, but rather the oak is brought out of the acorn. In the same way, a poet, a painter, a writer, a musician, a gardener or a farmer comes out of the child; those gifts are not put into the child. This is fundamental to the pedagogical approach that we adopt in order to provide children with a more holistic education. Spirituality, intellect, art, culture, aesthetics — all form part of that holistic vision.

Satish Kumar *is the founder of The Small School in the U.K., Director of Programs at Schumacher College, co-editor of* Resurgence *magazine, and the author of several books, including an autobiography* Path Without Destination *(William Morrow, 1999) and* You Are, Therefore I Am: A Declaration of Dependence *(Green Books, 2002). This article is based on an interview by Tim Grant, co-editor of* Green Teacher *magazine, with Satish Kumar in Toronto in October 2003.*

Environmental Industries Co-op Education

Students in this innovative program gain the knowledge and skills to put environmental values to work

Photographs by John Perry

by John Perry

Subject areas: science, language arts, mathematics, cooperative education

Key concepts: sustainable development, employment, business education partnerships, the six Rs, prairie restoration, community involvement, environmental assessment

Skills: identification and practice of employability skills, evaluation of potential careers, observation, research, synthesizing, résumé writing, speech making, report writing, laboratory techniques, computer use, environmental site assessment, sampling and identification of prairie species, water sampling and testing

Location: classroom, outdoors, cooperating industries' places of business

Time: one-semester or full-year program

In the early 1990s, our local business development group was worried about the economic direction of our Manitoba town and the two surrounding municipalities. The group's surveys had shown that the region's economic strength lay in the environmental industries sector but that growth was hindered by a lack of potential employees with relevant knowledge and skills. That assessment encouraged our area's "Focus 2000" group, consisting of educators, business people and government representatives, to develop a Grade 12 Environmental Industries Cooperative Education Program. We defined environmental industries as those whose products or services promote sustainable development by helping to create a healthy environment, economy and society. It was expected that this new program would increase awareness of environmental issues among students and the community, promote more school–community cooperation, and provide students with relevant, up-to-date job skills and training opportunities in the environmental field.

While the program was designed to attract students at all academic levels, special emphasis was placed on recruiting those who had dropped out of school or were at risk of doing so. We also wanted to attract young women and students from minority groups, who tend not to enrol in science and technology courses.

The Environmental Industries Cooperative Education Program ran in various configurations from 1994 to 2002: a full-year program of seven provincially accredited courses over two semesters, a one-semester four-credit program, and a three-credit mornings-only program. An English course in Language and Technical Communication was a regular provincial credit, while all others were provincially approved school-initiated courses. For each credit toward high school graduation, the student received 110 hours of instruction.

The following is a description of the courses, offered in the hope that these ideas may assist others in creating similar programs.

Environmental Industry courses

Students were able to enrol in three or four Environmental Industry credits each semester. Because I taught all of the courses, I was able to get to know the students and to tailor presentation methods and assignments to individuals' needs. We met for the entire morning each day, a timetable that ensured continuity and allowed us to schedule field trips, visit workplaces and bring in guest speakers without disturbing other teachers. In the afternoon, students who did not yet have a Grade 12 English credit had the option of taking Language and Technical Communication, a course specially designed for vocational students. For seven weeks each semester, students worked half days or full days at job placements.

Sustainable Development and Jobs: In this course, students were introduced to the concept of sustainable development, beginning with a look at what the local environment was like in the past. For the historical background, we studied the early works of Ernest Thompson Seton (author, artist, Manitoba's first naturalist, and co-founder of Boy Scouts of America), early maps, and a local program called "Recycling in the 1850s" that demonstrates how early settlers reused materials. We briefly reviewed the history of the concept of sustainable development and discussed the importance of Rachel Carson's *Silent Spring*, the Brundtland Commission's *Our Common Future*, and the Rio Earth Summit document *Agenda 21*. This led to a discussion of the ethics and challenges associated with sustainable development.

In preparation for their work placements, students were introduced to more than 200 jobs in the envi-
ronmental industry sector. In our area, these include conservation officer, biologist, forester, waste water treatment officer, ecologist, pollution prevention researcher and recycler. Students researched an occupation of their choice, using the library and the Internet, contacting Canada Employment and interviewing someone in the field. They then presented their findings to the class.

Chemical Handling and Research: The first aim of this course was to give students an in-depth understanding of safe chemical-handling procedures. Students received training from a local community college in the transportation of dangerous goods (TDG), for which they earn a TDG safety card that is recognized across North America. In cooperation with the Steelworkers Union and a local steel mill, students also took the Workplace Hazardous Materials Information System (WHMIS) course that is taught to all mill employees. Some students have reported that having both the TDG and the WHMIS certificates has been the deciding factor in their receiving job offers.

A second aim of the course was to have students learn the basics of report writing and how to use the Internet for research and business. One student assigned to work with a local auto recycler reported that her employer was using the Internet to answer bids for auto parts from as far away as Australia.

Laboratory Techniques and Theory: This course provided students with practical exposure to safety procedures in chemical laboratories. A major assignment was to conduct an inventory and safety evaluation of the chemicals in our high school's science department and to send the results to the appropriate safety committees. Students also studied the use of chemicals on farms and in households and considered the pros and cons of banning chemicals from agricultural use. Overall, this course helped to provide students with the skills and confidence needed to conduct themselves safely during their work placements and later in life.

English–Language and Technical Communication: Students who opted to take Language and Technical Communication had an opportunity to apply their learning by writing a 20-page report on an environmental topic of their choice. One requirement was that the report be useful to an outside group. Every finished report was bound and presented to the relevant group. Topics included aerial photography as a wildlife management tool, indigenous dance as an expression of respect for the environment, household recycling, green schools, farm chemical use, and new farm

technology, such as adjusting fertilizer delivery using Global Positioning System units on tractors.

Introduction to the Six Rs: This course provided an application of the theoretical concepts of sustainable development. The aim was to familiarize the students with all of the Six Rs — refuse, reduce, replace, reuse, recycle and restore — and to correct the common misconception that recycling is the most important of them. Examining each of the Rs in detail, students made connections to their own environment. They also examined at least one major related issue highlighted in the media.

Students then put the Rs into practice by becoming involved in the school's papermaking program, producing greeting cards on recycled paper. Students were also involved in the ongoing design and restoration of a wet and dry prairie habitat area behind the school. Besides planting, weeding and watering, they prepared the area for field trips by students at all grade levels. At the suggestion of one group of students, food was grown in an area adjacent to the prairie restoration area for the local food bank and soup kitchen. One fall, students harvested more than 100 kilograms (220 pounds) of produce.

Introduction to Environmental Assessment: This course acquainted students with one of the most innovative aspects of the burgeoning environmental industries sector. In examining the principles and issues of environmental assessment, we looked at the potential conflicts inherent in the interrelationship of the economy, the environment and the health of society. Students learned the Canadian Safety Standards Association's Phase 1 Environmental Site Assessment standards. They then applied these standards, along with their knowledge of WHMIS, by conducting safety checks of our classroom, their own kitchens and bathrooms, and the science department's storage area. Students' suggestions for improvements were one of the factors on which they were assessed. Some students subsequently conducted environmental assessments of their family farm or family business, leading to an increased awareness of safety and the correction of many minor problems.

Our interest in environmental assessment led us to conduct the United Nations sponsored Rescue Mission Planet Earth Indicators Survey. This involved an assessment of communities based on 16 indicators of sustainability. Since our area affords easy access to health care and education, receives minimal acid rain, and employs some progressive farming techniques, our overall assessment was quite positive. However, students identified as a matter of concern that access to public transportation was limited to peak hours, making us overly reliant on private automobiles.

Ecology Techniques and Theory: The main aim of this course was to familiarize students with the ecological side of environmental industries. The major strands were the principles of ecology, the identification and culture of common Protista, the identification of prairie plants, the pros and cons of an ecosystem approach to environmental management, and sustainable agriculture. To facilitate a hands-on approach, instruction was given in the use of microscopes, safe methods of handling bacteria, sampling techniques and related WHMIS procedures. Where practical, we integrated these strands with the prairie restoration and food bank/soup kitchen project.

Cooperative work placements

During each semester, students had a seven-week cooperative work period. This was divided into one three-week and one four-week placement, allowing students to experience two different jobs and work environments. Placements were determined by students' job research choices. Each morning from Monday to Thursday, they reported for the morning work shift at a local industry, where they were partnered with someone working in the environmental field that the student researched. These mentors explained what was involved in their jobs and what they liked or disliked about the work. Students could either work right alongside their mentor or be given their own tasks to perform under the mentor's supervision. On Friday mornings, students returned to school, where they compared experiences, made presentations and discussed ways of handling various situations.

Thirty-five employers matched our students with mentors, providing an opportunity for direct application of the skills learned in class. Students tested water quality for municipalities and First Nations reserves, dismantled cars, collected and sorted recyclable materials, and led environmental and historical interpretive walks. They even helped a conservation officer trap bears and clear beaver dams on flooding creeks.

Unifying case study

In order to make the course more relevant and challenging, each semester students did a case study on a subject that was often chosen from "hot" topics in the news. Topics included the controversial harvesting practices of a multinational forest company, over-fishing of cod off the east coast of Canada, envi-

ronmental problems associated with hog farms in and outside of our province, and pollution from a local coal-fired thermoelectric generating station. The case study theme became the major focal theme for all of the Environmental Industries courses in each semester. The students learned that balancing the three dimensions of economy, environment and health of society is not easy. The case study challenged students to evaluate media reports and their personal viewpoints, and to predict the evolution of the topic. It also created more work for the teacher, but the resultant relevancy and intellectual growth far outweighed the extra input required.

Results

The Environmental Industries program exceeded our initial expectations. Both students and community members became more aware of environmental issues, employment in local environmental industries increased, and students saw that what they learned at school was relevant to the world they would enter upon graduation.

Students from all academic backgrounds did well in the program. While some had always been on the honor roll, many academically weak students with previously poor attendance records found the desire and self-confidence to set goals and succeed. Female students, ranging in age from 17 to 39, accounted for more than half of the enrolment, and some were the first women ever to operate the equipment at their work stations. Some of our students were the first members of their families to graduate from high school. Some recruited friends, brothers, sisters and parents into the program. On average, our students received 1.5 job offers on graduation, some of which became career jobs or stepping stones toward post-secondary education. Some students went directly into the field of environmental industries. One graduate summed up her experience in the program by saying, "I learned about myself. I am capable of doing much more than I thought I could."

By increasing environmental awareness, creating partnerships between school and community, boosting local environmental industries and preparing young people to become productive members of society, the Environmental Industries Co-op Education Program represents a small step toward a more sustainable future.

Before retiring from teaching, **John Perry** *taught in Manitoba at various levels from Grade 3 to university. He now works as a consultant on sustainable development issues.*

Education for Sustainability:
An Ecological Approach

*Using nature's intelligent technologies and self-sustaining systems
as the model for a more sustainable human society*

by Marc Companion

Given the limits of Earth, reducing the human impact on the planet is arguably the most important challenge confronting present and future generations. For a growing number of designers and engineers, this means learning to create buildings, technologies and communities that produce no waste and make efficient use of natural resources. What better model could we have than nature itself?

For over three billion years, the natural world has sustained itself and its inhabitants using intelligent systems that have evolved though ongoing refinement. One can think of evolution as the ultimate research and development program, whereby designs continually adapt to create living systems that are truly self-sustaining. Living systems grow their own food, treat their own waste and use energy efficiently. They generate no pollution because everything is recycled through food webs that ensure nothing is wasted. By using loops and cycles rather than linear input–output streams, natural systems make extremely efficient use of resources. Biologically diverse ecosystems also possess self-regulating characteristics not yet found in our comparatively awkward human technologies. Such properties as the ability

to self-organize (form relationships to perpetuate the system), self-repair and self-replicate suggest that the whole is greater than the sum of the parts. In comparison, a pile of car parts on the floor will not organize itself into a functioning car, nor is the car able to repair itself or adapt to its surroundings.

Nature is high-tech. We all marvel at the complexity of our own bodies, and we know that many of our wonder drugs are pharmaceutical replicates of molecules that medicinal plants have been manufacturing for millennia. But did you know that, gram for gram, spiders' silk is five times stronger than steel? This recyclable wonder fiber is manufactured from renewable resources, such as mosquitoes and flies, in safe production processes that we do not yet understand. Scientists around the world, their laboratories filled with spiders, are attempting to discover what the spider has known for millions of years. Similarly, the adhesive industry would love to know what the mussel knows. In the wave-lashed surf of the ocean, mussels attach themselves to rocks using an extraordinary "glue" that works even when it is wet, a property not achieved by most of our toxic epoxies, resins and paints. Nature's computers are the highly evolved brains and nervous systems of living organisms. DNA reliably stores massive amounts of information, as do our own memories. Furthermore, nature has its own form of Internet, whereby unfathomably complex networks share information and nutrients just about everywhere, from the nervous systems in our bodies to the mycorrhizal fungi that extend from the roots of every plant.

Biomimicry is a cutting-edge science aimed at decoding the intelligent technologies that are ubiquitous in the natural world and applying this new understanding to human-made technologies. Note that this is not the same as biotechnology, the premise of which is to manipulate natural processes in order to create outcomes of our choosing, such as genetically engineered crops. Rather than trying to change natural designs, biomimicry aims to imitate them, following the same "rules" as nature and learning from the elegant ways these systems are built. The new inventions inspired by this partnership with nature will transform just about everything we do, from how we harness energy and heal ourselves to the way we do business and manufacture the products of the future.

Ecological design: A partnership with nature

In the emerging field of ecological design, natural systems are the inspiration for strategies to eliminate pollution, repair damaged ecosystems and make efficient use of natural resources. "Green" buildings, for example, are made of non-toxic materials and produce more energy than they use. In schools and neighborhoods, people are growing their own food, treating their own waste ecologically, and increasing biodiversity through the restoration of beneficial living systems in their backyards. Industry is redesigning its production processes to behave more like forests or prairies, whereby everything is valued as a resource and therefore recycled rather than discharged as pollution. Let's take a closer look at some of these exciting applications.

Water purification: In ecologically engineered water treatment systems, wastewater is cycled through a series of tanks containing biologically diverse communities of organisms that consume waste and digest organic pollutants in much the same way that natural wetlands purify water. In these "ecological machines," plants, snails, fish, bacteria and aquatic microorganisms feed on nutrients in the water, transforming wastewater into water that is clean enough to swim in, discharge into a river or recycle for reuse. A system operating at Corkscrew Swamp Nature Reserve near Naples, Florida, treats the sewage from the restrooms used by visitors. The treated water is as clean as the surrounding native swamp, and much of it is recycled for non-potable uses such as flushing toilets. Another ecological waste treatment system, at the Findhorn Foundation in Scotland, cleans the wastewater from a community of 350 people.

Because these systems are built onsite, wastes can be treated where they are generated rather than being transported across town. Furthermore, their biologically diverse ecosystems are stable and robust, able to adapt to changing waste streams and to break down a wide variety of nutrients, including harmful chemicals such as gasoline and caustic drain cleaners. These waste treatment systems also have multiple potential uses, especially if used to treat food waste rather than human waste. The nutrients from restaurant and cafeteria waste, for example, can be converted into products such as fish, hydroponic vegetables and agricultural crops. In schools, these systems can be used not only to treat waste, but also as living laboratories for hands-on learning.

Indoor climate regulation: Living organisms collectively help to regulate the climate of the planet by converting solar and geochemical energy into metabolic pathways. As a result, temperature is moderated, air and water systems are cleansed, and conditions are maintained to support the family of life. We can apply the same strategies to our own buildings by bringing ecosystems indoors to replace our inefficient heating and ventilating systems. Indoor living systems become the heart and lungs of a building, regulating indoor climate by moderating temperature, improving air quality and maintaining comfortable humidity. For example, "breathing walls" consisting of water, rock, frogs, fish, insects and plants act as biofilters that absorb indoor air pollutants.[1] At Stensund Folk College in Stockholm, Sweden, an indoor aquaculture system not only treats wastewater and produces fish, but is also a source of heat that is exported to other buildings on campus.[2]

In addition to the energy efficiency provided by nature's technologies, there are many other benefits of bringing ecosystems inside our homes and offices. "Sick building" syndrome is virtually eliminated as plants remove toxins from the air and add refreshing oxygen. The natural light and greenery of a living system make people feel better. In office buildings, for example, productivity is increased and absenteeism greatly reduced. In schools, generous natural daylight has been correlated with higher test scores and better attendance. There is growing evidence that even the sound of trickling water in the background can soothe hyperactive children and help them focus.

Repairing polluted bodies of water: Engineered ecosystems can repair and restore damaged aquatic environments. In many communities, streams and lakes are overloaded with surface runoff containing fertilizers and chemicals, or degraded by various land use practices. As a result, we find ourselves dealing with algae blooms, chemicals and heavy metals in the food chain, and loss of biodiversity in our lakes and rivers. In an emerging technology called the "Restorer," artificial islands of native wetland plants are floated on the surfaces of lakes and lagoons to digest excess nutrients. This seeding of native plants helps to replenish beneficial symbiotic bacteria and other organisms that once inhabited the body of water, thereby increasing biodiversity to healthier levels. Airlift bubblers circulate the water and sediments, creating gentle currents that pass excess nutrients over the floating ecosystem where they are taken up by plants and other organisms. Over time, as healthy populations of native organisms grow, balance is restored and the native ecosystem begins to take care of itself once again. The first Restorer was installed in 1991 on a 14-acre Massachusetts pond where it has cleaned the water and digested more than 50,000 cubic yards of organic sludge and sediments.[3] More recent applications of Restorer technology include treating slaughterhouse waste in a constructed lagoon in Maryland and digesting excess nutrients entering a golf course pond in Hawaii.

Ecosystems in the classroom

The idea of using nature as a model of sustainability can help to improve the way we teach about the environment. An indoor aquatic ecosystem, for example, is a versatile and interactive tool for learning how complex natural systems work and how our communities affect nature. Modeled after natural aquatic systems, an indoor system is sustained by photosynthesis, nutrient recycling and biodiversity. Like nature, it contains a variety of habitats and is capable of producing its own food and treating its own waste via complex food webs.

As a living laboratory, a classroom aquatic ecosystem offers almost limitless educational opportunities. By creating different kinds of habitat and observing what lives there, students can learn what living organisms need to survive. They can also safely vary conditions within the ecosystem to test hypotheses to all kinds of questions: What happens to carbon dioxide levels in the water if we cover the plants? How do aquatic invertebrates such as dragonflies behave at different times in their life cycle? How can we modify the hydraulics of our system so that the water flows faster? How will the system respond to excess nutrients if we introduce some of the pollutants that are affecting nearby streams and lakes?

Some of the curriculum areas that relate to the study of a classroom aquatic ecosystem include:

- physics (hydraulics, water properties, thermodynamics)

- organic chemistry and water chemistry

- biology (competition, natural selection, territoriality, population dynamics, taxonomy, adaptation, biotic and abiotic interactions, and ecotones)

- environmental studies (habitat needs, ecological relationships, water pollution and the watershed in our community)

From Mars to my schoolyard: The ecological school

In teaching the idea of sustainability, some of the more advanced explorations that may be taken with high school students include the concepts of homeostasis and self-regulation, the notion that nature is self-organizing, the recognition of patterns, fractals and systems thinking. (See "Roadmap for a Sustainable Future," page 43.) Not surprisingly, students are fascinated by such ideas. The study of space colonies is an engaging entry point into these explorations. Comparing the similarities and differences between Earth and the rest of the solar system (as we know it) provides insight into the workings of our own living planet. The study of space colonies also helps students think about the impact of human settlements on their surroundings. What does it take to support life? What are the needs of people in a space station or a colony on Mars? What are the needs of people living in my neighborhood? How can we support ourselves indefinitely with the limited resources available? Grappling with such questions helps students to evaluate, in an exciting way, the relationship of humans with their surroundings and critically analyze our built environment. It is also an important step toward developing skills for stewardship. Just as energy generation, food production and waste treatment are all essential in space, so too are these systems in our cities, schools and homes. A typical question that students move toward is "How can I make my school or house like a space station, so that it produces its own energy, grows its own food and treats its own waste?"

How *do* our school campuses measure up to the values and lessons we are teaching? Do our buildings improve water quality, enhance biological diversity and fit into the landscape, or are they constructed of toxic materials? Do they use non-renewable energy inefficiently? Do they discharge polluted water into the municipal sewer system for someone else to clean

Roadmap for a Sustainable Future

Developing an understanding of the world around us is linked to our ability to make decisions for the long term. In this example, an integrated science curriculum (left column) develops the skills for reducing our impact on the environment through activities such as habitat restoration, soil building and pollution mitigation. Futurist skills provide the context for the science learning by emphasizing stewardship, creating a common vision, thinking outside the box and mobilizing resources for change. The schoolyard becomes the laboratory for applying these ideas.

—by Jim Laurie, Gail Shaw and Marc Companion

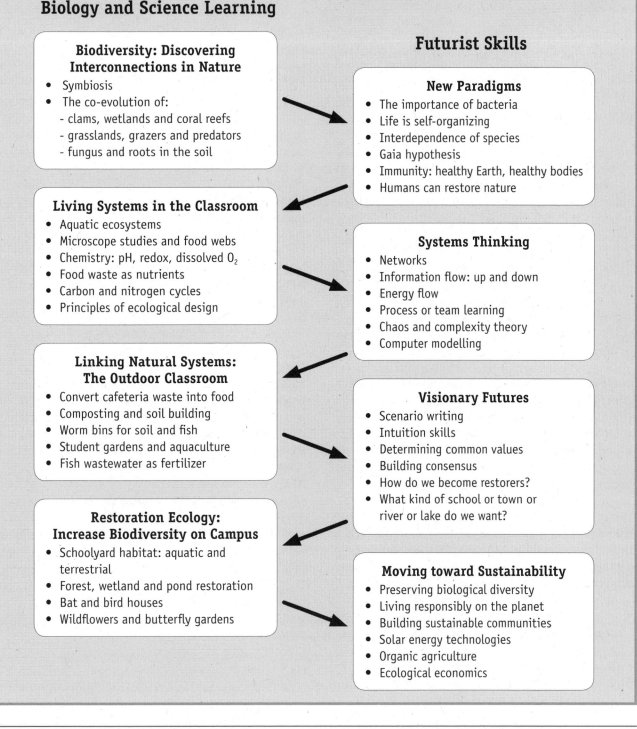

Biology and Science Learning

Biodiversity: Discovering Interconnections in Nature
- Symbiosis
- The co-evolution of:
  - clams, wetlands and coral reefs
  - grasslands, grazers and predators
  - fungus and roots in the soil

Living Systems in the Classroom
- Aquatic ecosystems
- Microscope studies and food webs
- Chemistry: pH, redox, dissolved O_2
- Food waste as nutrients
- Carbon and nitrogen cycles
- Principles of ecological design

Linking Natural Systems: The Outdoor Classroom
- Convert cafeteria waste into food
- Composting and soil building
- Worm bins for soil and fish
- Student gardens and aquaculture
- Fish wastewater as fertilizer

Restoration Ecology: Increase Biodiversity on Campus
- Schoolyard habitat: aquatic and terrestrial
- Forest, wetland and pond restoration
- Bat and bird houses
- Wildflowers and butterfly gardens

Futurist Skills

New Paradigms
- The importance of bacteria
- Life is self-organizing
- Interdependence of species
- Gaia hypothesis
- Immunity: healthy Earth, healthy bodies
- Humans can restore nature

Systems Thinking
- Networks
- Information flow: up and down
- Energy flow
- Process or team learning
- Chaos and complexity theory
- Computer modelling

Visionary Futures
- Scenario writing
- Intuition skills
- Determining common values
- Building consensus
- How do we become restorers?
- What kind of school or town or river or lake do we want?

Moving toward Sustainability
- Preserving biological diversity
- Living responsibly on the planet
- Building sustainable communities
- Solar energy technologies
- Organic agriculture
- Ecological economics

Left: A constructed wetland adjacent to a parking lot removes motor oil and other contaminants from stormwater runoff. Right: An ecological waste treatment system at the Findhorn Foundation in Scotland cleans wastewater for a community of 350 people.

up? What is their ecological footprint? What could we do to make our schools more self-supporting? Such inquiries can be part of an integrated curriculum that combines hands-on learning, group discussions, tours and field trips, group visioning and design work, and student presentations. As a starting point, students can find out the following:

Energy: Identify the school's energy needs. What energy sources supply the school? How are these energy supplies produced? How much energy is used monthly, annually? What is the school's energy used for (heating, cooling, equipment, lights, etc.)? What are the major consumers of energy on campus? What are the costs associated with these energy supplies?

Food: What foods are used on campus? How much does the school spend monthly or annually on food? Where do the foods come from and how far have they traveled before reaching the school? What percentage of food is imported from outside the campus? How are these foods produced and how do these agricultural processes affect the health of nature and local farmers?

Waste: What kinds of waste does the school generate? What activities create the waste? How much of each kind of waste is produced? How are wastes treated or where are they disposed of? How much does the school spend to dispose of the waste? How do the wastes impact the environment?

Schoolyard habitat: What species are present in our schoolyard? What used to live in this place before humans moved in? What kinds of habitat does our schoolyard have? How can we increase biodiversity in our schoolyard? In our neighborhood?

There are a great many projects that students can undertake to make their schools function more like natural systems. These might include building and installing solar panels to capture the sun's energy, planting native species in the schoolyard to increase biodiversity and provide wildlife habitat, composting cafeteria food wastes and converting their nutrients into organic vegetables, or creating schoolyard wetlands to filter runoff from roofs and parking lots. Students can create a plan for redesigning the school to minimize its impact on the natural environment. Encourage them to present their findings and recommendations, and help them to engage other community members in discussing how to create a place that is worthy of passing on to future generations. Such hands-on activities give students a sense of belonging and purpose while simultaneously making education more meaningful. With a keener understanding of natural systems and ecological design strategies, students will be better prepared to meet the challenges of life on an Earth of limited resources.

Marc Companion is an environmental education and international development consultant in Burlington, Vermont, and former education coordinator for Ocean Arks International.

Notes

1. See Becky Gillette et al, "The Living Wall: Urban Biofiltration," *E Magazine* 10:1 (January-February 1999), <www.emagazine.com/january-february_1999/0199inbrief.html>.

2. See EcoEng-online, International Ecological Engineering Society, <www.iees.ch/cs/cs_1.html>.

3. See Ocean Arks International, <www.oceanarks.org/nwt10rst_Restorer_Technology.php>.

RiverWatch

Learning About Ecosystems

❀ **Discovering Lake Management** by Matthew R. Opdyke

❀ **The Tantramar Wetlands Centre Project** by Chris Porter

❀ **Using Epiphytic Lichens as Bio-indicators of Air Pollution** by Andrew Kett, Sonia Dong, Heather Andrachuk and Brian Craig

❀ **Carbon Cycle: Measuring CO$_2$ Flux from Soil** by Robert Lessard, L. Dennis Gignac and Philippe Rochette

❀ **Tank Tips: A Freshwater Aquarium in the Classroom** by Rebecca Holcombe

❀ **Nitrogen Pollution: Too Much of a Good Thing** by David A. Bainbridge

❀ **Living Systems in the Classroom** by Mark Keffer

❀ **RiverWatch: Science on the River** by Cal Kullman

Discovering Lake Management

by Matthew R. Opdyke

Subject areas: biology, chemistry

Key concepts: aquatic life, characteristics of watersheds and lakes, aquatic habitat, water chemistry, algae, nutrients, eutrophication, conservation of water resources

Skills: observation, data gathering and recording, water testing, identifying algae, debating

Location: outdoors at a pond or lake

Time: 1 day to prepare equipment, go to the site, and conduct sampling of plant habitats, water quality and algae; 1.5 hours of class time for debates on water-quality conservation.

Materials: worksheets, plant and algae identification guides, water-quality testing equipment, compound microscope

A student collecting algae for examining under a microscope.

Teaching about lake management is an exciting way to get students interested in the environment and to provide them hands-on opportunities to learn about the biology and chemistry of lakes. This article offers instruction for three field activities that allow students to evaluate the health of a lake and learn the basics of lake management through a classroom debate.

Humans rely on lakes for drinking water, cropland irrigation, recreation and other uses. Additionally, lakes provide habitat for a variety of aquatic life, such as fish, microscopic animals called zooplankton, aquatic plants and algae. The fact that such a diversity of aquatic life, not to mention humans and other terrestrial organisms, all depend on lakes suggests the need to ensure that they are managed properly. Both Canada and the United States have enacted legislation

governing the quality and use of water resources, and both countries support the Great Lakes Water Quality Agreement to preserve water quality in the Great Lakes. However, lake management does not begin or end with formal legislation. Managing a lake requires the collaboration of many individuals, from those whose activities directly affect the lake to experts in chemistry, biology, natural resource management and socio-economics.

The most important concept to grasp when managing a lake is that lake management must begin in the watershed. A watershed is a specific area of land that drains water into rivers, lakes or other bodies of water. A lake is a reflection of its watershed because the nature of the landscape — its topography, geology, vegetation and use — influences the types of materials that enter it. Whenever possible, watershed sources of pollution are treated before problems within a lake are addressed. Consider a case in which excess nutrients enter a lake from rivers draining an agricultural watershed, resulting in an uncontrolled growth of algae in the lake. It would be poor management to add herbicides to the lake as a way of controlling algae growth, because considerable amounts of herbicide would be required, along with continuous treatments throughout the growing season to prevent a recurrence. A more appropriate action would be to encourage farmers to reduce the amount of fertilizer applied to their fields or to construct wetlands and grass buffer strips along rivers to capture nutrients from surface runoff.

The most pervasive water quality problem in the world is eutrophication, or the presence of excess nutrients such as phosphorus and nitrogen that disturb the balance of aquatic life. Excess nutrients accelerate the growth of aquatic plants, particularly algae, which grow faster and respond more quickly to changes in nutrients than do larger plants. An overabundance of algae reduces water clarity, and the decomposition of algae by bacteria reduces oxygen levels in the water. Another common and disruptive response to eutrophication is an increase in invasive plants. If invasive plants have already been introduced to a lake, an excess of nutrients can stimulate aggressive growth, allowing them to compete with and displace native plants.

The field activities proposed here concentrate on measuring three parameters associated with eutrophication in a lake: habitat resources, water quality, and algae diversity and abundance. These activities are best conducted at a small lake, one less than 30 hectares in area, so that the teacher can keep an eye on more adventurous students. If there are enough teachers and assistants, supervision can be made easier by separating students into groups of three to five with an assistant to supervise each group. Some of the chemicals in the recommended test kits should be treated with caution.

Investigating Habitat Resources

Time: 1 hour

Materials: aquatic plant identification guide, Habitat Resources Worksheet (see example)

Background:
The presence or absence of lake habitat features largely depends on the condition of the shoreline and whether nutrients are entering the lake by way of a river. If the shoreline is wooded or if rocks have been placed along the bank to prevent erosion, an abundance of submerged wood or rocks could be present. Some aquatic insects attach themselves to the undersides of submerged wood and rocks to escape predatory fish. In shallow waters, the surfaces of wood and rocks that are exposed to sunlight provide substrates for the colonization of algae, which are themselves fed on by several species of fish and aquatic insects.

In areas where nutrients enter the lake by way of a river and sunlight can penetrate to the lake bottom, aquatic plants will often grow in greater abundance than in deeper waters further from the nutrient source. Aquatic plants provide shelter from predators and serve as a food source for a diversity of aquatic life, such as the common carp and aquatic insects. In addition, young fish often find shelter in areas of dense plant growth, making aquatic vegetation an ideal breeding ground for many species of fish. However, an overabundance of aquatic plants or the presence of invasive plants may be detrimental to aquatic life. Invasive species such as Eurasian watermilfoil *(Myriophyllum spicatum)*, which is found throughout North America, may displace native plants and spread so extensively that fish breeding grounds are lost and food supplies diminished.

The methods frequently used by lake managers to curb the growth of invasive plants include treatment

Habitat Resources Worksheet

1. What are the two most abundant plants?
2. Are there any invasive plants? If so, list the names of invasive plants.
3. Do invasive plants outnumber native plants? If so, are invasive plants 25, 50, 75 or 100% more abundant than native plants?
4. Is water clarity impaired by the presence of algae on the water surface?
5. Is there sufficient plant cover to shelter fish from predators, and what type of plant provides the best shelter?
6. Besides plants, are there any other types of shelter for aquatic life along the lakeshore (e.g., large rocks)?

with herbicides, physical removal and biological controls. A systemic herbicide called fluridone is one option in the control of Eurasian watermilfoil, but it is non-specific and therefore has the tendency to kill native plants as well. More selective controls are to physically remove the plants by hand or to introduce weevils and beetles that feed specifically on watermilfoil. The success of these methods depends on the extent of watermilfoil growth and the investment in getting rid of the invasives. Physical removal must be done at least annually or watermilfoil will reestablish from seeds buried in lake sediments, whereas biological controls may be self-sustaining once the weevils or beetles are established and reproducing.

Introduction:

In this activity, students identify aquatic plants and assess habitat features at three different sites along a lakeshore. This simple observational task is a critical step in identifying potential threats to a lake. The locations of the study sites, as well as the area of shoreline and lake to be observed, largely depend on accessibility and the age of students. Preferably, the study sites should be within walking distance of each other and have features that provide diversity in habitats, such as shoreline development, woodlands or proximity to river inlets. A shoreline length of 15 meters and a distance out into the lake of 6 meters is sufficient for most sites.

The most challenging part of this activity is identifying the plants. It is essential to have a well-illustrated key to aquatic plants, such as *Through the Looking Glass: A Field Guide to Aquatic Plants* by Susan Borman et al. Information on aquatic plants can also be researched on the Internet: Texas A&M University, for example, has an excellent plant identification guide with pictures and descriptions of the ecology of aquatic plants (see Resources). It is also useful for the teacher to visit the lake before the field trip to get an idea of what plants are present. You may wish to construct a field guide specific to your lake by photographing the plants and pasting the photographs on paper adjacent to the plant names. If you have access to waders, students could collect plants, which would make identification easier.

Procedure:

1. Upon arriving at the lake, organize students into groups and give a brief introduction to the uses of the land surrounding the lake and the importance of investigating habitat resources, water quality and algae when considering how best to manage a lake.

2. Provide each group of students with an aquatic plant identification guide and a Habitat Resources Worksheet for each study site.

3. Explain that the groups are to rotate to three different study sites along the lakeshore. At each site, they are to observe the features of the lake habitat and answer the questions on the worksheet.

4. When the groups have completed the habitat study, either collect the completed worksheets for safekeeping or have students keep them until the end of the field trip.

Testing Water Quality

Time: 1 hour

Materials: table or other flat surface, water quality test kits or strips, plastic bottles, boat or waders, one Water Quality Data Sheet for each sampling site (see example)

Background:

Excess plant nutrients, particularly phosphorus and nitrogen, can lead to unhealthy growth of aquatic plants and algae in lakes. Several forms of phosphorus (organic phosphorus and phosphate) and nitrogen (organic nitrogen, nitrate and ammonium) can be found in lakes. The organic forms of these elements

Water Quality Data Sheet

Sample Location	Time of Sampling	Nitrate Concentration (mg/L)	Phosphate Concentration (mg/L)
river inlet	10:10 AM	1.1	0.3
forested shoreline	10:20 AM	0.4	<0.1
open shoreline for recreation	10:30 AM	0.7	<0.1

are contained in aquatic life and other organic material, such as leaves that are washed into the lake from the surrounding watershed. Of the inorganic forms, ammonium is rarely measured to any significant level in the surface waters, unless there is a source of ammonium pollution entering the lake. Concentrations of phosphate and nitrate are therefore the water-quality indicators used to identify eutrophication.

Under healthy conditions, the concentration of phosphate in freshwater lakes is typically lower than that of nitrate. For this reason, phosphate is the better indicator of eutrophication: an increase in phosphate will yield a quicker growth response in algae and aquatic plants than will a similar increase in nitrate. However, high concentrations of nitrate may indicate that nitrogen fertilizers are being washed from croplands into rivers in the watershed upstream of the lake. Generally, concentrations of phosphate and nitrate that exceed 0.1 and 0.5 milligrams per liter, respectively, are high nutrient levels that could result in eutrophication.

Introduction:
Phosphate and nitrate concentrations can be measured using nutrient test kits, which are available at many science supply stores. These are portable kits, unique for each nutrient being measured, containing step-by-step directions and all necessary supplies. The directions require the user to add a small packet of chemicals to a water sample, producing a color change. The color of the water is then compared to a color key on a chart indicating nutrient concentrations. An alternative to test kits is test strips, which require the user to dip a chemically treated strip into a water sample. Test strips are a better option for younger students and are typically cheaper than test kits. The disadvantage is that they are less accurate than the test kits.

Procedure:
1. Identify a central location among the study sites (the same sites used for investigating habitat resources) and set up a water-quality testing station consisting of a table, water collection bottles, a test kit or test strips and a Water Quality Data Sheet.

2. Have each group of students follow instructions for submerging a water collection bottle beneath the lake surface to collect water samples from each of the three study sites.

3. At the water-quality testing station, have each group analyze their water samples and record the phosphate and nitrate readings on the data sheet. This activity is the most demanding of the three because it requires attention to detail when conducting the water tests. If the groups have different results due to errors in analyses, the teacher will need to determine which measurements are the most accurate.

4. As an extension of this activity, students could use a long-handled dipper or similar apparatus to collect water samples at different depths at the center of the lake. In deeper water where sunlight does not penetrate, nutrient concentrations may be greater if algae are consuming the available surface nutrients.

Identifying Algae

Time: 1 hour

Materials: compound microscope and slides, plastic pipettes or straws, plastic water collection bottles, boat or waders, algae identification guide, Algae Identification Worksheets

Background:
The purpose of this activity is to introduce students to the lake's microscopic life by having them collect and view algae under a compound microscope. Through this activity, many students will get their first peek at a community of organisms that are a major food source for aquatic life and are the backbone to the survival of many fish.

In lake management, algae are seen as beneficial because they are an important food and energy source for zooplankton and fish. However, too much algae growth could indicate that a lake is eutrophic. An over-abundance of algae can clog water treatment facilities; cloud the water, thereby stunting aquatic plant growth; and produce undesirable tastes and odors. Additionally, when excess algae die and settle to the lake bottom, they are decomposed by bacteria, causing a reduction in oxygen concentrations that can suffocate fish and bottom-dwelling organisms. Low oxygen is a common problem in water bodies throughout the world, including Lake Erie in the Great Lakes, the Gulf of Mexico and the Gulf of St. Lawrence.

On average, lakes host more than 100 species of algae annually, of which 8 to 10 species account for 90 percent of the total algae population. The abundance and diversity of algae fluctuate with temperature, sunlight, nutrients and flow. In winter, the most common groups are dinoflagellates, small green algae, golden-brown algae and some diatoms. The fast-growing diatoms dominate in spring; green algae, dinoflagellates

Left: Students preparing to collect water samples from the center of the lake. Right: Students use chemical test kits to measure nitrate and phosphate concentrations in lake water samples.

and cyanobacteria are the most abundant in summer. Cyanobacteria frequently dominate in eutrophic waters when phosphorus exceeds nitrogen concentrations. This is due to cyanobacteria's ability, unique among algae, to convert atmospheric nitrogen to a biologically available form of nitrogen. This process is called nitrogen fixation.

In many cases, algae growth is strongly dependent on nutrient concentrations. In freshwater, phosphate is generally the nutrient that causes excessive algae growth. Phosphate originates from such sources as wastewater treatment plants, fertilizers applied to cropland and animal waste. When high phosphate concentrations originate from a wastewater treatment plant, management is directed toward reducing concentrations in the effluent. For example, constructing wetlands between the wastewater outflow and the receiving body of water allows aquatic plants to strip the phosphorus from the water. If the situation is more complex, with multiple sources of nutrients throughout the watershed that cannot be treated directly, methods must be found for reducing algae abundance within the lake. Some options are to increase flow through the lake to flush algae out a river outlet, to apply herbicides, and to grow wetland plants along the shoreline to reduce sunlight penetration into the water and absorb phosphorus.

Procedure:

1. Have students collect water samples. This can be done in the same manner as for the water-quality testing, and simultaneously if time is a concern. If possible, sample from both the open water and along the shoreline, as this may yield different types of algae.

For example, diatoms are more tolerant of shade than green algae. The volume of the sample is not critical: only a milliliter or two is needed for examination under a compound microscope.

2. If an electrical outlet is available at the field study site for illuminating samples on slides, students can view the algae in the field. Alternatively, have students observe and identify the algae in the classroom after the field trip. Use a plastic pipette or straw to transfer a drop of water to a microscope slide. One drop of water roughly equals one milliliter, so if students count the number of algae on their slide they can estimate the density of algae, expressed in abundance per milliliter. Examining algal density may prove beneficial if there are observable differences in water quality along the lakeshore (e.g., in an area adjacent to a forest, as opposed to a river inlet where the water has a high phosphate concentration).

3. Have students identify the algae in their samples by group (e.g., green algae, cyanobacteria, diatoms). This exercise usually requires the aid of a teacher or assistant who has basic skill in identifying algae using pictures. The Internet provides abundant resources for learning about algae. For example, Microscopy-UK offers an excellent online identification guide for algae groups. For a hard-copy reference, *A Beginner's Guide to Freshwater Algae* by Belcher and Swale is a serviceable identification guide. (See Resources list.)

4. Have each group record the names and density of each type of algae they identify, organized according to where the samples were collected (see Algae Identification Worksheet).

Algae Identification Worksheet

Sample Location	Time of Sampling	Groups of algae and their abundances per milliliter of water
river inlet	10:10 AM	green algae - 23
		diatoms - 11
		cyanobacteria - 5

Discussion of results

At the end of the field trip, collect all worksheets and check them for accuracy. Unavoidably, errors in plant and algae identification and water-quality measurement and recording will occur. Therefore, choose the most reliable data to use for a classroom discussion. The discussion should be initiated by the teacher, allowing students to interact with comments and questions while the teacher presents the results from the field trip. Once the results have been presented, the discussion can focus on how the results help determine the health of the lake. For example, a general absence of invasive plants, a diversity of algae (more than two groups)and sufficient habitat cover for aquatic life indicate a healthy lake. However, if floating mats of algae persist throughout the lake, and phosphate and nitrate concentrations are greater than 0.1 and 0.5 milligrams per liter, respectively, the lake may be eutrophic.

There are a variety of factors beyond those investigated in these activities that could lead to a lake's being assessed as healthy or unhealthy. The Internet provides many sources of information on how lake health is perceived and what it means for both humans and aquatic life (see Resources list). Additional discussion questions that might lead to interesting conversations include the following: How are aquatic organisms or humans affected by poor water quality? What additional tests could be conducted to determine the health of the lake? How might water-quality measurements and algae vary in different seasons?

Lake Management Debate

After discussing the results, separate the class into four or five groups. Assign each group a role to play in a discussion of how their lake should be managed to maintain or to improve its health. A variety of roles could be assigned, such as a farmer growing crops upriver from the lake, a mayor of a town that is located adjacent to the lakeshore, a fisherman and a manager of a wastewater facility that discharges into the lake.

Provide each group with a brief explanation of their job and ambitions (see Role Descriptions below). Then give each group 10 to 15 minutes to prepare a 5- to 10-minute presentation to the class on how the lake should be managed from their point of view. The remaining class period could be spent having the groups decide on a lake management action plan that would either be of most benefit to the lake or satisfy all of the roles included in the discussion.

Role descriptions

Farmer: The farmer's priority is producing the highest corn yield possible, which requires the application of nitrogen and phosphorus fertilizer on his fields. If the fertilizer is not applied, the crop yield will decline by 50 percent and the farmer will go bankrupt in five years. The lake is located one mile downstream from a river that drains his land and transports any fertilizer washed from the fields during rainstorms into the lake. The farmer wants to do his best to maintain the health of the lake. However, his priority is making a profit in order to support his family, and he cannot cut back on fertilizer.

Mayor: The mayor serves the public and must make decisions based on the needs of a large population. The lake serves as a water supply and offers recreational opportunities that provide tourism revenue for the nearby town. Therefore, good water quality is imperative. The mayor recognizes that managing the lake is a necessity, but wants to find a way to satisfy everyone in the lake's watershed.

Fisherman: The fisherman does not live within the lake's watershed, but frequently enjoys catching and eating fish from the lake. He supports all efforts at maintaining or improving the health of the lake, particularly since there are few other lakes in the area to fish from.

Wastewater facility manager: The manager of the wastewater facility has little incentive to improve the health of the lake. She realizes that nutrients are being discharged into the lake from the wastewater facility, but any efforts to reduce the nutrient discharge would cost her money. All of the waste being treated at the facility originates in the nearby town, and the manager recently spent a large sum of money enlarging the facility to accommodate the growing town.

Management options

There are numerous management options that students might consider. Depending on the flexibility of the group's attitude, the farmer can be stubborn and refuse to take any action or can apply for government grants to grow grass buffer strips along the river. Buffer strips can absorb phosphorus and nitrogen before they enter the river and flow downstream into the lake. An alternative is to grow a crop other than corn, one that is not dependent on fertilizer.

After hearing the farmer's decision, the mayor may respond by passing laws to limit fertilizer applications if the farmer is stubborn. Alternatively, the mayor could choose to address any problems at the lake instead of at the source. In some cases, this becomes a necessity, such as when there is a strong coalition of farmers in the watershed capable of blocking any laws that require a reduction in fertilizer applications. Management options for reducing nitrogen and phosphorus in the lake could include diverting some of the inlet flow from the river around the lake or constructing wetlands at the river inlet to absorb nutrients before they enter the lake.

Management options offered by the fisherman may include volunteering his time to physically remove invasive plants or, if there is excessive algae growth, lending his expertise in identifying what species of fish consume large amounts of algae. Unfortunately for the fisherman, he does not live in the watershed. Therefore, the farmer, mayor and wastewater facility manager may choose to ignore his opinions if improving the health of the lake becomes costly.

Although the manager of the wastewater facility has little interest in the health of the lake, she realizes that others will act and that the management action plan may be detrimental to her business if she does not recommend any alternatives. One alternative may be to increase taxes in the town to pay for constructing wetlands that would remove nutrients from the effluent before it enters the lake. This might be acceptable to the mayor and taxpayers, considering that the manager's facility is treating their waste. The manager could also apply for government grants to improve methods of removing nutrients from the waste effluent, or work with the farmer to transport some of the nutrient-laden waste to his fields for fertilizer.

The number of different roles and management options is endless. Discovering them and developing ideas on lake management is an activity that gets students involved in thinking about how communities interact about water issues and the importance of preserving natural resources. Together, the field trip and the classroom debate give students an introduction to the methods and challenges of lake management. The field trip is an excellent opportunity for hands-on learning about physical, chemical and biological aspects of lakes, while the classroom debate utilizes their results from the field trip to think critically about how we manage our resources and the difficulties in addressing everyone's opinions.

Matthew R. Opdyke is an Assistant Professor of Environmental Studies at Point Park University in Pittsburgh, Pennsylvania.

Resources

Aquatic Plant Identification

Belcher, Hilary and Erica Swale. Institute of Freshwater Ecology. *A Beginner's Guide to Freshwater Algae.* The Stationery Office Books, 1977.

Borman, S., R. Korth, J. Temte and C. Watkins. *Through the Looking Glass: A Field Guide to Aquatic Plants.* University of Wisconsin Press, 1997.

Microscopy-UK. *Pond Life ID Kit*, online at <www.microscopy-uk.org.uk/> (follow link to algae section of the online Pond Life ID Kit).

Texas Cooperative Extension, Department of Wildlife and Fisheries Science, Texas A&M University. *AquaPlant*, online plant identification guide with pictures and descriptions of the ecology of aquatic plants, <http://aquaplant.tamu.edu/>.

Lake Management

Aquatic Ecosystems by U.S. Environmental Protection Agency <www.epa.gov/ebtpages/wateaquaticecosystems.html>. Information on aquatic environments and the effects of water pollution.

Great Lakes Information Network (GLIN). Teach.GLIN.Net, <www.great-lakes.net/teach/>. Background on the Great Lakes and lake management issues in the region.

Herbert, P.D.N., Ed. *Canada's Aquatic Environments*, <www.aquatic.uoguelph.ca/>. Educational materials on aquatic life and the environments they frequent.

Washington State Lake Protection Association. *The Washington Lake Book*, <www.ecy.wa.gov/programs/wq/plants/lakes/book_contents.html>. Resource for understanding lakes, indicators for identifying water quality problems, and management options.

The Tantramar Wetlands Centre Project

High school students deliver wetland education programs to 4,000 schoolchildren annually at their school's restored wetland in New Brunswick

by Chris Porter

Subject areas: science (environmental, biology, chemistry, earth science), vocational education, technology (web design, media studies), music, art

Key concepts: wetlands, conservation, sustainability, biodiversity, water quality, populations, endangered species, invasive species, ecosystems, land use, disturbance, pollution, public education, careers

Skills: observing, measuring, recording and analyzing data, using laboratory and field equipment; waterfowl banding, tracking and trapping, species identification, controlling invasive species, canoeing, plant techniques, species surveys, field research, mapping, teaching and public speaking, equipment and facility maintenance, fundraising, public relations

Location: any wetland area

Time: one semester to establish program; training can be a regularly scheduled class or take place at lunch time or before and after school

Wetlands are the planet's second most biologically diverse habitats, and over half of world's endangered species depend in some way upon them for their survival. Wetlands can prevent damage due to flooding, help purify water and provide many recreational opportunities. Unfortunately, too many people still view wetlands as wastelands. While policies and regulations are in place in most jurisdictions to provide some measure of protection for wetlands, education can be a more powerful and long lasting approach to wetland conservation. The success of the Tantramar Wetlands Centre in New Brunswick clearly demonstrates this.

Tantramar Regional High School in Sackville, New Brunswick, has developed a wetlands education center that each year attracts thousands of students and teachers from across the Atlantic region. They come to participate in a variety of experiential programs that are delivered in large part by the Tantramar students themselves. The project has earned national recognition for its innovative approach to teaching and learning about the environment, and it has certainly captured the attention of the school's own student population, over 100 of whom are involved in the project. Known as "Wetheads," these students manage a unique facility that includes a restored wetland and a teaching facility where visitors are introduced to the importance of wetlands through participation in a host of hands-on activities, from banding ducks to trapping muskrats.

Designed as an outdoor classroom, the 15-hectare (37-acre) freshwater wetland impoundment allows great views of wildlife and immediate access to the water. A fully equipped wet lab and teaching theater are just steps away from the cattails in space that once housed the school's automotive program. With Tantramar's immediate proximity to the main highway connecting New Brunswick and Nova Scotia and its location just minutes away from the bridge to Prince Edward Island, there are over 60,000 students in three provinces that are less than an hour from the center.

Wetheads out early on a winter morning to drill holes in the ice so that visitors can sample invertebrates as part of the Winter in the Wetlands program.

History of the project

As in most parts of the world, wetland loss is a significant problem in eastern Canada. The Tantramar Regional High School is located on the edge of the Tantramar Marshes, a huge expanse of land that was almost entirely salt marsh in pre-settlement times. By the late 1700s, the Acadians had drained and diked the marshes, creating agricultural dike lands that still dominate the landscape today. As a result of these and other past and present land use practices, over 80 percent of the pre-settlement salt marshes have disappeared.

The Tantramar Wetlands Centre had its beginning in 1998, when school staff met with officials from Ducks Unlimited Canada, the Canadian Wildlife Service, the local school district, and the Province of New Brunswick to ask for assistance in creating a small wetland on the school's campus. The response was generous and immediate. Ducks Unlimited agreed to provide funding and engineering expertise to build the wetland, the Canadian Wildlife Service offered to provide building materials for pathways and viewing structures, and the

Town of Sackville volunteered to assist with their construction.

While conservation is central to the project's mission, the decision to restore a small area of wetland habitat was based on the school's desire to enrich the learning environment for its students and teachers. Specifically, teachers wanted to develop a program that would unite curriculum, teach a range of authentic skills, enhance the learning environment for students of all abilities and grade levels, and appeal to the broader community. Given the economic, environmental and cultural significance of the marshes in the Tantramar region and the close proximity of regional offices of both Ducks Unlimited Canada (DUC) and the Canadian Wildlife Service (CWS), the wetlands center had the potential to meet all of these objectives and to be a valuable resource for the benefit of Sackville residents. Led by the vision and determination of the school's principal, a steering committee comprised of teachers, students, school district administrators and representatives from both DUC and CWS began the planning process that would create the Tantramar Wetlands Centre.

One of the first steps taken was to become Tantramar Wetlands Centre Incorporated, a registered non-profit organization that would determine and guide the mission of the project and build the partnership base necessary to fund its construction and ongoing operation. Establishing this arm's-length relationship with the school district and Department of Education was a crucial step in raising the funds needed to build the center and in managing those resources for the strict benefit of the project. Tantramar Wetlands Centre Incorporated is governed by a board of directors made of up representatives from School District 2, Tantramar Regional High School, Ducks Unlimited Canada and the Town of Sackville. The administration and operation of the center is the responsibility of a lead teacher from the high school who serves as the board's executive director.

The school wanted students to be involved in all phases of the project. Therefore, prior to any construction being carried out, twelve Grade 9 students,

Left: Young visitors learn to identify tracks and scat before they head into the marsh on snowshoes. Right: Wethead student demonstrates the setup of a trap used in managing the wetland's muskrat population.

dubbed "the dirty dozen," were recruited to work with teachers and the project engineer on the design and planning of the impoundment. The 12 individuals were identified by their teachers as potential leaders who would attract others as the project grew. It was also felt that, as the youngest members of the student body, they would be able to see the project through all four years of high school.

While much of the initial work on the impoundment was done by machine, students and teachers cleared brush, moved gravel, planted hundreds of native trees and shrubs, built nesting boxes and seeded the newly created dikes to prevent soil erosion. Today, ten of the initial "dirty dozen" students are still with the project, and interest among others has grown quickly so that now more than 100 students participate each year. Some help manage the habitat, constructing nest boxes, maintaining a native plant nursery and winter bird feeding station, battling purple loosestrife, repairing minor damage, and trapping muskrats when necessary. Others gain valuable experience by working alongside wildlife biologists and field technicians from the project's conservation partners in a variety of research endeavors that include banding waterfowl, working on population surveys, conducting species inventories and monitoring water quality. The center's website is managed by the Wetheads, and any catering needs are carried out by students as well. The largest numbers of Tantramar students are involved in the delivery of programs for visiting schools.

Wetland programs

The center's programs are tied closely to seasonal changes in the wetland and are built around activities

and techniques practiced by wildlife biologists. "Wetlands Through Waterfowl" is a fall program that teaches young people about the importance of wetlands by focusing on the best-known wetland residents. The key component of this program is the experience of banding ducks. "Wetlands in Winter" teaches that wetlands are critical habitats even during the coldest months of the year. Participants learn to identify wetland species by their tracks and scat, and then head out to the marsh on snowshoes to practice these skills and observe how much activity there is, even in the winter. "Wetland Case Studies" are offered year-round, but are requested most often by groups visiting in the spring. Participants use field equipment and follow scientific protocols to examine a variety of chemical and biological parameters in order to assess the productivity and health of the wetland. Through these investigations, they learn first hand about the many threats to the quality of wetlands and the key indicators of damage.

Kids-teaching-kids model

Demand for these and other program activities did not take long to develop and it happened largely by accident. While the project was originally intended to be for the benefit of the Tantramar students and teachers, in the year following construction a few neighboring schools were invited to explore the new wetland. From the experiences of these first visitors, word of mouth has resulted in an annual invasion of over 4,000 students from the Atlantic provinces and Québec and from as far away as Texas. With so many visitors, the school made two decisions early on to ensure that its own students would continue to be the main beneficiaries of the project. Days were set aside for the exclusive use of the impoundment by Tantramar classes, and students were invited to become involved in the day-to-day operation of the center. Preparing the students for this responsibility became a key element of the project.

Training takes place both during and outside of the regular school day under the direction of Tantramar teachers and professional staff from the project's various conservation partners, who act as mentors and provide specific skill training. Pupils do not earn academic credit for their work with the center, nor is its operation connected to any specific courses. Because working at the center often results in the pupils being absent from regularly scheduled classes, teacher permission is the key requirement for eligibility. Crucial to the goal of maximum accessibility is the clear expectation on the part of the school's administration that teachers will encourage their students to take advantage of the center and assist them in making up missed work. In spite of the additional workload, each year more students are participating in wetlands activities, citing interest, enjoyment, training opportunities and, of course, time out of class as the main motivators. In the eyes of the Tantramar students, the wetlands center is a "happening place."

In addition to carrying out its own programs, the Tantramar Wetlands Centre now serves as a program provider for Ducks Unlimited Canada, New Brunswick's Department of Natural Resources, Green Street and Project WET. What makes the Tantramar model of delivery unique among environmental education models is its commitment to experiential programming and peer mentoring. The students who participate in program delivery do far more than lug equipment. The Wetheads have come to define the mission of this project. Passionate, enthusiastic and knowledgeable, these high school students have become great teachers and sincere advocates for wetlands. "Kids teaching kids" is very powerful pedagogy and it's what visitors consistently encounter at the Tantramar Wetlands Centre.

A group of Wetheads with a freshly banded duck about to be released.

Curriculum integration

Initially, the construction of a wetland provided the incentive to pilot a thematic approach to curriculum delivery. At the Grade 9 level, specific outcomes across a range of subjects were linked to wetlands and activities taking place in the building and operation of the center. This initiative provided a perfect opportunity to adopt changes that the provincial Department of Education was mandating, specifically a requirement that high schools move towards a team approach to curriculum delivery in the "Foundation Years" of Grades 9 and 10.

With increasing demand for programs at the wetlands center, the original cross-curricular approach in Grade 9 has evolved into a school-wide integration that sees different subject areas responding to the variety of needs created by the center. While the strength of the different subject connections depends largely on the individual teacher, technology students have managed the center's website, construction classes have taken responsibility for minor repairs, chemistry students routinely monitor water quality, culinary classes look after any catering requirements, theater arts students add energy to the education programs for visitors, and there has even been a wetlands choir to sing about Wetheads, muskrats and cattails.

Benefits

In addition to meeting its goals relating to curriculum, skills training and enrichment, the wetlands center is also making a major contribution to school climate. Wetheads represent all grades, abilities and — perhaps most importantly — all school groups, both formal and informal. The student council president, the captain of the football team and the homecoming queen are all wetlands regulars, and so are students who are not members of any team, club or social group. Some are classroom stars and some cannot cope in a regular classroom setting. The center offers something to the academic high flyers and to those who struggle to read and write. All of these students work together to manage the site and deliver its programs, and it is often not the classroom stars who give the orders. An initial lack of experience with nature tends to create a level playing field for the students, so that the usual school pecking order just doesn't apply to working in the wetlands.

Feedback from both students and teachers suggests the experiential nature of the wetlands center and its programs are providing effective environmental education. While largely anecdotal, these measures identify improved attitudes and understanding of environmental issues. Perhaps a better measure of the project's success in delivering environmental education can be found in the attention it has received from other environmental groups and organizations. In 2002, the Tantramar Wetlands Centre received the first National Award of Excellence in Environmental Education from the Canadian Network for Environmental Education and Communication (EECOM). The following year, the North American Wetlands Conservation Council at its national policy convention identified the project as a model for the delivery of wetlands education in Canada; and in 2004, New Brunswick's Department of the Environment presented the Tantramar Wetlands Centre Wetheads with a Provincial Environmental Leadership Award. Ducks Unlimited Canada and Green Street have recognized the project as a "Wetlands Centre of Excellence" for its leadership in environmental education, and this past year the Atlantic Provinces Council on the Sciences presented the Tantramar Wetland Centre with the Science Communication Award of Excellence in the high school category for its effectiveness in engaging young people in science.

Challenges

Establishing a wetlands center should not be viewed as something out of the realm of possibility for most schools. In fact, Ducks Unlimited Canada has been working successfully to initiate similar projects in other regions of Canada. Funding is certainly a constant challenge; but in Tantramar's experience, the core elements of environmental stewardship, education and youth have been very well received by potential sponsors. A hurdle that had to be overcome in the early days was a need to find technical expertise from outside of the school for some areas of the project. As it turned out, this support was readily available, and the project continues to benefit greatly from the role played by community volunteers. Perhaps the biggest challenge for the Tantramar Wetlands Centre has been maintaining the momentum within the school itself. Staff turnover results in an ongoing need to recruit new teachers to participate in the project. While the overall operation of the center is the responsibility

of one lead teacher, involving other staff members is crucial to attracting students. It is the large number of Wetheads who work in the center each year that demonstrate the project's validity and make it unique. The real challenge, then, has been to involve the right teachers, the magnets who attract young people, the teachers whose rooms are always full of students, both during and outside of class time. Tantramar's approach has been, "attract the right teachers and the students will follow," and so far, so good.

Any challenges and frustrations encountered along the way have been far outweighed by the environmental and educational benefits the project delivers. From an ecological standpoint, a biologically diverse, productive wetland ecosystem now sits on what was an abandoned hayfield. In addition to creating habitat for thousands of species, this unique setting provides learning experiences that not only promote healthy attitudes towards wetlands but instill in the thousands of youngsters who visit each year a conservation ethic that will last a lifetime.

Benefits to the instructional program of the high school have been just as profound. Teachers as well as students have an amazing resource that has the potential to enhance and extend learning in virtually every component of the school's curriculum. For some students, being able to participate in such hands-on programs as duck banding and trapping has meant the difference between staying in school and dropping out. Other students have acquired leadership and wildlife biology skills that have led directly to employment in the region's growing eco-tourism industry. Involvement in wetland education and research has helped many pupils form post-secondary and career plans.

This summer, as in each of the past eight years, the center is providing summer internships for its Wetheads. In addition to leading experiential programs, four students are monitoring a variety of wetland plants and animals, participating in wetland research, and carrying out routine maintenance in and around the impoundment. Much of their time is devoted also to improving their interpretive skills so that they can play an even greater role in the upcoming school year — when another 4,000 students and teachers will arrive in Sackville to "experience wetlands" at the Tantramar Wetlands Centre.

Chris Porter is the former director of the Wetlands Centre at Tantramar Regional High School in Sackville, New Brunswick. Now retired from teaching, he works as a consultant in sustainability education.

Using Epiphytic Lichens as Bio-indicators of Air Pollution

Photographs by Brian Craig (right and left), Sonia Dong (center)

by Andrew Kett, Sonia Dong, Heather Andrachuk and Brian Craig

Subject areas: science, geography, civics, mathematics, visual arts

Key concepts: lichen, biological monitoring, symbiosis, biodiversity, succession, indicator species, scientific protocol

Skills: conducting the scientific method, observation, taking scientific measurements, data synthesis and analysis, presentation skills

Location: outdoors

Time: 2-day introduction to lichen identification and monitoring; 1 day to organize equipment, go to the site, and complete sampling; 1 day data analysis; 1 or more days for extension (e.g., presentation, report, project)

Materials: air-quality monitoring equipment, guide to lichen identification, magnifying lens, tape measure, compass, data recording sheets

It can be a challenge to make environmental problems such as air pollution concrete and meaningful to students. Students learn the general concepts and the big causes and effects — greenhouse gases, acid rain, climate change — but in many cases the problems seem so huge and intangible that they have difficulty grasping how their own daily lives are linked to them. Indeed, teachers and students can both be in danger of missing the trees for the forest, of being too conceptual and overlooking the details, the "little picture." As educators, we need to make environmental problems relevant, local and concrete: that is, to show students how these problems affect the local environment in ways that can be seen and felt. When teaching about air pollution, one way to accomplish these goals is to have your class monitor air quality using lichens as biological indicators.

What exactly *are* lichens?

On first glance, lichens may appear to be a type of moss; but on closer examination they reveal themselves to be a unique life form. A lichen is composed of not one, but two organisms: a fungus and an alga, or cyanobacterium. The two organisms live in a symbiotic relationship in which the alga provides both partners with energy through photosynthesis and the fungus provides shelter and protection for the alga.

Approximately 20,000 species of lichens exist worldwide, about 3,600 of which are found in North America. Lichens cover eight percent of the Earth's terrestrial surface and they can grow just about anywhere: on soil, rocks, trees, even on human-made surfaces. They exist in some of the most extreme, inhospitable environments on the planet, including mountaintops, deserts and polar regions. While lichens often grow on trees and shrubs as epiphytes, they do not extract nutrients from the surfaces on which they grow, but instead absorb nutrients from the atmosphere. Lichens vary widely in size, color and shape. They also change color during the rain as they soak up water and produce food energy. This is one of the remarkable qualities of lichens, perhaps even the key to their survival in harsh climates: they can dry out completely, becoming very fragile and brittle, but will quickly rehydrate when moisture becomes available in their environment.

Lichens as bio-indicators

While harsh climates don't bother lichens, scientists have known for over 140 years that lichens are extremely sensitive to air pollution. They lack roots and so depend on atmospheric sources of nutrients. They also lack the protective waxy cuticle that plants have and so they are fully exposed to any pollutants present in the air. As they absorb nutrients, they also absorb air pollutants, and these accumulate in their tissues. Further, lichen morphology (unlike that of, say, a deciduous tree) does not change with the seasons, which means that lichens accumulate pollutants all year long.

Because they are so responsive to pollution and environmental change, lichens are useful as bio-indicators. Like the canary in the coal mine, they can provide us with warning signs of unhealthy environments. Studies have shown that the abundance and diversity of lichens decrease as urban development and industrial activity increase. Sulfur dioxide, in particular, has been strongly linked to declines in lichen populations. This common by-product of fossil fuel combustion apparently disrupts photosynthesis and the transfer of carbohydrates from the alga (or cyanobacterium) to

Lichen FAQs

What are lichens?

- Lichen = fungus (provides structure) + alga or cyanobacterium (provides energy through photosynthesis)
- Lichens are classified as fungi, even though they are made up of members of two different kingdoms
- Tree-dwelling types are called epiphytic lichens (*epi* = upon; *phyte* = plant)

What do lichens look like?

Lichens have three main forms: crustose (crust-like), foliose (leaf-like), fruticose (stem-like, shrubby). For photos and a detailed discussion of lichen biology, see <www.lichen.com/vocabulary>, a website that supports the book *Lichens of North America* by Brodo, Sharnoff and Sharnoff.

What do lichens "eat" and how/where do they grow?

- Lichens do not decompose, "eat," or otherwise harm trees; they trap nutrients directly from the air.
- Lichens grow 1–10 mm a year, and can live for up to 1,000 years.

- Lichens are opportunists: they are active when they are wet and dormant during hot, dry periods.
- Lichens can survive the harshest of conditions. There are 350 species in the Antarctic, where only two species of vascular plants are found.

How do lichens reproduce?

Lichens reproduce in three different ways: sexually, through the release of spores that form within bowl-like structures called *apothecia*; asexually through another type of spore that usually forms within tiny black "spots" on the lichen surface called *pycnidia*; and vegetatively through the fragmentation and dispersion of outgrowths such as *lobules*, *isidia* and *soredia*, each of which contains fungal and algal cells.

Heather Andrachuk

Brock University student learning to identify lichens as part of a "youth mentoring youth" training course run by Environment Canada's Ecological Monitoring and Assessment Network.

the fungus. Sulfur dioxide is also a major component of acid rain, which can make tree bark less hospitable to lichens. As the concentration of sulfur dioxide increases, lichen abundance decreases. Still, the populations do not vanish completely. Different lichens have different levels of tolerance to pollutants. Some can endure environments that are severely polluted, while others will perish in all but the most pristine conditions. Thus, through a simple study of the presence or absence of particular kinds of lichen, a class can make an accurate, scientifically valid assessment of the general air quality at a particular site.

Bio-monitoring projects

Many teachers integrate an air-quality monitoring project using lichens into their ecology units, chemistry or biology classes, or independent studies for upper year courses in high school. Related topics include ecology, pollution, climate change and biodiversity. Monitoring projects can even be linked to geography (mapping, Global Positioning System, environmental issues), math (data analysis), civics (environmental

action, informing the decision-making process) or art classes (photography, drawing, sculpture).

Because lichens have a considerable geographical range, studies can be carried out over large regions. And while lichens are slow-growing, they are extremely long-lived, so that studies can be long term. The depth and breadth of a monitoring project will depend on how involved you and your students want to become and your reason for monitoring. You may want only to get your feet wet, doing little more than getting out into the field to identify lichens and do a simple survey. Maybe you are interested in surveying lichens in order to assess air quality in an area near the school. Or you may want to answer a specific question about a pollutant source, or collect data that you can submit to a government or scientific database.

Since lichens grow year-round, monitoring can be performed any time of the year, but in the interests of avoiding inclement weather, it is best done in the warmer months of the school season. Because of the physiological changes that occur in lichens during rain or snow (they change color and become more difficult to identify), it is best to plan "rain dates" for field trips.

Species selection

Deciding which species to monitor and how to monitor them are perhaps the most important considerations when starting your project. For purposes of bio-monitoring, lichenologists have identified suites of indicator species for different forest types and developed field guides that present photos or drawings of the species accompanied by explanations of their unique features.[1] The lichens in each suite have a range of pollution tolerance, from very tolerant to very intolerant. Often, different suites of lichens are linked to particular monitoring methodologies, or protocols. Most suites have 15 to 20 species, but if surveying that many species is too complex an undertaking for your class, scientists have developed suites of as few as four species that can also be effective. And resources such as the enormous *Lichens of North America*[2] can guide teachers and students in identifying lichens not included in bio-monitoring suites.

Protocols

Teachers interested in beginning a monitoring project using lichens should take some time to read and reflect on different monitoring protocols. Generally, these are of two types, both of which focus on lichens growing on trees. The first type involves examining the entire trunk of a tree, up to about chest height, noting each species of lichen present and estimating its abundance. This method is particularly useful in areas with low lichen diversity and abundance, such as heavily polluted or urban areas. The second type of protocol considers only a portion of the tree trunk, which is usually marked off with a small grid or "ladder." This type of study is used extensively in Europe and in areas with high lichen diversity and abundance. Deciding which type of protocol to use can be difficult, as both have strengths and weaknesses. The ladder method enables students to assess abundance rapidly and easily, and has the advantage of being repeatable and more objective than the whole-trunk estimates of abundance. On the other hand, students using the ladder method may miss some of the species present at a site unless they sample many times.[3]

For classes undertaking small-scale projects, any protocol will likely be fine. Teachers interested in embarking on an extensive, multi-year project should contact local government, university or environmental groups for advice on protocol selection in their region. Using standardized protocols for collecting and reporting data is one of the biggest concerns in monitoring projects in which data is shared with others. Most government agencies have a lichen bio-monitoring protocol, and many are available on the Web (although often not in the most user-friendly language or form, particularly for students). A better bet for teachers is to contact regional environmental education or monitoring groups and organizations that have developed scientific monitoring protocols ready for classroom use (see page 62). These are usually written in comprehensible language and specifically designed for local student monitoring projects. In Canada, community monitoring groups, government agencies and post-secondary institutions are currently working in partnership to pilot a protocol that is similar to that used in Europe. This will allow students to compare their data with that of students in other schools across Canada.

Site selection

Many schools have at least a few suitable monitoring sites, such as parks, yards and cemeteries, within walking distance. Almost any treed site will do for a simple survey of lichens. If the aim of your study is to answer a specific question about a pollutant source, or if you intend to submit your data to an existing database, consider having a few different monitoring sites. All sites need to be relatively uniform because the type and density of the trees, the soil conditions and the major surrounding features can all affect lichen growth. Be sure to have students document each site well, drawing maps and, if possible, taking pictures.

Equipment and resources

The equipment for monitoring lichens is inexpensive and easily obtained. It is best to have students working in groups, and only one of each item is needed for each group. The equipment for each group should include:

- magnifying glass or lens, preferably 8–20x
- guidebook or key to lichen identification
- ruler and long tape measure
- compass
- datasheets on which to record information
- clipboard and pencil

Of course, the equipment list can be expanded if you happen to have unlimited resources or want to tailor your monitoring project. Certain protocols require defining the sampling area on the tree using chalk or a hanging grid of five 10 cm x 10 cm squares vertically aligned (students can easily make these "ladders" using paper, string, or, for more durable models, coathanger wire and lamp chain). A knife and some jars could be used to collect specimens for further study back in the classroom. A camera could be used to record site information. GPS equipment could be used to plot the sampling sites. And, most beneficial of all to the study, other air-quality monitoring equipment could be used in conjunction with lichen surveys, and the respective data compared.

Classroom and field resource materials enhance the learning experience for students, as well as the scientific validity of the data they collect. Species identification charts, data collection sheets and a detailed monitoring methodology will ensure that the data your students collect will be accurate and useful in comparison with data collected by academic and government monitoring programs. In addition, specialized teacher manuals can be used to plan lessons, conduct curriculum-linked activities, obtain background information and develop ideas for student action projects to improve their local environment.[4]

In order to ensure data quality, it is a good idea for teachers to obtain training in lichen identification. Many community groups provide training workshops for teachers, complete with classroom and field sessions and resources such as teacher manuals. Alternatively, some government agencies and community organizations provide teachers with trained postsecondary student volunteers who lead high school students through both in-class and outdoor field sessions. This "youth-mentoring-youth" model inspires and motivates youth with the possibilities of scientific endeavor and careers, and engages volunteers in valuable career-related work experiences while they are still in school.[5]

Sample project timeline

The following is a suggested timeline for a lichen bio-monitoring project.

1. *Project preparation:* Teachers and partners (e.g., local community or naturalist groups, academic institutions, government agencies) choose monitoring sites, schedule classroom and field sessions, gather background resources and equipment, and arrange for volunteers to assist with the project.

2. *Introduction to lichens:* Two in-class sessions of about 75 minutes each in which students learn about lichen biology and identification, and how to collect data in the field.

3. *Field work:* Two to four field sessions of two to three hours each. A typical data collection session would include:

a) site set-up. Choose five to ten trees of the same species. Record data about the trees (such as species and size) and the site (sketch a map, note the location, the date and time, weather and so on).

b) lichen identification. Identify the lichens present and record the data on a uniform data sheet. The abundance of each species may also be noted, depending on the protocol.

4. *Data analysis tutorial:* One session of about 75 minutes in which students learn how to analyze and interpret data using calculations such as the Index of Atmospheric Purity.[6]

Lichen Bio-monitoring Protocols

Citizens' Environment Watch, see "Air Quality Monitoring with Epiphytic Lichens" for a protocol, data sheets and a data analysis guide designed for school and community lichen bio-monitoring projects. <www.citizensenvironmentwatch. org/cew/resourceCentre/ protocols&manuals.html>

Ecological Monitoring and Assessment Network (Environment Canada) provides protocols for a variety of lichen-monitoring studies. These include lichen surveys using a small grid or "ladder" to determine diversity; mapping of lichen diversity and regional air quality using an Index of Atmospheric Purity; a photometric method of photographing lichens and looking at them digitally; and standardized collection procedures that allow for the analysis of metals and contaminants through the use of mass spectrometry, among other techniques. <www.eman-rese.ca/eman/ecotools/protocols/ terrestrial/lichens/intro.html>

The British Lichen Society, "The European Guideline for Mapping Lichen Diversity as an Indicator of Environmental Stress." Standardized European methods for monitoring air quality using lichens on tree bark. <www.thebls.org.uk/eumap.pdf>

USDA Forest Service, "Air Quality and Lichens: A Literature Review Emphasizing the Pacific Northwest of the United States. An excellent summary of lichen research and monitoring methods. <www.fs.fed.us/r6/aq/lichen/almanac>

5. *Action plan development and implementation and community dissemination of results:* This part of the project will vary, depending on students' and teachers' interests and time. (See "Taking action" below.)

This timeline is for a fairly comprehensive project. If you just want to introduce your students to lichens and take them outside to experience nature, community groups often provide half-day workshops for classes, along with preparation exercises and follow-up activities that teachers can incorporate into the classroom.

Taking action

After students have learned about lichens, and collected and analyzed their data, they often ask: "What do we do with all this data?" Within the classroom, making presentations and creating displays, information packages and brochures are just a few of the possible culminating activities. If students' analysis of the data shows that the local air quality needs improvement, they can take action by sharing their findings at a community meeting or by preparing a special display and presentation for a parents' night. Students may choose to make changes in their behavior that will reduce their impact on local air quality, or use their data to raise a red flag to governments to make changes in policies, or get involved in a large-scale monitoring study. They can invite the rest of the school community, and students from other schools, to become involved in monitoring or in actions such as planting trees or holding car-free days.

Monitoring air quality using lichens is a perfect way for students to participate in original, never-been-done-before research and to get better acquainted with their neighborhood. Students also learn about real issues that professional scientists face when conducting scientific studies: that there are possible sources of error, that one indicator doesn't tell you everything you need to know, that there is always the possibility for further study. Best of all, students get outside of the classroom and have the opportunity to get reacquainted with the particulars, the real nuts-and-bolts, of biological science: the trees and the sunlight and the air. The scientific theories, abstract concepts and the "big picture" have their place, but let's not forget that every theory was once just an observation. Every forest is really just a collection of trees. And before those trees existed, the ground was probably covered with lichens.

Andrew Kett *is an Education Specialist with Credit Valley Conservation in Mississauga, Ontario.* ***Sonia Dong*** *is the Executive Director of Citizen's Environment Watch, an organization in Toronto, Ontario, that trains and equips students and other volunteers to monitor local air and water quality.* ***Heather Andrachuk*** *is a graduate student in environmental studies at the University of Waterloo, Ontario, and former Outreach Science Advisor at the Ecological Monitoring and Assessment Network (EMAN).* ***Brian Craig*** *is a Project Manager with Parks Canada in southwestern Ontario, and former Senior Science Advisor for EMAN.*

Notes

1. For examples of lichen suites, see lichen identification field guides for mixed hardwood and boreal forests at the website of the Ecological Monitoring and Assessment Network of Environment Canada, <www.eman-rese.ca/eman/ecotools/protocols/terrestrial/> (follow links under "Lichen Diversity and Abundance"); and "Indicator Lichen Species and their Characteristics" at the website of Citizens' Environment Watch, <www.citizensenvironmentwatch.org/cew/resourceCentre/protocols&manuals.html> (follow "Guide to Indicator Species" link under "Air Quality Monitoring with Epiphytic Lichens").

2. Irwin M. Brodo, Sylvia Duran Sharnoff and Stephen Sharnoff. *Lichens of North America.* Yale University Press, 2001.

3. Robert Cameron, ecologist with the Protected Areas Branch of Nova Scotia Environment and Labour, personal correspondence, August 17, 2005.

4. See, for example, Margaret Peterson, "Lichens as Air Quality Indicators: A beginning lichen identification study" for Grades 6–8, Cooperative Institute for Research in Environmental Sciences, 2003, online September 27, 2005 at <http://cires.colorado.edu/education/k12/earthworks/teachers/petersonM.html>; and William C. Denison, "A Guide to Air Quality Monitoring with Lichens," Lichen Technology, Inc, 1973, online September 27, 2005 at <http://ocid.nacse.org/classroom/lichens/denison/>.

5. For example, Citizens' Environment Watch in Ontario matches trained volunteers (Monitoring Mentors) with classes to assist teachers in implementing monitoring projects. CEW also offers programs for youth outside of the school system and for community members/groups. See <www.citizensenvironmentwatch.org>.

6. A good resource for lichen data analysis is "Epiphytic Lichen Data Analysis," by Citizens' Environment Watch, 2002. It can be downloaded as a pdf file at <www.citizensenvironmentwatch.org/cew/resourceCentre/protocols&manuals.html>; click on "Data Analysis" under "Air Quality Monitoring with Epiphytic Lichens."

Resources

Brodo, I.M., S. Sharnoff and S. Sharnoff. *Lichens of North America.* Yale University Press, 2001.

Huckaby, L.S., ed. *Lichens as Bioindicators of Air Quality.* USDA Forest Service General Technical Report RM-224, Rocky Mountain Forest and Range Experimental Station, 1993.

Manning, W.J. and W.A. Feder. *Biomonitoring of Air Pollutants with Plants.* Applied Science Publishers, 1980.

Nash, T.H. *Lichen Biology.* Cambridge University Press, 1996.

Nash, T.H. and V. Wirth. "Lichens, Bryophytes and Air Quality." *Bibliotheca Lichenologica*, 30. J. Cramer, 1988.

Richardson, D.H.S. *Pollution Monitoring with Lichens.* Richmond Publishing. 1992.

United States Environmental Protection Agency, "Biological Indicators of Watershed Health." The focus of this report is watersheds rather than terrestrial systems, but it provides a good explanation of the use of bioindicators in monitoring environmental quality. Online at <www.epa.gov/bioindicators/>.

Carbon Cycle:
Measuring CO$_2$ Flux from Soil

Measuring soil respiration familiarizes students with an important component of the carbon cycle and makes the invisible mechanisms of soil biology and climate change more tangible

by Robert Lessard, L. Dennis Gignac and Philippe Rochette

Subject areas: biology, chemistry, science, mathematics

Key concepts: carbon cycle, greenhouse effect, soil respiration, soil organic matter, acid-base titration

Skills: using the scientific method, observation, taking scientific measurements, data synthesis and analysis, presentation skills

Location: outdoors or indoors

Time: 1 day for preparation and set up, 4–24 hours for incubation and sample collection, 1–2 hours of lab work for titration and calculations

Materials: air chambers, small yogurt containers, stoppered vials, titration equipment and chemicals (see "Materials" section below)

Teaching concepts that relate to environmental problems is not always easy since many of the underlying components may be abstract, complex or invisible. Such is the case with climate change and global warming. Greenhouse gases are virtually undetectable without the use of sophisticated gas-analyzing equipment that is unaffordable to most elementary and secondary schools. It is therefore difficult for students to realize the large amounts of gases emitted into the atmosphere. Students are told that greenhouse gas concentrations are increasing and that these changes are globally important since they will result in climate change. However, for many students,

Earth's atmosphere remains a mysterious black box. One way to demystify this concept is to have students measure carbon dioxide (CO$_2$) flux, or rate of emission, from soil to the atmosphere.

The activity that we describe here is designed for secondary school students and attempts to familiarize them with one aspect of the global carbon cycle: the production of CO$_2$ through soil respiration. It can also be used to demonstrate how the soil can become a sink for carbon, thus reducing concentrations in the atmosphere and alleviating the trend toward global warming. Furthermore, it presents a practical and inexpensive method for measuring CO$_2$ fluxes from soils.

Background

Soil respiration is defined as the production of CO_2 as a result of two processes: the breakdown, or oxidation, of carbon-rich organic matter by soil microorganisms, and respiration by plant root cells. The rate of CO_2 production is scientifically important because it provides an indication of the rate of breakdown of organic matter and therefore of the amount of soil carbon that is lost. Measurements of soil respiration help to determine the contribution of soil to the atmospheric CO_2 budget.

Carbon, an essential element for plant growth, is obtained from the atmosphere through photosynthesis. However, when plants die, their carbon-rich tissues are returned to the soil and decomposed by living organisms. Soil organic matter is therefore the sum of organic residues (plants and animals) at various stage of decomposition. Organic matter improves soil quality, helps prevent runoff, increases soil humidity and helps to moderate daily temperature fluctuations in the top layers of the soil. Soil organic matter also functions as an enormous storehouse for carbon: it is estimated that living organisms account for about one-quarter of all the carbon in terrestrial ecosystems, while the remaining three-quarters is stored in the organic matter contained in soils.

Soil carbon does not accumulate forever. It is released from the soil when organic matter is broken down by several types of aerobic organisms that use carbon for their own growth. This process liberates plant nutrients, which can then be taken up by living plants, but it also releases CO_2. The rate of microbial activity, and hence of soil respiration, is affected by soil temperature and humidity as well as by the quantity and quality of soil organic matter. Since all aerobic organisms release CO_2 as a result of the breakdown of organic molecules, and since there can be millions of these organisms in as little as a teaspoon of soil, soil respiration is an important source of atmospheric CO_2, contributing up to 100 billion metric tons of carbon to the global carbon cycle each year.

The increase in atmospheric CO_2 levels since the beginning of the Industrial Revolution is largely due to the burning of fossil fuels and changes in land use. Agricultural practices, often overlooked as a source of greenhouse gases, are responsible for approximately ten percent of greenhouse gases emitted by human activity in most developed countries. The quantity of carbon that is retained in the soil or lost to the atmosphere largely depends on the method of tillage used. When fields are plowed, fresh organic residues are thoroughly mixed into the topsoil. Under these conditions, microbial activity increases, resulting in more of the soil's organic carbon being turned into atmospheric CO_2. There is also a net loss of carbon when fields are left fallow. This is due in part to higher soil temperature and humidity, which accelerate decomposition, and also to the fact that no carbon is added to the soil during a year when there is no crop.

Sound land management practices help to conserve organic matter in soil, thus reversing the tendency of soils to lose their carbon to the atmosphere. One of these practices is no-till agriculture, which consists of seeding a crop in the residues of the previous year's crop. Studies show that the establishment of a permanent vegetation cover also contributes to the sequestration of carbon in the soil. Thus, along with reducing our consumption of fossil fuels, practicing good land management is another method of reducing the concentration of greenhouse gases in the atmosphere, by storing carbon dioxide as organic matter in the soil.

Since soil respiration plays such an important role in the carbon cycle, measuring it is a valuable component of effective teaching about the mechanisms that produce global warming. However, finding an inexpensive but effective method of measuring the CO_2 that is produced through soil respiration is fundamental. The method proposed for this activity is based on the ability of some alkaline compounds, such as sodium hydroxide (NaOH), to react with CO_2 from the air.

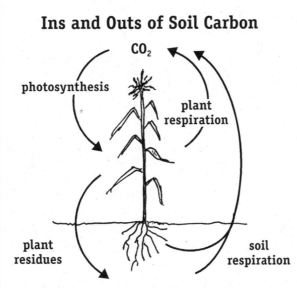

Ins and Outs of Soil Carbon

Much of the atmospheric carbon obtained by plants through photosynthesis is eventually stored in the soil as organic matter. Carbon is released back to the atmosphere through cellular respiration and the breakdown of soil organic material.

Experimental design

In this experiment, plastic containers are placed upside down on several sampling sites to act as air chambers in which CO_2 from the soil collects. A smaller container of NaOH is placed inside each air chamber to trap the CO_2. Alkali trapping uses the weakly acidic properties of CO_2 in an acid-base neutralization that produces carbonate:

$$CO_2 + 2Na^+ + 2OH^- \rightarrow CO_3^{2-} + 2Na^+ + H_2O$$

As long as there is an excess of OH^- ions (a result of NaOH dissociation), the equilibrium shifts towards the right, producing carbonate. Following an incubation period, the NaOH is collected and the carbonate is precipitated using barium chloride ($BaCl_2$) The quantity of CO_2 that is absorbed in the alkaline solution can then be measured using a simple titration.[1]

Materials

- air chambers, one per sample: 5-liter plastic pails, approximately 18 cm in diameter and 18.5 cm deep will work well

- NaOH containers, one per sample: small plastic yogurt containers, approximately 9 cm in diameter, cut to a height of approximately 4 cm. Any small plastic container can be used; however, to maximize the absorption of CO_2, the area of the opening of the NaOH container should be greater than 26% of the area of the opening of air chamber.

- one stoppered vial for each sample

- one or two flat boards (for control sites) measuring 30 cm x 30 cm, or larger

- electrical tape

- 250 ml Erlenmeyer flasks

- 10 ml and 25 ml graduated cylinders

- 5 ml pipettes

- 400 ml beakers

- 50 ml burettes mounted on retort stands

- 1 liter of 0.25 M NaOH

- 500 ml of 3 N $BaCl_2$ (1.5 M)

- 2 liters of 0.1 M HCl

- phenolphthalein indicator

Safety precautions

The solutions used in this activity are very corrosive. The sample collection sites should be fenced and have warning signs. Gloves, eye protection and lab coats or aprons should be worn whenever the chemicals are handled. At the end of the experiment, ensure that all solutions are properly disposed of in chemical waste containers.

Preparing solutions

NaOH: To prepare the 0.25 M NaOH solution, add 10 grams of NaOH pellets to 500 ml of distilled water. Swirl and then complete the volume to 1 L by adding more distilled water. Secure the stopper tightly to protect the solution from exposure to air.

HCl: To prepare the 0.1 M HCl solution, add 16 ml of concentrated acid to 1 L of distilled water. Swirl the solution and then add 1 L of distilled water to make a total volume of 2 L. It's a good idea to standardize the dilute acid using a 0.5 M NaOH standard solution. HCl and NaOH concentrations can be adjusted according to the anticipated CO_2 soil emissions. Lower concentrations of acid and alkali solutions are used if CO_2 emissions are expected to be low. To ensure best results, the HCl concentration is kept between one-half and one-quarter of the concentration of the NaOH.

$BaCl_2$: $BaCl_2$ is used in this experiment to precipitate the carbonate produced as insoluble $BaCO_3$. To prepare the 1.5 M solution, add 156.2 grams of $BaCl_2$ to 400 ml of distilled water and swirl. Then complete the volume to 500 ml. If $BaCl_2H_2O$ is used instead, 183.2 grams are needed to produce the 1.5 M solution.

Phenolphthalein indicator: The phenolphthalein solution serves as a pH indicator dye. Prepare a 1% solution by adding 1 gram of phenolphthalein to 100 ml of 95% (vol/vol) ethyl alcohol. Only two drops of this solution will be needed for each titration.

Selecting sites

Since the sample collection sites will have open containers of NaOH, they should be in an area where public access is limited. Select sites of approximately 50 cm by 50 cm in an area with little or no vegetation. Any soil may be used for this experiment as long as the surface of the ground is relatively flat. For best results, sample several locations that have different types of soil. The important variable that distinguishes the type of soil is the quantity of organic material it contains. Generally, if the soil temperature is high enough (> 10°C) and there is enough moisture, soils that contain the most organic matter will have the highest rate of soil respiration. After selecting suitable sampling locations, remove any vegetation from the sites at least 24 hours in advance in order to eliminate CO_2 that may be produced as the result of soil disturbance.

Option: If finding suitable sites is a challenge, a school-yard or lab experiment may be easier to manage. Growing beds packed with soil that is amended with different concentrations of organic matter can be used to simulate soils having different levels of carbon content.

Setting up collection chambers

Have students work in pairs, each pair being responsible for measuring the soil respiration at one sampling site. Assign one or two pairs of students to control sites. Controls are necessary in order to obtain a measure of ambient CO_2 in the atmosphere. This value will be subtracted from the quantity of CO_2 measured from soil samples in order to determine how much of the trapped CO_2 is contributed by soil respiration. Set up each sampling site as follows:

1. Measure and record the diameter of the opening of the air chamber in order to calculate the surface area that it will cover when placed upside down over the NaOH trap.

2. Position the NaOH trap approximately 4 cm above the soil. This is done by taping three small sticks approximately 15 cm in length to the sides of the container to act as a tripod (see Figure 1).

3. Place 25 ml of NaOH solution in the bottom of the NaOH trap (see Figure 2). The soil should not be disturbed during this step. In addition, students should not breathe directly on the surface of the liquid since this will contaminate it with CO_2. Due to the corrosive nature of NaOH, the 25 ml of solution for each trap should be transported in a stoppered vial to the study site.

4. Quickly place the air chamber over the trap and set its edges approximately 2 cm into the soil (see Figure 3). Some of the surrounding soil may be gently pushed along the edge to ensure a complete seal and prevent loss of CO_2 to the atmosphere.

5. Leave the chamber undisturbed for 24 hours, depending on the organic content of the soil. Soils that contain a large proportion of organic matter usually require less time than those that do not. The time must be accurately recorded in order to calculate fluxes.

Controls: Set up the control chambers in the same manner as the others, with the following exceptions. Lay a flat board on the surface of the soil to act as a barrier between the soil and the NaOH trap. Place the NaOH trap directly onto the board (do not elevate the trap on a tripod). Mount the air chamber over the

Figure 1: A plastic container cut to a height of about 4 cm serves as the NaOH trap. It is suspended above the soil on a tripod made of three sticks taped to the container.

Figure 2: The NaOH is transported to the study site in a glass vial and then poured into the trap.

Figure 3: The air chamber is a 5-liter plastic pail placed over the trap and pushed into the soil to a depth of 2 cm. Right: Soil surrounding the chamber is pushed around the edges in order to complete the seal.

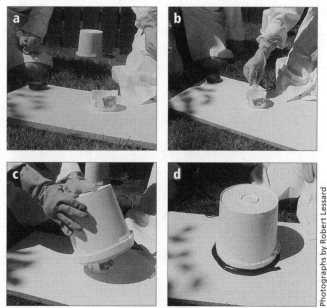

Figure 4: Control set-up. a) The NaOH trap is placed directly on a flat board. b) 25 ml of NaOH is poured into the trap. c) The air chamber is placed over the trap. d) The chamber is sealed to the board using black electrical tape.

Photographs by Robert Lessard

trap and seal the edges to the board using electrical tape (see Figure 4). Controls are left for the same time period as the treatments.

Figure 5: *At the end of the experiment, the chamber is gently removed and the NaOH is poured into a glass vial for transport to the lab.*

6. After the incubation period, collect the NaOH samples in suitably labeled vials. To do this, simply pour the liquid in the traps into the vials, making sure that none is lost and without breathing directly on it (see Figure 5). Then return the samples to the lab for titration.

Titration

Titrate each of the NaOH samples three times as follows.

1. Place a 400 ml beaker under a 50 ml graduated burette. Open the stopcock and rinse the burette a few times with distilled water. Add 50 ml of 0.1 M HCl to the burette and allow it to run through the tip. Close the stopcock and add 0.1 M HCl to the burette until the bottom of the meniscus is at 0 ml.

2. Place 5 ml of the NaOH solution from the sample into a 250 ml Erlenmeyer flask and add 10 ml of distilled H_2O.

3. Precipitate the carbonate contained in the NaOH solution by adding 10 ml of 3 N $BaCl_2$. The quantity of white crystals formed is proportional to the concentration of carbonate present in the alkali solution. The reaction, including $BaCl_2$, is:

$$CO_3^{2-} + 2Na^+ + Ba^{2+} + 2Cl^- \rightarrow BaCO_3 + 2NaCl$$

4. Add 2 drops of phenolphthalein indicator to the flask. This should turn the solution pink.

5. Place the flask under the burette. Slowly add drops of the HCl to the sample. After each addition, pause and mix the solution by swirling gently or stirring with a glass rod. When the color of the sample changes from pink to transparent (equivalence point), stop the titration and record the volume of HCl that was used.

6. Repeat the titration two more times for each sample. Find the mean volume of HCl required for titration.

Quantification of CO_2 concentrations in the samples

The quantity of CO_2 absorbed by the NaOH trap (QCO_2) for each sample is calculated as follows:

$$QCO_2 = (T - C)(N)(E)(Vtr/Vti) \text{ where:}$$

T = mean volume of HCl used to titrate the CO_2 in the control

C = mean volume of HCl needed to titrate the CO_2 in each of the samples

N = normality of the HCl used = 0.1

E = conversion factor: use 22 to obtain mg of CO_2, or 6 to obtain mg of C absorbed by the trap

Vtr = volume of NaOH in the trap in ml = 25 ml

Vti = volume of NaOH used in titration = 5 ml

Sample Calculations

In this example, NaOH that had incubated for eight hours was collected from a trap above a sampling site and from a control. The mean volume of HCl (0.1 N) needed to titrate the NaOH from the control was 36 ml; the volume needed for the soil sample was 30 ml.

CO_2 concentrations in samples

A conversion factor of 22 is used to calculate the quantity, in milligrams, of CO_2 absorbed by the NaOH trap. The volume of NaOH in the trap was 25 ml and the volume used for each titration was 5 ml. These values are entered in the equation $QCO_2 = (T - C)(N)(E)(Vtr/Vti)$ as follows:

T = 36 ml	N = 0.1 N	Vtr = 25 ml
C = 30 ml	E = 22	Vti = 5 ml

Thus, QCO_2 = (36 – 30)(0.1)(22)(25/5) = 66 mg of CO_2

CO_2 flux from the soil

Continuing with the above example, the diameter of the opening of the air chamber was 18.2 cm, or 0.182 m. The surface area of soil thus exposed was A = (π)(0.182/2)² = 0.02602 m². Since the incubation time was 8 hours, the CO_2 flux (FCO_2) = 66/(0.02602)(8) = 317.06 mg CO_2 m⁻²h⁻¹

Quantity and flux of carbon

To find the quantity of carbon absorbed by the trap, QC, use the formula with the conversion factor E = 6. The conversion factor is obtained by multiplying 22 by the portion of carbon in a mole of CO_2 (22 x 12g C / 44 g CO_2). This gives QC = 18 mg of carbon. The flux of carbon (FC) would thus be 18/(0.02602)(8), or 86.5 mg of carbon m⁻² h⁻¹.

Quantification of soil respiration

This calculation takes into account the surface area of the soil that was exposed and the incubation time. Soil respiration is calculated as the rate of CO_2 production by a surface area during a period of time and is then defined as the CO_2 flux (mg/m²/hr). The flux (FCO_2) is calculated as follows: $FCO_2 = QCO_2/(A)(t)$, where A is the area of exposed soil in square meters and t is the time of incubation in hours.

Extensions

1. Most of the CO_2 emitted at the soil surface is produced by microorganisms, and the warmer the soil, the more intensive the microbial activity. Soil temperature is therefore one of the most important environmental factors controlling the rate of CO_2 production in soils. By using temperature probes, students could measure this factor over several days. Students could then draw a graph of soil respiration as a function of soil temperature.

2. A second variable that affects soil respiration is the moisture content of the soil. The moisture content is easily measured by weighing soil samples, drying them in an oven at 60°C for 24 hours, and then weighing them again. The percent moisture content *(MC)* is calculated as: *MC = [(fresh weight − dry weight)/dry weight] x 100.*

3. Organic content is an important variable that affects soil respiration. The percent of organic content can be estimated by combustion, as follows. Remove a handful of the top 10 to 15 cm of soil from the study location. Heat a sub-sample of this soil at low intensity in a crucible to evaporate the water, and then weigh the soil to obtain the dry weight. Next, heat the soil at high intensity for a few minutes until the color no longer changes. Cool the soil and then reweigh it to obtain the burned weight. The percent organic content *(OC)* of the soil is calculated as: *OC = [(dry weight − burned weight)/dry weight] x 100.*

4. Other factors that change CO_2 fluxes from soils are quantity and quality of organic residues being decomposed. There are several ways in which organic soil amendments may influence CO_2 fluxes. For example, adding readily decomposable materials such as fresh manure, flour or even sugar to soil should generate higher fluxes compared to soils amended with substrates that decompose at a lower rate (wood chips, straw). Designing experiments in which the type and/or the quantity of organic matter added to soil changes will help students understand how organic amendments affect soil respiration.

Evaluation

At the end of the exercise, students should be able to measure CO_2 and understand that it is produced by soils and accumulates in the atmosphere. They should also understand that several factors, such as temperature and humidity of soils, affect their rate of CO_2 production. If extension activities 3 and 4 (see above) are used, they will also grasp the relationship between the amount and type of organic matter added to a soil and the quantities of CO_2 released to the atmosphere. A possible discussion question that students could reflect on is: How does returning more organic material to soils (crop residues, manure, etc.) increase agricultural sustainability *(elements of answer: reduced erosion, better retention of water and nutrients, higher intrinsic fertility, better soil aeration, less compaction)* and act on the total greenhouse gas balance?

Robert Lessard *is Principal at l'École canadienne-française in Saskatoon, Saskatchewan.* **L. Dennis Gignac** *is Associate Professor of Plant Ecology at the Faculté Saint-Jean of the University of Alberta in Edmonton.* ***Philippe Rochette*** *is an agrometeorologist at Agriculture and Agri-Food Canada in Québec City, Québec.*

Note

1. P. Rochette and G.L. Hutchinson, "Measurement of soil respiration in situ: Chamber techniques," in J. Hatfield and J. M. Baker, eds., *Micrometeorology in Agricultural Systems*, ASA monograph #47, Madison, WI: American Society of Agronomy, 2005, pp. 247–286.

References

Anderson, J.P.E. "Soil Respiration," in A.L. Page et al., eds. *Methods of Soil Analysis, Part 2.* ASA and SSSA, Agronomy Monograph 9, 1982, pp. 831–871.

Environment Canada. *CO2/Climate report — Summer 2003.* [online July 23, 2008] <www.msc-smc.ec.gc.ca/education/scienceofclimatechange/understanding/newsletter/co2_summer2003/2_e.html>.

Griffiths, Mary, Paul Cobb and Tom Marr-Laing. *Carbon Capture and Storage: An Arrow in the Quiver or a Silver Bullet to Combat Climate Change — A Canadian Primer.* Pembina Institute, 2005 [online July 23, 2008], <http://www.pembina.org/pub/584>.

Natural Resources Canada. *Carbon cycle.* Natural Resources Canada, 2005 [online July 23, 2008] <http://ecosys.cfl.scf.rncan.gc.ca/dynamique-dynamic/carbone-carbon-eng.asp>.

Rochette, P. and G.L. Hutchinson. 2005. Measurement of soil respiration in situ: Chamber techniques. p. 247–286. *In* J. Hatfield and J. M Baker, eds. Micrometeorology in agricultural systems. ASA monograph #47, American Society of Agronomy, Madison, WI.

Tank Tips:

A Freshwater Aquarium in the Classroom

A freshwater aquarium in the classroom offers both aesthetic appeal and the opportunity to integrate learning across many disciplines

Photographs by Rebecca Holcombe

by Rebecca Holcombe

Subject areas: cross-curricular, depending on lessons selected

Key concepts: cross-curricular concepts related to the care, observation and maintenance of a classroom aquarium

Skills: researching and selecting appropriate equipment and animals, leadership and ownership of the aquarium, academic skills as relevant to the specific lessons chosen

Location: classroom

Time: 1–2 hours to set up the aquarium, 1 hour of maintenance every 7–10 days

Materials: varies by aquarium set-up desired (generally includes: tank, hood, light, heater, filter, gravel, cleaning and water quality supplies, decorations and/or plants, fish)

Some of my favorite high school memories are of sitting in science class watching fish in aquariums. The counters bordering the classroom held about 20 tanks of different sizes, representing various freshwater habitats from all over the world. These aquatic communities included pink kissing gouramis, Mexican blind cave fish, a community tank of tetras, a three-foot-long African lungfish (who was hand-fed red worms once a day) and platties and swordtails who gave birth to endless schools of tiny fry. We watched the way the fish interacted and how their communities changed as new fish were added or babies were born. We helped change the water, maintain filters, feed the fish and design the "landscape" inside the tanks. The science classroom was always an interesting place to be, and the lessons I learned went far beyond science curriculum. I gained a very practical understanding of the effects of water quality and chemistry, developed a sense of ownership and responsibility towards the care of our classroom, and gained skills that have enabled me to enjoy a lifelong hobby of keeping tropical freshwater fish.

Today, I still keep tropical fish, both at home and at school, and enjoy sharing a classroom aquarium with my students. Teachers who are interested in adding a freshwater aquarium to their classroom will find that it offers both aesthetic appeal and the opportunity to integrate learning across many disciplines. Students may study chemistry as they learn how to test water quality, biology as they learn about the anatomy of a fish, math as they calculate how many fish can live in tanks of different sizes, and geography as they map the places in the world where their tropical fish came from. In addition to benefiting academically, students have the opportunity to learn and practice responsible behavior by helping to care for the fish and maintain the aquarium. Further, observations of the interactions of the fish provide excellent opportunities to discuss social relationships and classroom dynamics.

The following tips are intended to help teachers select aquarium equipment and freshwater tropical fish that are suitable for the classroom, and to link the classroom aquarium to various subject areas of the curriculum.

Selecting a tank

Aquarium tanks are available in many sizes and shapes, and range from the simple and low-cost to the very elaborate. The standard small tank holds 38 liters (10 gallons), but a slightly larger tank is easier to maintain because water chemistry will not fluctuate as rapidly in a larger volume of water. A 75- to 115-liter (20- to 30-gallon) tank is usually a good size for a classroom. Be sure to select a sturdy table or stand on which to place the tank and to position it near an electrical outlet and away from direct sunlight, heaters and air conditioners.

Every tank needs a lid to keep out dust and a light for easy viewing of the fish. If you are not adding live plants, the standard fluorescent lights supplied with most aquarium hoods will be sufficient for viewing your fish. The light should be set on a timer and turned on no more than 12 hours per day, in order to mimic the natural light cycle. If you want to have live aquatic plants in the tank, you will need to purchase a much higher quality light than is typically sold at pet shops.

Filters, heaters and air pumps

All tropical tanks need a heater and filter, and a wide variety of these are available on the market. A filter helps to keep the tank clean, aerate the water and maintain proper water chemistry. Most filters utilize several filtration methods: mechanical filtration, which removes solids such as dead plants and solid fish waste; chemical filtration, in which activated carbon or another medium removes organic pollutants chemically; and biological filtration, in which beneficial bacteria break down ammonia and nitrite into less harmful substances. The three most common types of filters are those that are submersed entirely in the tank, filters that hang on the back of the tank, and canister filters that are usually housed in a cabinet under the tank. By far the simplest and most user-friendly is the hang-on variety, as it is mechanically simple and easy to access for cleaning, and does not require complicated tubing and plumbing. A hang-on filter also provides adequate aeration (eliminating the need for an air pump), provided that it is large enough for the tank and is properly maintained.

An aquarium heater is necessary in order to maintain the water temperature in the range that most tropical fish prefer, between 24.5 and 26.5 °C (76–80°F). A fully submersible heater, rather than the kind that clips onto the top edge of the tank, is preferable, as the non-submersible variety will break if it is accidentally dropped into the tank.

Air pumps and air stones add pretty bubbles but are more decorative than functional. Although air pumps can help to add oxygen to the water, I would not recommend their use in a classroom as they tend to be noisy. However, if your filter is not the hang-on variety, it may not provide adequate surface turbulence to aerate the water and you may need an air pump.

Aquarium landscape

Designing the "aqua-scape" in the tank is a fun part of setting up your classroom aquarium and a great opportunity for students to learn about the habitat needs and preferences of different fish. Generally, fish need places to hide and several objects or structures in the tank that help them divide the space into homes and territories. Fish placed in a brightly lit, mostly empty tank are more prone to stress and disease than fish living in a tank with plenty of structures and hiding places. A favorable habitat also promotes natural behavior, and hence provides opportunities for students to observe natural interactions in the aquarium community.

Caves, rocks, plastic plants and driftwood are all good aquarium additions. Aquatic plants, too, are beautiful and beneficial additions to an aquarium, but be sure to check the specific care requirements of any plants you are considering. Two hardy, beginner-friendly live aquatic plants that will tolerate low light are Java moss *(Vesicularia dubyana)* and Java fern *(Microsorium pteropus)*. Both of these plants do well when they are anchored to a piece of driftwood (tie them on with fishing line). Be sure that all aquarium additions are non-toxic and insoluble. Many types of rocks, corals and seashells are not appropriate for freshwater aquariums because they slowly dissolve, releasing minerals that negatively affect the water chemistry. Granite, slate and sandstone are generally safe for aquarium use.

Aquarium decorations can be anchored in the substrate, which may be gravel or sand, two to five centimeters (one to two inches) deep. Avoid painted substrates, as the paint often flakes off over time; and avoid very large diameter gravel, as fish can become trapped in the spaces between the gravel pieces. If using sand as a substrate, purchase it from an aquarium shop and ensure that is intended for freshwater use (many shops sell sand for saltwater tanks that contains salts and minerals that will negatively affect water chemistry in a freshwater tank). Sand from a beach is

Tank maintenance includes changing 20 percent of water every two weeks.

not suitable since it will contain too much salt and organic material.

Choosing fish

There are many species of freshwater tropical fish and many color and form varieties within each species. The best choices for a classroom aquarium are peaceful community fish such as those in the tetra, gourami, danio, livebearer and rasbora groups. The needs of most peaceful community fish are similar enough that several species can live together. On the other hand, semi-aggressive or aggressive freshwater fish are more challenging to keep and greatly limit the diversity of species that can be kept in the same tank. (The websites listed provide in-depth information on the requirements of various species, including preferred lighting, water chemistry and recommended tank mates.)

Inviting students to participate in the selection of fish will encourage them to take an active interest in your classroom aquarium. Students can research behavior, adult size, habitat needs and other information about various species of fish. As there are hundreds of varieties, a good starting point is to make a list of the peaceful community fish that are available at your local pet shop. If you would like a larger selection of fish than is available locally, consider ordering through an on-line company, or ask your pet shop if they will make a special order for you. Be sure to purchase some livebearers (which give birth to live fry rather than laying eggs) if you want your students to watch generations of fish grow up in the tank (note that some fry will be eaten by larger fish if they are not removed and raised separately).

The number and size of the fish that you can accommodate is determined by the size of your tank. A typical aquarium can support one inch of fish per gallon of water (equivalent to 1 cm of fish per 1.5 liters). For example, a 20-gallon tank may contain only 17 gallons of water due to water displacement by gravel and decorations. These 17 gallons could support four two-inch fish and three three-inch fish, or any other combination that adds up to 17 inches of fish. Overstocking aquariums is a common cause of fish death, as it can lead to rapid fluctuations in water chemistry and result in dissolved oxygen levels that are too low for many types of fish.

Teachers will also want to consider the origin of their fish and the environmental implications of keeping exotic fish in the classroom. While it is possible to keep some varieties of native fish in the classroom, it is usually necessary to obtain them from the wild as they are not commonly available commercially. In addition, many species of native fish will grow far too large for a typical classroom aquarium and may require cooler, faster running water than it is feasible to provide. In many parts of the world, fish populations are dwindling due to habitat loss, over-fishing and water contamination, making wild collection of either native or tropical species undesirable. However, more than 800 varieties of freshwater tropical fish are captive-bred and tank-raised, primarily in the U.S. and Asia. (By contrast, only 10 percent of commercially available saltwater fish are captive-bred and raised, the remainder being harvested from increasingly endangered coral reefs and other marine environments.) When purchasing fish, look for dealers who specify the origin of the fish — whether tank-raised or wild-collected, and where they are from.[1] Researching and purchasing tank-raised fish provides an opportunity to talk with students about many environmental and ethical issues, including the distinction between wild and domestic animals and the ethical and environmental implications of the exotic animal trade.

Testing water pH.

Classroom aquarium challenges

Keeping an aquarium has many rewards, but when deciding to add a tank to your classroom it is also important to consider the challenges. Weekend, holiday and summer maintenance needs to be planned, as it is very difficult to move an aquarium home for the holidays. During short vacations, a timer and automatic feeder can be used to turn aquarium lights on and off and to feed the fish, but the tank should be checked every five days or so to make sure the equipment is working properly. Aside from vacation care,

normal tank maintenance includes changing 20 percent of the water every two weeks, monitoring water chemistry through regular water testing and basic care and cleaning of aquarium equipment (filter, glass, etc.). Testing and charting water chemistry and performing routine maintenance on the tank are good opportunities to involve students in the care of the aquarium.

Fish death is a challenge that most teachers will face at some point, and is not uncommon in the first few weeks when water chemistry is stabilizing in the tank. The manner in which death is handled by the teacher and students will depend on the age of the students. I believe it is best to establish with students from the start that, together, you will do your best to provide a good, healthy home and care for your fish responsibly, but that sometimes fish die and you will talk about it further if it happens. Fish death, although unfortunate, can provide opportunities for discussing feelings and life experiences, and how we learn and grow from those experiences.

Curriculum links

Once it is set up, a classroom aquarium can be integrated into many areas of the curriculum. Following are lesson and activity ideas for several subjects.

English literature: Read children's stories about fish and have students write their own stories based on observations of the classroom aquarium. *Clara and Asha*, a story by Eric Rohmann about a little girl with an imaginary fish friend, will inspire students to think creatively about fish beyond the aquarium. *Swimmy*, by Leo Lionni, provides opportunity to discuss diversity, problem solving and the value of teamwork. *Fish is Fish*, also by Leo Lionni, is the humorous story of a tadpole and a minnow who are born at the same time and look very much alike, but are surprised when they grow up to be different creatures with very different life experiences. *What's It Like to Be a Fish?* by Wendy Pfeffer is an excellent introduction to fish biology and life cycles for younger children.

Math: Many mathematical calculations are involved in setting up and maintaining a classroom aquarium. For example, students can calculate how many fish can live in tanks of various sizes, calculate the volume and surface area of the aquarium, learn to read water temperature on a thermometer and graph changes in water chemistry over time.

Science: Students may learn basic biology concepts through studying, labeling and drawing fish anatomy, and learn about habitats and ecosystems through researching and creating aquarium habitats similar to the native environments of particular fish. They may study fish adaptations by observing different mouth forms and feeding habits, and by considering how body shape and color may have been influenced by a fish's natural environment. As part of routine maintenance of the tank, students may test and chart water chemistry parameters and experiment with different types of filter media.

Many natural webs and cycles occur in a well-balanced aquarium, and these too may be studied, drawn and observed. For example, an aquarium with live plants will have a simple food chain, with plants as the primary producers, snails or herbivorous fish as primary consumers, and beneficial bacteria serving as decomposers. Aquariums with live plants also serve to demonstrate photosynthesis. A very important cycle in tanks with or without live plants is the nitrogen cycle, a process by which toxins such as ammonia and nitrites (from fish waste and decaying plants) are converted by beneficial bacteria into less toxic nitrates. Plants and animals use the converted nitrogen to grow, thereby completing the cycle. The levels of ammonia, nitrite and nitrate in the aquarium can be easily tested, making it possible to chart the progress of the nitrogen cycle in the aquarium.

Social Studies/Geography: Mapping the countries of origin of various tropical species is an excellent way to explore world geography. Various cultures may be highlighted by studying the history of fish keeping around the world (Japanese koi are a particularly good example).

Social Skills: Students can develop responsibility and ownership through participating in the care of a classroom aquarium. Additionally, observing fish behavior provides opportunity to talk about bullying, community, cooperation and other classroom dynamics that are reflected in the aquarium community.

Finally, a classroom aquarium can be used as a link to studies of the native fish in your area. Enjoyment of tropical fish in the classroom often sparks students' interest in learning where fish live in their local community, what their habitat is like and how human activities might affect them. My hope in sharing a classroom aquarium with my students is to teach responsible behavior towards and respect for living things, to provide interdisciplinary curricular connections and to inspire curiosity about the fish that are native to our community.

Rebecca Holcombe is an environmental educator and the Director of Community Programs for Common Ground High School and the New Haven Ecology Project in New Haven, Connecticut.

Note

1. Live Aquaria <www.liveaquaria.com> sells many captive-bred and tank-raised tropical fish and provides information about the origin of the fish they sell.

Resources

The Krib, <www.thekrib.com>. This website and community devoted to keeping tropical fish is an excellent source of step-by-step instructions for setting up an aquarium and in-depth profiles of many fish species.

Tetra Fish <www.tetra-fish.com/aquademics/>. This website has instructions for setting up and maintaining an aquarium and a section for teachers that includes lesson plan suggestions, printable activity sheets and online games for students.

Nitrogen Pollution:
Too Much of a Good Thing

Left to right: A. Chalmers, Gail Littlejohn, Paul McKay

by David A. Bainbridge

Subject areas: ecology and environmental science, history, mathematics

Key concepts: nitrogen pollution in aquatic and terrestrial ecosystems, eco-toxicity, biodiversity, systems dynamics, global change, ecological footprint

Skills: using the scientific method, using formulas, setting up experiments, observation, taking measurements, data synthesis and analysis

Location: lab, outdoors, greenhouse or grow light

Time: approximately 1 day to prepare, sampling over several weeks; 1 hour of class time per week

Materials: native and invasive grass seeds (native seed supply and garden supply or collect), sandy soil, nitrogen fertilizer, 1 gallon plant containers, water, plastic drink bottles, paper bags, hole punch, aquaria sealant, heavy duty clear small diameter tubing; Perlite and rye grass seeds in a 10 cm x 20 cm pan; filtered pond water; LaMotte or Hach dissolved oxygen test kit; *Euglena*, a species of green algae available from science supply houses

We often hear concerns expressed about exotic environmental risks such as chlorofluoro-carbons in the atmosphere, plutonium on satellites, mercury and cadmium in batteries, or the pesticides and herbicides in our groundwater. But it is becoming increasingly clear that disruptions in more basic processes may cause equally severe environmental problems. Rising levels of carbon dioxide in the atmosphere and the destruction of stratospheric ozone are two examples. Another is nitrogen pollution, which increasingly appears to be an environmental disaster both in water (where it has long been recognized) and on land.

Although nitrogen gas (N_2) makes up 78 percent of the air we breathe, it is often the limiting factor in the growth of plants because this large reservoir of atmospheric nitrogen cannot be used directly as a nutrient. Nitrogen gas is converted into chemical forms that can be used by plants through a process of nitrogen fixation that is carried out by bacteria. These include free-living cyanobacteria in soil and water, and bacteria that form and live in nodules on the roots of certain plants (Rhizobium bacteria in legumes such as beans, peas and clover; and filamentous bacteria called actinomycetes in alders, buffalo berries, mountain lilacs and a few other shrubs and perennial herbs). If you break open a root nodule from a clover or bean plant, it will be red inside if it is fixing nitrogen. These beneficial partners, or symbionts, convert nitrogen gas from the air into biologically available ammonia (NH_3). Ammonium ions (NH_4^+) may then be converted to nitrites (NO_2^-) and then to nitrates (NO_3^-) by aerobic bacteria.

After nitrogen has served its purpose in living organisms, vast armies of decomposers convert nitrogen-rich organic compounds, wastes, cast-off particles and dead bodies back into simpler compounds that are available to other plants and microorganisms. Other specialized bacteria, mostly anaerobic bacteria in the soil and in bottom sediments of lakes, oceans, swamps and bogs, then convert these inorganic forms of nitrogen back into nitrogen gas, which is released into the atmosphere to begin the cycle again. Nitrogen is also fixed by every lightning bolt, perhaps a kilogram per bolt. This makes up the critically important nitrogen cycle.

During pre-industrial times, nitrogen cycling is assumed to have been roughly in balance: measurements of nitrous oxide (N_2O) in ancient gas bubbles trapped in glacial ice show concentrations hovering around 285 parts per million (ppm). About 200 years ago, human activity began to throw this system out of balance. Since the Industrial Revolution began, the nitrous oxide level in the atmosphere has risen to approximately 310 ppm.

Several factors account for the dramatic increase of nitrogen in the environment. At the global level, the single largest source of added nitrogen is manufactured nitrogen fertilizer, which is made using large quantities of natural gas. In 2006 alone, more than 98 million tons of nitrogen fertilizer were used worldwide to increase crop growth. These crops are fed to animals and people, creating nitrogen-rich wastes. Over two billion tons of wet animal manure are produced each year in the United States alone. Much of it is not

Combustion of fossil fuel is the major contributor to nitrogen pollution in North America and other industrialized regions.

Gail Littlejohn

treated, and the move toward industrial production of meat and eggs results in the concentration of enormous quantities of these nitrogen-rich wastes in small areas. The failure of just one pig waste storage lagoon in North Carolina resulted in the release of 25 million gallons of nitrogen-rich material into local waterways. When accidents like this occur, or when floodwaters breach manure lagoons or collect nitrogen-rich material from fields, extensive pollution can result not only in fresh water but also in coastal regions downstream.

Nitrogen also concentrates in cities and towns, in human wastes as well as pet droppings and lawn fertilizers. Yet most sewage treatment systems remove only half of the nitrogen from human wastes, and stormwater runoff from fertilized lawns and golf courses is usually not treated at all. Like the runoff from fertilized farmland, it carries nitrogen compounds directly into local streams and lakes. These non-point sources are very difficult to control, although the use of buffer strips of natural vegetation and trees along water courses is very helpful.

On a global scale, the planting of immense acreages of leguminous crops has also played a role in the nitrogen pollution problem by increasing biological nitrogen fixation. Crops such as peas and beans have been calculated to add 34 million tons of biologically available nitrogen to the world environment every year.

The major problem in most developed areas is the nitrogen added to the environment from burning fossil fuels, estimated at 20 million metric tons each year. Burning coal and wood mobilizes the nitrogen in the fuel, while burning gas, diesel and natural gas adds nitrogen largely by oxidizing nitrogen gas in the atmosphere. In the United States, more than 3.2 million tons of nitrogen are deposited from the atmosphere each year as wet deposition in fog, rain and snow, or as dry deposition in droplets, gases and particulates. The largest sources of nitrous oxide in North America are coal- and oil-fired power plants and industries, many of which pollute large areas downwind. Locally, automobiles, trucks, buses, planes, leaf blowers, lawn mowers and jet skis are often the most significant sources. These nitrous oxides combine to form particulates that fall as dust or are caught up and deposited in rain. Much of the dark dust that settles on cars in urban areas is composed of nitrogen-rich particulates. These little particles add up. The average nitrogen deposition rate in central Europe is now 15 kilograms per hectare per year. Studies in the UK showed that one species is lost for every 2.5 kilograms of added nitrogen per four-square-meter plot.[1] In automobile-dominated areas such as southern California, annual nitrogen deposition can reach almost 80 kilograms per hectare, considerably more than the world average application of nitrogen fertilizer on crops. If you drive 16,000 kilometers a year, you may be adding as much as 32 kilograms of nitrogen pollution to your local environment.

Like the more widely recognized increases in greenhouse gases, increased levels of nitrogen can have profound effects on the biological world; but because nitrogen is a natural component of ecosystems it was not recognized as a threat for a long time. Many thought higher concentrations would be beneficial, an idea that was reinforced when nitrogen studies in several ecosystems showed increases in growth and productivity. But impact studies typically evaluate changes over only about five years, a period that is too short to reveal slow and cumulative changes. Where the effect of excess nitrogen has been studied for long periods, its impact has been shown to be nothing short of catastrophic. By favoring plants, algae and organisms that are highly responsive to nitrogen, an excess of nitrogen reduces diversity and limits the ability of ecosystems to cope with stress.

A study that began in the 1850s at Rothamsted Experimental Station in England, has shown dramatic declines in the diversity of grassland plots treated with nitrogen at levels well within current deposition rates.[2] As Table 1 shows, these changes occurred slowly and

Table 1: Impact of Excess Nitrogen on Biodiversity

Short term impact

Years	Nitrogen input — # species in plot		
	43 lbs N/acre	86 lbs N/acre	129 lbs N/acre
6	33 species	28 species	28 species
16	43 species	30 species	16 species

Long term impact

Years	Nitrogen input — # species in plot		
	43 lbs N/acre	86 lbs N/acre	129 lbs N/acre
21	48 species	27 species	15 species
47	39 species	24 species	na
63	31 species	16 species	8 species
93	20 species	16 species	3 species

–Data from studies at Rothamsted Experimental Station, England

would not have been apparent had the study continued for only a few years. During the first 15 to 20 years, species diversity increased in most plots with added nitrogen. But over the long term, very negative impacts were observed, with diversity dropping from 30 species to three in plots that received the highest nitrogen input.

A 12-year study in Minnesota grasslands showed similar declines in species diversity and changes in community composition.[3] Species richness declined 50 percent and bunch grasses were replaced by weedy European grasses. Recent reports from Sweden, where deposition can exceed 100 kilograms per hectare, are equally alarming. In some areas, the beneficial mycorrhizal fungi have produced no fruiting bodies (mushrooms) for the last six years. This will have profound effects on forest ecosystems.

In aquatic ecosystems, the problems caused by excess nitrogen are equally grave, yet may take many years to develop. High levels of nitrogen cause waterways to become eutrophic, a condition in which excess nutrients lead to rapid growth of both algae and the microbes that feed on them. When these organisms die, decomposing bacteria digest the dead organic matter and consume large amounts of oxygen in the process. Lower oxygen levels can, in turn, kill fish and microorganisms. In eutrophic waters, species diversity may decrease, and less desired organisms, such as toxic varieties of algae, may increase. Thus excess nitrogen may directly or indirectly lead to problems like the dangerous outbreak of the toxic microbe *Pfiesteria piscicida* in Chesapeake Bay and along the eastern coast of the United States. The outbreak appears to be the result of additions of nitrogen from massive poultry and pig farms, but it may also reflect nitrogen deposition from the air and runoff from farm fields.

What can be done about nitrogen? Unfortunately, the solutions are not easy. We can reduce the nitrous oxide emissions of power plants and cars. We can drive fewer miles, ride a bicycle, move closer to where we work, and avoid using machines powered by two-stroke motors such as mowers, snowmobiles and scooters. We can eat less meat and choose free-range beef and chicken rather than industrially produced animals. We can limit our use of nitrogen fertilizer and adopt agricultural practices that rely more on organic matter and biological nitrogen fixation. Where appropriate, we can add slow-to-decompose carbon-rich materials (like sawdust) to the soil to tie up added nitrogen. We can also preserve and construct wetlands to filter excess nitrogen from water.

Studies of the long term effects of nitrogen on ecosystems and waterways are urgently needed, as are new efforts to reduce future impacts. It is also important that interdisciplinary teams cooperate on studies between countries where pollution drifts occur, such as between Canada and the United States, the United States and Mexico, and Scandinavia and the United Kingdom. At present, however, funding for such research is minimal. In the United States, the National Science Foundation's Long Term Ecological Research Program receives only $10 million a year — less than one-third the cost of running a mediocre major league baseball team and about the same as the cost of running an international race car team for one year. Funding should be at least $500 million and could be raised by imposing a nitrogen impact fee on gasoline sales, airport operations and ship traffic. A gasoline tax of a few cents per gallon would provide millions of dollars for long term impact studies and environmental restoration and treatment to offset nitrogen pollution.

The nitrogen pollution problem provides a good example for teaching about the insidious nature of some types of environmental damage, and it high-

Nitrogen Oxide Emissions (U.S.)

On-road vehicles	38%
Electricity generation	22%
Equipment	21%
Fossil fuel combustion	11%
Industrial processes	5%

Nitrogen Fertilizer Use (World)

Year	Million tons
1970	31.8
1980	60.9
2000	88.0
2006	98.2

Sources: U.S. EPA, 2002; FAO, 2007

lights the importance of monitoring long term changes and the need for consideration of sustainability in everything we do. It also demonstrates the cumulative impact of many small actions and the need to consider nitrogen pollution as part of our ecological footprint. Finally, it points to the value of simple, low-cost research in a time when many people consider super-computers and super-colliders as the forefront of science. The best research we have on nitrogen impacts was done with paper and pencil and 100 years of careful observation.

David A. Bainbridge *is Assistant Professor and Environmental Studies Coordinator at United States International University in San Diego, California.*

Notes

1. C. J. Stevens, N. B. Dise, J. O. Mountford and D. J. Cowing, "Impact of Nitrogen Deposition on the Species Richness of Grasslands," *Science* 303 (2004): 5665:1876–1879.

2. W. Brenchley, *The Park Grass Plots*, Rothamsted Experimental Station, Hertfordshire, England, 1956.

3. D.A. Wedin and D. Tilman, "Influence of Nitrogen Loading and Species Composition on the Carbon Balance of Grasslands," *Science* 274 (1996), pp. 1720–1721.

References

Allen, E. B., P.E. Padgett, A. Bytnerowicz and R. A. Minnich. "Nitrogen deposition effects on coastal sage vegetation of southern California." In A. Bytnerowicz, M.J. Arbaugh and S. Schilling, eds. *Proceedings of the International Symposium on Air Pollution and Climate Change Effects on Forest Ecosystems, Riverside, California.* General Technical Report PSW-GTR 164, Albany, California, Pacific Southwest Research Station, USDA Forest Service, 1996.

Ayers, R.U., W.H. Schlesinger and R.H. Socolow. "Human Impacts on the Carbon and Nitrogen Cycles." In R. Socolow, C. Andrews, F. Berkhout and V. Thomas, ed. *Industrial Ecology and Global Change.* Cambridge University Press, 1997, pp. 121–156.

Investigating Nitrogen Pollution:
Activities and Models

Nitrogen Pollution from School Commuters: A Study in Impact Analysis

Purpose: Standards for auto exhaust emissions are stated in grams of NO_2 per mile or per kilometer. By molecular weight, NO_2 is about 30 percent nitrogen. We can therefore calculate the contribution that cars make to nitrogen pollution by estimating the distance driven each year. In the U.S. the annual total is an amazing 3.2 trillion kilometers (2 trillion miles). If you drive 16,000 kilometers a year, you may be adding as much as 32 kilograms of nitrogen pollution to your local environment.

As a class project, have students determine how much nitrogen their families contribute to the local environment by driving cars. Ask students to estimate how many kilometers their families drive each year and, if possible, find out how many grams of NO_2 per kilometer their cars produce. Older cars may produce more than 2 grams per km, while the best new cars can be as low as 0.12 grams per km. Have students use the following calculation to determine their individual impact, and then average the driving and emissions data to determine the impact of the class as a whole.

Grams nitrogen/year = (Number of cars) x (average km driven per year) x (average grams of NO_2 emissions per km) x 0.30

Nitrogen Response in Native and Introduced Species

Purpose: An excess of nitrogen may at first appear to benefit ecosystems by increasing productivity, but over the long term it can reduce biodiversity by favoring plants, algae and organisms that are highly responsive to nitrogen. The following experiment tests whether some species of local plants are more responsive to excess nitrogen than others.

Materials: 15 five-liter (or one-gallon) containers; sandy soil; at least 15 seeds each from two local shrubs or grasses, one a native species and one an introduced species; houseplant fertilizer.

Procedure:

1. Fill the containers with a sandy soil that has few nutrients.

2. In each pot, plant three seeds from the native shrub or grass and three seeds from the non-native species (six seeds per pot).

3. Divide the pots into five groups of three. Treat each group of three pots with one of the following doses of fertilizer: none (control), one-half the recommended dose, the recommended dose, twice the recommended dose, and three times the recommended dose.

4. Monitor germination and growth. Develop tables of data on factors such as germination rate and height of plants. At the end of the experiment, dry and weigh the plants to obtain data on biomass. Calculate the means of each variable and test for the significance of any observed differences.

5. Discuss the potential impact of nitrogen pollution on biodiversity in your region. What species are likely to be favored in conditions of excess nitrogen?

Nutrient-loading Model

Purpose: This nutrient-loading model illustrates how the application of fertilizers on land influences plant and algae growth in aquatic ecosystems through runoff and infiltration. The model allows students to generate and investigate questions related to what can happen to aquatic ecosystems if nutrients applied on land are directly discharged into a lake or stream that has no buffer zone of riparian plants to absorb them. The discharge of excess water from the receiving bottle into a flat of rye grass illustrates differences in the growth of wetland plants receiving the nutrient-rich water. Removing water from the test and control bottles for dissolved oxygen analysis lets students investigate the effect of nutrient enrichment on a chemical parameter that is extremely important to aerobic aquatic organisms. This can serve as a discussion point for how riparian vegetation and wetlands help buffer the potential impact on lakes and rivers.

Materials and equipment: Three two-liter clear plastic soda drink bottles; hole punch, aquarium sealant, heavy-duty clear ½-inch tubing; Perlite and rye grass seeds in a 10 cm x 20 cm pan; filtered pond water; LaMotte or Hach dissolved oxygen test kit; *Euglena*, a species of green algae available from science supply houses.

Constructing the models: Make at least two models, one for the test conditions and one to be the control. For each model, cut and assemble three clear plastic soda bottles as follows:

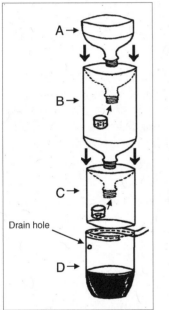

1. Cut the tops off of two bottles, leaving a short 3 cm sleeve on one bottle top (see section A in diagram) and a longer 15 cm sleeve on the other (section B). Drill or punch holes in the caps and replace them on the spouts of the cut-off tops.

2. Insert the short-sleeved top (section A) into the long-sleeved top (section B), as shown in the diagram.

3. Use the bottom half of a cut-off bottle as the receiving bottle (section D). Form a drain hole for overflow by using a hot nail or a single-hole punch. Position the hole approximately 5 cm from the top edge of the receiving bottle.

4. In order to elevate the top portion of the model high enough for water to drip into the receiving bottle, tape a 12 cm section from a third bottle onto the receiving bottle (see section C).

5. Create a "wetland" for each model by planting rye grass seeds in a Perlite substrate in a 10 cm x 20 cm pan. Insert a length of clear tubing into the overflow hole and position the tube so that it drains into the pan. Seal the tube at the overflow hole with aquarium sealant.

Nutrient input

1. Put washed Perlite into the top half of each model. Plant the Perlite substrates with rye grass seeds that have been soaked for an hour to speed up germination.

2. Cover each model with a paper bag for three days. Keep the seeds moist with distilled water.

3. After the seeds have germinated, remove the paper bags. Pour 60 ml of pond water into the top funnel of each model so that it drains through the Perlite into the receiving bottle at the bottom. If you wish to speed up algal growth, inoculate the water in the receiving bottles with equal amounts of a culture of *Euglena*, a species of green algae.

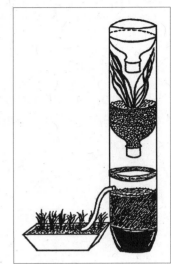

4. Expose the models to a light source, such as a grow light or fluorescent light, or place the models in the window if you are conducting the experiment during the spring. Be sure that the test and control models receive the same amount of light.

5. Make a stock solution of fertilizer by adding 2 grams of a houseplant fertilizer to a liter of distilled water. Then make a weaker solution of 5% stock (5:100). Every 2–3 days, add 20 ml of the 5% solution to the test models, and 20 ml of distilled water to the control model. If clean rainwater is available, it can be substituted for distilled water in both the fertilizer solution and the control. This will simulate a natural situation in which rainwater washes fertilizer into groundwater and then into lakes, rivers or wetlands.

6. In three to five weeks, algae will grow in both the treated and control models; however, the nitrogen-treated models will have more growth. Discuss how each model might respond over a long period of time. Compare the growth of plants in the "wetlands" and discuss how nutrients influence wetland plants and what wetlands do to buffer nutrient runoff from the land.

Dissolved oxygen test: Nutrients increase the growth of algae. Like all plant cells, algae produce oxygen through photosynthesis during daylight hours but also use oxygen from the water in order to carry out aerobic respiration. At night and on overcast days, these plants use up more oxygen than they produce. After the plants die, additional oxygen is needed by the bacteria that decompose the dead organic material. In nutrient-enriched lakes and ponds with prolific algal growth, levels of dissolved oxygen can drop so low that fish and other aquatic organisms cannot survive.

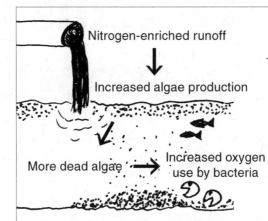

After an obvious algal growth has developed in the nutrient-enriched test bottle (in 3–5 weeks), the models can be used to illustrate how increased populations of aquatic plants can lower the amount of dissolved oxygen in the water:

1. Remove water from both the test bottle and the control using a syringe. Gently discharge the water into a 60 ml or smaller BOD (biochemical oxygen demand) bottle for testing dissolved oxygen with a LaMotte or Hach test kit or Chemetrics test strips.

2. Test the water from each model after both have been exposed to a full day of daylight. Test again after the models have been covered or placed in the dark for 12 hours, ensuring that they are sampled as soon as they are removed from the dark.

Extended math activity: Weigh the pond water in each trial. Filter and dry the materials. Weigh dry materials to find biomass. What is the ratio of polluted water to biomass?

Discussion: Compare the changes in the levels of dissolved oxygen in each model. In which model was there a greater decrease in dissolved oxygen during the dark period? Which model had the highest level of dissolved oxygen after a full day of light? Have students explain the differences they observed. Discuss the implications of losing wetlands, which act as buffers by taking up nutrients that enter rivers and lakes in runoff. Discuss the ways in which human activities on land speed up the eutrophication process in waterways.

— *"Nitrogen Pollution from School Commuters" and "Nitrogen Response in Native and Introduced Species" were developed by David A. Bainbridge. The Nutrient Loading Model was developed by Dr. Kevin Curry, biologist at Bridgewater State College in Bridgewater, Massachusetts. Accompanying instructions and activities were developed by Barbara Waters and Faith Burbank for the Massachusetts Bays Watershed Education Teaching Program.*

Living Systems in the Classroom

Making an aquatic ecosystem for the classroom is an engaging project and a springboard to discussing concepts of ecology, biology and hydraulics

Photographs by Mark Keffer

by Mark Keffer

Subject areas: ecology, botany, zoology, environmental science, physics (hydraulics)

Key concepts: aquatic ecosystems, biodiversity, bioremediation, phytoremediation, microcosms

Skills: observation, construction of models, long-term observation, adapting models, designing experiments

Location: indoors, with outdoor collection of materials

Time: 2–3 hours to assemble materials; 2–3 hours to put system together; several weeks to months running the system

Materials: plastic tubs, clear vinyl tubing, grommets, air bubbler, hose inserts, living materials from nearby ponds or other aquatic environments, optional aquarium pump, water-quality sampling kits

A "living machine" or aquatic living system is an excellent teaching tool, offering hooks to many concepts in science, environmental studies and other areas of the curriculum. It can be used to purify water, treat wastes, raise fish, grow vegetables or to do all of these at the same time, depending on how it is designed. It is a great focus for inquiry and cooperative learning, provides a lot of fun, and helps students develop the kind of do-it-yourself confidence that is not always inspired by textbook experiments.

The easiest way to describe an aquatic living system is as several aquarium tanks linked to each other, such that water and materials move from one to the next. Instead of a single tank with a complex mix of habitats and niches, a living system has several tanks in which distinct habitats flourish in relative isolation but are connected to other habitats by the flow of water between cells. By isolating "cells" that contain different habitats, we increase the opportunity to learn about the unique characteristics of each habitat and open the door to a much larger set of ideas. The following is a look at some of the main concepts related to living systems and a brief explanation of the steps in setting up your own classroom system.

Concepts: habitat, niche, biotic and abiotic factors, optimum point, range of tolerance

Living systems have a number of different containers or "cells" that contain aquatic life. Water flows from one container to the next, distributing nutrients, wastes and microorganisms among them. Different containers have different conditions and contain different substances, thereby providing a diversity of habitats and niches. For example, in the system described here, one cell contains pond muck while another contains emergent plants. The roots of the emergent plants provide surface area for the attachment and sheltering of bacteria, snails and other organisms. The pond muck provides habitat for many organisms also, but they are a different set from those in the emergent-plant cell. Other systems could be designed to have a "floor" of forest leaf litter, or a chunk of turf cut from the schoolyard, or sand from a streambed or beach. Conditions can be varied in different cells by changing the temperature, the amount of light, the presence or absence of bubbling, the amount of shelter for insects and so on.

By varying the biotic and abiotic conditions within cells and then examining the life that proliferates under those differing conditions, students can observe concrete examples of such concepts as optimum conditions, range of tolerance, habitat and niche. Each different set of environmental conditions has a unique and diverse group of organisms that favor it. If an environment changes so that it is no longer suitable for an organism, the organism has only two choices: move somewhere else or die. It is a clear example of what happens in the real world when organisms lose their habitat.

Concepts: trophic levels, food chains and webs, biodiversity, populations, communities, stability

Through the flow of water, microorganisms and nutrients can move freely from cell to cell. Over time, organisms find the area to which they are best suited, stay there and, if conditions are right, proliferate. Greater biodiversity increases the complexity of the food webs present, and this increases the ability of the system to withstand such challenges as the addition of harmful materials, a sudden change in temperature, the loss of a particular species, or a power outage during which the air pump or bubbler gets cut off.

Concepts: nitrogen and carbon cycles, the importance of microorganisms, photosynthesis, respiration, excretion, metabolism, symbiosis

Living systems provide excellent opportunities for students to explore the chemical cycles of life, as well as symbiosis and interdependence among organisms. In an indoor living system, as in the natural world, the wastes of one organism become the nutrients for another. For example, while fish may be the most visible inhabitants of the system, their existence depends on many other inhabitants and interactions. Fish excrete ammonia as a waste product; and if this ammonia builds up in the water, it can kill them. Nitrifying bacteria living in the water change ammonia into nitrites and then into far less toxic nitrates. The nitrates then become fertilizer for plants in the system. By taking up the nitrates through their roots, plants help purify the water. Plant roots also provide extensive surface area for the attachment of the nitrifying bacteria. Plants may further encourage this symbiosis with bacteria by exuding substances (such as sugars) through their roots that nourish the bacteria and help them continue their work of converting ammonia to nitrate.

Concepts: open and closed systems, sustainability, interrelations within the biosphere

Living systems are self-sustaining. Once they are successfully running, they produce their own food and treat their own wastes, the only inputs being light and perhaps air from a bubbler.

Concepts: hydraulics, flow rates, water pressure, potential energy

The many possible configurations for connecting cells and re-circulating the water between them provide opportunities for students to investigate hydraulics and related concepts. For example, students can experiment with flow rates by adjusting the height of water, the amount of water that is raised or the diameter of the tubes through which water flows.

Making a simple desktop living system

There are three main requirements in setting up a living system in the classroom. First, you need containers. Just about any containers can be used, as long as they will hold water and (in most cases) allow light to enter. Second, you need to get water to flow from one container to the next. This can be done by siphoning ("over-the-wall" connections) or by using fittings to make a "through the wall" connection. Third, you need a means of moving water from one container to the next. Most of this movement will be accomplished by gravity, but somewhere along the line, water will have to be lifted. This lifting of water can be done with either a pump or an airlift.

Containers

Plastic tubs, plastic garbage cans and pails will all work as containers for the cells of the system. Glass aquariums are not recommended since drilling holes in glass requires special equipment and it is very easy to shatter it. The containers do not have to be the same shape or size, although this may make things more convenient. The instructions here are for a system that uses four 55-liter semi-transparent rectangular plastic tubs measuring about 45 x 45 x 64 centimeters, readily available from stores selling large storage tubs. Large 19-liter water jugs with their tops cut off also work well, and they fit into a smaller space. (You may be able to obtain defective but usable water jugs inexpensively from drinking water suppliers.) Cylindrical containers such as drinking water jugs provide magnification for viewing the life inside. However, if the jugs are too small, the curvature of the wall makes it difficult to get a good seal on through-the-wall connections.

Check your containers for leaks before setting them up, and note that containers may bulge when full of water. Also be sure that your location will support their weight when they are full of water. Water is heavy! One liter of water has a mass of one kilogram (8.4 pounds per U.S. gallon). A 55-liter tub, when two thirds full of water, will weigh about 37 kilograms. Weight is a consideration when moving tubs, too, as the handles on flimsier containers might not be able to support the weight of water when they are filled. It is therefore a good idea to empty tubs at least partially before attempting to pick them up by the handles.

Siphoning versus over-the-wall connections

Water can move between cells in many different ways. At the simplest, water can pour from one container into the next. This invites spillage, but might be an interesting way to mimic natural stream "riffle" conditions. Water can also be siphoned over the top of one container into the next. This requires a siphoning tube and has the advantage that you do not need to drill holes in the walls of your containers. Once you get the water flowing in a siphon tube, it will continue to flow up and over the wall of the container through the tube as long as the source of water is higher in elevation than the lower end of the tube. However, if the flow in the siphon is interrupted for any reason (e.g.,

if air gets into the tube), then somebody will have to start the flow again. This has the potential to be disastrous if the interruption occurs at night or when no one is around to restart it.

It is generally safer to drill holes in the walls of the containers and connect containers to each other with tubing or pipe. This method is much less likely to cause spillage. The disadvantage is that you must drill holes and that leakage around the holes must be prevented. The grommet–pipe insert system described below is easy, reliable, quick and does not require caulking.

Airlifts, pumps and bubblers

An airlift is a simple and effective device for raising water from the lowest point in the system back up to the top. It requires only plastic tubing and an inexpensive aquarium bubbler. Airlifts use differences in water pressure to lift water: when air is injected deep in the water column, the aerated water is lifted, since the density of the unaerated water below the air bubbles is greater. As the bubbles rise, they expand, enhancing the effect. If the water and bubbles are channeled inside a tube, the water within the tube is raised above the surface of the surrounding water.

Airlifts have the advantages of not becoming clogged with solids as a pump would, and of aerating the water as it is lifted. A source of oxygen is important both for fish and for the bacteria that turn ammonia into nitrate. Another advantage of airlifts is that living organisms are less likely to be damaged when moving through an airlift than when moving through a pump. The main disadvantages of airlifts are that they cannot lift water very high or move water as quickly as a pump might. In the system described here, an airlift would be able to lift water a maximum of about 10 to 15 centimeters. However, this amount of lift is easily enough for the system to work.

Four main variables affect the movement of water in an airlift system: the amount of air injected; the depth at which the air is injected; the amount of friction in the tube; and the amount of lift above the surface that is required. The diameter of the tube used for the airlift also has an effect. In the setup described below, all tubes are one-half inch in diameter.

The movement of water from cell to cell helps organisms move around so that they can find their optimal living conditions. Faster flow rates between cells can be used to mimic conditions found in natural rushing streams; slower flow rates can be used to mimic conditions found in ponds and wetlands. If the flow rate between cells is too slow, organisms will not be able to move quickly enough between cells in order to find their optimum conditions. If the flow rate is too fast, fragile organisms might be damaged or might not be able to "keep their footing" in their optimum spots.

Generally, an aquarium pump will produce much higher flow rates than an airlift. If you desire a system that has a rushing flow, it is therefore best to use a pump. The higher the pump must send water, the slower the flow will be. Pumps are usually sold with a chart that suggests the flow rates possible at different head heights. Flow rates should be such that the entire volume of water in the system is exchanged in a period of 24 to 36 hours. The airlift system described in this procedure runs at roughly this speed. It is not necessary to get a high-volume pump. For most systems, a small aquarium pump in the $20 to $30 range should suffice.

System layouts

The diagram "Sample System Layouts" shows two simple plans for a living system. Both systems produce a difference in water height. The greater the height of water, the greater the gravitational potential energy. The highest elevation of water in the system is called the head height. It doesn't matter if the water is higher because the water *within a cell* is higher or if the *cell itself* is higher. In general, the flow rate through the system depends on three main things: the head height (how high the water is raised); the amount of water that is raised to that height; and the thickness of the tubes through which the water flows. Increasing any of these three factors will lead to faster flow of water through the system.

The following is a quick and easy method for setting up a system that uses through-the-wall connections to carry water from one cell to the next and an airlift to raise water so that it can circulate between the cells. The instructions given here describe a system that resembles System 2 in the diagram. This is just one possibility for a successful system. Part of the fun (and instructional value) of setting up a classroom system is in improvising and experimenting.

Materials

- four 55-liter rectangular plastic tubs (many other types of containers can be used; see "Containers" above)

- power drill with hole saw for cutting holes in tubs

- ¾" hole saw

- 2.3 meters of transparent vinyl tubing of ½-inch inner diameter: four 30 cm lengths (for connecting cells to one another); six 10 cm lengths (for outlets); one 50 cm length (for airlift)

Sample System Layouts

System 1

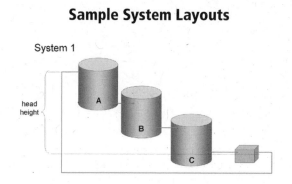

System 1: *Water falls by gravity from cell A to the lower cells. A pump returns the water from cell C back to cell A. Advantage: Water flows faster between cells. Disadvantages: A pump is required because an airlift usually cannot lift water this high; if the pump stops, most of the water in cells A and B will overflow into cell C.*

System 2

System 2: *The cells are all at the same height. Water from cell C is returned to cell A, and this raises the level of water in cell A. The higher water level in cell A provides the force to push water into cells B and C. Advantage: This amount of lifting can be done by an airlift; if a pump is used and the pump stops, there will be no significant overflow. Disadvantage: Flow rates are slower, although adequate.*

- 1 stainless steel hex nut with a ½" inner diameter (used as a weight for airlift tube)

- eight rubber grommets with outside diameter 1⅛", inside diameter ⅝", groove thickness 1/16" and groove diameter ⅛" (buy extras, since the rubber tends to dry and crack over time, especially when exposed to sunlight; see Resources section for suppliers.)

- eight plastic ½" hose inserts, at least 2 inches long (also called hose connectors; available from hardware stores that sell plumbing supplies)

- three plastic ½" elbows, 90 degrees, hose connectors

- aquarium bubbler and/or pump (see notes on pumps and bubblers above: a pump can be used to achieve faster flow rates, in which case the bubbler becomes optional)

Left and center: In a four-cell system, the holes in two of the tubs are "left-handed" and in the other two they are "right-handed." Right: A hose insert placed within a grommet provides a watertight connection without caulking, allowing for easy disassembly.

- 1.3 to 2 meters of vinyl tubing for bubbler (the tube size must match the bubbler: usually ⅛")

- inverted crate, box or other surface on which to place the bubbler so that it is elevated to the height of the jugs

- fish (goldfish work well) and other organisms (obtain these *after* the system has been running successfully for a few days with plain water)

- plants, mud, soil and pond water

Procedure

1. Drill ¾" holes in two walls of each tub. Holes should be about two-thirds of the way up the side of the tub. For the most tightly packed arrangement of tubs, position the holes in a "right-handed" orientation (on the north and east sides) in two of the tubs, and position them in a "left-handed" orientation (on the north and west sides) in the other two tubs. This allows tubs to be placed in a two-by-two arrangement as shown in the illustration "Four-cell Setup."

2. Insert rubber grommets into the holes. If the edges of the holes are jagged, sand them lightly using coarse sandpaper.

3. Place the hose inserts into the grommets. This is much easier to do if both the grommet and the hose insert are wet. If sticking is a problem, lubricate the hose insert with glycerol. (Dish soap works well, as long as all traces of the soap are washed away before starting the system.) Position the hose inserts midway through the grommets, so there is roughly as much of the insert on the outside of the tub as on the inside.

4. Choose an area that gets lots of light, and arrange the four tubs, or cells, as shown. Tubs should be about 20 to 30 cm apart. Tubs can be set on the floor or on a table, as long as the table can accommodate the weight of water in the tubs (approximately 147 kilograms or 325 pounds). Designate one of the tubs to

be the one that contains the airlift — this will be "cell 1." (It doesn't matter which tub, although it should be one closest to wherever the bubbler will be situated.) Connect the tubs using a 30 cm length of hose between one tub and another, attached to the outside of the hose inserts. (See diagram "Four-cell Setup" for overall view of the system.)

5. Attach two 10 cm lengths of hose to an elbow to make an "L."

6. Designate one of the holes in cell 2 to be the outflow, and the other to be the inflow (see diagram "Four-cell Setup"). Attach one end of the "L" to the inner side of the hose insert that makes the outflow. Orient the "L" such that the open end is pointing down, towards the bottom of the tub. Positioning the outflow hose lower in the container will keep surface vegetation and detritus from blocking the outflow to the next cell. It will also encourage water from lower in the cell to circulate to the next cell, rather than only the top layers of water exchanging.

7. Repeat Steps 5 and 6 for cells 3 and 4.

8. On the fourth tub (cell 1), attach the 50 cm tube to the inner side of the outflow. This tube will form the airlift. As much of this tube as possible should be submerged in water.

9. Place the stainless steel nut around the distal end of the 50 cm airlift tube (the end farthest from the hose insert). This will act as a weight. Without a weight, the injection of air bubbles will cause the tube to float, which will greatly reduce the airlift effect. The airlift works best if it is a smooth S-shaped curve, as shown in the diagram "Airlift Tube." (The airlift hose in the "Four-cell Setup" diagram is shown with elbows for ease of drawing. However, these elbows slow down the flow in the airlift.)

10. Insert the bubbler tube 2.5 to 3 cm into the airlift tube. To ensure that the bubbler tube stays in place, you may need to cut a small hole in the airlift tube, and insert the bubbler tube into the hole in the airlift tube there. This should be 2.5 to 3 cm from the distal end of the tube. The air injection should be done as deep as possible without allowing air bubbles to come out the distal end of the airlift tube. Any bubbles

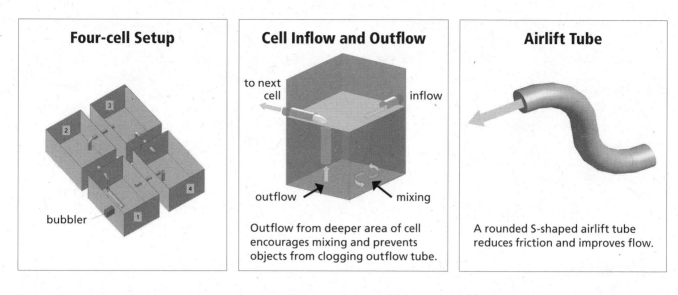

Four-cell Setup	**Cell Inflow and Outflow**	**Airlift Tube**

Four-cell Setup

bubbler

Cell Inflow and Outflow

to next cell

inflow

outflow

mixing

Outflow from deeper area of cell encourages mixing and prevents objects from clogging outflow tube.

Airlift Tube

A rounded S-shaped airlift tube reduces friction and improves flow.

escaping from the distal end will reduce the efficiency of the airlift. If bubbles start to escape from the distal end of the airlift tube, push the bubbler tube up into the airlift tube a little farther, until no more bubbles escape.

11. Fill the system with water up to the level of the holes (about two-thirds of the volume of the tubs). If the grommets have been installed properly, water should not leak out around the hose inserts.

12. Elevate the bubbler so that it is higher than the water level (and note that the bubbler should *never* be submerged!). If the bubbler is not elevated and for some reason the airflow stops, water can siphon back through the air tube into the bubbler, which will likely damage it.

13. Start the airlift by turning on the bubbler. Water should start to bubble from the airlift cell (cell 1) to cell 2. As water is pumped from cell 1 to cell 2, water will enter cell 4 from cell 3 to replace it. Although the flow rate is slow, with careful adjustments it is possible to get flow rates of up to 100 ml/minute. This rate of flow would exchange the entire volume of the system in about 24 hours. Possible adjustments include increasing the airflow and removing any kinks or pinches in the airflow tube. Increasing the airflow will increase the flow rate up to a point; continuing to increase airflow past that point will not increase the flow rate of the water. Kinks or pinches in the airlift tube will reduce the flow rate.

14. Once the system is set up, run it for a few days with water only before adding plants or animals. This will give you an opportunity to find and fix any leaks around the hoses and grommets. If there are leaks, they can often be fixed by ensuring that all tubes and grommets are firmly seated. These few days will also

give the water a chance to de-chlorinate. (Note that any time you intend to add water to the system, you must let it sit out for 24 hours first, since chlorinated tap water can kill or injure fish and microbial populations.)

Adding life to the cells
Cell 1: Floating vegetation

Cell 1 contains floating vegetation such as duckweed, or azolla. These are commonly found in ponds or available from garden centers that sell aquatic plants. Cell 1 will act as a "refuge" for these plants. In time they will spread across the surface of the cell, at which point some can be transferred to cell 2 for the fish to eat. This shows how the system can be self-sustaining over time, with the fish being fed from the plants that grow naturally in it. (It does not matter which of the four cells contains the floating plants. However, it is best not to have the airlift or pump in the cell that has the fish, as they can become caught in the airlift or pump.)

Cell 2: Fish

Leave this cell empty for now. Put fish into it only after the system has been running with the plants for a few days. Goldfish from a pet store are a good choice since they are inexpensive and, if they survive the transition, quite hardy. However, make sure that the fish are not so small that they could get into the tubes. If possible, mix your system's water with the fish water gradually, in a separate container, to allow the fish to acclimate to their new home.

Cell 3: Emergent plants

For cell 3, select plants that have submerged roots and stems. Examples of emergent plants are taro, papyrus, calla lilies and peace lilies. These grow well and are likely to be available from aquatic garden centers. Start with 2–5 stems of any of these. Roots are needed as well, since they are the regenerative structures of these plants.

Cell 4: Pond muck

For cell 4, collect 2–3 cups of pond muck and water from a nearby pond, possibly with cattails or other marshy grasses.

Many other configurations are possible for adding life to the cells, depending on what you want the system to be able to do and illustrate. (See section on Modifications to the standard system.)

Observations

Careful, organized and detailed observations of the living system will increase students' interest in its progress. Once the system is running and the flow rate adequate, have students start monitoring the number of plants, the size of leaves, the types of insects and invertebrates present, the presence or absence of snails, and any other organisms or changes that can be observed in the system.

It is very helpful to test the nitrogen levels in the cells, especially in the fish cell. Inexpensive kits can be purchased from aquarium stores. The most important tests are those for ammonia, nitrite and nitrate. Ammonia and nitrite are toxic to fish, but under good conditions are transformed by nitrifying bacteria to nitrate, a much less toxic form of nitrogen that can be taken up by plant roots as a nutrient. Tests are colorimetric (students compare the color of the water in a test tube to a standard color chart) and easy to perform. Regular observation of ammonia, nitrite and nitrate levels are very instructive for explaining the fate of wastes and nutrients in the system. Tests should be done daily over a period of several weeks.

Living Systems FAQs

How many cells?

Systems should have a minimum of three cells. Beyond about eight cells, a system may become difficult to manage.

How big should cells be?

A minimum volume is about the volume of a large drinking water jug, roughly 19 liters (5 U.S. gallons).

Should systems be designed by teachers or by students?

If students design it, they will have an opportunity for creative input and are more likely to become invested in the project. However, allowing the students to do the designing usually takes longer and produces more varied results. A good compromise is for the students to choose the containers and plan the flow pattern, and the teacher to help with connecting the cells to one another. Leakage and improper connection of cells are the largest sources of trouble.

How can organisms be kept from moving from one cell to another?

Small organisms should be able to move freely from one cell to another in order to find the niche that suits them best. Fish can be prevented from migrating out of their cell by placing screening over the tubes. Screening over tube inlets can also reduce the number of snails that congregate in the tubes. (Snails, if present, tend to accumulate in the tubes. If screens are used, it is helpful to use easily removable and replaceable ones and to keep a test-tube brush handy to push the snails through the tubes.

Is it better to have all cells on the same level or at different levels?

Both setups have advantages and disadvantages. If cells are on different levels, the water falls further and therefore must be raised further. This requires energy. The small amount of lift needed for a system in which cells are all on the same level can be done with an airlift. The larger amount of lift needed for raising water in a multi-level system would probably require a pump. If a pump is used, it might also be necessary to add a bubbler to provide enough oxygen to the system.

An interesting challenge for students is to try to move and aerate the water without using electricity. Students may investigate other power sources, such as human power and wind power, or revisit some of the means of storing and releasing energy that predated electricity — such as flywheels, counterweights or springs.

What should I do with the inhabitants of the system when I want to stop running the system?

If there are fish, recruit someone to take them home and take care of them! If any species in your system are invasive, do not dump them into any natural waterways. Consult your closest agricultural extension office to see if any of your species are on a list of invasive or nuisance species in your area.

Collecting living organisms with which to "seed" the system is one of the most fun parts of this project. Keep in mind that the greater the diversity of your system, the greater the chance that it will succeed. Think of it as transplanting miniature ecosystems into a new home, rather than simply collecting specimens. Over time, populations of different insects, algae and other creatures will rise and fall. It won't always be possible or even desirable to predict exactly what organisms will be present, and that is one of the most interesting parts of a living system. Have fun, experiment, and don't let an occasional spill deter you.

Activities and investigations

1. Observe the system over time, recording and drawing the organisms in different cells.

2. Use the system to grow shrimp, crayfish, fish or other aquatic species.

3. Use the system for aquaponics (an integration of fish culture and hydroponics). Fish wastes can provide the fertilizer for growing plants, such as flowers or vegetables (tomatoes and basil make a nice combination).

4. Compare the ability of two or more similar systems to break down a certain contaminant or waste product, such as organic waste, ammonia or phosphates. These are easily measured with the following standard water-quality tests.

Organic waste: Biochemical oxygen demand (BOD) reflects the amount of organic nutrient in the water that could provide food for bacteria. As bacteria break down this organic material, they absorb oxygen from the water and put carbon dioxide into the water. This results in a low-oxygen environment that is detrimental or lethal to other aquatic animals. The BOD test measures how much oxygen disappears from water over a specified time period and assumes that the more organic nutrient that is present, the more oxygen will disappear from the water. High BOD measurements usually indicate contamination from sewage, animal feedlots, urban runoff, or other industrial or agricultural processes. In this investigation, a useful analog for sewage is reconstituted powdered milk: it is inexpensive and can be reliably prepared to a wide variety of concentrations.

Ammonia: Ammonia is a waste product of many aquatic animals. When its concentration gets too high, it becomes toxic, and aquatic species may die. Healthy ecosystems have bacteria that turn ammonia into nitrates, which are far less toxic. Two similar recirculating systems could be compared for their ability to break down a small amount of ammonia.

Phosphates: Phosphates are commonly present in fertilizers and urban runoff. Excess phosphate in a water body often leads to eutrophication, in which there is a short-lived "explosion" of plant growth, followed by plant death and decomposition. This decomposition, done by bacteria and fungi, chokes the water of oxygen. Students could compare the ability of similar recirculating systems to absorb a pulse of phosphate.

5. Compare two standard systems in which the only difference is the flow rate. Use a bubbler in one and a higher-powered pump in the other.

6. Investigate the effect of biodiversity on the ability of a system to withstand stress. Set up two systems with identical cell configuration, volume and flow rate, and the same kind of bubbler or pump. Designate one system as the "full life system" and seed it with many kinds of living matter, including different plants and soil and muck samples from different sites and conditions. In the other "modified system," put fish, sand that has been sterilized (baked in an oven for one hour at 400 degrees F), and plants that have had their roots rinsed thoroughly with water from a garden hose set at high-pressure spray. Take regular and frequent water samples from each system to measure ammonia, nitrites and nitrates. It may be of interest to measure pH also. After making initial observations and measurements, introduce some form of stress to the systems. For example, you could stop flow and aeration by shutting off the bubblers, shield the systems from light, add some form of waste or contaminant, or make some other change in both systems. Continue to monitor and measure the systems. Note that this is a long-term experiment that needs to run for two to three months.

Modifications

- Include cells that replicate other kinds of natural environments, such as a forest floor, desert, wetland or ocean shore community. Provide some cells that have ample "hiding spaces" for aquatic organisms. Use cells of varied shapes, some being wide and shallow, some narrow and deep. Include a cell that has pump on a timer to simulate a "spray zone" on a rocky seashore or lakeshore.

- Create a system with cells that fill and empty on a periodic basis, mimicking natural wetland flushings in tidal pools, salt marshes or freshwater estuaries. The systems could make use of tipping buckets, as described in Adey (see Resources).

• Include an anoxic/anaerobic cell for accelerated waste breakdown or compost breakdown. In this case it might be of interest to include an odor trap. This consists of a screen with cedar chips piled on top to absorb odors, placed over the top of the cell containing wastes.

• Develop a system that changes its flow depending on whether it is sunny or dark. For example, a system that uses a bubbler all the time, but additionally is augmented with a solar-powered pump during the daytime.

• Develop an "atrium" system that will be installed in a prominent location to provide the sound of running water and an eye-catching educational display of ecological interactions.

Mark Keffer teaches high school biology in Vermont. He completed a masters' degree on Living Machines with Dr. John Todd at the University of Vermont, and formerly taught high school biology and environmental sciences in Waterloo, Ontario.

Resources

Adey, W.H. and K. Loveland. *Dynamic Aquaria: Building Living Ecosystems.* Academic Press, 1998. Foundations and development of the field of constructed ecosystems; includes information on the algal turf scrubber and the tipping bucket.

Andrews, W.A. *A Guide to the Study of Freshwater Ecology.* Prentice-Hall, 1972. Excellent source of information, background and classroom activities in aquatic ecology.

Beyers, Robert J. and Howard T. Odum. *Ecological Microcosms.* Springer-Verlag, 1993. Extensive background on the ecology, measurement and study of microcosms for very in-depth readers.

Mitchell, M.K. and W. B. Stapp. *Field Manual for Water Quality Monitoring* (10th edition). Thomson-Shore Inc. An excellent how-to manual for all the most common water-quality measurement techniques.

Supplies

Grommets with the specifications mentioned in the instructions are available in bulk from Manufacturers Rubber Supply Company, 7B Commercial Drive, Brentwood, NH 03833, 1-800-727-7763, <www.manuf-rubber.com/grommets.html>, product number 31450. Grommets are also available from many hardware stores, but at a higher price.

RiverWatch:
Science on the River

Students take to aquatic laboratories to test the waters of their local rivers

Guy Pollard

by Cal Kullman

Subject areas: environmental science, chemistry

Key concepts: aquatic ecosystems, water quality monitoring, wastewater treatment, water use conflicts, stewardship

Skills: water safety, observation, taking scientific measurements, data synthesis and analysis

Location: outdoors on navigable rivers

Time: 1 day on the river, plus pre- and post-trip activities

Materials: signed acknowledgement of risk form, bus transportation, qualified raft guides/interpreters, rafts, paddles, rubber boots, raincoats, throw bags, personal floatation devices (PDFs), first aid kit, cell phone, river access, shoreline study sites, wastewater treatment plant access and tour, water quality testing kits, instructions, waste bottles, goggles, disposable gloves, invertebrate nets, sorting trays, identification chart, bacteria testing kit, Petri dish, pipette, identification sheet, data collection sheet, storage bins, lunches, drinks

The rivers that flow through our cities and towns intimately link all aspects and inhabitants of our watersheds. In every community, we must deal with the impact of upstream users and at the same time acknowledge the water requirements of users downstream. The health of a river is thus an environmental report card that marks our cumulative impact on and stewardship of terrestrial and aquatic ecosystems. For this reason, local rivers are a rich teaching resource for educators looking to help students relate abstract concepts of science and ecology to the real communities in which they live.

In 1995, a group of four educators sensed the irony of teaching a text-oriented unit on aquatic ecosystems at schools located only kilometers from a real river, and thus began dreaming of a real-world river study. As science teachers and avid paddlers, we wanted our students to experience the rivers that we loved to kayak and canoe. We also saw an opportunity to offer our students an exciting way to fulfill the field study component of the provincially-mandated environmental quality unit. We imagined students traveling along the river aboard large inflatable rafts equipped with water-quality testing equipment, and later in the classroom analyzing data to construct a picture of river health. Over the next 14 years, this dream became a reality in a very big way. What began as a pilot trip for three classes led to the formation of a non-profit company running an award-winning river-monitoring program in which 7,000 students across Alberta participate annually.

RiverWatch

When we first began designing the RiverWatch field study, responses to a pre-project survey of colleagues around the province echoed our dissatisfaction with the provincial environmental quality unit. The unit was often left to the end of the year, covered quickly because time ran out, and required water-testing equipment that was generally not available in junior high schools.

Rather than create a new curriculum or text for an already packed science year, we set out to design a fun, hands-on field study that would dovetail with the existing science curriculum and textbook. We sought advice on routes and testing procedures from local fish hatchery staff. We found that we could rent or borrow all the necessary water-testing and rafting equipment at a reasonable cost from sources such as the city waterworks lab, the university outdoor program center and local canoe clubs.

Once equipped with a river route, rafts and testing kits, we piloted the project with 90 students in the spring of 1995 and then sent program information to every junior high school in Calgary and outlying school districts. That next fall, 22 teachers and more than 500 students spent a day on the river. By 2008, RiverWatch programs were being delivered in Calgary and Edmonton with four full-time management staff and 24 seasonal guides using two equipment buses, two raft trailers and 12 rafts. Annual participation is targeted to grow over the next decade to 20,000 students.

The RiverWatch Program

To ensure that students get the most out of their time on the river, RiverWatch programs have a pre-trip component that prepares students for what they will see and do during the field study and a post-trip analysis and interpretation of results.

Pre-trip preparations

Before attending the field study, students are presented with the question "How healthy is your river?" They then research components of river ecosystems and learn what aspects of water quality can be measured for a diagnostic "check-up" of river health. An online pre-trip survey measures student knowledge of the river, water quality tests, invertebrates, environmental issues and stewardship actions.

The pre-trip resource materials provided online include background information on phosphates and their impact on aquatic environments, water-quality testing procedures and invertebrate identification, as well as newspaper articles on local rivers. A family newsletter outlines the purpose of the trip, its costs and hazards, and the clothing and participation requirements. Different perspectives on river use are conveyed through presenting the views of native elders, anglers, ranchers, environmental lawyers and presidents of power and irrigation companies. Data collected previously from all sections of the river is available through an online, interactive charting option.

On the river

The actual river trip takes about six hours, during which students perform a number of water-quality tests and observe wildlife and human activities that have an impact on the health of the river. The rafts are aquatic laboratories equipped with water-testing kits for measuring pH, temperature, dissolved oxygen, turbidity, phosphates, nitrogen and coliform bacteria. Water samples are tested at two study sites for comparison of water quality above and below a point source of pollution, such as a wastewater treatment plant. Students also collect and identify samples of invertebrates as water-quality indicators.

The program uses a ten-kilometer section of river — not very long, but it includes a variety of shoreline stops that give students a close-up view of stormwater outfalls, bridges, weirs, golf courses, industrial sites, wastewater treatment facilities, nesting colonies of bank swallows, beaver lodges, cormorants and geese. We take care to avoid littering, disturbing birds' nests, running over fishing lines and kayaks, removing invertebrates or dumping untreated chemical waste.

The use of rafts is a key element in making the field study an enjoyable highlight for students. In some school field programs, rivers are studied through a series of bus stops and shoreline observations; but this requires re-focusing each time students step off the bus into the natural world. Continuously floating a length of river, on the other hand, gives students seamless contact with the environment and presents opportunities to highlight physical changes, to view wildlife and to observe evidence of human impact that is not visible from a bus. Using rafts to float students along a river also provides an element of organization, focus and control. The rafts create small, workable groups of 10–15 students that develop a sense of community and teamwork. Students are "in" the river, but not wet; and they are focused on paddling and maneuvering the raft rather than engaging in horseplay.

Our float trips use Class I rivers with clear channels, easy-to-avoid obstructions, no construction debris, no overhanging trees and no rapids. The rivers have minimal boat traffic and have access sites with bus parking and boat trailer ramps. Safety being a top priority, we cancel or postpone float trips as the river level and floating debris increase in late spring. Students are too young to sign waivers and their parents cannot sign on their behalf. However, we inform parents and students of potential hazards in a PowerPoint presentation, video, trip newsletter and shoreline briefing. We insist on good behavior from students. Non-swimmers are seated near the guide, and students must wear personal floatation devices zipped and tied at all times while in the raft and wading or working along the shoreline. Feet must be kept inside the raft to avoid

Top: Students tour a tertiary water treatment plant where ultraviolet light is used to destroy microorganisms. Bottom: Invertebrate nets are searched for nymphs, worms and beetles that are indictors of water quality.

Guy Pollard

falling overboard or scraping against river obstacles. Students are briefed on what to do if someone falls overboard. Guides watch for weather changes such as rain showers, lightning and wind storms. Qualified and trained staff equipped with first-aid kits and cellular phones complete our safety preparations.

A river float trip is a big adventure for students. Sun hats, shorts, day packs, lunches and drinks can make for an atmosphere of a day at the beach. In the first 100 meters and five minutes of a raft float, at least one student inevitably exclaims "This is the best field trip I've ever been on!" While it isn't a whitewater thrill, students find there is a great deal to see, hear and smell around every bend.

Back at school

Once back at school, students use their collected data to evaluate the health of the river. The differences in water quality that were noticeable on the river become even more evident in graphs. For instance, graphing the data collected below the city wastewater outfall can show an increase in water temperature, a decline in dissolved oxygen, and populations of aquatic nymphs being replaced by snails and leeches — all indicators of decreased water quality. At the end of the study, the online pre-trip survey is repeated to measure changes in students' knowledge and attitudes related to the river and environmental quality.

Online presentation of data gives students and teachers access to water-quality results obtained by schools above and below their own sampling locations. This data opens the door to comparative analysis and evaluation of river ecosystems from source to mouth. The program also has the potential to foster "river pal" exchanges through which students in communities along the length of the river share information, insights, stories and projects.

A self-sustaining program

Following the success of the first year, the river study was made readily accessible to any interested school through a not-for-profit company that secured grants, obtained liability insurance, purchased equipment and hired staff. Each season, we train and employ guides for the trips, who are hired on the basis of their paddling and first-aid certification, university training in science or environmental studies, and enthusiasm for and experience with working with young people. Legal counsel is provided on a pro bono basis from a local firm believing in good corporate citizenship. Grants from corporations and all levels of government have enabled us to purchase equipment and hire staff. Municipal wastewater treatment plants provide a secure home for our equipment and are important facility sites on the tour.

RiverWatch is now well established as the most intensive and widespread environmental field study program in Alberta, with four full-time staff, 24 seasonal river guides and an annual operating budget of $630,000. Through a blend of user fees, corporate sponsorship and grants, the program has been financially sustainable for 14 years. Salaries and wages are the greatest expenditure of the program, which has a staff-to-student ratio of one to seven. A fee of $35 per student covers half of the ongoing costs of staffing, insurance, equipment maintenance, lab materials and office expenses. Individual schools may reduce the student fee through fundraising, parent council support or by paying a portion of the fees from their own science budgets. However, the fees still present a barrier to full participation in some jurisdictions, and corporate sponsorship is continually sought to remove a portion of the overhead operating burden shouldered by students. Our goal is to subsidize RiverWatch staffing, equipment, resources and program delivery so that student fees decrease to $20 per student.

RiverWatch has transformed what was once a "left-to-the-end" reading unit with few lab activities into an award-winning environmental monitoring experience that combines physical challenge and adventure with hands-on, real-world science. Through training and mentoring young staff, the program provides professional development in environmental leadership. For teachers wanting to conduct field studies, having these program leaders alleviates the need to be jacks-of-all-trades with paddling and first-aid certification, field research experience, field management skills and interpretive knowledge.

For students, the day spent floating on the river is often the first close-up view they have ever had of this vitally important resource flowing through their communities. More significantly, it is likely the first time they have considered their own impact on the river and on the lives of all other inhabitants downstream. It is our hope that these young people will go on to become good stewards of our rivers and ultimately contribute to a better quality of life for all.

*Cal Kullman is the Executive Director of RiverWatch in Edmonton, Alberta, and co-writer of the original version of this article with **John Dupuis** and **Tessy Bray**. These three, along with Guy Pollard, are the founders of RiverWatch. For more information or advice, contact: RiverWatch, Suite 433, 17008–90 Avenue, Edmonton, AB, T5T 1L6, (780) 590–5330, <www.riverwatch. ab.ca>.*

Starting a RiverWatch program?

RiverWatch

Educators wishing to establish a RiverWatch program are advised to team up with a non-profit organization that already works with schools, rather than undertake the difficult work of assembling the assets of incorporation, offices, funding, staffing and a board of directors. For the sum of approximately $15,000, a program can equip itself with one six-meter self-bailing raft fully equipped with paddles, PFDs, raincoats, rubber boots, oar-rigs, first-aid kit, throwbags, lifelines, science kits and invertebrate nets.

Anne Hansen

❀ **Eco-economics in the Classroom** by Susan Santone

❀ **Measuring Your School's Ecological Footprint** by Julie Sawchuk and Tim Cameron

❀ **Choosing Our Future** by Jan Cincera

❀ **Linking Trade, Human Rights and the Environment** by Tricia Jane Edgar

❀ **Planet Transit Game: Profit or Survival?** by Georgi Marshall

❀ **Global Morning: A Consumer Awareness Activity** by Mary Gale Smith

❀ **The Debate About Hemp: A Role Play** by Sara Francis

❀ **Teaching About Biodiesel** by Richard Lawrence

❀ **Making Biodiesel from Waste Vegetable Oil** by Alison K. Varty and Shane C. Lishawa

❀ **Small-scale Science** by Alan Slater

❀ **Green Driving Lessons** by Tim Altieri

Eco-economics in the Classroom

Ecological economics offers teachers and students opportunities to explore such vital and timely topics as consumption, population, climate change and development

Illustrations by Tom Goldsmith

by Susan Santone

Subject areas: social studies, economics, environmental studies

Key concepts: carrying capacity, resource use, waste production/assimilation, product lifecycles, incentives, subsidies, externalities, price versus cost, indicators and measurement

Skills: analyzing and interpreting data, generating and investigating questions, connecting cause and effect, developing reasoned positions, making informed decisions, communicating information, conducting community research

Location: classroom with optional research in the community

Time: 3–5 class sessions and time for research out of class

Materials: global environmental data and information about economic policies at the local, national or global levels; for simulation activity, see page 101

il spills are good for us!" declares a high school student to an audience of parents and civic leaders. "And so are crime and divorce!"

The girl's provocative statements elicit uneasy laughter from the crowd as they realize that she is right: oil spills, divorce and crime are good news when measured by the purely monetary terms of the Gross Domestic Product, the "character" played by the girl

in a thought-provoking skit. The student's presentation followed a series of lessons on ecological economics, an approach to the economy that is gaining support from environmentalists and business leaders alike. When tested against the science of ecology, conventional market ideas often fall short. From the narrow focus on profits to the belief that unfettered growth is both desirable and possible, some of the most basic economic assumptions simply cannot be reconciled with nature's fundamental laws of limits, interdependence and balance.

Take, for example, the Gross Domestic Product (GDP). As the student's skit made clear, the GDP counts as positive any activity in which money is spent. When it comes to clear cuts, oil spills, divorce and crime, the GDP sees only the financial "upside" — the timber sales, clean-up costs, legal fees and other dollars spent. The negative impacts of these activities, such as resource degradation and social decay, are ignored. Moreover, the GDP ignores the many life-sustaining services provided by nature, such as pollination, erosion control and carbon dioxide absorption. Thanks to this selective accounting, decision-makers cheer each rise in the GDP while simultaneously ignoring the erosion of the environmental and social capital on which the economy ultimately depends.

As an instructional approach, ecological economics ("eco-eco") offers teachers an opportunity to explore such vital and timely topics as consumption, carrying capacity, climate change and development. Students grapple with issues through an integrated social-scientific perspective, just as they will need to do as citizens and workers. Because ecological economics exposes the environmental and social impacts of economic choices, it offers a systematic, thorough paradigm that is ultimately more useful than traditional economics for understanding and solving interconnected problems.

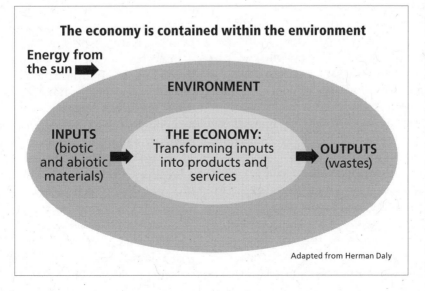

Ecological economics enables students to acquire, integrate and apply meaningful knowledge across several disciplines. Given the potential complexity, it's wise to teach major ideas in a sequence that helps students construct a layered understanding. The following is an introduction to several essential ideas of ecological economics and a description of sample activities that high school teachers can use to teach them.

Essential Idea 1:
The economy exists within a larger ecosystem

Ecological economics rests upon a fundamental assumption: that human activity, including economic activity, exists within larger ecosystems. As the diagram shows, all human activity (including the economy) requires drawing materials from an ecosystem and putting wastes back into it. (Note: The placement of the economy in the center reflects the fact that it is contained by the larger biosphere. This is not meant to suggest that humans are the most important species or that the natural world exists for their needs only. It is important to clarify these ideas with students.)

An investigation of human–environment interdependence can easily start with students' everyday lives. For example, you can give students a category such as transportation and ask them to list all forms of transportation they have used in the past few days (e.g., bus, car, walking, bike). For each form of transportation, students should state the energy source, try to trace it to its origin, and identify where the wastes will go. For example, gas in a car could be traced to oil, which could have come from the Middle East, Venezuela or another country. The wastes (emissions) will go into the atmosphere and then possibly be absorbed by trees or other carbon "sinks." The same approach can be taken with electronics (What is your cell phone made of?

The economy is contained within the environment

Energy from the sun ➡

ENVIRONMENT

INPUTS (biotic and abiotic materials) ➡ THE ECONOMY: Transforming inputs into products and services ➡ OUTPUTS (wastes)

Adapted from Herman Daly

Where did those components come from?) or food (What did you eat yesterday? Where did the ingredients come from? Where will it go when you dispose of it?) Depending on your students' prior knowledge, it's likely that they will not know the answers to the questions; thus, the activity can be used as an introduction to raise awareness, fill gaps in knowledge and generate further questions for exploration.

As a next step, students can examine the concept of the ecological footprint, a measurement of the amount of land required to provide all the resources needed to sustain a population's (or individual's) consumption and to absorb all the waste. Using an online calculator (e.g., <www.myfootprint.org>), students can take a quiz to measure their own footprint. Lessons built around the quiz and the data underlying it can thus serve as a foundation for ecological economics.

The above activities are all entry points to help students understand the core ideas of ecological economics: that all materials come from the environment and that all wastes go back into it.

Essential Idea 2:
Products have a "life cycle" that begins with materials extraction and ends with disposal, reuse or recycling. There are many environmental and social impacts at each of these stages.

Once students know that they depend on resources to meet their needs, it is easy to connect this to the topics of manufacturing and product life cycles. To begin, students can create timelines that track a product's components from the extraction of raw materials to final disposal. A timeline for a sports shoe, for example, extends 200 million years into the past (the origins of the oil in the vinyl) and thousands of years into the future (the time it will take for plastic to break down in a landfill). This activity encourages students to raise questions about the production and disposal of everyday items, their often-hidden environmental impacts and the scarcity of resources.

As a next step, students can research the "life cycle" of specific items, from the extraction of raw materials to disposal. To provide structure, give students the steps of a product's life cycle as the basis for the research: extraction of raw materials, processing/manufacturing, transportation/distribution, consumption and disposal. For each stage, students should identify raw materials, energy and labor used (inputs), wastes produced (out-

puts), and the role of the environment as the source of the inputs and the "sink" into which the outputs go. For further guidance, provide students with short readings on how different products are made, and have them work with the texts to identify the materials, labor and energy used at each stage, as well as wastes produced. Books such as *Stuff: The Secret Lives of Everyday Things* by John C. Ryan and Alan Thein Durning, provide concise and interesting "stories" of different products. An Internet search on "item + life cycle" will also yield many examples, although some may be technical.

As students learned through calculating their ecological footprint, ecosystems are limited in their ability to provide resources and absorb wastes. This presents challenges for manufacturers. To explore this, teams of students can "manufacture" placemats, greeting cards, posters or other items from paper and paint with the aim of creating as little waste as possible (see "Eco-Economics: A Manufacturing Challenge," pages 101–102). Points are awarded for production techniques that minimize waste and pollution while still producing an attractive and useful product. Through discussion questions after the exercise, students can consider the challenges faced by manufacturers as well as the impact of being evaluated on their efforts to reduce waste. Most students acknowledge that without an incentive (being evaluated), they would have been much less likely to consider the problem of waste. This leads into an examination of the economic concept of externalities (see below).

The study of product life cycles can introduce students to industrial ecology, an engineering field focused on designing industrial systems that operate on the principles of natural systems. Students can, for example, research cutting-edge, green approaches to manufacturing that are now in use by such major companies as Ford, Interface and 3M. Arranging industrial practices on a spectrum is a useful way to help students evaluate different approaches touted as environmentally friendly. Consider, for example, approaches to reducing waste. Points on the spectrum might include recycling, reduction (reducing waste by using materials more efficiently) and elimination (redesigning production processes so that wastes are used as inputs, resulting in a "closed-loop" system).

Students can also research and evaluate the ways in which various companies address the problems of industrial pollution and greenhouse gas emissions. While reducing pollution and emissions through efficiency is good, eliminating the problems by phasing out toxic substances and fossil fuels is even better. When studying these topics, science classes can focus on the chemistry of emissions or the impacts of pollution on air, water and soil. Social studies students can concentrate on incentives, policies and other economic factors influencing business choices. Once students understand the impacts of a range of practices, they can research particular companies' environmental practices and identify their impacts, costs and benefits. As another project, students can create peer-education materials for environmentally-preferable purchasing based on criteria they develop from their research.

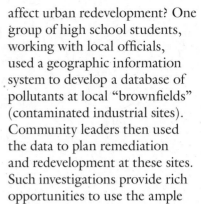

Essential Idea 3:
Price and cost are not the same.

Students (and teachers!) often ask why the more "environmental" choice is often more expensive. Students can explore the issue by investigating the difference between price and cost and the concept of externalities. A popular topic with teenagers — cars — can begin the activity. First, have students calculate the cost (the dollar amount) of purchasing and operating a car. Then ask them to generate a list of some potential other costs of driving: the environmental and social impacts they do not pay for, such as carbon emissions, wear on roads, pollution and health care. This simple activity helps students realize that much of the true cost of driving is absorbed by the public and that this hidden subsidy makes auto use and many other activities artificially cheap. This provides a clear introduction to the concept of externalities — the unintended consequences and impacts of an action.

To deepen their learning, students can evaluate the intended and unintended environmental impacts of policies in the school or school district and write a position paper to suggest changes. A high school civics student, for example, researched the district's policy for purchasing paper. Upon discovering that environmental impacts were not among the selection criteria, the student recommended that at least 25 percent of the paper purchased by the district be recycled and chlorine-free.

Students can likewise investigate local or national policies that have hidden environmental costs. What, for example, is the impact on soils and wetlands of urban planning policies that allow sprawling development rather than encouraging clustered housing? How do policies to address industrial contamination affect urban redevelopment? One group of high school students, working with local officials, used a geographic information system to develop a database of pollutants at local "brownfields" (contaminated industrial sites). Community leaders then used the data to plan remediation and redevelopment at these sites. Such investigations provide rich opportunities to use the ample primary-source data available on the Internet and in government documents and other sources.

Essential Idea 4:
Economic indicators should account for social and environmental costs.

No study of economics would be complete without exploring the criteria by which we measure economic success. The Gross Domestic Product, one of the leading economic indicators, is a good place to start. As an introduction to the concept, students can identify and describe the purpose of indicators used in everyday life, such as grades, test scores and job evaluations. Next, they can identify common economic indicators such as the unemployment rate and consumer price index, or environmental indicators such as air-quality ratings and bacteria counts at beaches.

Once students understand the role of indicators, they can continue by evaluating the accuracy of the Gross Domestic Product — one of the most important economic barometers — in light of social and environmental goals. Ask students to identify and compare the social, environmental and economic impacts of various activities, such as crime as opposed to volunteer work, driving as opposed to walking, and growing vegetables as opposed to buying them. Students will discover that crime, for example, generates economic activity and thus adds to the GDP even though it is clearly detrimental to society. Likewise, although walking has obvious environmental and health benefits, it is considered economically "worthless" because, unlike driving, no money is spent to do it. These and other examples reveal that many beneficial activities are ignored by the GDP while many negative activities benefit the economy — a contradiction that calls into question the emphasis placed on the GDP as a barometer of national well-being.

Students can likewise explore the links between the GDP and the environment by considering the value of the services provided by nature. What is the dollar value of the pollination provided by insects or of the water purification provided by wetlands? (As with other topics, data is available on the Internet as well as from other sources.) This investigation easily leads to the question of how (or whether) the value of nature's life-sustaining services is counted in the economy by the GDP. Of course, the point is not to suggest that nature is only as useful as the dollars we can attach to it, but rather to demonstrate that nature's economic value is ignored by traditional economic theory and entrenched economic policies.

Teachers can extend the GDP activities by researching another measure, the Genuine Progress Indicator (GPI). Like the GDP, the GPI measures the monetary value of transactions and activities. However, unlike the GDP, the GPI subtracts the value of negative activities, such as crime, pollution and the depletion of natural resources, and adds the value of positive activities, such as volunteer work and the services provided by ecosystems. Whereas the GDP measures economic activity only, making no distinction between good and bad, the GPI measures a nation's combined economic, social and environmental progress by distinguishing between "goods" and "bads."

By comparing the GDP and the GPI, students learn that our combined social, economic and environmental progress, as measured by the GPI, is declining even as the GDP continues to rise. This calls into question the practice of measuring economic, social and environmental indicators separately as if they were unrelated. To apply their knowledge, students can use community data to develop and research indicators in health, transportation, the environment, education and other categories. The resulting community "report card" can be organized around key questions, such as: Where are we now on this indicator? How did we get here? Where would we like to be? and How do we get there? This activity provides another opportunity for students to use primary-source data from government agencies, research institutes and other sources.

Ecological economics offers teachers an accessible entry point for addressing some of today's most important issues. By requiring evaluation of economic choices in light of their environmental and social impacts, the topic provides opportunities for science and social studies educators to integrate content and develop challenging investigations. Moreover, ecological economics enables students to apply their knowledge in meaningful ways, making learning highly motivating and engaging. Whoever thought economics could offer so much?

Susan Santone *is the director of Creative Change Educational Solutions in Ypsilanti, Michigan, and the author of* Economics for the Common Good: A Curriculum for Building a Sustainable Economy.

Resources
Curriculum
Maier, Mark H. and Julie A. Nelson. *Introducing Economics: A Critical Guide for Teachers.* M.E. Sharpe, Inc., 2007. This is a very user-friendly teacher's guide to understanding some of the ideological slants in K–12 economics books. Provides ideas and resources for teaching economics through lenses that emphasize the environment, human rights and democracy. See summaries at <www.introducingeconomics.org>.

Eastern Michigan University and Creative Change Educational Solutions. *Designed by Nature.* Online at <www.emich.edu/biology/DbyN/index.html>. A middle school curriculum on product life cycles, green design and ecological economics.

Websites
<www.bsr.org> Business for Social Responsibility is a nonprofit organization that helps companies design and implement socially responsible business policies, practices and processes.

<www.carbohydrateeconomy.org> The Carbohydrate Economy Clearinghouse provides information on products derived from plants and the cutting-edge companies and cooperatives that are producing them.

<www.newdream.org> The Center for a New American Dream addresses consumption and media issues.

<www.creativechange.net/resources/area/resource_economy.htm> Creative Change Educational Solutions. Resources on ecological and sustainable economics.

<www.ecosystemvaluation.org> Ecosystem Valuation explains the basic methods of ecosystem valuation, with examples and case studies.

<www.enviroliteracy.org/article.php/1320.html> The Environmental Literacy Council. A concise description of ecosystem valuation with links to other useful sites.

<www.greenpages.org> The Green Pages is the online version of Co-op America's popular National Green Pages directory of socially and environmentally responsible businesses, products and services.

<www.interfaceinc.com> Interface is an innovative carpet manufacturer that pioneered the leasing of carpets to businesses in order to reuse materials, eliminate waste and reduce pollution.

<www.naturalcapitalism.org> Excerpts of Natural Capitalism, in which authors Paul Hawken, Amory Lovins and Hunter Lovins offer a prescription for a new industrial revolution and profiles of innovative companies working to meet the challenge of resource scarcity.

<www.naturalstep.org> The Natural Step organization uses a systems framework to help organizations, individuals and communities take steps towards sustainability.

<www.newuses.org> The New Uses Council promotes the development of new products from renewable forestry, livestock, marine and agricultural resources.

<www.rprogress.org> The Redefining Progress site has information about the Genuine Progress Indicator, which assigns values to ecosystem services, volunteer work and other things not currently counted by the GDP.

<www.responsibleshopper.org> Responsible Shopper. Ratings of the performance of companies on a range of issues such as labor practices and pollution.

Eco-Economics: A Manufacturing Challenge

In this hands-on simulation, students must produce placemats, greeting cards or a poster with as little waste and pollution as possible — an environmental challenge faced by many manufacturers.

Guiding question: How can scarcity affect production practices?
Time: 15 minutes to prepare, 45 minutes for activity
Materials: For each group of four students, 1 paint brush, 1 piece of construction paper or plain white paper, 1 cup of water, sheets of newspaper, paper towels, 2 colors of tempera paint, one light and one dark (e.g., yellow and black), Production Worksheet (see page 102)

Procedure

1. Arrange students' desks in groups of four. Make sure each group has adequate work space. Distribute the materials.

2. Explain to the students that they will "manufacture" placemats, greeting cards, a poster or other item with the aim of creating as little waste as possible. Have each group choose a company name and assign roles (see Production Worksheet).

3. As a class, read through the design guidelines on the worksheet. Emphasize important criteria, opportunities for earning points and possible deductions. As noted under guidelines 5 and 6, explain that after they produce their products they will measure and record the amount of wasted paper and the pollution levels of their water. Bonus points will be awarded to the team(s) with the least amount of waste and the cleanest water.

4. Allow 15 to 20 minutes for students to produce their items. During this time, circulate among the groups to make sure students are on task. You can also begin awarding points for creative production techniques (guideline 3) or deducting points for not cleaning tools (guideline 2) or using "illegal" tools (guideline 4).

5. When the teams are finished, have them display their placemats and tools and measure and record their waste paper and record the pollution of their water as noted under guidelines 5 and 6. Award points for the most creative design (guideline 1) and deduct points for not cleaning tools (guideline 2).

Reflection

Discuss the groups' responses to the following reflection questions:

1. What challenges do you think engineers, manufacturers and designers face? Had you ever thought about these issues before? *(Possible responses: How to use materials efficiently, how to handle waste and minimize pollution.)*

2. What difficulties arose for your group in the process? *(Record responses.)*

3. What strategies did you use to reduce waste and keep the water clean? *(Possible responses: Tried to use as little paint as possible; cleaned the brush on the wasted paper so as not to get the water dirty.)*

4. What would have made it easier to reduce waste and keep the water clean? For example, what tools could you have used? What information would have been helpful? *(Possible responses: Other tools could have been useful, such as a painting tool that does not absorb as much paint as a brush. Help students consider how the right equipment can help manufacturers reduce waste and avoid pollution: for example, car companies have improved spray-painting equipment in order to reduce waste. Emphasize that access to information can play a role: manufacturers must know about pollution-prevention strategies in order to use them.)*

5. If you hadn't been evaluated on how clean the water was or the amount of waste you produced, do you think you would have paid as much attention to these issues? Why or why not? *(Students will likely respond that they would not have paid attention to waste or pollution if they hadn't been evaluated on it. This raises the question of how incentives affect economic behavior. Without penalties for wasting resources, or rewards such as tax breaks for increasing efficiency, business may ignore these issues. Moreover, current economic policies often reward environmentally destructive behavior. Subsidies for mining and logging, for example, can make recycling more costly than using "virgin" metal and paper.)*

6. Provide examples of how your team worked together.

7. What new questions did this activity raise for you?

Extension: Have students investigate emerging "green" industrial production practices by researching a company that is taking steps to reduce waste and pollution. Examples include: Johnson and Johnson (reduction in packaging and paper use); Cargill and Dow Chemical (biodegradable plastics); Interface Carpet (leasing and recycling of carpet tiles); Kafus Environmental Industries (natural-fiber materials).

Adapted from *Economics for the Common Good: A Curriculum for Building a Sustainable Economy* by Creative Change Educational Solutions.

Production Worksheet

Guiding question: *How can scarcity affect production practices?*

Background: Manufacturers face many challenges in deciding what resources to use in production and how to handle waste and pollution. In this activity, you will work in teams to manufacture a placemat with as little waste and pollution as possible.

Choose a name for your company: _____

Assign each person in your group a role:
- The Production Engineer will cut the paper to size and, with input from the group, decide what to do with the leftovers.
- The Artistic Director will use paint to decorate the placemats, with input from the group.
- The Sanitation Engineer will provide advice on how to minimize waste and pollution.
- The Communications Director will record the group's responses to the questions.

Design guidelines	Points
1. Create an attractive placemat that is 20 cm x 15 cm (8" x 6"). Each placemat must be decorated with at least two colors of paint. Decorations must cover at least 25 percent of the placemat's area (one side only). **You get 10 points for following these directions; points are deducted for not following them. The most creative design receives 10 bonus points.**	
2. You must clean the brush when changing colors and when you are finished. You get 10 points for thoroughly cleaning your tools between colors and at the end of the activity. **Up to 10 points may be deducted for dirty tools.**	
3. **Up to 10 bonus points will be awarded for creative techniques that reduce paper waste and minimize water pollution.**	
4. Use only the material you were given! **Up to 10 points will be deducted for using your clothes, desk, skin, etc., to clean or paint.**	
5. Waste as little paper as possible; any paper left after the activity will be counted as waste. Your work surface will be covered in newspaper, but you must try to keep it as clean as possible. Any newspaper that gets dirty will be considered waste. When you are finished, measure your dirty and/or leftover paper and record the amount in square centimeters here: _____ **The team with the least amount of dirty or wasted paper gets 10 bonus points.**	
6. When you clean your brush/tools, keep the water as clean as possible so that you minimize pollution when the water is dumped. When you have finished the activity, measure your pollution by dipping your brush in the leftover water and painting this box: **The team with the cleanest water gets 10 bonus points.**	

Reflection questions: Discuss these questions with everyone in your group. The Communications Director will write down the key ideas to turn in.
1. What challenges to you think scarcity presents for engineers? Had you ever thought about these issues before?
2. What difficulties arose for your group in the process?
3. What strategies did you use to reduce waste and keep the water clean?
4. What would have made it easier to reduce waste and keep the water clean? For example, what tools could you have used? What information would have been helpful?
5. If you hadn't been evaluated on how clean the water was or the amount of waste you produced, do you think you would have paid as much attention to these issues? Why or why not?
6. Provide examples of how your team worked together.
7. What new questions did this activity raise for you?

Measuring Your School's Ecological Footprint

A two-part activity for determining the environmental impact of a school and exploring routes to greener, more sustainable practices

by Julie Sawchuk and Tim Cameron

Subject areas: science, math, business (packaging and marketing), consumer studies

Key concepts: ecological footprint, waste management, recycling, resource conservation, green space

Skills: collecting data, sorting materials, measuring weight, recording and calculating results, auditing, surveying, use of significant digits, communicating results, researching, interviewing

Materials: copies of the "How Green is Your School?" survey and the "Ecological Footprint: Audit Data and Translation" chart, pencils, clipboards, measuring tape or meter stick; for waste audit, large space with tables for sorting waste, plastic sheets for tables, large plastic tubs, clear plastic garbage bags, latex gloves, safety goggles, weigh scale, markers, tape

Have you ever wondered how your high school would fare in an environmental audit? During the past decade, many student environment clubs have reduced waste in their schools by recycling and reusing materials, and many school boards have taken steps to make buildings

more energy efficient. Yet few teachers, students or administrators would assert that their schools are as environmentally friendly as they could be. Even those who have made great strides are often surprised to discover how much more could be done.

The High School Ecological Footprint activity is designed to help students gain a better understanding of the impact of their school on the environment and to learn what they can do to make their school more sustainable. It requires a bit of work, but the results will be enlightening! The activity is completed in two phases: a survey of current practices at the school, and an audit of resource consumption and waste that enables students to calculate the school's ecological footprint.

Background

Ecological footprint analysis is a form of environmental impact accounting that gives an estimate of the total area of land required to support the consumption and assimilate the waste of a given population. Developed in the early 1990s by Mathis Wackernagel and William Rees, the concept has been widely applied as a means of determining the sustainability of communities. By relating the goods and services we

use to the amount of land and water required to produce, deliver and dispose of them, ecological footprint analysis measures the demand that a particular lifestyle places on the Earth's resources. It also provides a means of comparing a nation's environmental impact with that of others. For instance, while a land area of 7.6 hectares is needed to support the lifestyle of a typical Canadian, the average ecological footprint in the United States is 9.6, in Mexico it is 2.6, and in India it is a mere 0.8 hectares per person.[1]

In calculating an ecological footprint, resource and land use are divided into categories of consumption, such as food, housing, transportation, products and services. The footprint of our food, for example, is based on the amount of land required to grow the crop or raise the livestock; the energy (both human and mechanical) required to produce it; additional inputs, such as water, pesticides and packaging; and the distance the food travels to reach our tables. Similarly, the footprint of our transportation is determined by calculating the area of land needed to produce the materials and fuel used in manufacturing and operating vehicles, to build roadways, and to absorb the carbon dioxide and other gases emitted by the combustion of fossil fuels.

Survey of current practices

As a preliminary activity, have students complete the "How Green is Your School?" survey (see page 106). Through this assessment of the school's current environmental practices, they will be able to determine where the best efforts are being made and where improvements are needed in the areas of waste management, energy and water conservation, food, products and services, transportation and green space.

Resource and waste audit

In order to calculate the ecological footprint of the school, students must collect data on the waste produced and the resources consumed in providing energy, water, and transportation to and from school. These data are recorded on the "Ecological Footprint: Audit Data and Translation" chart (see page 107). They are then multiplied by conversion factors that translate the audit results into a measure of the area of land required to provide each resource or service and to assimilate each type of waste.

Most of the information for the audit can be obtained through surveying students and staff, consulting with custodial or other maintenance staff, and performing a waste audit. The chart is designed so that the completion of each section leads to useful

Julie Sawchuk

Students can reduce energy consumption in the school by planting trees to provide shade in summer and a windbreak in winter.

conclusions and insights. For example, the waste audit will reveal how much waste could be diverted from landfill by recycling and from where in the school it came.

The following guidelines correspond to the six sections of the "Ecological Footprint: Audit Data and Translation" chart.

Energy: Consult maintenance/buildings staff at your school or board office to determine the total energy consumption at your school last year for heating, lighting and other energy needs. Include in your audit all of the energy sources used in the school, including oil, natural gas, electricity, solar power, wind power and any others.

Water: Consult maintenance/buildings staff at your school or board office to find out much water was used last year at your school.

Transportation: Survey students and teachers to find out how they get to school and how far they travel. For each mode of transportation (car, bus, rapid transit or subway, streetcar, bike, walk/roller blade), determine the number of "person kilometers:" that is, the total of the various round-trip distances traveled by those who use that mode of transportation.

Collect the waste from every room of the school and weigh each bag before sorting its contents.

Sort the waste into categories.

Transfer the sorted waste to labeled collection bags.

Find the total weight of each type of waste collected.

Mieke Foster, TDSB

Land Use: Take a physical measurement or consult the school's blueprints to determine the area of land, in square meters, occupied by the school building(s), including portables and outbuildings, the schoolyard and the parking lot(s).

Food: Calculating the dietary footprint of the school population is possible, but it is a complex and time-consuming process. For this analysis, students can simply multiply the number of people by the North American average, which is shown on the chart.[2]

Waste Management: Complete this section by performing a waste audit (see instructions below) of the entire school, including the kitchen and cafeteria. The information required includes:

Bags of garbage: The number of large bags of garbage produced in the school in one day. This is a baseline figure for comparison in future audits.

Recyclables in garbage: The weights of all recyclable materials (paper, glass, aluminum, steel and plastics) that are placed in the school's garbage bins in one day.

Current recycling: The weights of the recyclable materials (paper, metal/glass) placed in the school's recycling bins in one day.

Performing a waste audit

In this activity, students collect, sort and weigh one day's accumulation of garbage and recycling from every room of the school, including the cafeteria, washrooms and staff areas. To avoid interrupting "waste routines" and thus possibly skewing the results of the audit, do not publicize the activity until after collection day. This means that only a core group of trusted students, such as members of a school environment club, will be involved in collecting the waste from each room at the end of a school day. Other students, or an entire class, may be enlisted to help sort the materials the following morning.

Safety guidelines: Gloves, goggles and direct supervision are essential in this activity. Washroom garbage (e.g., paper towels) should be weighed only, not sorted, and its contents assumed to be compostable. Caution students to be on the alert for sharp objects, particularly when they are sorting cafeteria waste. Ensure that students wash their hands and arms well when the audit is complete.

Materials: large space with tables for sorting waste, plastic sheets for tables, large plastic tubs, clear plastic garbage bags, latex gloves, safety goggles, weigh scale, markers, tape

Time: 2 hours at the end of a school day to collect waste and bring it to a central sorting area; 3–4 hours the following morning to sort materials

Procedure:

1. In separate bags, collect the contents of every garbage can and recycling bin in the school, including those in washrooms and the cafeteria. Clearly label each bag, recording the room and container (garbage or recycling) from which the materials were taken.

2. Set up a sorting room with several large tables covered by plastic sheets. On each table, place plastic tubs for separating the waste into categories.

(continued on page 108)

How Green is Your School?

This survey will help you to establish a baseline from which you can work to reduce your school's ecological footprint. The maximum point values for the questions reflect the impact of those practices and show where you can make the biggest reduction in your school's footprint.

Instructions: For each question, answer "always" (full points), "usually," "sometimes," "rarely" or "never" (0 points), and assign the number of points that fits best.

Waste Management

1. Does your school encourage the use of both sides of paper? (0–2) _____
2. Are recycling boxes placed near every garbage container? (0–3) _____
3. Are materials and supplies collected for reuse in art classes? (0–2) _____
4. Are materials from home collected for reuse in art classes? (0–2) _____
5. Are hazardous materials collected and disposed of properly? (e.g., batteries, printer toner, auto or woodshop waste, paint, glues, solvents) (0–8) _____

Energy

1. Does your school have an energy conservation program (e.g., are lights and computers turned off when not needed?) (0–8) _____
2. Are air vents and windows kept free of obstructions? (0–5) _____
3. Has the school been designed or retrofitted for energy efficiency and conservation? (0–12) _____

Water

1. Does your school have a water conservation program (e.g., does it have low-flow faucets, water-saving toilets, and rain-collection barrels for watering lawns and gardens?) (0–3) _____
2. Does your school promote water conservation and awareness? (0–2) _____

Products and Services

1. Does your school purchase "eco" cleaning products that are safe for the environment? (Ask the custodial staff/purchasing department.) (0–3) _____
2. Does your school purchase recycled paper and paper products? (0–5) _____

Transportation

1. Does your school have anti-idling signs posted at drop-off zones and receiving bays? (0–5) _____
2. Do students and staff respect smog alerts by leaving their cars at home and using more sustainable transportation? (0–2) _____
3. Does your school support sustainable transportation (organizing carpools, installing bike racks, providing public transit information)? (0–13) _____

Green Space

1. Does your school have a natural area (gardens, greenhouse, many trees), which reduces energy consumption by reducing lawn maintenance and the amount of pavement? (0–2) _____
2. Does your school have shade trees, which help reduce energy consumption by protecting buildings from seasonal elements such as wind, sun and snow? (0–3) _____

Food

1. Does your cafeteria purchase locally grown food whenever possible? (0–15) _____
2. Has your school participated in litterless lunch campaigns? (1–5) _____

Scoring

0–25 There are many great things you can do to make your school a greener place.

26–50 You have made some inroads, but have many more green initiatives to explore.

51–75 You are doing well and working hard towards greening your school.

76–100 Great work! Your school is a shade of green already!

Ecological Footprint: Audit Data and Translation

	Audit result	Multiply by translation factor	Result in hectares
Energy			
Oil (liters)		0.000001391	
Natural gas (m3)		0.001255	
Electricity (kwh)		0.0000125	
Solar (kwh)		0.00000233	
Wind (kwh)		0.00000181	
Water			
Liters used in school last year		0.00000167	
Transportation			
Car (person km)		0.00015	
Bus (person km)		0.0000173	
Streetcar (person km)		0.000008	
Subway (person km)		0.0000043	
Bike/walk/rollerblade (person km)		0.0	
Number of students and staff		0.3 (resources per person to build and maintain roads)	
Land Use			
School buildings (m²)		0.00001	
School yard (m²)		0.00001	
Parking lot (m²)		0.00001	
Food			
Number of students and staff		2.9 (average hectares per person for food resources in Canada and U.S.)	
Waste Management			
Bags of garbage		Used as baseline only; no calculation	
Recyclables in garbage:			
Paper (kg)		0.0010	
Glass (kg)		0.00067	
Aluminum (cans) (kg)		0.00333	
Steel (kg)		0.00083	
Plastic (kg)		0.00167	
Paper collected for recycling (kg)		0.0006	
Metal/glass collected for recycling (kg)		0.0013	
Number of students and staff		0.01 (energy used for waste collection and processing)	
Number of students and staff		0.8 (resources to process other forms of waste; i.e. paint, motor oil, etc.)	

Total Hectares: _____ (multiply by 2.4711 for acres)

Note: For the most accurate results, maintain all significant digits in your calculations.

3. Begin by sorting the bags containing waste collected from garbage containers. In an accessible area away from the tables, place a series of labeled garbage bags into which the sorted waste will be placed. You will need one or more bags for each of the following categories and subcategories:

- recyclable materials, including cardboard, box board, newspaper, fine paper, glass, aluminum, steel, and separate bins for each type of plastic that is recycled in your area

- compostable materials, including food scraps and paper towels

- materials that are not currently recyclable in your area, such as some plastics, Styrofoam, juice boxes and milk cartons

- hazardous waste

- garbage (anything that cannot be sorted into the categories above)

4. Sort one bag of garbage at a time at each table. First record the weight of the bag and the room it came from. Then sort the waste into the various categories and record all of the types of waste found in the bag. Because bags are sorted individually, it will be easy to determine which rooms in the school are producing the most garbage and should be targeted for reduction strategies. Before going on to the next bag of garbage, transfer the sorted materials into the corresponding collection bags.

5. When all of the garbage is sorted, record the total weight of each type of waste collected on the "Ecological Footprint: Audit and Translation" sheet.

6. Repeat Steps 2–4 for the recyclable materials that were collected from recycling bins. Divide them into categories of paper and metal/glass, and record the total weight of each category on the audit sheet.

Communicating findings

The High School Ecological Footprint activity will yield valuable information that students can share with other students, teachers, school administrators and the school board. The following are some ways of communicating the results.

- Demonstrate how much of the school's garbage is actually recyclable by displaying the sorted contents of a typical garbage bin in the school foyer.

- Make a presentation to administrators showing how much money the school could save by taking such simple measures as turning off lights.

- Create a poster comparing the environmental costs of the various methods of transportation used to get to school.

Taking action

The information obtained in the waste audit can be used in a variety of statistical calculations and year-to-year comparisons. For instance, students might track and graph the percentages of recyclable materials that are being recycled, as well as monitor changes in the overall volume of waste produced in the school. The learning that takes place during an audit is not only about what waste consists of and how much is produced, but also about changing the way it is dealt with in the school. Out of the process can come a variety of waste-reducing projects, such as the following:

- a large and creative display of findings

- a link on your school's web site

- a written report of results and recommendations to the school administration

- an improved paper, bottle and can recycling program

- a battery recycling program

- a litterless lunch campaign

- a composting program

Other follow-up activities and projects

- Conduct an energy audit of the school to determine where lights could safely be turned off and to identify windows that are broken or require weather-stripping.

- Initiate a school-wide "turn-off-the-lights" campaign by creating posters and making announcements.

- Install rain barrels around the school to collect water for use on gardens and lawns.

- Survey the school for leaky faucets and continuously running toilets and water fountains, and learn how to fix them.

- Conduct an anti-idling campaign around your school: post signs to inform drivers to turn off their engines, save fuel and spare the air.

- Make announcements about smog-alert days and encourage staff and students to carpool and take public transit.

- Create a reward program for teachers and students who carpool regularly.

Mike Foster, TDSB

• Conduct a "Keep Your Car Running Clean" workshop for students and teachers (run by the auto shop class).

• Conduct a letter-writing campaign asking food distributors to use less packaging on their products.

• Tour a supermarket to determine where popular lunch foods come from and how far they have traveled. Work with the cafeteria staff to purchase locally produced foods.

• Research the purchases make by the school (e.g., paper and cleaning products) and find similarly priced eco-friendly alternatives.

• Create signage for the photocopy room reminding teachers to double-side photocopies.

• Track the recyclable materials that leave your school to see where they end up.

• Establish a community garden and have a sale of native seeds and plants to raise money for it.

• Increase schoolyard biodiversity by planting a butterfly garden and making bird nesting boxes, bat boxes and butterfly houses.

• Plant evergreen trees on the north side of the school to shelter the building from winter winds; plant deciduous trees on the south side for shade in summer.

• Participate in a Yellow Fish Road program[3] around your school neighborhood to help keep toxic substances out of local waterways.

• Challenge another school to calculate their own ecological footprint and compare your results. This will provide you with a great incentive to reduce your own and come up with new and inventive strategies for doing so.

Julie Sawchuk is the Science Department Head at Listowel District Secondary School in Listowel, Ontario. *Tim Cameron* is the former Hamilton-Guelph (Ontario) Greening High Schools Coordinator for Youth Challenge International. The High School Ecological Footprint was developed in cooperation with the late **Eric Krause**, environmental technician and planner for the City of Toronto.

Notes

1. Ecological footprint calculations based on 2003 data. See Chris Hails, ed., WWF International, *Living Planet Report*, Switzerland, 2006, pp. 31–32.

2. For calculating the dietary footprint of a class of students, see "Food to You," *Green Teacher* 45, December 1995, pp. 10–14.

3. Participants in Trout Unlimited Canada's Yellow Fish Road program paint yellow fish next to storm drains and distribute brochures to remind people that any substance entering storm drains will likely end up in a local water body. Visit <www.yellowfishroad.org> for more information.

Resources

Rapport, David J., Bill L. Lasley, Dennis E. Rolston. *Managing for Healthy Ecosystems*. CRC Press, 1999.

Ryan, John C. and Alan Thein Durning. *Stuff: The Secret Lives of Everyday Things*. Northwest Environment Watch Publications, 1997.

Wackernagel, Mathis and William Rees. *Our Ecological Footprint: Reducing Human Impact on the Earth*. New Society Publishers, 1996.

Choosing Our Future

An activity that stimulates discussion of preferred and probable futures

Illustrations by Tom Goldsmith

by Jan Cincera

Subject areas: social science, environmental studies

Key concepts: future, limits to growth, new technologies

Skills: discussion and presentation skills, critical thinking

Location: indoors

Time: 1½ hours

Materials: large blackboard or chart paper; for each group of three to five students, one set of the eight scenarios (see page 112) cut into strips, one extra blank strip of paper; articles or excerpts related to the eight scenarios (optional follow-up)

Forecasting Congress is a discussion activity intended to initiate discussion of problems in our world and society, our personal responsibility for them and our choices for the future. It can be a starting point for discussions of technological dilemmas or such problems as poverty and resource depletion. The activity can also be used to assess and compare students' degree of technological optimism, skepticism and radicalism. The game has been used often in global and environmental education, but it could also be used in economics, sociology and history. While it is suitable for students of age 15 and up, teachers may wish to simplify or otherwise modify the descriptions of the future scenarios presented, depending on the maturity, discussion skills and knowledge of their students. Presenting the game at the beginning of a course creates the opportunity to refer to it in the ensuing lessons; but the game could also be played at the end of a course to describe the directions confronting us at the present crossroads.

Goals

We can never know the future, but we can consider the risks and problems that it may hold and what we can do now to create a better future. In this activity, students are confronted with eight scenarios that present different faces of the future. The activity asks them to consider which visions of the future they would prefer, which are most probable, and what would need to change in order for the most preferable scenario to become the most probable scenario. Choosing the "best" scenario is not important: the value of the game is in the discussion itself.

Procedure

1. Divide the class into groups of three to five students. Distribute a set of scenario strips and one extra blank strip to each group. Ask the students to read the scenarios and discuss them within their group. Tell them that if they think a possible future scenario is missing from the set, they may add it by writing it on the blank strip they have been given.

2. On the board, draw two diamond shapes side by side. Within each diamond, draw lines to create nine boxes, as shown in the diagram. Label one diamond "Preferences" and the other "Probabilities."

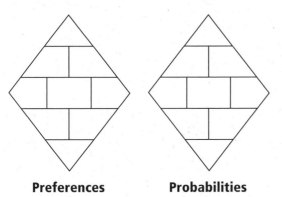

Preferences   **Probabilities**

3. Ask half of the groups to rank the future scenarios according to their preference. They should arrange their strips in a diamond pattern, placing the most desirable future scenario at the top, the second and third most desirable scenarios in the second row, and so on, with the least desirable future scenario at the bottom. Ask the other groups to rank the scenarios according to what they think is probable, placing the most probable future scenario at the top, the second and third most probable scenarios in the second row, and the least probable scenario at the bottom.

4. Ask the groups to read their rankings aloud and then write them in the appropriate diamond charts on the board or on large chart paper. Each group may complete their own chart or you may decide to have the Preferences and Probabilities groups collaborate on their rankings to arrive at a consensus.

Debriefing

Begin debriefing the session by identifying the scenarios that have been placed in the same row on both the Preferences and Probabilities charts. For each of these scenarios, discuss why students consider it a preferable or probable future. Questions might include: Have you observed or read anything that suggests that this scenario is probable? Have you heard about any scientific research that might lead to the future depicted in this scenario? Why would this be a good (or bad) future for people? and Would you like to live in such a society? If there are no preferable and probable scenarios placed on the same level, discuss why this is the case. Ask what would need to change in order for the most preferable scenario to become the most probable scenario? What can we do to help make those changes?

To aid in the discussion, you may provide additional information about the scenarios (see "Background for teachers," below).

Follow-up

As a follow-up to the game, distribute articles and excerpts from literature that is connected to the scenarios. Ask students to identify which of the scenarios their excerpt corresponds with and to comment on the readings, stating which of them is the most interesting or appealing, and why.

This activity sometimes leads students to feel pessimistic about the future. If this happens, remind them that the future is not a given, that we create the future through our choices. It is up to us to decide whether to amend the troubles in the world or resign ourselves to them.

Background for teachers

All of the scenarios presented in Forecasting Congress have a basis in real-world situations or in the writings of various philosophers and futurists. The following is a brief background that teachers may wish to build upon in developing discussion points for use with students.

Doomsday: The doomsday scenario sounds a bit fantastic. Nevertheless, some believe that the world has been close to devastation for at least 50 years. They point to the risk of nuclear war during the Cold War era and, more recently, terrorist attacks and the threat of biological and chemical warfare. You might discuss religious groups that believe in doomsday or our dependence on fragile and fallible technologies, such as the worldwide web of computers.

Scenarios of the Future

Doomsday: Powerful weapons and technologies, environmental degradation and an accumulation of social problems will result in the fall of human civilization. The Earth will be devastated, many people will die and most of human knowledge will be lost. For those who do survive, living conditions will be harsh and primitive.

Overshoot and collapse: Exhaustion of natural resources, stress on food and water supplies and other environmental problems will result in conflicts between North and South and East and West. Economies will regress, and populations and consumption levels will decline. People will become poorer but eventually will be able to solve their problems.

United peoples: New communication technologies will enable people to find common solutions to problems and eliminate disparities among regions. People from all nations will begin to see themselves as members of a global village and work together on wise stewardship of the planet. Many contemporary problems will vanish; however, people will lose some of their personal freedom in the name of collective interests.

Omnipotent individual: Advances in biotechnology, genetic engineering and information and communication technologies will lead to a magnificent growth in human abilities. Life expectancy will increase and we will develop new abilities, such as the ability to communicate telepathically and access global databases of information through microchips implanted in our bodies. We will colonize space and be capable of rebuilding our own bodies. Differences in the level of development among countries will cause some countries to dominate others; but over time, these differences may become smaller.

Technological slavery: New technologies will become so complicated that only a few experts will be able to manage them. Major decisions will be generated by computer programs, while people occupy themselves with trivial matters, high levels of consumption and virtual games. Transnational corporations will be stronger than elected governments. People will be well-fed and satisfied, but will not have the freedom to change their lives in any significant way.

Sustainable development: Despite difficulties, people will succeed at finding a fragile balance between environmental, social and economic interests. People in wealthier nations will reduce their level of consumption, and clean technologies will be developed and promoted, leading to a satisfying standard of living for people all over the world. There will be a revolution in knowledge and no concern about risks or calamities in the near future. Democracy will flourish, and citizens of green cities will actively participate in decision-making.

Successful globalization: Technological progress will solve contemporary social and environmental problems. Intercultural differences and economic disparities will be eliminated by free markets. Western concepts of human rights and democracy will deeply influence other cultural regions.

Unexpected breaking point: Something unexpected will influence human history. Extraterrestrials will land on Earth, or scientists will develop something completely new, such as teleportation — the instantaneous transmission of objects from one place to another. This event or discovery will profoundly change human history and start a new era.

Overshoot and collapse: The overshoot and collapse scenario is derived from the classical work *The Limits to Growth* (1972) and its sequel *Beyond the Limits: Confronting Global Collapse, Envisioning a Sustainable Future* (1992) by Donella Meadows and Dennis Meadows. Based on computer models of population growth and resource use, the authors predicted that if we do not limit economic growth, we will exhaust the carrying capacity of the planet within 100 years, resulting in the precipitous collapse of economies and food production.

United peoples: The united peoples scenario comes from the works of James Lovelock (the Gaia hypothesis, which states that Earth is a living, self-regulating organism) and Pierre Teilhard de Chardin (we are evolving toward a global consciousness, or noosphere, which will unite all people) and from theoreticians on cyberculture. You might ask students if they have cyberfriends from distant parts of the world whom they have never met in person.

Omnipotent individual: The omnipotent individual scenario is a reflection of the idea that humans represent a transitory stage in the evolution of intelligence and that technological advances will enable us to improve our physical, emotional and intellectual characteristics. This idea is underpinned by scientific discoveries of the last decade, especially in the field of robotics or genetics. (Find examples of such discoveries in newspapers or popular journals; and visit the website of the Extropy Institute, a movement to promote this vision of future.)

Technology slavery: Students may already know about the technology slavery scenario. Refer to authors in the cyberpunk branch of science fiction (for example, William Gibson) or to the movie *The Matrix*. Ask students whether they believe that artificial intelligence is a threat or an opportunity. Investigate neoluddism, a movement to refuse modern technology. Compare it with luddism, a 19th-century movement with similar goals. Compare and contrast the technology slavery scenario with the previous two scenarios, which are much more optimistic.

Sustainable development: Inform students of the history of the notion of sustainable development (Rio Declaration on Environment and Development, Earth Summit 1992) and its principles and basic document (*Agenda 21*). Discuss the post-Rio development (World Summit on Sustainable Development in Johannesburg in 2002) and the problems associated with implementing sustainable development as policy.

Globalization: Discuss globalization and its impact on, for example, non-European cultures or the rise of fundamentalism. You could mention the thesis of Samuel Huntington on the clash of civilizations (in future, cultural differences will be a dominant source of world conflict) or the optimistic visions of Francis Fukuyama (the modernization of nations will lead to free-market liberal democracy).

Unexpected breaking point: The unexpected breaking point scenario reveals the unpredictability of the future and may be the most probable of all. Twenty years ago, who could have predicted the expansion of communications though technologies such as the Internet and mobile telephones? Remind students that the future is not predetermined. The unexpected breaking-point scenario is a source of threat but also a source of hope and new opportunities.

Jan Cincera is an instructor in the teacher education program at the Technical University of Liberec in the Czech Republic. He focuses on active methods of teaching in the fields of global and environmental education.

References

Agenda 21. The United Nations Conference on Environment and Development, 1992. Online at <www.un.org/esa/sustdev/documents/agenda21/english/agenda21toc.htm>.

Extropy Institute, <www.extropy.org>. A non-profit organization devoted to the exchange of ideas on the use of technology to overcome human limitations and improve human life in the future.

Fukuyama, Francis. *The End of History and the Last Man.* Penguin, 1992.

Huntington, Samuel P. *The Clash of Civilizations and the Remaking of World Order.* Simon & Schuster, 1996.

Lovelock, J. E. *Gaia: A New Look at Life on Earth.* Oxford University Press, 1987.

Meadows, Donella H. et al. *Beyond the limits: Confronting Global Collapse, Envisioning a Sustainable Future.* Chelsea Green Publishing, 1992.

Meadows, Donella H. et al. *The Limits to Growth: A Report for the Club of Rome's Project on the Predicament of Mankind.* Universe Books, 1972.

Linking Trade, Human Rights and the Environment

Illustrations by Tom Goldsmith

by Tricia Jane Edgar

Subject areas: geography, social studies, science

Key concepts: human rights, social justice, environmental and social impact assessment, life-cycle analysis, economics, history

Skills: oral and written presentation skills, social science research, original research, data analysis, life-cycle analysis, observation and reflection

Location: indoors

Time: 2–3 class periods plus independent research and presentations

Materials: paper or objects to represent land in The Land Game, scissors, example of life-cycle analysis, sample sheets with products students may want to study. If desired, examples of products, stories and product information. Poster boards and paper for poster presentations, if desired

How is a healthy environment connected to human rights? A healthy environment *is* a human right. Without clean water, fresh air and fertile soil for growing food, it is hard to get an education, raise a family or work for a better society. A healthy environment is the foundation of a sustainable society and economy.

Yet in many areas of the world, the right to live in a healthy environment is compromised by resource extraction and manufacturing processes that pollute the air, water and soil, and provide little benefit to local communities. The consequences are often tragic. In 1995, for example, Nigerian writer and activist Ken Saro-Wiwa was executed because he spoke out against the environmental devastation of his homeland by multinational oil companies. As oil pipelines were built across their land, his people, the Ogoni, had died from hunger and disease. All the while, consumers around the world were fueling their homes and cars with oil from the Niger Delta, most of them oblivious to its social and environmental impacts

Industry and trade are powerful tools. When used well, they support human rights, contribute to social stability and foster practices that sustain the natural environment. At its best, the manufacture of goods requires no more resources than can be renewed, and the waste from one activity becomes the raw material for the next.

It creates employment and enriches people's lives, helping them feed and clothe themselves and supplementing what they themselves produce. Under these conditions, health, education and culture flourish, and people become linked in a thriving economic community in which one person's need matches another's product.

Then there is trade at its worst. In this scenario, resource extraction and production leave a community poorer than before, its soil, water and air deteriorated. Some profits go to local people in the form of low-wage incomes, but most leave the community. With their environment damaged and wages low, it is difficult for people to feed themselves, let alone support a flourishing culture and educate their children. Trade such as this does not link people in positive ways. Consumers know little about the people and places that created the products they use, and those who create the products benefit little from the trade relationship.

If we are to help make trade a positive tool that sustains environments and supports human rights, a first step is to learn about the origins of the products we use. Our cell phones, shoes, bananas … where and how are they produced? How do they affect people and places around the world? The following activities introduce the concept of human rights and help students understand that human rights and social stability are compromised when the environment is compromised. Through life-cycle analysis of everyday items, students discover the environmental and social impacts of the things we buy and are encouraged to research alternative products and processes.

Bill of Rights

In our busy lives, we seldom stop to consider what makes our existence possible. This exercise challenges students to examine the necessities of life and introduces the concept and diversity of human rights. Students then create a bill of rights that ensures that everyone is able to enjoy these rights.

Time: 30 minutes

Materials: chart paper or blackboard

Background:
In 1948, the United Nations developed the Universal Declaration of Human Rights, a document that outlines the "inalienable rights of all members of the human family." These include civil and political rights, such as the right to free speech and the right to organize. They also include social and cultural rights, such as the right to form a family or own property.

The Universal Declaration of Human Rights was a starting point. Many other documents followed. In 1972, the Stockholm Declaration linked human rights and environmental protection. It declared that people have the right to live in a world where the physical environment supports a dignified life. Each person also has the responsibility to protect and improve the environment in order to ensure the well being of future generations.

Procedure:
1. Give the class the following scenario: *You are marooned on a new planet, one that is very similar to Earth. You are responsible for developing rules for your new society.*

2. Ask the students to list at least five things they will need to survive and be happy. These might be physical needs, such as food; they might be social needs, such as friends; or they might be psychological needs, such as love. Students may include some silly ideas, but must have at least five serious ideas. Allow five minutes for them to complete their lists.

3. Divide the class into groups of three or four. Ask the members of each group to pool their ideas and create a new list of the rights that they all agree are important.

4. Ask the groups to use the rights they have selected to design a bill of rights that ensures everyone's needs are met. For example, if it is agreed that everyone needs food, the bill of rights might read, "On our planet, everyone has the right to have three meals a day." If they decide that people need friends, they might say, "On our planet, everyone has the right to choose their friends."

Students should think also about civil and political rights. These are the rights that help people organize and speak out in order to get what they need. For example, if people do not have enough food, they might organize a farmers' cooperative. If they do not feel physically safe, they might lobby for laws and community support to reduce crime.

Allow 15 minutes for the groups to draft their bill of rights and prepare to discuss them with the class.

5. As each group presents their rights to the class, organize the rights into categories, such as social, economic, cultural and civil rights. Include a column

on "the right to a healthy environment." Ask which of these rights they consider most important. Why?

6. After compiling the groups' ideas, your class will have a document that likely bears some similarity to the United Nations Universal Declaration of Human Rights (online at <www.un.org/Overview/rights.html>). Review the UN Declaration and discuss differences and similarities between the students' list of rights and those in the Declaration. If differences are noted, discuss possible reasons for these differences. Is anything missing from the Declaration?

Point out that the UN Universal Declaration of Human Rights does not make a direct connection between human rights and a healthy environment. This connection was made in 1972 in the Declaration of the United Nations Conference on the Human Environment, commonly known as the Stockholm Declaration.

7. Brainstorm things that could prevent people from having certain human rights. For example, a government may make laws that prohibit people from forming unions. A natural disaster might prevent people from obtaining enough food. Environmental damage such as water contamination might threaten people's health.

8. Brainstorm ways in which societies ensure that people have rights. For example, societies have constitutions, laws and law enforcement, as well as advocacy organizations, civil society organizations and unions. These documents and organizations work to achieve a balance between individual rights and the good of society at large. Individual civil and political rights, such as freedom of expression and freedom of speech, allow people to work for other human rights.

The Land Game

People thrive when they live in a healthy environment with ample resources to support social, cultural and economic activities. The Land Game, which is similar to musical chairs, helps students understand the connection between a healthy environment and a healthy society. The game shows how scarcity of resources and stress on the environment can cause social unrest, and how people can work together to solve environmental and social problems.

Time: 45 minutes, with debriefing

Materials: 8½" x 11" paper (10 sheets more than the number of students), music CD and player or other music source

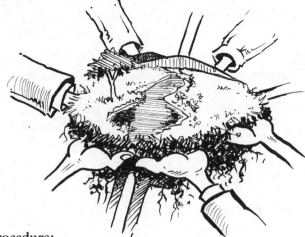

Procedure:

1. Before the activity begins, find or clear an area large enough for your group to walk around in. Place pieces of paper on the floor, one or two meters apart. Begin with about 10 more pieces of paper than there are students in the class.

2. Ask the students to position themselves so that each person is touching one of the pieces of paper with a toe or some other part of the body. More than one person can touch the same piece of paper.

3. Introduce the game by telling the students that in this activity they will play the role of farmers in a developing country who rely on sales of their crops to support their families. Explain that the pieces of paper on the floor represent arable land. When the music starts, they are to move around planting seeds and hoeing their fields (demonstrate these actions). When the music stops, they must find a piece of land and touch it. Anyone who cannot find space on a piece of land must leave the game and go to the side of the room as an observer.

4. Start the music and let it play for 30 seconds or so. Then remove one piece of land and stop the music. As you remove each piece of farmland, you may wish to give a reason for the loss (you could make dice with different reasons on each face and roll a die each time you remove land). Reasons for removing land might include the following:

• The government has rezoned this land for a new housing development.

• A lumber company has deforested the nearby mountainside, causing flooding and erosion in your fields.

• The government has leased this land to a multinational company for growing export crops.

• Your fields are situated near gas wells, and methane seepage from the wells is killing your crops.

Start the music again and repeat the rounds until there is only one piece of land left. At that point, you may stop and debrief the class or go on to play round two (see Step 5) and debrief both activities at once.

5. Return all of the pieces of land to the floor. Explain that in the second round, no one can go to the sidelines. Everyone must use the land that is available. It is interesting to watch how a class grapples with the need to fit everyone on the remaining land. However, if you feel that this needs pre-teaching, explain that, once again, land will become limited, but this time they must work together to use and steward the land that remains. Ask the groups to think of one or two plans for doing this, and discuss the plans as a class before the game begins again.

Debriefing

Reorganize as a class and discuss the following questions:

• What do the pieces of paper symbolize?
(In the game, the pieces of paper symbolize land. However, they can represent a variety of things that people need from the environment, such as food, water and fuel.)

• How did you feel during the first activity?
(Students may have felt frustrated or competitive, or experienced any number of other feelings. Discuss the reasons for these feelings.)

• What in real life might this activity symbolize?
(When resources such as clean water and fertile land are scarce or inaccessible, people may have difficulty meeting their basic needs. A scarcity of resources can cause feelings of insecurity and frustration and even lead to social unrest or conflict between land users.)

• Why are resources scarce?
(Scarcity can occur as a result of natural disaster, overuse or degradation of a resource, or political decisions that result in inequitable access to resources. Since we live on a finite planet, all non-renewable resources are naturally limited. Even renewable resources, such as water and forests, can be polluted or damaged and take a long time to recover. Political decisions, such as the privatization of common resources, can make resources scarce for some.)

• What happened in the second game? How did it differ from the first game?
(In the second game, students had to find a way to fit everyone onto the remaining land. They may have stopped to talk about how best to do this. They may have created a resource management agency. They may have even organized to take back some of the land that was removed.)

• In real life, what are some ways to solve the problems of resource scarcity?

(Individually, or in community, we can work to minimize our use of resources and find ways to recover them, such as by recycling or reusing waste products. If the resources are renewable, we can work to replenish them. Governments can develop laws and other policies that encourage people to conserve resources and ensure equal access to resources. We can also create organizations that help manage resources. For example, community forests allow people to be the managers of their local environment, working collaboratively to steward a precious resource.)

Extensions

• On the back of each piece of paper (land), write one of the rights from the students' Bill of Rights (e.g., the right to clean water, clean air, adequate food, a place to live and education). At the end of the game, turn over the pieces of paper to reveal the rights that were taken away as each piece of land was removed. Brainstorm the ways in which loss of land or livelihood can be linked to the loss of other rights.

• Ask two or three students to play the role of a social elite or powerful corporation who has the right to decide how land will be used. They will perform the task of stopping the music and removing the pieces of land, explaining as they do their reason. For example, they might decide to drill an oil well or lay a pipeline.

Hidden Lives: Life-cycle Analysis of Everyday Objects

This exercise demonstrates that consumer goods have social and environmental impacts and introduces the concept of product life-cycle analysis.

Time: One class period, with a follow-up independent assignment

Materials: "Hidden Scandals, Secret Lives" handout (see page 118), "Tell their Stories: Life-cycle Analysis Poster" handout (see page 119), poster paper

Background:
Just as we have human rights, we also have a responsibility to safeguard the rights of others. As consumers of products, we are all participants in global trade, and our choices shape environments and societies throughout the world. It is our responsibility to become conscious consumers: to learn about the impacts of the products we use and to make choices that support a

(continued on page 120)

Hidden Scandals, Secret Lives

Hidden scandals and secret lives...there is a story behind every product that you own. To understand all of the impacts of a product, you need to look into its past and learn about its life cycle. A product's life begins when the materials it is made from are mined, harvested or extracted. These raw materials are combined with energy and labor to create a product. There may be several stages of production. For example, gold may be formed into bars, which later become jewelry. After the product is made, energy is used to transport it to distribution centers and then to stores. Sometimes the use or consumption of the product also uses resources. For example, during the time that you own a favorite piece of clothing, you will wash it many times and this requires water and energy. Finally, the product wears out and either goes to a landfill as waste or becomes raw material for a new product.

Cotton T-shirt

Although your favorite T-shirt is made of natural fiber, it is likely anything but natural. In fact, it took about 150 grams of synthetic pesticides and fertilizers to grow the cotton it is made of. Cotton is the world's most heavily sprayed crop, accounting for one-quarter of all insecticides used. Most of the pesticides sprayed on cotton are toxic to humans and other animals, and half are carcinogens. These substances get into the air, water and soil where cotton is grown, accumulate in plants and animals, and cause serious health problems for farm workers and those who live near cotton fields. Less than 0.5 percent of the world's cotton is grown organically. And whether organic or not, cotton is a thirsty crop, requiring 7,000 to 29,000 liters of water for each kilogram produced.

After harvest, cotton is processed to remove seeds and debris, compressed into bales, and transported to mills where it is spun into thread and woven into cloth. Cotton textiles are usually dyed and often treated with chemicals such as fire retardant and formaldehyde to reduce wrinkling and fading. The fabric is then sewn into garments. Many of the cotton T-shirts on our store shelves are made in developing countries, often by low-paid workers in "sweatshop" factories. During the time that you own your T-shirt, you will use water and energy to wash and dry it many times. Later, you might pass it on to a friend or a charity; or, if it wears out, you might use the cloth as a polishing rag. Eventually, however, it is likely to be thrown away: in the United States alone, three million tons of fabric goes to the landfill every year.

Gold necklace

There may be gold in the hills, but is it worth mining? In South America and on Africa's Gold Coast, gold mines contaminate water and damage the health of humans and animals. Gold extraction and refining is a complex process involving chemicals and electricity. Gold is mined from surface deposits or veins, or may be extracted during the production of other metals.

In South America, small-scale gold miners use water cannons to extract gold from surface mines. The water blasts away fragile soil and vegetation, creating holes that fill with water, attracting mosquitoes that spread malaria. Sometimes miners use mercury to extract gold. Much of the used mercury goes into local rivers, where it changes into methyl mercury. This form persists in the environment and accumulates in the food chain. Miners and local residents affected by mercury poisoning develop tremors and brain damage. In large-scale gold refining, cyanide is used to purify the gold. In Peru, where a large gold mine drains into four watersheds, local people say that the cyanide-polluted water is destroying their pastures and killing their animals.

Once gold is extracted and refined, it is made into bars and shipped around the world. Most gold remains in bars, as global currency. The rest is made into jewelry or medical or electronic equipment, or is combined with other metals.

Online resources for further study:

Centre for Economic and Social Rights, <http://cesr.org/>. Environmental and social impacts of the gold industry.
Human Rights Watch, <http://hrw.org/>. Human rights in the gold industry.
OXFAM America, <www.oxfamamerica.org/>, search "gold mining." Articles and research on the environmental impacts of gold mining.
The World Gold Council, <www.gold.org>. Gold industry.

Tell their Stories: Life Cycle Analysis Poster

Telling the Story

1. Choose one of the products listed below and create a poster that tells its story.

Gold necklace: Gold mining often involves the use of toxic chemicals.
Cotton T-shirt: Cotton is the most heavily sprayed crop in the world.
Can of motor oil: The search for oil can cause conflict both within and among countries.
Banana: Workers spray pesticides without adequate protective equipment.
Coffee: Forests are cleared for plantations, damaging local habitat, soil and water.
Computer: Developing countries process toxic electronic waste.
Plastic toy: PVC plastics cause cancer and kidney and reproductive disorders.
Cell phone: A metal found in cell phones fuels war and the destruction of habitat.

2. Describe and illustrate the life cycle of the product from the time its raw materials are mined or harvested through production, transportation, consumption or use, and disposal. Answer these questions:

• Where do the raw materials come from?
• Who lives in the area where the product is made?
• Who makes the product?
• What materials, energy and labor are used during different parts of the product's life cycle?

Identifying Impacts

3. Once you have learned about your product's life cycle, try to identify a few of the impacts the product has on people and the environment.

• What are three ways that this product affects the environment? Describe environmental impacts that occur at different stages in the product's life cycle.
• What are three ways that this product affects people? At least one example should show how an environmental impact of the product hurts or helps local people. Think also about ways in which the product affects local cultures and economies.
• Think back to the Bill of Rights that the class made. What human rights are affected by this product? Are the impacts positive, negative, or both positive and negative? For example, gold mining helps people make a living but may make it difficult for them to lead a healthy life.

Making Change

4. Include in your poster actions that are being taken, or could be taken, to change the way this product affects people and the environment.

• What are people doing about these impacts in the place where the product is made?
• What are people doing globally, as individuals or as part of an organization?
• What can you do?

There are many ways to make change. As consumers, we can choose not to buy a product. We can use products that are made locally, fairly, or with more ecologically sound materials and processes. We can also volunteer with nonprofit organizations that raise public awareness of the impacts of products, promote fair trade, and lobby industry and governments for changes in the way products are made.

clean environment, a sustainable economy and a flour-ishing society for all. Introducing students to product life-cycle analysis gives them a tool they can use to guide their choices as consumers.

Life-cycle analysis is the tracking of a product and its environmental and social impacts, from the time the raw materials are mined or harvested, through production, transportation, consumption and, finally, disposal or recycling. Although it is hard to quantify all of the potential impacts of a product, life-cycle analysis is a useful concept because it allows us to make better informed choices as consumers. We may feel good about buying organic bananas, but a life-cycle analysis will reveal that a great deal of greenhouse gas is emitted in transporting them to us, and might lead us to consider purchasing locally grown fruit instead.

Procedure:

1. Give students the handout "Hidden Scandals, Secret Lives." Review it with the class as a preface to the assignment. Using the example of the cotton T-shirt or gold necklace, draw a chart or schematic on the board as you identify the various stages in the product's life cycle (e.g., for a gold necklace, extraction, refining, forming into bars, shipping, reforming into a necklace, packaging, marketing and transportation to retail store). For each of these stages, brainstorm with the class the potential environmental and social impacts.

2. Give students the handout called "Tell Their Stories" and review the requirements of the independent research assignment. The students are to develop a poster that tells the story of an everyday object. The poster can take the form of an illustrated timeline, flow chart or web that shows the impacts of the product as it progresses through the different stages of its life cycle.

Explain that it may be difficult to find information about the life cycle of a particular brand of product because much of this information is proprietary. Instead, students should describe a possible or a typical life cycle for the product they choose. For example, research on the gold necklace might reveal that some of the world's gold comes from South America. Students could research the impact of gold production in South America and investigate how gold is processed and transported.

Younger students who are just learning about research can work with one of the examples provided in the "Hidden Scandals, Secret Lives" handout. They can identify the environmental and social impacts outlined in the case study, add some of their own, and research alternatives using the suggested resources.

Each poster should contain:

- a summary of the product's story, or life cycle, accompanied by illustrations

- a description of at least three environmental impacts at different stages in the product's life cycle

- a description of at least three ways in which the product affects people

- a description of ways in which the product supports or hinders human rights

- a description of actions being taken to reduce or eliminate negative impacts of the product (suggest to students that they research the work of local or global organizations or individuals who are working to make these changes)

- a strategy for personal change (things the student can do to reduce the negative impacts and increase the positive impacts of the product)

The completed posters can be the basis for a short class presentation, or the posters can simply be exhibited for all to see. As extensions, students could develop mock advertisements that describe the impacts of a product and suggest alternatives.

Tricia Jane Edgar *coordinates education programs at the Lynn Canyon Ecology Centre in North Vancouver, British Columbia.*

Resources

Reducing environmental impact

Center for a New American Dream, <www.newdream.org>. Information on changing consumption habits and conserving resources at home and school.

Rees, William and Mathis Wackernagel. *Our Ecological Footprint*. New Society Publishers, 1996.

Ryan, John C. and Alan T. Durning. *Stuff: The Secret Lives of Everyday Things*. Northwest Environment Watch, 1997.

Human rights

Amnesty International, <www.amnesty.org>. Reports on human rights issues around the world.

Human Rights Internet, <www.hri.ca>. Teaching resources on human rights.

Human Rights Watch, <www.hrw.org>. Reports on human rights issues around the world.

United Nations, Universal Declaration of Human Rights, 1948, <www.un.org/Overview/rights.html>.

Fair trade

Global Exchange, <www.globalexchange.org>. Fair trade and the impact of trade on human rights.

Oxfam, <www.maketradefair.com>. Oxfam's "Make Trade Fair" campaign website has examples of fair trade around the world.

Planet Transit:
Profit or Survival?

A game of choices and consequences for Grades 9 and up

by Georgi Marshall

Subject areas: social studies, civics

Key concepts: industrialization, sustainable development, natural resource use, carrying capacity, tragedy of the commons, profit and loss, green technologies

Skills: negotiation, decision making, systems thinking

Location: large open area indoors or outdoors

Time: 90 minutes for activity; 30 minutes for discussion

Materials: enlargement or overhead transparency of "Planet Transit Accounting" chart (see page 124) with "EI Penalty," "LR fee" and "GT Price" sections covered so that they can be revealed one at a time. For each "planet" of 7 or 8 students: 1 cushion (or piece of cardboard) per group member, plus two additional cushions; 25 beads (or other objects to represent money); one set of Industry Cards (see pages 125–26); chart paper; marking pens

Prem Center Magic Eyes Barge Program

E ight teenagers are squeezed together awkwardly on five cushions — their planet! Things didn't start out this way for the team, who are now very vocal as they enter the last round for a chance to see if they can rebalance life aboard planet "Karabaw Deeng." Citizens of another planet, "Man Overboard," gaze over smugly, as they have ample space to sit, with nine cushions. They are carefully hiding their list of development choices from the other two planets and hoarding a large amount of money (beads) in a bowl. The citizens of the third planet, "Fried Rice," are struggling to make decisions. They have seven cushions to sit on, but they possess a smaller amount of money than "Man Overboard."

It is difficult for most of us to imagine running out of natural resources. We may experience minor shortages of out-of-season produce and other goods, but these shortfalls are easily overcome if we are willing to pay higher prices to purchase these items from elsewhere. What happens, then, when the natural resources of our planet become so depleted or deteriorated that there is no "elsewhere" and we have no money to buy our way out of the problems we have created? Planet Transit is an extremely animated game that raises students' awareness of the environmental impact of the industries that support our comfortable lifestyle. In planet teams, students are taken through three industrial eras, beginning in the early 20th century. At the start of each era, they must decide what industries to invest in to bring economic development to their planet. However, the outcome is not as simple as "development equals prosperity." As we know, planets have carrying capacities and cannot tolerate exploitative development forever. As the game proceeds from one era to the next, the consequences of investing in polluting or environmentally destructive industries are revealed and students must choose between profit and survival.

Suitable for Grades 9 and up, Planet Transit was developed in Thailand as a means of engaging students in a geography unit on industrialization. It was first played aboard a boat that runs along the Chao Phraya River, Thailand's source of vitality, and was inspired by hearing older people tell stories of once swimming in and drinking from the river (which one would certainly not do today!). From the deck of the boat, students could see and even smell some of the industries they were "investing" in, such as the food market, a beer factory and numerous restaurant boats, and could observe for themselves how development over time can damage natural environments.

Planet Transit evokes greed, frustration, mediation and much laughter. Most important, it is a good starting point for discussions of industrialization, sustainable development, natural resource use, and concepts such as carrying capacity and the "tragedy of the commons." Be prepared for a game of animation, transition and consequence.

Chork Dii! (Good luck!)

Facilitation roles

The following roles may be played by one or more facilitators.

Leader: The Leader distributes materials at the beginning of the game, explains the game, introduces each round, and graphs the profit and loss of each planet (if a graph is used) as the game proceeds.

Banker: The Banker collects the money (beads) paid for investments at the beginning of each round and distributes the profits at the end of each round.

Environmental Impact Agent: The Environmental Impact Agent prompts participants for ideas about the environmental impacts of various industries, reveals the penalties for these impacts, and removes land (cushions) accordingly.

It is recommended that the facilitator(s) circulates among the groups throughout the game, recording students' comments and reactions for use as discussion points in the follow-up discussion.

Getting set for round one

1. Divide the group into three or four "planet" groups. The group size will vary with class size, but seven or eight is a good number because it is challenging for students to make decisions in a group this large.

2. Give each group a large sheet of paper and marking pens, which they will use to record the industries they invest in during each round. Have each group give its planet a name and write the name at the top of their paper.

3. Give each group one cushion (or piece of cardboard) for each member and two extra cushions that represent common land. Instruct the students to join their cushions together and sit on them, ensuring that all body parts are aboard their "planet." This creates a sense of dependence on their planet.

4. Give each group one bead for each member (e.g., a group of eight receives eight beads). The beads represent money, in this case the return from their crops during the last season.

Game overview

The game is played in three rounds representing three different periods in history: 1900–1920, 1920–1960 and 1960–2010. At the beginning of the game (in 1900), the citizens of each planet are all small-scale farmers. They possess land (one cushion per person, plus two extra cushions) and a small amount of money (a quantity of beads equal to the number of group members) to be used for the development of their society. Each planet starts with the same amount of money and land, and then operates independently in making decisions about investments. The objective of the game is to have as much money (beads) and as much land (cushions) as possible by the end.

In introducing each round, the leader may wish to evoke the atmosphere of the period by wearing a costume and describing, or asking students to describe, what was happening around the world at that time.

Selecting investments

At the beginning of each of the three rounds, the groups have 2–5 minutes to select the industries they wish to invest in for economic development during that era. They may choose to remain farmers throughout the game, but a variety of other industries are presented for their consideration (see Industry Cards). Six choices are available in round one, and new investment possibilities (Industry Cards) are added each round. The groups record their choices on chart paper, *keeping them secret from the other groups*, and then pay the Banker one unit of money (bead) for each industry. If they wish, they may invest more than one bead in a single industry, in which case their profits — and environmental impacts — for that industry will be multiplied.

Since industries generate different levels of financial return, varying amounts of money can be made. However, students need to be wary of the hidden costs of their decisions: the environmental impacts of some of the industries are punishable by loss of land. It may seem straightforward for planets to avoid investing in these industries. However, during rounds one and two, the future environmental consequences are not revealed until after the students have made their investments (a situation that raises discussion of the lack of environmental awareness during that time in history). Furthermore, the temptation of profit often exerts a strong pull toward a particular investment, despite its potential consequences.

Assessing environmental impacts

After the groups record their investment decisions, the Banker distributes the anticipated profits (beads) according to profits stated on Industry Cards. But just as the groups are enjoying the wealth that comes with development, the Environmental Impact Agent steps in to reveal the environmental impact penalties (i.e., land to be forfeited) resulting from industries that damage the environment. The agent then removes the appropriate number of cushions from each planet (refer to the "Environmental Impact Penalty" column on the Planet Transit Accounting chart). For example, a group who invested in the coal industry will receive a six-bead profit, but will lose four cushions — a penalty they were unaware of when investing in and reaping the profits of their coal mine. For each industry resulting in an environmental impact penalty, the agent asks: "Why is this penalty appropriate?" and "What impacts would this industry have on the environment?"

When land is lost, students are forced to squeeze onto their reduced cushion space to avoid "falling off their planet." This makes the game fun and instills a feeling that actions have consequences. It also make the game more lifelike, as it reflects the ramifications of the destruction of natural resources, such as the present-day struggle for access to fresh water. Experiencing the consequences of their decisions after each round provides an incentive for the groups to make better-informed decisions about what to invest in the round(s) that follow.

Restoring land

By the third and final round (the period 1960–2010), some of the planets may be in trouble. Having nearly run out of land (cushions), they realize that money alone is not going to win them the game. Fortunately, there is a way for groups to recover land so that their planets are not completely wiped out: cushions can be gained back by giving a certain number of beads to the bank. This represents spending money on pollution cleanup and land restoration in order to undo some of the damage that has been done in previous rounds. (Refer to the "Land Restoration" column on the Planet Transit Accounting chart for the suggested number of beads to be paid for each cushion regained.) In addition to paying fees, the groups are required to state their plan for land restoration (e.g., planting trees) or for making changes to reduce the impact of an industry (e.g., switching to cleaner manufacturing processes or reusing waste byproducts).

The opportunity for land restoration takes place *before* investing in round three; therefore, there is no chance to fix environmental damage resulting from decisions made in the third round. However, before the third-round purchase of industries commences, students are informed that in this final round green technology options are available for each industry. They may pay the regular purchase price of one bead per industry, or they may opt to pay the higher green technology price (as shown on the Planet Transit Accounting chart). If they choose green technologies, the environmental impacts of the industries they invest in will be halved. This instigates discussion of the costs and benefits of their investments.

Planets in transit

A twist occurs at the end of the final round when the groups are ordered to move from their cushions to the planet next door. This can evoke mixed emotions or outright chaos, as some students will have identified strongly with their objectives and be very angry to be forced to live on a planet their neighbors were controlling — and destroying (some planets might not even exist anymore!). Of course, the opposite may also be true. This finale raises discussion of not-in-my-backyard attitudes, of disparities in access to natural resources, and our collective responsibility for the management of resources.

Debriefing

The results of each round and the responses of students throughout the game provide great points for discussion.

As a first debriefing point, ask students how they felt when they were asked to move to the other planet. Then ask how the move to another planet represents living together on Earth. We all live on the same planet and rely on the same resources for survival, yet some use (and abuse) more than others. Refer to the concept of the "tragedy of the commons:" that we all suffer the consequences of development that damages our shared natural resources.

An effective way to extend the discussion is with a recap of comments made by students during the game. These are comments that the facilitator has heard and recorded as students discussed their investments and responded to the resulting profits and penalties. Discuss the concept of carrying capacity: of having limited land for producing what we need and absorbing our wastes. This can be linked with an ecological footprint calculation (using, for example, an online calculator) or lead to a follow-up project on ways to reduce what we consume and waste on the planet. Discussion can also include national policies and international agreements on the protection of species and natural areas, trade, and greenhouse gas emissions. Finally, discus-

sion can touch on green technologies and the short term and long term costs and benefits of our choices.

Variation: The Industry Cards provided may be substituted with others that are more relevant to your area. An alternative is to work as a class at the beginning of each round to create a list of industries that reflect that era and to determine appropriate profits for each. The facilitator playing the role of Environmental Impact Agent will need to determine the environmental impact penalties of the industries in order to keep these hidden from the groups until the end of the round. This can be a spontaneous, creative and enjoyable way to play.

Georgi Marshall has spent the past ten years working in the fields of environmental education, waste management and community development in Australia, Southeast Asia, Africa and Canada. She currently resides in Tasmania, where she runs an organization developing pedal-powered activities and technology for community sustainability, energy awareness and health.

Planet Transit Accounting

Round 1 Industries 1900–1920	Profit (beads)	Environmental Impact (EI) penalty (cushions)	Land Restoration (LR) fee (beads/cushion)	
Cattle Farm	2	1	4	
Coal Mine	6	4	6	
Craft Making	1			
Market Vending	1			
Produce Farm	1			
Sawmill	4	2	8	
Round 2 Industries 1920–1960				
Cement Factory	5	2	5	
Fish Canning Company	5	2	5	
Fruit Farm	4	2	4	
Furniture Manufacturing	2			
Hydroelectric Plant	9	4	8	
Pulp and Paper Mill	8	4	7	
Restaurant	3	1	3	
Round 3 Industries 1960–2010				**Green Technology (GT) price (beads)**
Car Manufacturing	10	5		5
Chemical Company	12	5		6
Hotel Chain	12	4		6
Tourism Operation	8	2		4

Industry Cards

Round One (1900–1920)

Cattle Farm: As a cattle farmer, you work long hours and constantly struggle to keep your cattle fed. However, you love working on the land and you are your own boss.
Profit: 2 beads

Market Vending: Working in the local market, you sell products made in your community. You can sell fruits and vegetables when they are in season and you use banana leaves to wrap your products.
Profit: 1 bead

Coal Mine: You have tapped into a fairly new resource that has a high rate of return. You can employ many people for a relatively low wage. However, the work can be dangerous and often people are killed in accidents at the mine.
Profit: 6 beads

Produce Farm: As a farmer, you work long hours and are in constant struggle with weather and insects. It is the only life you have known as you carry on the traditions handed down from your father.
Profit: 1 bead

Craft Making: You weave baskets and brooms from reeds growing on the riverbank and sell them around the city. You make enough money to buy produce, but you also depend on fishing for sustenance and you trade fish for other goods.
Profit: 1 bead

Sawmill: There is always a demand for wood and there seems to be enough wood to keep your company in business for a long time.
Profit: 4 beads

Round Two (1920–1960)

Cement Factory: The construction business is booming and your company can barely keep up with the demand for cement. However, the river sand is being depleted in the area you have been dredging, so you will have to relocate in order to find more sand.
Profit: 5 beads

Furniture Manufacturing: This small company uses local resources and employs local people.
Profit: 2 beads

Round Two (1920–1960)
(continued)

Pulp and Paper Mill: Your industry cuts down a great deal of timber and uses huge amounts of water from the river and does not always put the water back the way it found it. However, you create a lot of employment and your profits are high.
Profit: 8 beads

Fruit Farm: Your company is known worldwide and makes a good profit, but you use lots of fertilizers and pesticides to keep production levels up.
Profit: 4 beads

Hydroelectric Plant: This industry dams rivers in order to generate power to satisfy the demand electricity. Although it is very profitable, the impact on the environment is big.
Profit: 9 beads

Fish Canning Company: You use many natural resources in your production, but you employ many people and the profit is good.
Profit: 5 beads

Restaurant: Yours is a small but successful restaurant business. You buy food and supplies from the local market.
Profit: 3 beads

Round Three (1960–2010)

Car Manufacturing: The number of cars on the road is growing and your company is starting to introduce more fuel-efficient models, but this will have an impact on your profit because it takes research and time. You think that, in the long run, your company will remain competitive.
Profit: 10 beads / EI: 5 cushions / GT: 5 beads

Hotel Chain: You have a big chain of posh resorts that cater to the very rich. You use energy-efficient bulbs to cut costs, but the waste and sewage produced in your properties is more than you can deal with and much of it is disposed of improperly.
Profit 12 beads / EI: 4 cushions / GT: 6 beads

Chemical Company: Your company is a key player in supplying chemicals to a variety of other industries, such as paint companies and prescription drug manufacturers.
Profit: 12 beads / EI: 5 cushions / GT: 6 beads

Tourism Operation: You are a new operator in a very competitive business. In order to establish yourself, you offer a different type of "eco" adventure, taking tourists on expeditions "off the beaten track" into remote wilderness areas. Your business is getting bigger.
Profit: 8 beads / EI: 2 cushions / GT: 4 beads

Global Morning:
A Consumer Awareness Activity

by Mary Gale Smith

Subject areas: home economics/family studies, business education, social studies

Key concepts: implications of consumer choice, social justice

Skills: critical thinking, locating countries on a map

Location: classroom

Time: one hour for the activity, one or more classes for follow up

Materials: map of the world, push pins or tacks, ball of yarn, copies of the scripts, (optional) examples of products mentioned in the script to be used as props during the reading

Tom Goldsmith

C onsumer goods link us to all parts of the world. Yet, as consumers, we tend to buy what we want without much thought of where the goods come from or the consequences of our choices in human, environmental, social and economic terms. This activity is designed to raise students' awareness of the extent of our global interdependence and to encourage responsible consumer action. It begins with the reading of a script that tracks the origin and impacts of products used or consumed by a typical North American on a typical workday morning. The script is a springboard for discussing the implications of our choices as consumers and the questions we can ask and the actions we·can take to become more informed and responsible consumers.

Global Morning script

The Global Morning script has two alternating parts. One part is a first-person narrative describing a typical morning routine, from waking up and eating breakfast to leaving for work or school. The other part is a commentary that examines the origins and impact of the products used or consumed during that typical morning. The script can be read in various ways; for example:

• Four students may present the script in front of the class. One student reads the narrative script, stopping at the end of each numbered sentence or phrase. At each pause, the second student says, "Stop!" and then reads the corresponding commentary. The third student locates the countries mentioned on a map and marks them with a pushpin or tack. The fourth connects the pins by winding a piece of string or yarn from each pin back to the home country.

• The class can be divided into groups of three, and each group assigned to prepare and present one of the sections of the script. One student in each group reads the narrative part, one reads the commentary, and one locates the places on the map.

As an alternative to reading the commentary script provided here, students could be assigned to research, write and present their own commentary on the consumer goods mentioned in the narrative.

Part one: Narration

1. I awoke this morning at seven o'clock to the ringing of my alarm clock.

2. I padded across my warm rug ...

3 ... pulled on a track suit, laced up my cross-trainers and went for my morning run.

4. Returning home, I showered and cleaned up.

5. Then I dressed quickly in my favorite cotton T-shirt and blue jeans.

6. I boiled water for my coffee (or cocoa), sliced a banana over my bran flakes, spread peanut butter on my toast, and then sat down to eat breakfast.

7. Shortly after 8:30, I grabbed my eco-fleece jacket.

8. I left home and drove to a nearby gas station.

9. While driving to work (or school), I tuned my new portable media player to the music I had recently downloaded to make the trip more enjoyable.

10. In just a few hours of my life, I have consumed raw materials from most parts of the world and used products made in many places both locally and globally. I have depended on the rest of the world. I have made global connections.

Part two: Commentary

I awoke this morning at seven o'clock to the ringing of my alarm clock.

1. Stop! You have just encountered the global. Your clock was assembled in Brazil from components produced in Japan, Mexico and Germany. It was shipped from Brazil to Canada in a Greek-owned ship that was manufactured in Sweden, licensed in Liberia and staffed by a Portuguese crew.[1]

I padded across my warm rug . . .

2. Stop! Your warm carpet was made in either India or Pakistan in a carpet industry that uses bonded child labor. In theory, these children are working to pay off loans made to their parents, but in reality the children are slaves because the terms of the loans make them debts that can never be repaid. The children are exploited because they are the cheapest labor available and because they have nimble fingers, keen eyesight and the ability to sit in the same position for hours. Frequently such working conditions lead to leg and back deformities, water retention in the knees, swelling or infection in the fingers, breathing problems, lung infections and tuberculosis.[2]

. . . pulled on a track suit, laced up my cross trainers and went for my morning run.

3. Stop! You are now wearing the global. Your track suit may have been made in an export-processing zone in the Philippines by women working in factories where conditions contravene Article 23 of the United Nations Declaration of Human Rights, the right to just and favorable conditions of work. These women work long hours for extremely low wages under a quota system, in conditions that include crowding, insufficient ventilation, exposure to health risks such as chemicals and airborne fibers, and physical abuse. They have few breaks for attending to physical needs. If they complain, they are fired.[3]

Your training shoes may have been made by children in Indonesia's large footwear industry, where thousands of children work at gluing shoes in poorly ventilated workshops. The glues contain dangerous chemical substances that can cause headaches, addiction and serious health problems. Most of the children have dropped out of school in order to help support their families.[4]

Returning home, I showered and cleaned up.

4. Stop! Some of your shower products are made by multinational corporations that also manufacture environmentally unsustainable products (e.g., disposable diapers) or are involved in practices that are morally and legally questionable (e.g., marketing infant formula as a replacement for breast milk in developing countries, where mothers may have no choice but to mix the formula with contaminated water or dilute it to make it last longer, which can result in disease and death).[5]

However, some of your shower products are made by companies that are committed to social responsibility and environmental sustainability. By choosing to purchase these products, you are supporting companies that are working to reduce the environmental impact of their operations and to ensure fair wages and healthy working conditions for those who make their products.

Then I dressed quickly in my favorite cotton T-shirt and blue jeans.

5. Stop! Again you are wearing the global. Your T-shirt was made by the largest manufacturer of cotton T-shirts in North America. The cotton was grown in the United States, spun into yarn in Canada, and then shipped to Honduras where it was knitted, dyed, cut and sewn. This company has been very successful because it has adopted the strategy of using cheap labor in the maquiladoras[6] of Mexico, Central America and the Caribbean. Workers get paid about ten dollars a day if they meet production targets, but the targets are often much higher than is possible to complete in an eight-hour day.[7]

Your blue jeans, like your T-shirt, were made of cotton grown in the United States. The cotton industry uses enormous quantities of water and more pesticides than are used on any other crop. Your jeans were produced in Mexico, where the majority of the workers live in poverty because their wages are so low they cannot afford basic necessities. Mexico's lax enforcement of environmental laws allows textile companies to dump dyes into lakes and rivers, polluting the groundwater that supplies nearby farms. Every day, workers are exposed to toxic substances, such as fumes from caustic soda and chlorine, and are in contact with enzymes, detergents, peroxide, oxalic acid and sodium bisulphate used to bleach, shrink, soften and texturize the denim fabric.[8]

I boiled water for my coffee (or cocoa), sliced a banana over my bran flakes, spread peanut butter on my toast, and then sat down to eat breakfast.

6. Stop! You are now eating the global. The peanuts may have come from Senegal, the coffee from Colombia, Costa Rica, Peru or Ethiopia, and your cocoa from the Côte d'Ivoire. The sugar may have come from the Dominican Republic, but more likely it is a domestic product made from sugar beets rather than sugar cane. The banana came from Honduras, one of several Central American countries that have been called "banana republics" because their economies, which are dominated by large foreign companies, depend on one main export crop, such as bananas. The banana producers in these countries receive only a small fraction of every dollar

that we spend on bananas.[9] In developing countries, sugar, peanuts, coffee, cocoa and bananas are examples of cash crops that are often grown on land previously used for subsistence farming. No longer able to grow their own food, farmers are forced to buy food, but often cannot afford to do so.[10]

The rising demand worldwide for coffee and chocolate has many environmental and social consequences. Coffee and cocoa farmers are usually paid a pittance for their beans, and the profits go to food processors and distributors in wealthy countries. In the Côte d'Ivoire, the world's largest producer of cocoa, low cocoa prices drive farmers to employ children because they are the cheapest labor available. Between 100,000 and 200,000 children work in the Côte d'Ivoire's cocoa industry, about ten percent of them victims of human trafficking or enslavement.[11] By buying fairly traded coffee and chocolate, consumers can guarantee that farmers get a fair price and do not exploit their laborers. Some fairly traded coffee is "shade grown" under the canopy of the rain forest, rather than on cleared land. This maintains the forest for migratory songbirds, so you may find shade-grown coffee advertised as being "bird friendly."

Your cereal and toast are products of North America, and the organic milk for your cereal came from a local dairy. In choosing local and organic products, you are avoiding the environmental costs of long distance transportation and supporting sustainable agriculture.

Shortly after 8:30 I grabbed my new eco-fleece jacket.

7. Stop! Your new jacket was made by a clothing company in California that is trying to minimize the environmental impact of its operations. The eco-fleece fabric is made of used plastic pop bottles that have been cleaned, melted down and extruded into fibers that can be spun into yarn. It took about 25 two-liter clear plastic bottles to make the fabric for your jacket.[12] Recycling the bottles in this way means that less plastic ends up in landfill sites.

I left home and drove to a nearby gas station.

8. Stop! Now you are driving the global. The average car contains as many as 30,000 parts that come from all over the world. The glass and the radio may have come from the United States or Canada, the cylinder head, carburetor and headlights from Italy, the starter, alternator and windshield washer pump from Japan, and the battery and mirrors from Spain.[13] The gas you buy was extracted and refined in your country, but the price you pay for it is influenced by weather, wars and other events in oil-producing nations around the world. You

save money, however, because your car is a new gas–electric hybrid that is three times more fuel-efficient than a typical sports utility vehicle.

While driving to work (or school), I tuned my new portable media player to the music I had recently downloaded to make the trip more enjoyable.

9. Stop! Your old media player is probably languishing in a landfill, contributing to the ever-increasing problem of toxic waste. Many electronics manufacturers are being pressured to take back and recycle their products. By downloading music, you are reducing your consumption of the energy and raw materials used in manufacturing and packaging compact disks, and keeping these materials from ending up in a landfill.[14]

In just a few hours of my life, I have consumed raw materials from most parts of the world and used products made in many places both locally and globally. I have depended on the rest of the world. I have made global connections.

10. Stop! Let's consider how our consumer choices affect the environment and other people. We need to purchase goods in order to live, but what are the implications of our choices?

Debriefing

After the script has been read, debrief the activity by asking questions such as the following:

1. How do your consumer decisions affect the lives of others?

2. How do consumer decisions affect our lives?

3. What assumptions guide our purchases? For example, do we assume that cheaper is better, or is it more important to ensure that people are treated fairly and the environment is not harmed? What values form the foundation of these assumptions?

4. What does it mean to be a globally responsible consumer? Do we have an ethical obligation to be globally responsible consumers? Can we afford to be globally responsible consumers?

5. What should be done about the negative effects of consumerism? How could we change our consumer habits to make them more environmentally and socially responsible?

Becoming informed consumers

In this activity, students brainstorm questions that they think should be asked (and researched) before

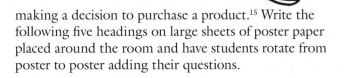

Tom Goldsmith

making a decision to purchase a product.[15] Write the following five headings on large sheets of poster paper placed around the room and have students rotate from poster to poster adding their questions.

Environmental (e.g., Does producing, packaging, transporting or disposing of the product pollute the environment or draw excessively on non-renewable resources?)

Economic (e.g., Did the growers or producers get a fair wage for their labor? Does purchase of the product help to support local economies in the place or origin? Who is profiting? Is anyone losing out?)

Social (e.g., Was the product produced by child labor? Does the product enhance the quality of life of the individual or society using it? Does the company's advertising of the product undermine cultural values or stereotype any group on the basis of gender, ethnicity or other characteristic?)

Legal (e.g., Does the company respect trade union rights? Is the product being "dumped" — that is, sold for less than fair market value — in other countries, making it impossible for producers there to compete? Are environmental laws being violated?)

Health (e.g., Does use of the product damage people's health? Does its production expose workers to toxins or otherwise cause them ill health? Will disposal of the product threaten the health of humans or animals, or contaminate water, air or soil?)

Taking action

Have students brainstorm actions that we can take to become responsible consumers. This may be done as a group activity, with each group recording their suggestions on chart paper that can be posted for sharing. The following list of actions has been compiled from a variety of sources[16] and can be used to supplement the actions suggested by students. Each action suggested could be examined for its consequences to oneself and others.

• Buy less and live more simply.

• Increase your knowledge by researching the products you use.

• Support alternative trading organizations.

• Buy locally from cooperatives and small businesses.

• Boycott companies that act unethically and products that are over-packaged or cannot be recycled. Write letters to companies informing them of your choice not to purchase their products and explaining why.

• Boycott products from countries that do not protect the environment or the rights of their citizens.

• Penalize pollution by buying environment-friendly products.

• Lobby politicians and government officials to change laws and regulations that are unjust or damage the environment.

• Give and invest with thought, supporting socially and globally responsible organizations and investments.

• Join organizations that take action for the betterment of human beings and the environment.

Other follow-up activities

1. Students could review the Global Morning script and, for each seemingly negative example, make suggestions for more environmental, socially just choices (e.g., instead of driving, take public transport, walk or bike; when purchasing T-shirts and jeans, look for "union made" or "organic cotton" on the label; substitute locally grown fruit for bananas).

2. Students could choose a particular consumer item to research and write a report using the title "What if _____ could talk?" The task would be to the follow item from cradle to grave.

3. Students could choose or be assigned topics to research, such as the following:

• Research a particular corporation to see if it has developed a code of corporate social responsibility or conducted an environmental assessment of its operations.

• Research organizations or communities that have initiated "Sweat Free" or "No Sweat" policies and find out what these policies entail.

• Investigate advocacy organizations that are committed to ethical principles and social justice (e.g., Free the Children, No Sweat Apparel, Maquila Solidarity Network, European Clean Clothes Campaign, Ethical Trading Action Group, Labour Behind the Label, Transfair, Oxfam).

Mary Gale Smith teaches at the Faculty of Education at the University of British Columbia in Vancouver. This activity is a modification of "A Day In My Life" by Graham Pike and David Selby, in Global Teacher Global Learner, *Hodder and Stoughton, 1988.*

Notes

1. Graham Pike and David Selby, *Global Teacher Global Learner*, Hodder and Stoughton, 1988, p. 288.

2. Linda Peterat, *Work: Children, Women, and Men in Families*, Canadian Home Economics Association, 1991, pp. 22–23; Moira Farrow, "By buying that oriental rug, you might be helping to enslave a child," *The Vancouver Sun*, March 8, 1992, p. B2; Canadian student Craig Kielburger founded Free the Children in response to the murder of a 12-year-old bonded laborer from Pakistan who spoke out against child slavery. The organization works to free children from abuse and exploitation and to provide them with educational opportunities. See <www.freethechildren. org>.

3. Lorraine Gray, director, *The Global Assembly Line* (film), Educational TV and Film Centre, 1986.

4. International Labour Organization, "Fighting Child Labour in Indonesia: ILO Launches New Programme," May 5, 2004 (online August 15, 2008, <www.ilo.org>).

5. Ben Corsen, Alice Tepper Marlin, Jonathan Schorsch, Anita Swaminathan and Rosalyn Will, *Shopping for a Better World*, Ballentine, 1990. See also John Elkington and Julia Hailes, *The Green Consumer's Supermarket Shopping Guide*, Victor Gallancz, 1989; and Joan Helson, Kelly Green, David Nitkin and Amy Stein, *The Ethical Shopper's Guide to Canadian Supermarket Products*, Broadview Press, 1992.

6. The term *maquiladora* was originally associated with milling, but is now used to refer to product-assembly factories in Mexico, Central America and the Caribbean. Maquiladoras began in Mexico over 30 years ago when the Mexican government allowed U.S. firms to set up assembly plants on the Mexican side of the border, import raw materials and components duty-free, have them assembled by local workers, and then export the finished products back to the U.S. For manufacturing companies, the benefits of the maquiladoras are low wages, a lack of environmental or labor

regulations, low taxes, and few if any import duties. Some of the products assembled in these factories are apparel, electronic goods and auto parts. Source: <www.maquilasolidarity.org/>, website of the Maquila Solidarity Network.

7. Maquila Solidarity Network and the Honduran Independent Monitoring Team, *A Canadian Success Story? Gildan Activewear: T-shirts, Free Trade and Worker Rights*, Maquila Solidarity Network, 2003; see also Peterat, p. 47.

8. See Maquila Solidarity Network and The Human and Labour Rights Commission of the Tehuacan Valley, *Tehuacan: Blue Jeans, Blue Waters and Worker Rights*, Maquila Solidarity Network, 2003; "The Big Jeans Stitch-up," *New Internationalist* 302, June, 1998; Maquila Solidarity Network, "The Journey of a Jean," February 2, 2007 (online August 15, 2008, < http://en.maquilasolidarity.org/en/node/677>); and Tanya Lloyg Kyi, *The Blue Jean Book: The Story Behind the Seams*, Annick Press, 2005.

9. Philip White, *The Supermarket Tour*, Ontario Public Interest Research Group, 1990, p. 15.

10. Linda Peterat, *Food Security and Staple Foods and Food Forms: Choices, Changes and Challenges*, Canadian Home Economics Association, 1991; see also Anup Shah, *Behind Consumption and Consumerism*, 2005 (online March 29, 2007, <www.globalissues.org/TradeRelated/Consumption.asp>).

11. Rupert Taylor, ed., "Food," *Canada and the World* 57:2, 1991, pp. 14–31; *Birdsong & Coffee: A Wake Up Call* (film), Old Dog Documentaries, 2006; Save the Children Canada, *Children Still in the Chocolate Trade: The Buying Selling and Toiling of West African Children in the Multi-Billion Dollar Industry*, 2003 (online May 4, 2007, <www.savethechildren.ca>). For information on fair trade products, see TransFair Canada <http://transfair.ca> or TransFair USA <http://transfairusa.org>.

12. John Flinn, "Want to be ultra-chic? Then try the sweater that's simply garbage," *The Vancouver Sun*, September 21, 1993.

13. Nigel Harris, "Halfway to Liberation," *New Internationalist* 204, February 1990, pp. 18–20.

14. National Geographic, *The Green Guide*, <www.thegreenguide.com>.

15. Linda Lusby, "The New Consumerism," Canadian Home Economics Association, March 1991.

16. See David McConkey, *Choices: A Family Global Action Handbook*, Star Printing, 1987; Philip White, *The Supermarket Tour*; and S. Shaw, "Shopping for the Planet: The Green Consumer," *New Internationalist* 203, January 1990, pp. 4–23.

References

Print

Brower, M. and L. Wade, *The Consumer's Guide to Effective Environmental Choice: Practical advice from the Union of Concerned Scientists*. Three Rivers Press, 1999.

Goodwin, N., F. Ackerman and D. Kiron, eds. *The Consumer Society*. Island Press, 1997.

Menxel, P. *Material World: A Global Family Portrait*. Sierra Club Books, 1994.

Ryan, J. *Seven Wonders: Everyday Things for a Healthier Planet*. Random House, 1999.

Ryan, J. and A. Durning. *Stuff: The Secret Lives of Everyday Things*. Northwest Environmental Watch, 1997

Wackernagel, M. and W. Rees. *Our Ecological Footprint: Reducing Human Impact on the Earth*. New Society Publishers, 1996.

Websites

<www.davidsuzuki.org> The website of the David Suzuki Foundation has information on environmental issues and reducing our ecological footprint.

<www.worldwatch.org/pubs/goodstuff/> Worldwatch Institute, *Good Stuff? A Behind-the-Scenes Guide to the Things We Buy*.

<www.youthxchange.net/main/home.asp> The youthXchange website, sponsored by UNESCO and UNEP, has a variety of world statistics and other information to assist youth groups, NGOs and teachers in raising awareness of sustainable consumption.

The Debate About Hemp:
A Role Play

In this role play, students explore the controversy surrounding the commercialization of industrial hemp. This format could be used for researching points of view surrounding any controversial issue.

Lambton County Museum

by Sara Francis

Subject areas: social studies, environmental science

Key concepts: propaganda, THC, crop yields, overproduction, self-sufficiency, advocates, legalization, multiple perspectives

Skills: debating, critical thinking, character development

Location: indoors

Time: 70 minutes for role play; additional time for optional prior research

ndustrial hemp is a crop that has the potential to alleviate several environmental problems, yet this potential is constrained by its association with its recreational cousin, marijuana. The issue of legalizing hemp production has generated much discussion in recent years, and there is no better way to learn about it in a classroom than through a mock debate. Through developing characters whose opinions represent real positions in the hemp debate, students are able to explore the issues and to arrive at their own perspectives on the future of hemp.

This mock debate has been used with a class of first-year environmental science students at the post-secondary level, but could be undertaken successfully by students in Grades 9–12. The characters include environmentalists, hemp business entrepreneurs, people opposed to pesticide use, lumberjacks and woodlot

Hemp requires no pesticides and can be made into fabrics that are stronger and more absorbent than cotton.

owners, pulp and paper company owners, petroleum company owners, farmers, representatives from the government agencies for health and agriculture, anti-drug lobbyists, and a hippie still living in the Sixties (this is always the most entertaining character, although closely rivaled by the lumberjack!). There may be complaints when someone is assigned a character whose point of view is contrary to their own, but in my experience, these are the same students who, at the end of the activity, say they had the most fun and learned the most from having to defend a different perspective.

Before starting the debate, students will need time to develop their roles, based on the character sketches provided. Note that the roles are deliberately opinionated! Students should first read the section "Industrial hemp: background notes," which provides basic information that will help them develop their characters' positions. Ideally, time can then be allocated for additional research (see Resources section) that will enable participants to strengthen their characters further. The entire activity could be undertaken in one class period; in that case, the teacher will likely need to intervene from time to time with extra information.

Hemp has a fascinating history on this continent and a potential to help solve some of our most serious environmental problems. This activity will provide teachers and students alike with the opportunity to make an informed decision on the agricultural production of industrial hemp.

Industrial hemp: background notes

In 1994, researchers in Canada began raising the first legal crops of industrial hemp to be grown in North America in nearly 50 years. This agricultural research, done under strict permits from Health Canada, was followed in 1998 by the Industrial Hemp Program, under which farmers in Canada may obtain licenses to grow hemp commercially. In recent years, a few states in the U.S. have passed similar legislation. Despite the fact that hemp is only now being reintroduced, it has a lengthy history in North America, reportedly beginning in the Acadian region of Nova Scotia when Jacques Cartier's apothecary brought hemp seeds from Europe in 1606. During the 1600s, the new colonies in North America were under contract to supply hemp fiber for the sails and rigging used on the ships of the French and British navies. By 1630, hemp had become a staple crop in both the United States and Canada, and many hemp farmers and mills prospered. The long outer fibers of the plant were used to make clothing, cordage and paper, and its seeds and oil were used for cooking and lighting.

Hemp continued to be a profitable crop until the late 1700s. However, with the advent of steam power, which reduced the need for sails and rope, and with the invention of the mechanical cotton gin, which made cotton fiber more cost-efficient than the more labor-intensive hemp fiber, the market for hemp declined. Demand for hemp fiber was further threatened by the development of chemical–mechanical processes of pulping trees for fiber. Similarly, the invention of synthetic materials made from petroleum reduced the market for hemp cellulose and hemp seed oil.

Industrial hemp farming might have remained uneconomical had it not been for the invention, in 1917, of a fiber-separating machine called a decorticator. This device reduced the labor needed to separate hemp fibers and made available the previously unused short-fiber core of the hemp stock. These new efficiencies in processing hemp offered the potential of hundreds of new hemp products and promised farmers a "new billion-dollar crop."

The resurgence of industrial hemp in the 1920s was short-lived, however. It is now believed that leaders in the chemical and pulp and paper industries, threatened by hemp's new industrial possibilities, set about

Left and right: Hempola Valley Farms, oilseedworks.com; center: Sara Francis

Hemp seed oil is used in food, cosmetics, paints, fuel and biodegradable plastics.

to discredit it by equating it in the public mind with its recreational cousin, marijauna. Up until that time, the clear distinction between industrial hemp and marijuana had always been acknowledged. While both varieties are known in scientific terms as *Cannabis sativa L.*, industrial hemp has little or none of the chemical tetrahydrocannabinol (THC) that gives marijuana its recreational and pharmaceutical potential. The lower level of THC in industrial hemp (one percent or less) is a natural genetic variation developed through selective breeding, and it eliminates the possibility of the plant being used for recreational purposes.

Despite this known difference between industrial hemp and marijuana, there were massive propaganda campaigns in the United States during the late 1920s and early 1930s to incite fear of marijuana and to convince the public and the government that industrial hemp and marijuana were the same thing. Stories appeared in newspapers about immigrants smoking marijuana and subsequently stealing, vandalizing and even committing murder. Such stories, now believed to be fabricated, made their way to Canada where there were debates in the House of Commons about the danger of marijuana falling into the hands of children.

In 1937, the United States enacted the Marihuana Tax Act to ban marijuana. Although the Act was not intended to interfere with industrial hemp, its effect was to create so much suspicion and red tape that hemp farms and factories were put out of business. Canada followed suit in 1938, banning both the recreational and industrial varieties of *Cannabis sativa*. In both countries, the possibility for further development of a legitimate industrial hemp industry was eliminated, and the distinction between industrial and recreational hemp was blurred in the public mind. It is this failure to distinguish between the two varieties that is the cause of the present controversy.

Hemp today . . . and tomorrow?

This "billion-dollar crop" is now beginning to resurface as farmers look for new sources of income and North Americans become more concerned about the

environmental degradation caused by the pulp and paper industry. The attention that hemp is gaining is in large part due to its potential as an alternative to wood-fiber paper and petroleum-based products. Hemp plants produce two types of fiber, bast and hurds, which have different uses. Bast fiber is a material of very high quality that can be used in textiles and premium paper products. The hurds can also be used for paper, as well as for animal bedding, insulation and construction materials. Some construction materials made from hemp are twice as strong as wood and concrete. Hemp seeds can be eaten or crushed for oil that can then be used in food, cosmetics, paints and other commercial products, such as clean-burning diesel fuel and biodegradable plastics. It is estimated that hemp has thousands of commercial uses.

An exciting aspect of the hemp plant is that it has the potential to alleviate some environmental problems. One of the main problems associated with pulping tree fiber is the use of chlorine compounds to dissolve lignin, the organic glue in wood, and to bleach the fibers white. Hemp contains less lignin than wood, and its fibers are naturally light in color, thus reducing the need for dissolving and bleaching compounds. Where bleaching is required, hydrogen peroxide has been shown to be a less damaging but effective agent.

Another major advantage of growing hemp instead of trees is its superior yield. One hectare of farmland can produce approximately 10 metric tons of hemp (total dry matter) in one year. In the same time, one hectare of softwood forest produces less than two metric tons of fiber. Put another way, one hectare of hemp annually yields five times as much fiber as one acre of trees of harvestable age (trees require a minimum of 20 years' growth for paper purposes.) As the public becomes more aware of the soil erosion and the loss of wildlife habitat and water quality caused by the pulp and paper industry, more attention may be paid to hemp as a less harmful alternative.

Besides attractive yields, hemp offers other environmental advantages for those concerned about conventional farming practices. Hemp requires less water

(continued on page 138)

Roles in the Hemp Debate

Industrial hemp advocate

• You firmly believe that hemp can replace any product made out of trees or petroleum.
• The legalization of industrial hemp will greatly improve environmental quality, as the plant is naturally resistant to disease and requires no pesticides, herbicides or genetic modification
• The best fertilizer for hemp is animal manure; hemp growing therefore provides a "sink" for this resource.
• You see numerous possibilities for hemp to create new industries that will provide new jobs and a better economy.
• You are able to distinguish between industrial hemp and recreational marijuana. While you would not object to legalizing marijuana, this is not the focus of your debate.

Member of the public opposed to the legalization of hemp

• You are fundamentally against legalization of hemp, whether it is industrial hemp or recreational hemp.
• You believe that the legalization of industrial hemp will make it easy for people to grow recreational hemp hidden within the crop.
• You believe this supply of illegal recreational hemp will find its way into the hands of children.
• You believe that people will try to smoke industrial hemp products (paper, clothing).
• You know that a marijuana crop will bring in much more money than an industrial hemp crop, and you doubt that farmers would bother to grow industrial hemp.

Lumberjack

• You have worked in the forests all your life and you love your job. You are not prepared to give it up to grow hemp.
• You don't want to see yourself and your friends lose their jobs because of industrial hemp production.
• You do not believe that hemp is the miracle crop. You are skeptical of the claims that hemp does not require pesticides and herbicides.
• You are concerned about the environmental implications of growing hemp, such as the energy required for harvesting and the toll on the land from continuous farming. Hemp is an annual crop that is harvested every year, whereas trees are harvested at a minimum age of 20 years.

Rural entrepreneur or worker

• You want to initiate a rural development project in the town where you grew up.
• You are excited about the possibilities of hemp: you think that the farmers in this town could cultivate hemp and sell it to a nearby textile plant.
• This would be a new type of farm community, where all the farmers operate in a co-operative.
• This could be a welcome economic opportunity for this community, bringing lots of jobs and money.

Woodlands manager at a pulp and paper company / Owner of a small woodlot

• You do not see anything wrong with growing and harvesting trees. They are a renewable and sustainable crop.
• You do not believe there are any negative environmental effects associated with intensive forest management.
• You believe that herbicides and pesticides are needed to ensure optimum conditions for growth.
• You believe that clear-cutting is the best method of harvesting trees and managing the land.
• You do not believe that hemp will ever be able to supply all the pulp needed in your province or state
• You are worried that if pulp mills convert to hemp you will be out of a job.

Tobacco farmer

• Your family has been farming for generations and you would like to continue farming in order to support your family.
• You are looking for a new crop to grow because tobacco is no longer profitable for your 100-hectare farm. You could make about $750 per hectare for hemp fiber.
• You need to improve your soil's fertility, and hemp may be the crop that can do this.
• Hemp chokes out weeds and its deep taproots break apart the soil, allowing greater access to nutrients.

Hemp advocate still living in the Sixties

• You would like both industrial and recreational hemp to be legalized.
• You are often accused of supporting the industrial hemp lobby only because you really want recreational hemp legalized.

Environmentalist concerned about the loss of forests

• You are looking for an alternative to using trees to make paper.
• You believe that intensive forest management (which includes clear-cutting) has numerous negative environmental effects. These include soil erosion, stream sedimentation and the intensive use of pesticides and herbicides.
• As an annual crop, hemp can provide more fiber in one year than an equal area of harvestable 20-year-old trees. You believe that switching from wood fiber to hemp fiber for paper products can increase fiber production while helping to preserve forest lands.
• You are impressed by the fact that hemp requires no pesticides or herbicides, and that animal manure can provide sufficient fertilizer for its growth.
• You are impressed that paper made from hemp fiber requires fewer chemicals for bleaching and processing than paper made from tree fiber.
• You are annoyed by those who cannot separate industrial hemp from the issue of recreational hemp.

Department of Agriculture policy advisor

• You are intrigued by new developments and opportunities surrounding industrial hemp.
• You are extremely concerned about the social and economic welfare of farm workers.
• You are extremely concerned about the degradation of soil and are aware that intensive farming practices contribute to it.
• You are impressed that hemp improves soil quality and gets rid of weeds.
• You are concerned that if caution is not taken in legalizing hemp then recreational hemp will proliferate.

Department of Health policy advisor

• You played an important part in the development of the Industrial Hemp Regulations, which regulate the issuing of licenses to cultivate industrial hemp and include strict penalties for the cultivation of recreational hemp.
• You have influence with the Minister of Health, who in turn has the authority to create the regulatory framework under which fiber hemp may be grown.
• You are extremely cautious about legalizing industrial hemp.
• You want recreational hemp to remain illegal, with heavy fines or other penalties for its cultivation and use.

Owner of a pulp and paper company

• You feel threatened by the possibility that hemp fiber could replace tree fiber.
• The only way that you will support legalization of hemp is if you think it will benefit you.
• You may support the incorporation of hemp fiber into tree fiber if it would be profitable.
• You are not yet convinced that hemp is an ideal fiber for papermaking, and you don't want to invest in something that could prove to be only a fad.
• You do not want to sever your ties with the woodlot owners who supply you with wood fiber.

Environmentalist concerned about the use of pesticides in making cotton textiles

• Cotton production is one of the most chemically intensive agricultural processes. About half of the pesticides used in the United States are sprayed on cotton plants. Pesticides used on cotton may be contaminating groundwater as well as increasing cancer rates.
• Hemp can be used to make the same textiles as cotton, yet it does not require pesticides.
• Hemp fabrics are more effective than cotton in blocking ultraviolet light.
• Compared to cotton, hemp fiber is stronger, more lustrous and absorbent, and more mildew-resistant.

Entrepreneur / Inventor

• You are fascinated by the thousands of practical products that can be made from hemp.
• You are extremely anxious to have industrial hemp legalized so that you can start patenting products and make millions of dollars! (You should choose a hemp product and describe how you could develop it.)
• You may or may not have environmental concerns that are motivating your decision to make a certain product.

Owner of a petroleum company

• Your company supplies petroleum to the cosmetics industry.
• You think the legalization of hemp will severely threaten your industry because hemp oil may be substituted for petroleum. You will do anything to prevent hemp's legalization unless you see how it could be advantageous to you.
• Depending on the information presented during the debate, you may continue to oppose the legalization of hemp or you may be convinced otherwise.

than cotton and it has few natural pests, thus requiring fewer pesticides than cotton and many other crops. It grows so densely that it effectively chokes out competing plants, thus reducing or eliminating the need for herbicides. In fact, hemp was often grown to clear fields of weeds prior to planting other crops. The crop does require fertilizer to facilitate fast growth, but animal manure has been found to be the best fertilizer for hemp. This does not alleviate environmental problems associated with excess nitrogen, but it reduces the need for farmers to purchase chemical fertilizers.

Switching to hemp could also resolve another dilemma: North American farms produce too much food. Overproduction lowers farm gate prices and drives marginal farmland out of production. Thus hemp and other fiber crops, such as switchgrass, could invigorate the economies of less productive farm regions. Indeed, the fact that hemp is a bulky product to transport means that hemp fields and mills will have to be in close proximity. This could help to develop regional self-sufficiency.

Hemp advocates fear that if we do not develop a commercial hemp industry soon we will miss out on a huge economic opportunity. Many European countries have been growing commercial hemp for years; and while industrial hemp can now be grown in Canada and a few U.S. states, farmers operate under strict government regulations. It will be impossible to develop a hemp industry and define markets for hemp products until we are able to grow large-scale commercial plots. It is presently in the hands of the government to remove restrictions for commercial crops. Your participation in this debate will help to determine the future of industrial hemp in this country.

Sara Francis *lives in Dartmouth, Nova Scotia, where she works in the health and wellness field.*

Resources

Print

Herer, Jack. *The Emperor Wears No Clothes.* Online at <www.jackherer.com/chapters.html>. Information on all aspects of *Cannabis sativa L.*, making it a good place to start (but don't take everything at face value).

International Hemp Association. *Journal of Industrial Hemp.* Hayworth Press. Contains reports of current and scientific industrial research on hemp from around the world. IHA, Postbus 75007, 10710AA, Amsterdam, The Netherlands, <www.internationalhempassociation.org>.

Rosenthal, Ed. *Hemp Today.* Quick American Archives, 1994. Information on growing and processing industrial hemp.

Roulac, John. *Industrial Hemp: Practical Products — Paper to Fabric to Cosmetics* (3rd edition). Hemptech, 1998, <www.hemptech.com>. A handy little book chock full of information.

Websites

Search on "industrial hemp," as many websites cover both industrial and recreational hemp.

<www.agr.gc.ca> Agriculture Canada and <www.hc-sc.gc.ca>Health Canada. Background information on hemp and Canada's Industrial Hemp Regulations.

<www.hemptrade.ca> The Canadian Hemp Trade Alliance. A national coalition of farmers, processors, marketers and researchers; website contains information on products that can be made from hemp.

<www.thehia.org> Hemp Industries Association. A non-profit trade organization representing hemp companies and researchers; the website's education section has links to current news and research, resources for public education, and FAQs.

<www.votehemp.com> Vote Hemp. Reports and up-to-date information on legislation governing agricultural hemp.

Teaching About Biodiesel

Richard Lawrence

by Richard Lawrence

Subject areas: chemistry, automotive technology, plant science

Key concepts: renewable energy, transesterification

Skills: measurement, titration

Materials: research media, common and hybrid vehicles

As it becomes more and more obvious that our dependence on fossil fuels is fouling the air, endangering our health and changing the global climate, the quest for clean and renewable energy sources is underway. During the transition away from fossil fuels, teachers will play a critical role in educating about alternative forms of energy. Biodiesel is one renewable fuel that makes this learning fun and engaging. Students always enjoy the hands-on experience of making something useful, but how often do they get to start with a bucket of used fryer grease — crispy bits of French fries and all — and end up with a fuel that can power their car or school bus?

Running engines on vegetable oil is not a new concept. In fact, the original compression-ignition engine, designed in 1895 by Rudolf Diesel, ran on peanut oil. Since then, the diesel engine has been modified to use a dirty by-product of gasoline manufacturing — what we now call diesel fuel. Today's diesel engines can be operated on vegetable oil, but pure vegetable oil is too viscous to be used without modification of the engine. While it is neither practical nor economical to overhaul the millions of diesel engines currently in use, something can be done to lower the viscosity of the oil. Biodiesel is vegetable oil that is processed in order to break apart its molecules and reduce its viscosity, thereby becoming a fuel that can be used in any diesel engine, either alone or mixed in any proportion with regular petroleum diesel.

Making biodiesel

The making of biodiesel is a two-part process called transesterification. An alcohol such as methanol is mixed with a catalyst such as sodium hydroxide (lye) to make sodium methoxide. The methoxide is then mixed with vegetable oil, such as corn or soybean oil. In the resulting chemical reaction, the triglycerides that make up vegetable oil are broken down to produce methyl ester (biodiesel) and glycerol (glycerin). Glycerin, being the heavier of the two components, settles to the bottom of the vessel, allowing the biodiesel to be syphoned off the top. Biodiesel and its by-product, glycerin, are both compostable and safe to wash down the drain of any school laboratory — they might even clean out the pipes! Biodiesel is also the safest of all fuels to handle and store, due to its high flash point (150 °C), non-toxicity and biodegradability. But, of course, a much better way for students to "dispose" of biodiesel is to put it in the gas tank of any diesel-powered school bus or car.

National Renewable Energy Laboratory

While the process of making biodiesel is straightforward and requires only vegetable oil, alcohol, a catalyst and standard laboratory equipment, it does require safe handling of toxic substances (alcohol, lye and sodium methoxide) and knowledge of such procedures as titration. Teachers wishing to have students make small batches of biodiesel in the school laboratory are therefore advised to do some prior research to determine the method most appropriate for their students' skills. (See "Making Biodiesel from Waste Vegetable Oil," page 141.)

Biodiesel in the curriculum

Making fuel from waste vegetable oil is exciting and empowering for students. Once they have learned about the benefits of biodiesel, they may wish to put their knowledge to practical use by encouraging their school district and local government agencies to consider fueling their fleets with biodiesel. Since petroleum diesel exhaust is toxic and carcinogenic, and contributes heavily to global warming, biodiesel is an economical alternative for school bus fleets looking to clean up their act.

Science class is the most likely setting for learning about biodiesel, but the topic can be incorporated easily into social studies (analyzing the politics of renewable energy), math (calculating reductions in carbon dioxide emissions), English (writing informative

articles for school or local newspapers), automotive technology (testing the performance and emissions of different concentrations of biodiesel), and agriculture (studying the oil productivity of different plants). Biodiesel is also a terrific topic for extracurricular projects in science and environmental clubs. An alternative fuel with a very promising future, biodiesel offers a means of teaching about alternative energy that is interdisciplinary, fun, practical and empowering for students.

Richard Lawrence is the Education Coordinator for Cape and Islands Self-Reliance, a non-profit environment and energy education organization in Cape Cod, Massachusetts.

Resources

Books

Alovert, Maria. *Biodiesel Homebrew Guide* (Edition 10.5). Self-published, 2007, <http://localb100.com/book.html>.

Carter, Dan M. and Jon Halle. *How to Make Biodiesel.* Low-impact Living Initiative (LILI), 2005

Estill, Lyle. *Biodiesel Power: The Passion, the People, and the Politics of the Next Renewable Fuel.* New Society Publishers, 2005.

Pahl, Greg. *Biodiesel: Growing a New Energy Economy.* Chelsea Green Publishing, 2004.

Tickell, Joshua, *From the Fryer to the Fuel Tank: The Complete Guide to Using Vegetable Oil as an Alternative Fuel,* 3rd edition, Tickle Energy Consulting, 2000. This is a highly recommended, comprehensive reference on biodiesel.

Websites

<www.b100supply.com> Bio100 Supply LLC. Information, kits and supplies for making biodiesel.

<biodieselamerica.org> Biodiesel America. Site developed by educator Joshua Tickell, author of From the Fryer to the Fuel Tank, includes information, resources, community forums and news stories.

<www.biodiesel.org.au> Biodiesel Association of Australia. A non-profit organization that was founded to ensure that biodiesel is established and flourishes as a common alternative to diesel fuel in Australia.

<http://journeytoforever.org/biodiesel.html> Journey to Forever. Lots of information about biodiesel and the best site for biodiesel recipes.

<www.biodiesel.org> National Biodiesel Board. The national trade association representing the biodiesel industry and the coordinating body for research and development in the U.S.

<www.eere.energy.gov/afdc/> U.S. Department of Energy, Alternative Fuels Data Center. U.S. government site with over 3,000 documents on alternative fuels (including biodiesel) and alternative-fuel vehicles.

<www.veggiepower.org.uk> Veggiepower. A site for do-it-yourselfers, featuring homemade biodiesel processors and diesel engine modifications that allow the use of straight vegetable oil.

Making Biodiesel from Waste Vegetable Oil

by Alison K. Varty and Shane C. Lishawa

Subject areas: chemistry, plant science

Key concepts: renewable energy, transesterification, titration, viscosity, density, cloud point

Skills: measurement, titration, lab procedures

Materials: refer to list accompanying each procedure

Biodiesel is a promising renewable fuel that can be used with little or no technology conversion in diesel engines and fuel-delivery systems. Made primarily from plant seed oils, biodiesel has many environmental benefits, including lower emissions of carbon dioxide and other air pollutants than petroleum fuels,[1] provided the crops that produce the oil are grown on land already in agriculture.[2] However, there are drawbacks to growing crops for fuel oil. If the oil from all of the soybeans (a major fuel oil crop) grown in the United States were made into biodiesel, it would meet only six percent of the United States' demand for diesel oil.[3] Furthermore, wide-scale planting of fuel crops, whether for biodiesel

or for other crop-derived fuels such as ethanol, threatens food security and puts pressure on fallow lands and native ecosystems.[4] And when land is cleared to grow crops for biofuels, the reductions in carbon dioxide emissions are dwarfed by the carbon dioxide emitted as biomass is burned or decomposes.[5] In contrast to biodiesel made from virgin oil, biodiesel made from waste vegetable oil has few of these drawbacks.

In our course titled Solutions to Environmental Problems: Biodiesel, at Loyola University Chicago, students construct, staff and maintain a biodiesel lab to make biodiesel out of waste vegetable oil. Our education students have had great success working on biodiesel education in high schools. The topic connects naturally with many key concepts in chemistry (combustion, density and states of matter), biology (photosynthesis, energy and the carbon cycle) and environmental studies (climate change, air pollution, farming, land-use change and alternative energy).

Making biodiesel is hands-on and engaging, and maintaining a small-scale biodiesel reactor engages students in design and construction and develops technical skills necessary for the growing number of "green collar jobs." Most importantly, a biodiesel laboratory provides students with a means to make tangible reductions in emissions of carbon dioxide and other air pollutants. By taking waste vegetable oil generated in a school's kitchen and turning it into biodiesel that can be used in school maintenance equipment, school buses, or for heating, students help to decrease the carbon footprint of the school.

Constructing a biodiesel lab requires a serious commitment from the whole school community. It also requires a space with adequate ventilation (100 percent fresh air intake); a functioning fume hood; a flammables cabinet for storing methanol, which is one of the necessary reagents; and hazardous chemical pick-up service or a plan to use the glycerin, a by-product of the reaction. (The glycerin contains a significant amount of methanol that can be recovered through distillation and reused; the purified product can be used to make soap.) The plans to build the small-scale biodiesel reactor that we use can be found at the Loyola University Chicago website <www.luc.edu/biodiesel>. In addition to the initial costs of building this small-scale biodiesel reactor (approximately $500), a school will need to prepare for ongoing maintenance and reagent costs which will vary depending upon the quantity of biodiesel produced.

Although constructing a biodiesel reactor offers valuable opportunities for design and research, biodiesel can be made on a smaller scale in canning jars or separatory funnels as described in the activities below. The protocol for making, washing and dehydrating biodiesel in a large reactor follows the same basic steps and can be found at <www.luc.edu/biodiesel/pdfs/Biodiesel_laboratory_procedure.pdf>.

Making biodiesel from waste vegetable oil

Biodiesel is made through transesterification, a reaction that esterifies and cleaves the fatty acids from a glycerin molecule in the presence of a catalyst (see Figure 1). The recipe for making biodiesel from virgin vegetable oil is simple: to 1 liter of vegetable oil, add 200 ml of methanol and 3.5 g of sodium hydroxide (the catalyst).

The recipe is more complicated when making biodiesel from waste vegetable oil. The chemical properties of an oil that has been heated in a deep fryer in the presence of watery foods, such as frozen potatoes, differ from those of virgin oil. In the presence of water and heat, hydrolysis occurs as fatty acid chains are broken off of the glycerin portion of the triglyceride molecule, forming free fatty acids. With the addition of these

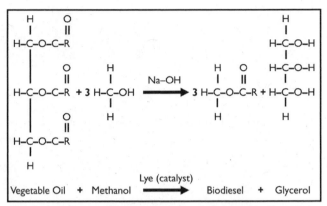

Figure 1: Transesterification reaction by which biodiesel is synthesized from vegetable oil

acids, the pH of the oil decreases and it becomes necessary to increase the amount of lye in the recipe in order to neutralize the oil. To calculate the quantity of additional lye needed, one must determine the amount of free fatty acids in each batch of waste vegetable oil. This is done by titration.

Titrating waste vegetable oil

Materials: safety goggles and gloves, 10-50 ml of phenolphthalein indicator solution, 100 ml of 99% isopropyl alcohol, three 50 ml beakers, one 10-50 ml burette, ring stand with burette holder, 500 ml container of sodium hydroxide drain cleaner, 1 liter de-ionized or distilled water, funnel, pH paper, 250 ml waste vegetable oil

Procedure:
Put on safety goggles and gloves.

Preparing the analyte solution

1. Measure 10 ml isopropyl alcohol into each of three 50 ml beakers.

2. Add 2-3 drops of phenolphthalein solution to the alcohol in each beaker and swirl to mix.

3. Add 1 ml of feedstock oil to each beaker and swirl to dissolve.

Preparing reference solution

1. Dissolve 1 gram of sodium hydroxide in 1 liter of distilled water.

2. Using a funnel, pour the solution into the burette.

Performing titration

1. Place one of the beakers of analyte solution under the burette.

2. Record the initial quantity of reference solution in the burette.

3. Slowly add the reference solution ~ 0.5 ml at a time to the oil/alcohol solution.

4. Swirl the beaker.

5. Continue to add reference solution to the oil/alcohol solution until the solution turns light pink and stays pink for ~30 seconds.

6. Stop.

7. Record the volume of reference solution used (in ml) as follows: Remaining volume – Initial volume = Reference solution used.

8. Repeat the procedure twice and record the quantity of reference solution used for both trials.

9. Average the volume of reference solution used in the three trials (T).

10. Use the formula below to determine the amount of catalyst and reagents to use to make biodiesel from this waste vegetable oil. For every 1 liter of oil, add 200 ml methanol and X grams of sodium hydroxide, where X = T + 3.5 grams.

Making biodiesel

After the appropriate amount of catalyst (sodium hydroxide) has been calculated, you are ready to make biodiesel. These instructions will make 500 ml batches, but the recipe can be scaled up or down by multiplying the oil, methanol and sodium hydroxide by the same factor.

Materials: methanol (it is not necessary to use laboratory grade methanol; it can be purchased as race car fuel or fuel line antifreeze at a lower price), sodium hydroxide, waste vegetable oil, quart-sized canning jars with lids, separatory funnel capable of holding >120 ml of liquid

Procedure:
Put on safety goggles and gloves.

Making sodium methoxide

1. Under the fume hood, pour 100 ml of methanol and 0.5X grams of sodium hydroxide into a quart-sized canning jar. (X = the value obtained in Step 11 above.)

Measuring catalyst for a biodiesel reaction.

Richard Lawrence

2. With the lid sealed tightly, shake the contents of the jar until all of sodium hydroxide is dissolved. Note: The reaction is exothermic and you may feel some heat coming from the solution. A small amount of pressure will build up as well. After shaking the solution for several minutes, open the lip under the fume hood to release the pressure.

Making biodiesel

1. Measure 500 ml of waste vegetable oil.

2. Pour this into the jar with the sodium methoxide.

3. Carefully shake the mixture for at least 10 minutes.

4. Pour the mixture into a separatory funnel and let it sit overnight (you will begin to observe a separation between the glycerin and the biodiesel after 15 minutes; the glycerin is more dense and will settle to the bottom of the jar).

5. When you return in the morning, you will see that a distinct layer of glycerin has formed on the bottom of the separatory funnel (it will be darker in color). Open the stopcock to pour off the glycerin.

Washing the biodiesel

The biodiesel you have made contains small quantities of leftover catalyst (by definition, the catalyst is not incorporated into the product), glycerin and methanol. These impurities may reduce fuel performance, but all are water-soluble and can be removed by washing the fuel with water.

Equipment: safety goggles and gloves, pH paper capable of measuring between pH 7 and 12, a spray bottle full of water (de-ionized or distilled water is preferable), small beakers, vinegar

Procedure:
Put on safety goggles and gloves.

1. To wash the crude biodiesel, gently spray water inside of the separatory funnel using a spray bottle. You may want to swish the water around by very gently agitating the mixture. Be sure the stopper is secure.

2. Put the separatory funnel back on the ring stand.

3. Almost immediately, you should see a separation between the water and the biodiesel. The water is

denser than the biodiesel and will settle to the bottom of the funnel. After 5–10 minutes, remove the cork and turn the stopcock to drain the water.

4. Dip the pH paper into the wash water to check the pH of the wash water.

5. Record the pH. The pH is typically very basic at first (~10) due to the residual sodium hydroxide in the biodiesel.

6. Repeat steps 1–7 until the wash water is neutral (~7). Record the pH for each trial.

7. Before disposing of the wash water, add a small quantity of vinegar to neutralize it.

Dehydrating the biodiesel

After washing, the biodiesel will appear cloudy because water molecules will be suspended in it. Water will reduce fuel performance and must be removed by dehydrating. This is done by bubbling air through the biodiesel. The suspended water molecules bond to the rising air bubbles and are brought to the surface where they evaporate.

Equipment: aquarium bubbler, silicone or PVC tubing (biodiesel dissolves rubber!)

Procedure:
Dehydrate the biodiesel by bubbling air through it with an aquarium bubbler for approximately 12 hours. Discontinue dehydration when the biodiesel appears clear.

Testing fuel quality

Many things can go wrong in the production process. For example, an incomplete reaction would result in bound glycerin remaining in the fuel. This would increase the viscosity of the fuel and could damage an engine. The simple biodiesel quality-control tests described below not only inform the production process, but have the potential to teach students important concepts in chemistry and physics.

Determining density

The mass per unit volume or density of biodiesel affects fuel consumption, as the amount entering the combustion chamber of the engine is volumetric. The density of biodiesel will be increased by residual glycerin and decreased by residual methanol. It is possible to measure the density of biodiesel using a glass hydrometer. Because density is related to temperature (in general, density will decrease as temperature increases), it must be measured at a constant temperature.

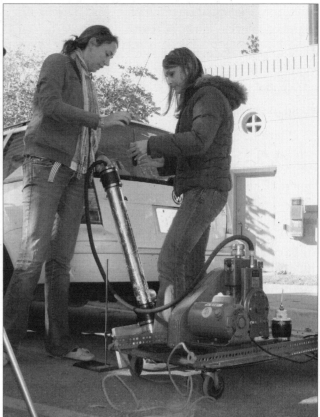

Matthew Kordonowy

Students test gas and particulate tailpipe emissions in order to compare emissions from diesel and biodiesel blends.

Equipment: glass hydrometer that reads between 860 and 900 kg/m^3, 500 ml glass cylinder, 450 ml of biodiesel

Procedure:
1. Heat or cool ~420 ml of biodiesel to 15 °C.

2. Pour the biodiesel into a 500 ml glass cylinder.

3. Carefully drop the hydrometer into the oil with the lead weight down and the density scale up.

4. Carefully, read the density of the hydrometer. Make sure you view it at eye level, ignoring the meniscus (the fluid that creeps up the wall of the cylinder and the hydrometer).

5. The density of biodiesel should be between 860 and 900 kg/m^3.

Testing viscosity

The resistance to flow, or viscosity, of the finished biodiesel provides important information about its quality. High viscosity indicates high levels of glycerin in the biodiesel. This can have an impact on an automobile's fuel injector pumps by increasing resistance to fuel flow. It can also lead to storage problems: the excess glycerin may settle to the bottom of fuel storage containers. We use a viscometer, a piece of glassware with a calibrated capillary tube, to measure viscosity. Viscosity is determined by recording the amount of time it takes the biodiesel to flow through the capillary tube. Viscosity is dependent on temperature (it increases as temperature decreases) and thus must be measured at a constant temperature.

Equipment: Ubbelohde viscometer, hot plate, 2000 ml graduated cylinder, ring stand with clips to suspend the viscometer in the waterbath, ~30 ml of biodiesel, two syringes, one to apply suction and the other to load the silicone tubes of the viscometer

Procedure:
1. Follow the instructions provided with the viscometer.

2. Place 2010 ml of 40 °C water into the clear plastic 2000 ml graduated cylinder. Place the cylinder next to a ring stand.

3. Load the viscometer with biodiesel (it is convenient to use a syringe connected to the viscometer with a silicone tube).

4. Submerge the viscometer in the waterbath and align it vertically on the stand.

5. Leave the biodiesel sample in the water bath for approximately 10 minutes.

6. Using a syringe, apply suction and pull the biodiesel sample into the bulb above capillary tube.

7. Remove suction from the viscometer until the sample drops away from the lower end of the capillary tube.

8. To obtain efflux time, measure the time required for the meniscus to pass between the two marks indicated in the instructions (this will likely take between 2 and 10 minutes).

9. To calculate viscosity of the biodiesel in centistokes, multiply efflux time in seconds by the viscometer constant (0.01).

10. The viscosity of biodiesel should be between 1.9 and 6 centistokes.

Testing cloud point

Cloud point describes the temperature at which a cloud or haze of solid crystals appears in biodiesel; it marks the beginning of a phase change from liquid to solid. Clouding will affect how the fuel flows through the fuel system at cold temperatures. The cloud point depends on the chemical composition of the oil used to make the biodiesel. For example, trans-fats and saturated fats tend to cloud at higher temperatures than unsaturated fats. Operating an engine below the fuel's cloud point can potentially block fuel lines and clog fuel filters. This test involves cooling a sample of biodiesel and examining it visually for clouding.

Equipment: 100 ml of biodiesel, 100 ml beaker, foam cork with a hole in it (to fit the thermometer), thermometer, ice, salt

Procedure:
1. Measure 100 ml of biodiesel in a beaker and pour it into the cloud point test jar.

2. Cork the vessel with the foam cork and place a thermometer through the hole in the cork so that it rests above the bottom of the test jar.

3. Prepare cold water bath: half-fill a 1-liter beaker with packed ice and add 20 grams of table salt to the ice. Stir vigorously and monitor the temperature until it reaches ~ −10 °C.

4. Place the test jar in the cold water bath.

5. Allow sample to sit in the bath for 1 minute.

6. Observe the biodiesel and the temperature every 30 seconds.

7. Record the temperature at which the biodiesel begins to cloud (you will start to see a creamy whiteness in the fuel, usually toward the bottom of the jar).

Alison K. Varty *coordinates and co-teaches the STEP classes taught through the Center for Urban Environmental Research and Policy at Loyola University Chicago.* ***Shane C. Lishawa*** *teaches with her and manages the Biodiesel Lab.*

Notes

1. J. Hill, E. Nelson, D. Tilman, S. Polasky and D. Tiffany. "Environmental, Economic, and Energetic Costs and Benefits of Biodiesel and Ethanol Biofuels." *Proceedings of the National Academy of Sciences* 103 (2006), pp. 11206–11210.

2. T. Searchinger, R. Heimlich, R.A. Houghton, F. Dong, A. Elobeid, J. Fabiosa, S. Tokgoz, D. Hayes, T. Yu. "Use of U.S. Croplands for Biofuels Increases Greenhouse Gases through Emissions from Land-use Change." *Science* 319 (2008), pp. 1238–1240; and J. Fargione, J. Hill, D. Tilman, S. Polasky, P. Hawthorne. "Land Clearing and the Biofuel Carbon Debt." *Science* 319 (2008), pp. 1235–1238.

3. Hill et al., 2006

4. Searchinger et al., 2008.

5. Fargione et al, 2008.

Small-scale Science

*A "small is better" technique that dramatically reduces the quantity
of chemicals used in science labs*

Photographs by Alan Slater

by Alan Slater

Subject areas: science, environmental studies

Key concepts: environmental awareness, safety, green chemistry

Skills: microscience techniques

Location: indoors/outdoors

Materials: microplates and plastic pipettes

I was a research and development chemist in the petrochemical industry just when concerns about pollution began to arise. A common attitude then was that "the solution to pollution is dilution." Dump the offending material into the landfill, river or air and forget about it. We all did this in our daily lives, too — paints and cleaning agents went down the drain, raw sewage ran into the sea. In the science classroom lab, large five-pound (now two-kilogram) bottles of chemicals were "used up" each

year. Many of us can probably remember a science class when a large spill occurred or some apparatus exploded. Then, at the end of the period, it was all washed down the sink or put into the garbage.

In the good old days, we would allot at least $600 per course for lab materials in our high school. Now we have a hard time spending $100 for the 1,000 science students who use the chemicals and related equipment in our courses. This is because we now do most of our experiments on a small (micro) scale. Microscale science is the most exciting, innovative technique I have seen in over 30 years of teaching science and chemistry, and it is sweeping the globe. Using a drop of solution no bigger than this small dot • and grains of solid the size of this dash —, we can get the same lab results as in the past, while reducing the quantity of materials we use by at least 10 times and often 100 times or more.

Although microscience has the most impact in chemistry classes, it has applications in general science and biology classes and wherever chemicals are used. It addresses issues of pollution, waste disposal, lab safety and our attitudes toward the environment, yet at the same time maintains the "hands on" experience and saves time for both the teacher and student. Everyone, including the environment, is a winner!

Equipment

About 20 years ago in the United States a group of very creative teachers saw the latest plastic technology used in medical labs and envisioned the potential uses of this simple plasticware in chemistry. Only two very basic pieces of equipment are needed to start with: a well plate and a pipette. Although both are regarded as disposable in the medical field, they can be reused many times in school. Some well plates have been in service for over 10 years; and while pipettes do not usually last that long, they are made of recyclable plastic.

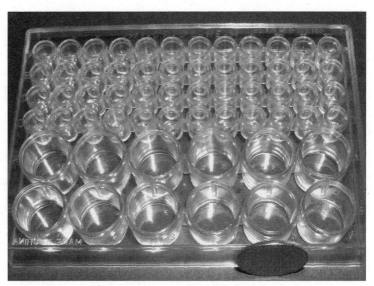
Combination reaction well plate designed for high school use.

Sizing up Microscale Science

To micro-size means:

Increased safety, because small quantities of chemicals (0.02 milliliters of solution or 1–2 grains of solid) are used and students have more control over a reaction.

Less waste, because such small quantities are used that waste and disposal is minimized.

Less storage space needed for materials, as only small amounts need to be stored, whether as solutions or in solid form. A solution for a whole class can be stored in one micropipette. The classroom chemical inventory will be reduced by at least 90 percent, and probably much more.

Less breakage, because the basic equipment is plastic and quite durable.

Money saved on chemicals and equipment. A well plate can last ten years or so, and a 500-gram bottle of chemical could last 1,000 years or more.

Faster cleanup and much less water used in washing up.

Less distilled water needed, thus saving both the cooling water and the energy used in distilling.

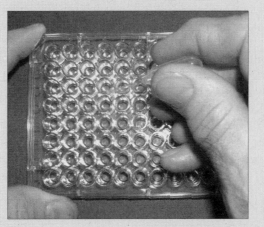

Time saved in doing experiments and, as a result, many students want to, and do, repeat lab experiments. Instead of cleaning up and rushing on to another class, students have time within the same period for post-lab reflections and for entering and manipulating numerical data on a computer spreadsheet. More time can be spent on designing experiments and developing higher order thinking skills.

Time saved by the teacher in preparing for a class, as only small quantities of materials are needed and there is very little equipment to move around. For example, one can carry all the solutions for about ten labs in one small tote box.

What are the drawbacks? Very few, but...

• You need a good electronic balance reading to 0.001 grams for high school quantitative work. If not, you must make either more highly concentrated solutions or larger volumes of stock solutions.

• As with any new method, new techniques must be learned.

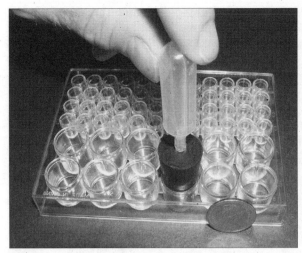

Producing and collecting gas in a well plate.

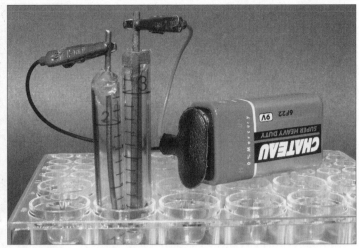

Easy setup demonstrates electrolysis using only 5 ml of solution.

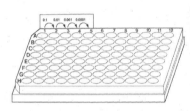

The most common **well plate** in use is the 96-well plate, which is equivalent to 96 test tubes. There are also 24- and 6-well plates, as well as combination reaction plates designed specifically for use in high school science. Combination reaction (or dual well) plates consist of half of a 96-well plate (i.e., 48 small wells) and half of a 24-well plate (i.e., 12 larger wells), and some are made of a plastic that is resistant to organic chemicals. Each well on a 96-well plate can hold about 0.3 milliliters of solution (12–16 microdrops), and the rows and columns are labeled. The 24-well plate replaces beakers in most experiments, with each well having a volume of less than 4 milliliters.

Well plates are typically made of polystyrene, which is very durable and easy to clean. Stubborn stains can be removed with cotton swabs and water (most organic solvents should be avoided except on the organic-resistant comboplates). As polystyrene is non-wetting, dilution procedures and cleaning can be done quickly and effectively. Stirring can be done using toothpicks or plastic stirrers. Typically, the plates cost two to six dollars each.

The **pipettes** are made of polyethylene and can be purchased to dispense as many as 50 drops per milliliter. Thus a single drop can be as small as 0.020 milliliter, or 0.020 grams. Often one drop is all that is needed for an experiment in which 10 milliliters or more might have been used before. The pipettes are non-wetting and easily cleaned, and can deliver very accurate drops when handled correctly. They can also be cut to make a variety of other pieces of equipment,

such as the simple distillation apparatus described below. There are four types of pipettes normally used. In bulk, these cost five to eight cents each.

Experiments

With these two very simple pieces of equipment — a well plate and a pipette — students can easily do a whole range of experiments, such as testing the density of liquids, solubility curves of a solute such as potassium nitrate, chromatography of water soluble inks, collecting and testing various common gases, electrolysis of various ionic solutions and fuel cells, and testing foods for proteins. Here are some brief examples:

• White solids from the supermarket can be analyzed and unknowns determined.

• Any gas can be produced and collected safely and quickly with a well plate, a one-hole stopper and a graduated pipette (see photo). For example, oxygen can be made from a well-known bleach, hydrogen peroxide, using a simple mineral, pyrolusite rock. This is a catalyst and can be is reused many times. The oxygen can even be tested with a glowing toothpick! Even hydrogen/oxygen mixtures can be exploded safely with this apparatus.

• Electrolysis of many solutions can be done in 5 to 10 minutes with 5 milliliters of solution (see photo). A similar apparatus, using graphite electrodes, can electrolyse a magnesium sulphate solution (Epsom salts) to make hydrogen and oxygen. Disconnecting the battery and using a multimeter can show a fuel cell with a voltage around 2 volts. The cost is only about $5.

• Two graduated pipettes can be cut up and, with a

syringe plug and plastic T, made into a simple distillation apparatus that can be used in a hot water bath.

• For labs involving the dilution or neutralization of solutions (e.g., acid/base), the numerical scale across the top of the well plate is ideal for use as a scale of concentration or pH. One creative Grade 12 student used a 96-well plate and pipettes to determine the relative amount of active ingredient present in various consumer products such as aspirin, juice or wine.

When I first tried this new method, I used an old semi-micro lab and scaled it down from big drops to one small drop. The results were just as good but quicker and easier for the students to do. Then I began asking myself, "Why do I use so much? Can I use 10 or even 100 times less?" In almost every case, the answer was a resounding yes. Where I previously used 10 milliliters of a solution and a graduated cylinder, I could use 0.1 milliliter (5 drops) dispensed from a small pipette — a 99 percent reduction in chemical use. Even labs that could not be done in a well plate could still be scaled down by at least 10 times. A reaction using 200 milliliters was simply modified to use 20 milliliters and done in a smaller container. Where I once used 50 liters of distilled water for a lab, I now needed only 5 liters. With about $100 worth of plasticware and a questioning mind, I could reduce our chemical use by 90 to 99 percent! This meant my chemical waste was also reduced by 90 to 99 percent. My old two-kilogram bottles and even my 500-gram bottles have now become dinosaurs.

Students in the lab are constantly exposed to ways of reducing their use of materials. In fact, it is often a game to see who can do a reaction with the minimum number of drops. If there is a spill, it is usually no more than one milliliter — hardly a horrible mess to clean up — and it provides an example of reduction at the source. How easy is it to clean this up in our lab compared to dealing with it at the sewage plant or cleaning it up later downstream.

Except for a final rinse of the plates or pipettes, students put no waste materials down the sink. What little waste is generated has been reduced further by constantly finding new processes that use up this waste. For example, waste copper solutions can be saved and the copper ions later removed by adding scrap iron (iron nail in the lab).

My students have enthusiastically embraced this new way of doing labs. They are not alone: through my involvement in microscience techniques, I have presented workshops across North America, England and Africa. There is global interest in this, and certainly many uses of small-scale science in developing countries where science education might otherwise go down the road we traveled many years ago.

Our biggest problem in the classroom now is sewage gas! There is so little cleanup water going down our drains that the traps are in danger of drying out and thus letting the sewer gas back into the lab.

Alan Slater is a retired science/chemistry teacher who has given workshops across North America and England on microchemistry and microscience and received a number of awards for his work in this area. He is co-author, with Geoff Rayner-Canham, of Microscale Chemistry (Addison-Wesley, 1994), a microchemistry lab manual and teacher's guide for high school chemistry. He lives in St. Mary's, Ontario.

Supplies

Canada

Boreal Northwest <www.boreal.com>, search on "microchemistry." A good source of microchemistry kits, equipment and lab manuals.

United States

Educational Innovations <www.teachersource.com>, search on "microscale" for a list of well plates and pipettes available.

Kemtec Educational Products <www.kemtecscience.com/Chemistry.htm>, see Microchemistry section under "Chemistry Kits."

Flinn Scientific. PO Box 219, Batavia, IL 60510-0219, 1-800-452-1261, flinn@flinnsci.com, <www.flinnsci.com>. Best source of equipment and lab books in the U.S. Their catalog has a wealth of ideas.

Green Driving Lessons:
Oxymoron or Opportunity?

Illustrations by Tom Goldsmith

by Tim Altieri

Subject areas: driver's education, science, math, social studies, communication arts, computer technology, consumer education

Key concepts: air pollution, natural resources, operating temperature, emission-control devices

Skills: data synthesis and analysis, research, presentation skills

Location: indoors, outdoors for vehicle demonstrations

Despite great strides by automobile manufacturers in reducing fuel emissions, air pollution from cars continues to increase because more people are driving and they are spending more time on the road. Ground-level ozone, much of it from automobile emissions, now threatens the health of communities across North America. According to the American Lung Association, in 2005 nearly half of all Americans lived in counties with levels of air pollution that put them at risk for respiratory disease.[1] In Canada, government scientists estimate that air pollution causes over 5,000 premature deaths annually.[2]

As millions of adolescents come of driving age each year, conversations between adults and young drivers

are often dominated by such issues as reckless driving and high insurance rates. Earth-friendly driving techniques and expectations that link new driving privileges with minimizing air pollution are often missing. "Green driving" may seem an oxymoron, and indeed there is no question that young people should be encouraged to take the bus, cycle or "hoof it" whenever possible. Driving consumes fuel, creates emissions and adds to traffic congestion; and traffic tie-ups force drivers to spend even more time on the road, burning up more gas and spewing more pollutants. Congestion also motivates politicians to approve more road construction, which paves over green space and encourages sprawl. For these reasons, one could argue that driving should be avoided at all costs. Another viewpoint holds that if kids are going to join the millions in the ranks of lifelong drivers, then parents and educators should encourage driving habits that minimize fuel consumption and emissions.

At the high school level, when most kids are intrigued with cars, there is nobody in a better position than teachers to impress upon young drivers the importance of Earth-friendly driving. Driver education teachers can easily incorporate green driving lessons into their programs. With a little creativity, teachers of many other disciplines can legitimately address this topic in their curricula, too.

Eco-tips for young drivers

Traditional driver education courses stress the operation of vehicles in accordance with the rules of the road — laws that are intended to prevent accidents and keep traffic moving in order to avoid roadway congestion. A green driving course builds on those strengths by linking the topics of safety, maintenance and operating costs to environmental impacts. For example, student drivers typically are taught to maintain a safe distance between their own car and the vehicle in front of them. The standard reason for doing this is to ensure that there will be sufficient time to brake in case the car ahead makes a sudden stop. A green driving lesson would emphasize the safety rationale for this rule of the road, but would also point out the environmental impact of tailgating — that the repeated cycle of over-acceleration and braking associated with tailgating wastes fuel, generates more engine emissions than necessary, and results in more particulate-producing wear on brake linings.

Another area where issues of safety, cost and environment come together is the practice of maintaining the recommended air pressure in tires and rotating tires at regular intervals. The purpose of this is to diminish tire wear and to ensure safe traction. Well-maintained tires make it easier for drivers to control their cars in adverse conditions, but they also reduce fuel consumption and emissions. Many driver education courses already teach the safety advantage and economic reasons for these maintenance procedures and can easily emphasize their environmental impact as well.

Such eco-tips as proper tire maintenance have their roots in an important resource for designing green driving lessons that is only as far away as a teacher's own glove compartment. Most automobile owner's manuals have diagrams showing the locations of oxygen sensors, air filters, catalytic converters and other emissions control devices. Discussing these auto parts is an excellent way of connecting students' interest in driving to lessons in chemistry, physics and environmental science. Emissions control devices also serve as great examples of how car design has improved to meet tougher government environmental regulations.

Another important eco-tip found in an owner's manual involves the correct way to start the engine. The improper start-up of hundreds of automobile engines every morning can have a huge impact on a town's air quality. A faulty start causes unburned fuel to pass through the engine and through a cold catalytic converter. Older cars with carburetors require a press of the gas pedal when the engine is cold, but newer cars with fuel injectors do not need a tap on the accelerator unless the temperature is below freezing. If an engine is already warm when a car is started, feeding it too much gas by pressing the accelerator only wastes fuel and increases emissions. Applying this basic knowledge when starting their cars, drivers can lessen their environmental impact.

Several green tips relate to engine temperature. Just as the human body has a healthy temperature, a car engine has an optimal operating temperature. The closer the engine is to this temperature, the more efficiently it will operate. And the more efficient the engine, the more power it will have, the less fuel it will consume, and the less harmful gas it will emit. Conversely, operating a cold engine, as frequently happens on short trips, results in more air pollution and leads to more visits to the mechanic for tune-ups and parts replacements. On short trips when a vehicle is not driven long enough for the engine to warm up, moisture is not evaporated from the exhaust. As a result, water lies in the exhaust system and causes premature rusting of the pipes and catalytic converter. Rust can create holes that allow carbon monoxide to leak into the car interior, causing illness, drowsiness and even death.

Engine temperature affects the operation of catalytic converters also. The job of a catalytic converter is to intercept unburned hydrocarbons, carbon monoxide and nitrous oxides and change them into less harmful chemicals such as water and carbon dioxide. Catalysts, the chemicals that initiate and speed up these reactions, work properly only at about the temperature of a warm engine. Therefore, a cold engine pollutes a great deal more than a warm engine.

Because an engine warms up faster when it is doing work (moving the vehicle), it is especially important not to let a car idle on cold days simply to warm up the interior. To warm up the engine quickly, one must get the car moving. This means adjusting the seat and mirrors and putting on seat belts before starting the engine. In addition, since the car's interior heater functions by taking heat away from the engine, keeping the heater off for a few minutes (and using the car-seat heaters, if available) will help the engine to heat up faster. In cold climes, an engine-block heater or oil-pan warmer on a timer can also be used to reduce the time it takes the engine to warm up. Backing the car into the driveway or parking space at the end of a trip while the engine is warm helps avoid the idling that occurs when the car is backed out cold at the beginning of the next trip. These small steps will get the car moving and the catalytic converter working more quickly.

Green Driver Pledge

While I use, take care of, and/or own a vehicle, I pledge to take the following actions to reduce my environmental impact:

Before driving:
• Take the bus, bike, walk or car pool with other drivers whenever possible.

• Read and understand the owner's manual in order to operate the vehicle efficiently.
• Reduce the number of cold starts and short trips each week by combining errands.
• Avoid overloading the vehicle with people or cargo.
• Minimize idling by adjusting seats and mirrors and buckling passengers up before starting the engine.

While operating the vehicle:
• Start the vehicle according to instructions in the owner's manual.
• Warm up the engine quickly by moving the car forward in order to get emission-control devices warm enough to function.
• Brake slowly and avoid quick acceleration to conserve fuel and reduce emissions.
• Use cruise control and avoid tailgating to save gas and brake linings.
• Obey speed limits: the faster the car goes, the higher its gas consumption and emissions.
• Reduce drag by removing or replacing unnecessarily large mirrors, wide tires and luggage racks, and by closing the windows at high speeds to create a more streamlined surface.
• Conserve tire treads by avoiding quick acceleration or fast, tight turns (no tire squeals).
• Turn right on red lights (when legal) instead of idling the car and causing others to idle unnecessarily.
• Avoid idling in long lines, such as in drive-throughs, at road construction sites and after big events.
• Anticipate animals being on or near the road, especially around dusk, at the edges of woods and near water and food sources.

• Keep passengers from littering, including smokers who might be inclined to toss cigarette butts out car windows.

At the pump:
• Always turn the engine off while fueling and check the oil and tire pressure regularly.
• Use the correct fuel, as designated in the owner's manual, and never top off or overfill the tank.
• Minimize the time the gas cap is off the tank in order to reduce gas evaporation.
• Make sure the gas cap is tight and replace it immediately if it is lost or begins to leak gas vapors.

Maintaining the vehicle:
• Follow the air, oil and fuel-filter replacement and tire rotation instructions in the owner's manual.
• Check for and eliminate tire problems, such

as poor alignment, worn treads, and over- and under-inflation.
• Look for leaks of oil and other fluids, and smell for gas vapor leaks and eliminate them.
• If the owner's manual approves, use synthetic motor oils, which do not need to be changed as often as petroleum oils.
• Have all car fluids and parts recycled, including the entire car when it is no longer operable.

After each trip:
• Back into the driveway or parking space to decrease idling with a cold engine at the start of the next trip.
• Park in the shade on hot days and behind a sunny wind block on cold days.
• Watch for other green driving tips and share them with other drivers.

Curriculum links

Green driving lessons need not be confined to driver's education classes, but lend themselves nicely to an interdisciplinary or team-teaching approach. Here are a few ideas:

• Math students could calculate the cost of purchasing, driving, maintaining and disposing of a car through a typical vehicle's lifespan, or research and compare the cost, fuel consumption and emissions of different models to determine which cars are most economical and least polluting.

• Geography lessons could focus on regions of the world where crude oil is extracted and refined, and the journey that oil takes from extraction to the local gas station. Students might study the environmental impacts at each step of this journey, or research the ways in which reliance on automobiles affects land use planning and the design of communities.

• History classes may examine the growth of the automotive industry and associated labor movements, car designs and advertising. Students may also look at how oil interests affect government policies, and at the waste and pollution caused by wars in oil-producing regions such as the Persian Gulf.

• A social studies unit may focus on the environmental impacts of various forms of transportation. As a lesson in consumer awareness, students can check Consumer Reports and other independent testers to research the fuel consumption and emissions of different vehicles. The creation of cartoons spoofing the use of sports utility vehicles and pickup trucks to do jobs suitable for more fuel-efficient vehicles can be a source of classroom fun.

• Technology classes can learn about hybrid fuel technologies, and a representative from a local transportation company may be invited to talk about the use these new technologies in their fleets. A representative from a trucking company could show students how global positioning systems are used to monitor the speed, fuel consumption and location of trucks in order to save money and fuel.

Spreading the word

There are a number of ways in which students can teach others what they've learned about greener driving techniques. For example, students could make an educational board game or computer game in which players roll a die and move along a highway. Squares containing green driving tips earn players "lighter impact points," while landing on polluting, bad-habit squares earns players "pollution points." At the end of the game, the winners are rewarded with good or excellent air quality, and losers with poor or severely polluted air. Students can also share green driving tips by writing articles for the school or local newspapers, or by creating an educational video or pamphlet. Making posters and placing them in local car repair shops or dealerships is also a great way to spread the word. Students may be inclined to design a website on the topic, complete with links to other sources of information. They may even be encouraged to lobby their school board and government to include green driving techniques in the school curriculum and state or provincial driver's license testing.

At the conclusion of a green driving course, students can be invited to sign a pledge to operate and maintain their cars in ways that reduce their impact on the planet. The pledge may contain 10 or 20 simple statements reminding drivers of environmentally friendly driving tips (see "Green Driver Pledge" example). Students can even write their own pledges. "Greener Driver" pins can be given to those who agree to sign and adhere to the pledge. Such pins, displayed on book bags and jackets, make superb conversation pieces that give students plenty of opportunities to share what they have learned with other drivers.

Many driving eco-tips seem like small details, but when one considers the combined effect of millions of drivers over time wasting fuel and polluting the air, it is easier to understand that small changes could have a huge impact. If people develop greener driving habits while they are young, the environmental impact of their driving over a lifetime will be less significant. Teachers who encourage new drivers to develop greener driving habits can have a positive impact on the pollution crisis facing millions of people.

Tim Altieri is a public school administrator and county park naturalist in Lancaster, Pennsylvania.

Notes

1. American Lung Association, "State of the Air 2005," <http://lungaction.org/reports/sota05_cities.html>.

2. Environment Canada, "Tracking Key Environmental Issues: Air Quality," 2005, March 24, 2007, <www.ec.gc.ca/TKEI/air_water/air_qual_e.cfm>.

Resources

Ryan, John C. and Alan Thein Durning. *Stuff: The Secret Lives of Everyday Things*. Northwest Environment Watch, 1997.

Sikorsky, Robert. *Car Tips for Cleaner Air*. Perigee Books, 1991. Describes strategies to reduce car pollution and includes graphs, diagrams and a good glossary.

Prem Center Magic Eyes Barge Program

❀ **Green Mapmaking** by Robert Zuber and Wendy E. Brawer

❀ **Connecting Students with Special Needs to the Environment**
by Lynn Dominguez and Mary Lou Schilling

❀ **Exploring The Earth Charter** by Linda Hill

❀ **Walking into Wonder** by Cynthia Macleod

❀ **Building Green** by Jennifer Wolf

❀ **Ancestral Arts** by Elizabeth Lorentzen

❀ **GIS in the Classroom** by Marsha Alibrandi

❀ **Voices of the Land: A Course in Environmental Literature** by Emma Wood Rous

❀ **Social Justice and Language Arts** by Christopher Greenslate

❀ **Designing a Green City** by Iori Miller and Susan Sheard

Making Interdisciplinary Connections

Green Mapmaking

*Mapping the richness of their communities motivates young people
to make them healthier and more desirable places to live*

Regina Weir

by Robert Zuber and Wendy E. Brawer

Subject areas: Earth science, ecology, biology, language
arts, technology/media, geography, social studies

Key concepts: sustainable development, food systems,
alternative transportation, biodiversity, localization, cultural awareness, social equity, new media, urban planning,
eco-design, sustainable energy

Skills: observation/investigation, expressive narrative and
image development, eco-literacy, critical assessment, new
media production, cross-cultural communications, mapmaking

Location: indoors and outdoor community settings

Time: varies depending on the scope of the school/commu-
nity investigation and the complexity of the resulting maps

Materials: notebook, compass, drawing instruments, printed
base map or reference map, posterboard; optional (but recommended) resources include Green Map Icon Posters (download
at GreenMap.org/icons) and Green Map Modules (download
at GreenMap.org/youth), digital camera, computer

Youth are often discouraged by discussions of
environmental degradation, but they are also
inspired by stories of extraordinary efforts
being made every day in schools and communities to
reclaim and maintain the health of local environments.
It is important for young people to see first-hand
abandoned lots being transformed into beautiful, productive gardens; parklands, wetlands and waterfronts
being restored for exploration and recreation; habitats
for wildlife being preserved and extended; people
using bicycle lanes and shopping locally at farmers'
markets and eco-oriented retail outlets. Our youth
need both to see and to help create hopeful resources
that change the face and improve the health of urban
and rural environments.

One means of bringing students into closer contact
with the wealth of natural, cultural, recreational and
civic resources in their communities is to encourage
them to create Green Maps®, compelling visual repre-
sentations of local environmental and cultural sites (see
"Students' Guide to Green Mapmaking," pages 159–
160). Green Mapmaking offers reinforcement for lessons in geography, civics and science, sharpens powers

of observation and eco-literacy, and promotes cooperative learning. But perhaps most important, Green Mapmaking heightens students' awareness of, interest in and commitment to their hometowns. Few of our communities can truly thrive without the energy, creativity, enthusiasm and even impatience of our young people. The more they know how rich and special their hometowns are, the more motivated they will be to preserve and enhance that richness. Through Green Mapmaking, students gain confidence in their ability to help make their neighborhoods healthier, more attractive, more desirable, more sustainable places to live.

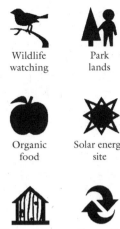

Wildlife watching

Park lands

Organic food

Solar energy site

Eco-building

Reuse site

The Green Map System

The Green Map System (GMS) is an award-winning, globally connected, locally adaptable framework for promoting community sustainability. Since 1995, GMS has provided a variety of resources to assist teams of youth and adult volunteers in creating maps to represent and share the ecologically and culturally significant places, projects and organizations in their home communities. Through the interactive Green Map website (Greenmap.org) and its online exchange, presentation and tool center "The Greenhouse," as well as through books and other resources in multiple languages, GMS helps youth and adults worldwide communicate compelling and inspiring stories of community change.

While the selection of sites included in each Green

Cuban students plan their map using chalk, modeling clay and Green Map Icon stickers.

Map is up to the local mapping team, all use a shared visual language, a set of more than 125 icons that symbolize various types of ecological and cultural sites. Among the natural and built features highlighted on Green Maps are:

- gardens, parks, places of natural beauty, wildlife habitats and zoos

- farmers' markets, eco-businesses and sustainable economic developments

- pedestrian zones, bike lanes, mass transit and car-free options

- cultural resources, historical features and eco-tourism destinations

- solar and other renewable energy sites

- important cultural, civic, governmental and health resources

Joining the Global Green Map System

By registering their mapping project with Green Map System (GMS), teachers and students become part of a global network of Green Mapmakers and gain access to a diverse array of mapmaking resources. Registered mapmakers can publish both their completed map and a project profile (which includes the reasons for making the map, key community findings and map impacts), thereby providing inspiration for other mapmakers worldwide. Mapmakers can also share images and outreach materials they have created, promote their events, and exchange ideas and activities with other youth.

Once officially registered, mapmakers may use the copyrighted Green Map Icons (in font or sticker formats), as well as the GMS logo and widely recognized name, Green Map® (which is a registered trademark to be used with permission). Green Map requests a modest sliding fee to help support ongoing efforts; however, educators and youth group leaders may exchange a service (such as translation or contributing an activity or curriculum resource) or request a scholarship in lieu of registration fees.

To register as a Green Mapmaker, visit <www.greenmap.org> and go to "Participate" section. If you have questions before registering, contact Green Map System, PO Box 249, New York, NY 10002, info@greenmap.org.

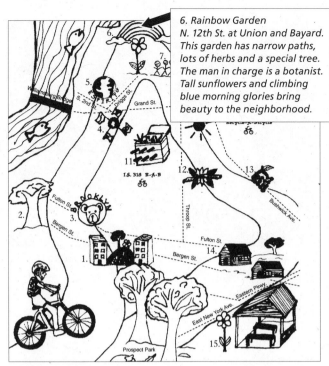

6. Rainbow Garden
N. 12th St. at Union and Bayard.
This garden has narrow paths,
lots of herbs and a special tree.
The man in charge is a botanist.
Tall sunflowers and climbing
blue morning glories bring
beauty to the neighborhood.

Students in North Brooklyn mapped 15 community gardens accessible by bicycle. A legend (see inset) describes each garden.

• bioregional, geological and other natural features

• water, power and waste infrastructures

• environmentally-sound architecture and significant design projects

• toxic hot spots and pollution sources

Mapmakers decide which of these categories they wish to chart and may create their own icons to better describe unique local features. They then decide together how to disseminate their completed Green Map — in a mural, on a website, in a community center or as printed maps.

From its inception, GMS has promoted the idea that students can become community investigators, creating maps of local neighborhoods while in some instances contributing to the larger city maps produced primarily by adult designers. For example, students in Seattle are being inspired to create healthier communities through the Homewaters Community Mapping Project. The Robeson County (North Carolina) Green Map project is helping Native American and other rural youth to discover, appreciate and protect their unique biological and cultural assets. Students in Podravja, Slovenia, are using Green Mapmaking to rediscover the "forgotten knowledge" in their communities. And in Tororo, Uganda, youth are helping to promote food security while raising awareness of the need for community involvement in protecting the area's fragile ecosystem. These are only a

few of the exciting projects in over 50 countries that are changing the way people interpret and appreciate their hometowns.

Like most of us, young people are habituated to their surroundings: the more time they spend in a place, the less they tend to see it. For Green Mapmakers, "seeing" a community means being aware of the things that most of us take for granted or ignore altogether: rhythms of growth and decay, seasonal transformations in the natural and built environments, local flora and fauna and what sustains (and threatens) their habitats. It also means asking the questions that many of us ask only infrequently: Where and how is our food grown? What happens to our waste? What cultural resources do we have in our region? Who in the community is working on bicycle lanes or other transportation alternatives? What plants and animals are native to our area? Bridging the gap between the questions students can already answer about their hometowns and what they will need to know to promote healthier, more sustainable communities is an essential motivation for GMS's work around the world.

Through participation in the growing network of Green Mapmakers, students are increasing their visual assessment and communication skills, and learning science, art and civics in creative ways. Most important, they are discovering a vast array of local cultural and ecological sites of which they were largely unaware. Creating their own Green Maps is an opportunity for young people to explore and interpret this richness in their local areas and to develop the skills to replace environmental degradation and neglect with stewardship and community renewal.

Robert Zuber *is a senior organizational and fundraising consultant with Green Map System. He also serves a variety of other organizations including the Center for International Media Action, New York Theological Seminary and the United Nations Emergency Peace Service project.* ***Wendy E. Brawer*** *is an award-winning eco-designer and founding director of the Green Map System, where she has both supervised the growth of the global Green Map System and developed the New York City "Green Apple Map" projects.*

Resources

Green Map System. *Green Map Atlas*. A multimedia anthology of the stories and strategies behind the making of ten Green Maps in Asia and North America. Free download at <www.GreenAtlas.org>.

Lydon, Maeve, GroundWorks. *Mapping Our Common Ground/Mapeando Nuestra Tierra Común*. Common Ground Community Mapping Project with Green Map System and Mapas Verdas Americas, 2007, ISBN 0-9738728-8-8 (English), ISBN 0-9738728-9-6 (Spanish). This 60-page guide offers community mapping stories and methodologies, samples of community maps, workshop outlines and design ideas. Available in the U.S. from the Green Map Store <GreenMap.org/store> and in Canada from LifeCycles Project Society, <www.lifecyclesproject.ca>.

Students' Guide to Green Mapmaking

This guide integrates both Green Map System iconography and the educational resources available at GreenMap.org.

Getting started: Start by choosing an area to explore. Discuss the target audience (e.g., neighbors, city residents, tourists, students, planners and policy makers) and determine the general goals for your Green Map. Consider how and where your map will be displayed, shared and distributed. Should you plan to make more than one version of the map? Should you use multiple formats for your completed map (paper, online, etc.)?

Brooklyn Tech students with green map.

Emma McGregor-Lowndes

Surveying the area: In small teams, scout around and find special places in your community, especially those that can be described by the GMS icons. You might begin by looking at green businesses, eco-smart transportation alternatives, recycling or reuse sites, cultural and historic places that define your community, and gardens and natural areas.

Write a short survey to help gather more information from community members about wildlife, significant organizations, public transportation, cultural sites and other green places in your area. Do people of different age groups suggest different kinds of sites?

Check the library and online for resources on local tourism and natural and cultural history. Check with community and governmental offices, including planning boards and the parks department, to find out who is working behind the scenes to create and conserve a healthier environment. Check school, community and online bulletin boards for information on eco-events that might lead you to discover more green sites or greening initiatives underway in your community or region. Consider inviting a local expert to your class to help deepen your understanding of the sites and resources you have discovered.

Recording green site information: While you are in the field, use notebooks or index cards to keep track of the category, name and location of each green site. Some places may be very small, but if they are important for the environment, or just make you feel good about

being outdoors, record them for placement on your map. Write a few sentences about special features of the landscape and make sketches or take photos to capture the sites' key elements. Collect notes on noises and smells, as well as general impressions of the health and physical beauty of the area. Take down contact information for your sites (if available), which can be used by readers of your map who are looking for recreational, educational or volunteer opportunities.

Your map can point out any polluted toxic hot spots, too, along with blight sites that mar your environment. Be aware of the effects of pollution and neglect on residents in your neighborhood. Make note of the category, location and name of each toxic hot spot. You may need to get advice from a local environmental group to identify these polluted places. If you decide not to include toxic hot spots on your map, you can write an article about these sites for the school newspaper or website and suggest actions your peers can take to address pollution in your community. Discuss ways you can use your Green Map to help identify areas in your neighborhood that need more government resources and public attention.

Completing and organizing your list of sites: Share your list with your class. Are there any categories you missed? Do you need to conduct more research? Should additional recreational, cultural or historical places be included? When the list is complete, organize the green sites by type of site or by location. If possible, transfer the information into a computer database to make the data easier to use now or add to later. Some sites will require two or more icons to describe them fully, and you may want to create new categories and symbols in cases where the icons provided by GMS don't describe all the special places you've found. Add your newly-created icons to your Map Profile (at GreenMap.org) so they can be included in the list of locally-produced icons to be shared worldwide.

Making your map: Begin drafting your map by tracing a base map or drawing a diagram of your area. Use a copy machine or tracing paper to create a working map. Select colors and design elements that will enhance the map but will also reproduce well. Identify your map's geographic boundaries so that people seeing it for the first time will understand where your neighborhood is situated. Consider how users will navigate the map and how to draw attention to the most important features.

Place the icons in the appropriate places on your map. To identify each site by name, you can: a) put the site's name on the map next to the icon; b) number each icon on the map and put a numbered list of names (perhaps with additional site details) along the side; or c) place numbers on the map and put both icon and site name in a numbered list on the side. Registered mapmakers can download several useful resources for design and communication from GreenMap.org.

Your Green Map should tell the story of your neighborhood's ecology in a condensed and inviting way. Consider different ways to present the key information about each site. This might include poems, brief essays, or photos and drawings that will encourage people to discover new things about your community. You can place text on small pieces of paper on the working copy so they are easy to reposition. Be sure to include on your map:

- a key, which is a list that defines each icon and explains how to read the map

- an arrow pointing north, the scale of the map and the date of its creation

- a list of the members of your mapmaking team and the sources for the information listed on your map

- the Green Map System copyright ("Icons © Green Map System, Inc. 2003. All rights reserved. Green Map® is a registered trademark and used with permission"). You can also add the GMS logo.

- a title block or logo, as well as your own copyright (if desired) and your contact information

- a white border (at least 1 cm) around the map

When everything has been placed on your working map and you are happy with its appearance, copy or trace over it to create a clean, finished Green Map. Alternately, a computer-based map can be created from your data and images using a scanner and graphic design, desktop publishing or GIS (geographic information systems) software.

Sharing your map: Consider strategies for sharing your map with your school community, other schools nearby, community groups and elected officials. A large, colorful copy of your Green Map can be posted on a kiosk or bulletin board, or you can make a mural. You can share printed copies in the form of a folding map, postcard or poster (ask a local printer for help or photocopy the map and add color highlights by hand). Your map can also be photographed and posted on the Internet. Send or deliver your map or Internet map address to friends, relatives and the green businesses and other organizational sites listed on the map.

Send a press release or other background information about your project to local newspapers. Hold an event to publicize your map's completion, such a as a tour or presentation. Create a photo presentation, poster or mural to encourage everyone to visit the green sites you have discovered. Share your map worldwide through GreenMap.org and through the exhibits, books and presentations made by Green Map partners (take part in the online Mapmakers Exchange to learn more about these opportunities). Through the display and distribution of your map, you will be sharing knowledge of important resources and relationships in your community, teaching others the things that you have worked so hard to teach yourselves!

Evaluating your map: Draw some conclusions from the work you have done. What have you observed about the relationship between nature and our cultural (built) environment? What new things have you learned about the place where you live? What was your favorite part about making a Green Map? What was most difficult? What surprised you most? What was the strangest or most interesting thing you learned about your local environment? How does the number of green sites in your community compare with the number of toxic hot spots, blight areas or other problem sites? Can you think of ways to tip the balance in favor of a healthier, greener community? What can you do personally to change things for the better?

Keeping your map fresh: Update your Green Map from time to time to refresh your perspective on community sustainability and document how your community might have changed. Many people will suggest sites to be added to your map and you will continually notice new places to add as well. Keep notes in a safe place until you are ready to begin the new edition. Updating the Green Map could be a project that next year's students or club members take on.

Adapted with permission from resources at the Green Map System website <www.greenmap.org>.

Connecting Students with Special Needs to the Environment

by Lynn Dominguez
and Mary Lou Schilling

Subject areas: science, special education, outdoor education

Key concepts: recycling, waste management, water quality, water cycle, watersheds, habitats, toxins

Skills: decision making, constructing models, observation, taking scientific measurements, action taking, lifetime activities

Location: indoors and outdoors

Time: 5-week program of one or two hours daily; field trips to local parks, stores, river/lake

Materials: water-quality testing equipment, outdoor recreation equipment (canoes, paddles, personal floatation devices), consumable supplies (paper, tape, glue, poster board)

Special education class teams up with Central Michigan University students for field studies.

Environmental educators know that positive outdoor learning experiences assist in the development of environmental stewardship. But outdoor experiences are often regarded as luxuries for students who have a disability. Their school day already includes life and work skills, in addition to traditional academic subjects, and adding environmental education may seem impossible. Yet most people with a disability are capable of independent or semi-independent living, and, like all citizens, need to understand the impact of their daily actions on the natural environment. Far from being an "add-on," environmental education can be integrated into the curriculum in ways that supplement and enrich the learning experiences of students with disabilities.

We had the opportunity to offer a five-week environmental education program to high school students in a transition-to-work, special education class. These students, from 16 to 26 years of age, had a variety of disabilities, including Down syndrome, learning disabilities, fetal alcohol syndrome, mild and moderate mental retardation, emotional impairments and mild physical impairments. The goal of our program was to increase the students' knowledge of environmental issues, such as waste management and water quality, and to help them understand the impact of their environmental decisions on community life. In the following, we describe highlights of our program and offer teaching hints and recommendations that focus on educating people with special needs about the environment. Although ours was a self-contained special education class, the techniques described can be applied to any science or environmental education classroom to facilitate inclusion of students with special needs.

Our environmental education program ran two hours daily for five weeks. The facilitators were university students majoring in environmental education and therapeutic recreation, who volunteered through a partnership between the high school and the university.

The program was initially implemented in the classroom and progressed to include field trips to local parks, most of which were within walking distance of the classroom. The parks provided access to a river, fields and woodlots, thus allowing students to explore a variety of habitats. Riverfront access also provided opportunities for water-quality testing, paddling instruction and river cleanups (a lifeguard was present for the river cleanup and canoeing).

While special education resources for environmental education are limited, many hands-on activities designed for elementary-level students can be successfully adapted for older students. Local rangers and other natural resource personnel can be invited to share their knowledge, and interpreters and nature center staff can help in adapting and developing lessons for people with special needs. In developing lesson plans, we adapted a variety of environmental education activities, giving special emphasis to hands-on discovery methods and techniques. Curricular content included the following four thematic areas:

Air, water and soil: Activities included discussions of the benefits of clean air, water and soil; the impact of air, water and soil pollution on humans and wildlife; how to keep the environment clean; and garden and tree planting. This thematic area was used to introduce many concepts that were built upon in the following sections of the program. For example, a "web of life" activity was used to integrate the concept of habitat and the interconnections between humans and wildlife.

Water cycle and watersheds: This area of instruction included an activity demonstrating the water cycle, an action-oriented activity exploring the impact of toxins on wildlife and natural habitats, and the construction of watershed models that demonstrated how toxins are carried in a water system and potentially into drinking water.

Recycling and product packaging: Activities in this thematic area focused on identification of recycling symbols and codes, knowledge of recyclable items, sorting of recyclable products, creative or homemade strategies for recycling, and product purchasing to minimize unnecessary packaging.

Water-quality testing and river clean-up: This curricular area included water-quality testing, an introduction to the Adopt-a-Stream program, a river cleanup, and instruction in canoe paddling, which was intended to facilitate the river cleanup and introduce students to a potentially lifelong outdoor recreation activity.

Tips on exploring the outdoors

Environmental education activities that promote hands-on exploration in the outdoors are uniquely suited to meeting the learning needs of students with disability. The following tips should help you as you explore the outdoors with your students:

1. Develop buddy systems that allow people without disability to assist people with disability. This technique was particularly helpful in our work with people with mental retardation, fetal alcohol syndrome and Down syndrome. The buddy system provided instructional assistance, enhanced safety and fostered inclusion. Buddies can be recruited from local schools, colleges, seniors' organizations or community groups.

2. Focus on the process rather than on the outcome of the activity. For example, during a paddle down a river, encourage students to become aware of the natural habitat rather than placing primary focus on the length of the trip and the quality of the paddling stroke. This is particularly helpful when working with people with more severe disability.

3. Repeat and review more often than you would with regular students, especially when teaching more complex and abstract concepts. To reduce boredom, use a variety of approaches to teach the same concept or skill. For example, when we discussed the water cycle, students drew the water cycle on the board, participated in a role-playing activity in which they became parts of the water cycle, created posters tracing the cycle of a raindrop, and taught a water cycle activity to early elementary students.

4. Identify the strengths of the students in order to focus on abilities rather than disabilities. For example, the building of watershed models allowed students to work cooperatively in teams. Some were able to visualize the final product and were best at directing tasks,

others were good at manipulating the small objects used in model construction, while others enjoyed "making it rain" on the model. Everyone on the team contributed to the final outcome, a working watershed model.

5. Encourage participation by all students in the class. Active participation reinforces abstract concepts that are first introduced in the classroom (e.g., water quality) and then applied outdoors (e.g., water testing). This also assures interaction between group members to enhance communication and social skills.

6. Consider both mental and chronological age when selecting activities. The content must be appropriate for the students' mental age, while the process (e.g., leadership style, equipment used, instruction location) needs to be consistent with their chronological age. In other words, it is important to respect students' chronological age while directing information to their mental age. We found, for example, that the board game Candy Land, intended for four- to eight-year-olds, could easily be adapted for teenagers whose chronological age exceeded their mental age. We kept

the color-coded game path and flash cards for moving forward, but destination cards that showed such points as the "peppermint forest" and "ice cream sea" were changed to show people involved in environmentally responsible actions, such as recycling or planting a tree. Cards that showed oil spills and glass bottles being thrown in the trash were used to move participants backwards on the board. The card showing the final destination depicted a local park where the students had recently participated in a trash cleanup.

7. Use field trips as sensory learning experiences to help students become more aware of the environment. Encourage students to touch, smell and listen (especially with their eyes closed). We found that most of our students had never been encouraged to listen to natural sounds around them, or to smell flowers, touch trees, or plunge their hands into cold river water.

8. Provide the most normal learning environment possible. Students with cognitive impairments do not easily transfer information presented in the classroom to the natural environment. Therefore, we created

In-class activities to demonstrate environmental concepts

Web of Life (ecological relationships): After discussing the components of habitat (food, shelter, environmental factors), students form a circle. One student, holding a ball of yarn, names a wild animal (e.g., a hawk). Other students then name something the animal needs to survive (e.g., prey items such as mice and voles, trees, nesting sites, clean water). As students contribute ideas, the ball of yarn is passed around the circle until it forms a web connecting each student to all the others. Then the instructor proposes various scenarios that would have an effect on one or more of the components. The student who is affected gives a tug on the yarn, and everyone who feels the tug, tugs back. This activity helps

students understand the connections among the various components in a habitat.

Down the Drain (waste management): Students are instructed to bring from home the packaging of a product that they or their family routinely wash down the drain, such as toothpaste, shampoo, laundry soap, drain cleaner and dishwashing detergent. Students share information about the items and sort them into toxic and nontoxic categories. The instructor then leads a discussion on the correct ways to dispose of toxic household chemicals, and the students construct their own educational posters related to proper disposal of such chemicals.

Watershed Models (water flow and pollution): Students work in small groups to construct watershed models in pans. Aluminum foil and wooden blocks are used to shape hills, ponds and a river that flows into a large lake. Paper cups with small holes punched in the bottom are used to create rain. Students observe rain falling on the hills and running over the contours of the land, collecting in the river and traveling to the lake. Point and non-point sources of pollution are illustrated by placing drops of food coloring or a pinch of colored drink crystals on top of some of the hills. Students can trace the path of the pollutants throughout the watershed by watching the water change color.

the most functional learning environments possible: for example, water quality testing was done at the riverbank. We found that the students learned and applied skills with greater ease when they were actively involved outdoors.

9. Adapt activities to the physical impairments of the individual. The following adaptive strategies promote success.

• For people with vision impairment, use tactile boundaries, brightly colored objects and specific visual cues.

• For those who are hard of hearing, provide extra visual aids, avoid hand gestures, and assure proper lighting and positioning. Be aware of secondary medical conditions (e.g., cardiac problems, asthma and diabetes) that may restrict or limit participation. Seek the advice of a medical practitioner where appropriate.

• When a person demonstrates decreased strength and endurance, reduce the length of activity sessions and build in rest periods. When a person demonstrates decreased balance, it may be appropriate to provide a wider base of support, lower the center of gravity or use stability bars. If a person displays decreased coordination, you may wish to increase the size of the equipment and use lightweight, stable equipment.

10. Teach new concepts at the beginning of a session when participants are most alert. The majority of students we worked with had varying levels of mental retardation, and we found this technique assured attention to tasks and improved learning.

11. Use step-by-step instruction. Activities may need to be broken down into sequential training steps to accommodate students' attention deficits and to assure success.

12. Remember that success and fun are the basic ingredients of any recreational or environmental education activity. Make activities fun so that students will maintain their enthusiasm and want to return to your outdoor classroom.

Outcomes

Both students and their classroom teachers were highly motivated and enthusiastic participants in our program. Students said that they had never before been asked how they felt about the environment. Teachers reported continued discussions and homework projects centered on environmental concerns during the program. Most exciting to us was the long-term involvement of the students in environmental activities after our program ended. The students developed and implemented a one-hour environmental education session on the water cycle for a second grade classroom. Additionally, one group continued doing river cleanups.

A new group of students has now entered the transition-to-work classroom, and our outdoor and environmental education students at the university will continue their involvement by partnering with the class to provide environmental programs that are integrated with and supplemental to the classroom curriculum. By providing opportunities for all students to learn about the environment and their impact upon it, teachers can play an important role in helping students move into the community as better prepared, environmentally responsible, informed citizens.

Lynn Dominguez and *Mary Lou Schilling* are instructors in Outdoor and Environmental Recreation and Therapeutic Recreation at Central Michigan University in Mt. Pleasant, Michigan.

Resources

Local agencies and programs

• Local park and recreation agencies with therapeutic recreation programs
• Community colleges with teacher education programs
• Natural resource agencies
• Local universities with outdoor and therapeutic recreation programs

Websites

<www.recreationtherapy.com/tractv.htm> Therapeutic Recreation Directory (activity ideas for recreation therapy)

<www.accesstr.com> Access to Recreation (adaptive equipment)

<www.spokesnmotion.com> Spokes 'n Motion (adaptive equipment)

<www.abledata.com/abledata.cfm> Able Data (assistive technology)

<www.pvamagazines.com/sns/magazine/article.php> Sports 'n Spokes magazine (published by Paralyzed Veterans of America)

Print

American Forest Foundation. *Project Learning Tree: Environmental Education Activity Guide, Pre-K to 8*. American Forest Foundation, 2006.

Bialeschki, M.D. "Environmental Education Needs of Special Populations." *Journal of Environmental Education*, 13:1, 1981, pp. 39–44.

Brannan, S., A. Fullerton, J. R.Arick, G.M.Robb and M. Bender. *Including Youth With Disabilities in Outdoor Programs: Best Practices, Outcomes, and Resources*. Sagamore Publishing, 2003.

Carter, M. J., G.E. Van Andel and G.M. Robb. *Therapeutic Recreation: A Practical Approach* (3rd ed.). Waveland Press, 2003.

Cornell, Joseph. *Sharing Nature With Children II*. Dawn Publications, 1989.

Environmental Protection Agency. *Let's Reduce and Recycle: A Curriculum for Solid Waste Awareness*. EPA Publication 530-SW-90-005, 1990.

National Wildlife Federation. *Access Nature*. National Wildlife Federation, 2001.

Western Regional Environmental Education Council. *Project WILD Activity Guide*. 2001.

Exploring The Earth Charter

A series of experiential education activities for guiding students through The Earth Charter

by Linda Hill

Key concepts: Earth community, diversity, sustainable global society, respect for nature, universal human rights, economic justice, peace, equality, global partnerships, tensions between diverse values, balancing human needs with nature's needs, personal and collective responsibility

Skills: working together, achieving common goals, observing, multi-sensory listening, shifting perspectives, connecting abstract issues to personal experience, reading comprehension, cooperative learning, divergent thinking, meditation, visualization, connecting with nature, debriefing

Location: indoors and outdoors

Time: 10 hours or more for all six activities

Materials: copy of The Earth Charter for each student (download from <www.earthcharter.com>) and additional materials as noted below for each activity

Making meaningful connections with The Earth Charter can be a challenge for students, and for teachers as well. The Earth Charter is a comprehensive and detailed document, and the sheer number of interconnected issues in its 4 main themes, 16 principles, and 61 sub-principles can seem overwhelming. In 2003, when a group of us decided to take on the challenge of guiding youth to explore The Earth Charter, one of our members, a 15-year-old student, commented, "The role of the document is to bring together many countries with huge issues that we can't even begin to comprehend. The sixteen sub-headings carry so much meaning in themselves that you could have an entire conference on just one of them .... The Earth Charter, I agree, is an excellent document, but much too complex for our age group."

In response to this concern, we considered using one of the simplified versions of The Earth Charter that have been written for young people.[1] However, we soon realized that none of them matches the powerful beauty of the original text. So we stopped searching for simpler words and chose direct experience as the best

I had never before heard of or was interested in The Earth Charter, but through this past couple of days, I have never been so overwhelmed with compassion for diversity and a desire to help this world and the people in it.

I learned that The Earth Charter encompasses all the important aspects of us, as humans living on this planet. It states how we can live with each other and the rest of the world in a positive way.

Exploring the Preamble
Move Forward Challenge

Key concepts: critical moment, to move forward, diversity, human family, Earth community, sustainable global society, respect for nature, universal human rights, economic justice, peace, responsibility

Skills: working together, strategies needed for achieving common goals.

Location: indoors or outdoors

Time: 10–20 minutes

Materials: copy of The Earth Charter for each student

The preamble to The Earth Charter states, "To move forward, we must recognize that in the midst of a magnificent diversity of cultures and life forms we are one human family and one Earth Community with a common destiny." This activity, adapted from an improvisational theater exercise,[2] encourages students

teacher. We set out to develop or adapt participatory activities that would provide opportunities for students to make spiritual, emotional, personal and practical as well as cognitive connections with The Earth Charter. The following activities have been field-tested in our four-day intergenerational Earth Charter Camps held each autumn. We have found that they work very well with youth and can be easily adapted in many ways and for any age group. We have used them successfully with adults of all ages and with children as young as six. As these comments from high school students show, young people find this experiential approach to learning about The Earth Charter to be interesting, relevant and inspiring:

Exploring The Earth Charter made us realize how much our lives are connected to the Earth.

The Earth Charter is a widely recognized international declaration of fundamental principles for building a just, sustainable and peaceful global society. It is the result of one of the most ambitious multicultural and multilingual global consultation processes ever attempted. In the decade following the 1992 Earth Summit in Rio de Janeiro, representatives of the world's governments, religions, diverse cultures, and grassroots and non-governmental organizations collaborated in drafting and redrafting the ethics and principles that should govern human conduct on the planet. The result is a powerful synthesis of political action that goes far beyond the International Declaration of Human Rights to consider both people and the environment. The Earth Charter contains 16 principles addressing the themes of respect and care for the community of life; ecological integrity; social and economic justice; and democracy, non-violence and peace. Since the release of the Charter in June 2000, this "people's treaty"

has been endorsed by UNESCO, the World Conservation Union and over 2,500 other organizations — governments, businesses, faith groups, educational institutions and non-governmental organizations around the world. The Earth Charter is central to the United Nations Decade of Education for Sustainable Development, 2005–2014.

In the classroom and community, The Earth Charter can be used to raise awareness of global interdependence and as a basis for discussing values and responsibilities, both individual and collective, in an interdependent world. It may lead to brainstorming how the principles it outlines can help in solving local problems. It may even prompt questions about the values and assumptions of the curriculum. The following pages present a series of experiential, cross-curricular activities that can be used to guide students through each section of the Charter, the full text of which can be downloaded in many languages at The Earth Charter website <www.earthcharter.org>. — *Editors* to think about the challenges of working together and the strategies needed for achieving common goals.

Procedure:

1. Have students take turns reading the first paragraph of the preamble aloud.

2. Instruct students to line up side by side and to walk together — in step — toward the same destination without talking (for example, from one side of a gymnasium or field to the other). Other than reminding students not to talk, do not give any more instructions or advice as they attempt to move forward to a common destination.

3. After a few minutes of this non-verbal experimenting, gather in a circle, discuss what is working and what isn't, and plan strategies. For example, you and your students may decide to work on this challenge in small groups, and build up to moving forward as one large unit. You may decide that all should lead with the same foot and keep step with the person to the left or right as the group moves.

4. Try the exercise again and then gather in a circle to debrief. Ask students to take turns connecting their experience to the first paragraph of the preamble to The Earth Charter. Some examples of insights shared by students that we have worked with are:

You really have to pay attention to each other if you are going to the same place.

It's easier for a small group of people to be in step than for a big group to work together.

Sometimes I wished that we could have elected one leader and just followed that person instead of all trying to figure it out together.

The more we practiced, the easier it was to move forward together.

Getting To Know Other Living Beings

Key concepts: we are part of a community of life; we live within ecological systems

Skills: observing, multisensory listening, shifting perspectives, concern for all living beings

Location: outdoors in a natural area

Time: 40 minutes or more

Materials: copy of The Earth Charter and interview questions for each student

The second paragraph of the preamble reminds us that "Earth, our home, is alive with a unique community of life." This activity for getting to know the living beings in your community is adapted from one by Joseph Cornell, an inspirational nature educator who uses the power of relationship building to reduce prejudice against nature.

Procedure:

1. After reading the second paragraph of The Earth Charter, "Earth Our Home," send students outside on short solo journeys in a nearby natural area with instructions to find another living being to interview. This could be a tree, a squirrel or any other living being, or a larger living system such as a body of water.

2. Encourage students to ask the following questions (silently or aloud), one at a time, and then write down the answers that come to them as they watch, listen and try to understand the perspectives of other beings who share Earth, our home.

- How old are you?

- What forces of nature and uncertainties have you experienced in your life?

- From your viewpoint, what does the Earth provide for you that is essential for you and your kind to survive and for your species to evolve?

- What do you need in order to preserve your health?

- What finite resources are you concerned about?

- What can people like me do to help protect your vitality, diversity and beauty?

3. Invite students to debrief by sharing their answers and insights with the rest of the group. One group of high school students who spent an entire morning interviewing living beings, were inspired to collaborate in writing a poem by contributing one verse each as they shared what they learned from their encounters with living beings in nature (see sidebar, page 168).

Equality Tag

Key concepts: patterns of competitive production and consumption, injustice, equality, inequality, trends are perilous but not inevitable, forming global partnerships, interconnected challenges, forging inclusive solutions

Skills: observing, connecting abstract issues to personal experience, debriefing

Location: gymnasium or grassy field

Time: 20–30 minutes

Materials: copy of The Earth Charter and two slips of paper for each student, bandanas to tuck into waistbands, nametags

In this activity, students explore the global situation and the dominant patterns of competitive production and consumption by comparing two different ways of playing tag.

Procedure:

1. Hand out name tags and encourage students to use each other's names during the debriefings.

2. Read aloud the third paragraph of the preamble, "The Global Situation."

3. Have students play the traditional version of tag: one or two players who are "It" run around chasing the other players; students who get tagged are sent out of the game; and the last one or two players to be tagged become "It" for the next round. As an alternative to tagging (and to avoid arguments over who was and wasn't tagged), hand out bandanas for students to tuck into waistbands; the players who are "It" pull the bandanas.

4. After two or three rounds, facilitate a debriefing discussion in which students reflect on what this children's game teaches about the effects of the dominant patterns of production and consumption on the global situation. Some of the types of comments you may hear are: *"The fastest runners always win, as in survival of the fittest," "I can't run very fast so I always get tagged. It feels a lot like going extinct,"* and *"Playing tag is a lot like war."*

5. Read the last sentence of the paragraph titled "The Global Situation" to remind your students that "These trends are perilous — but not inevitable." Then read aloud the fourth paragraph titled "The Challenges Ahead." Inform the students that they are going to play another version of tag, called Equality Tag,[3] which explores the concepts in the paragraph they have just read.

Explain that in Equality Tag, everyone is 'It' and everyone has the same goal: to tag two people whose names they will draw in a minute. They do not tag by touching these two people. Instead, they tag by positioning themselves — and keeping themselves positioned — equidistantly between the two people whose names they picked. This position might be the central point in a line between the two people or one point of a triangle. Players can go anywhere they like within the boundaries of the game so long as they are an equal distance between the two people they are responsible for tagging. Ask for two volunteers and demonstrate this new way of tagging.

6. Give two slips of paper to each student and have them print their names on these slips. Place the papers face down in the middle of the circle. For example, if there are 30 students, there will be 60 slips of paper in the middle of the circle.

7. Ask students to pick up two slips of paper, making sure that they have the names of two different people. If they pick their own name or two slips of paper with the same name, they must put one back and select a different slip of paper.

Cooperative Poem

A group of high school students cooperatively wrote this poem by contributing one verse each as they shared what they learned from their encounters with other living beings.

I lay in the open
Rain falls
In my eyes
Relaxing
Clearing all worries
From my mind.

When the wind blows
I can feel
It blows on
All my tiring feelings.
It invites
People, animals, insects, fish
To be part of it.

Realize
Most people
Just look at them
As plants
Although they
Are living beings also.

Learn
Nature wants to be
Seen
Touched
Felt
Not destroyed.

Look around
Realize
Plants hurt
Limbs missing
Tops broken
Close your eyes
Hear a lot more.

Sound of branches
In the breeze
Rustle the earth
Distant calls of ravens
All drift
Like whispers
To my ears.

Wild
And free
Trapped
With disability
Just like me.

Nice to be in the woods again
Like a child
Discovering new things
Learning there is
No such thing as
Living forever.

Caution students not to reveal the names they have chosen until the game is over. Once they have silently read and remembered the names on their slips of paper and secretly located the two students they are to tag, collect the slips for use in the second round.

8. Without further discussion, play the game. As students try to center themselves between the two people they are responsible for tagging, everyone will begin to circulate, each movement triggering many others in an active, interdependent fashion.

9. After students have played for a few minutes, gather in a circle to talk about what happened and share strategies. Participants may mention the importance of knowing each other's names, maintaining wide-angle vision, and constantly adapting to what the others do.

10. Pool the names again, ask students to pick two new names, and play a few more rounds. The game will speed up and slow down and sometimes even stop on its own as everyone gradually finds a stable place to stand, only to speed up again when someone explores what happens when they shift positions. Students may suggest new ways of selecting the players to tag or other rules they want to try. Follow students' suggestions so long as they remain relevant to the goals of exploring partnership, care, interconnectedness and inclusiveness. Stop playing when you feel that the students are fully engaged in the game, but before everyone gets bored.

11. Gather in a circle and give students opportunities to discuss the lessons they have learned about the challenges involved in forging inclusive solutions. The following are comments that we have heard:

I couldn't figure out who was trying to tag me, but I knew that I was important to at least two people in the group.

Instead of trying to have one winner, everyone was winning all the time.

I felt like we were all connected and included. Maybe this is the way all the other plants and animals on Earth relate to each other already?

If you are new to cooperative games, you may find it helpful to do some trial runs with a few willing students before you play Equality Tag with an entire class. The rules are simple and the only thing you can do wrong is to stand around explaining so long that there is no time left to play. State the rules, demonstrate, do the selecting and start playing. If you have students with mobility or vision challenges, be sure to encourage them to play both forms of tag and share their insights. You will find that there are many ways for students to interact with you, the activity, and with each other, and you can never completely predict the outcome. Do not be discouraged if a game does not go exactly as you hoped it would. Play in a spirit of respect, choice and fun, and then accept whatever lessons are learned. The most important aspect of experiential learning is to give students opportunities to share what they observed and realized during the experience.

Exploring Earth Charter Principles
Balancing Our Universal Responsibilities

Key concepts: tensions between diverse values, balancing human needs with nature's needs, overview of Earth Charter principles

Skills: reading comprehension, connecting abstract concepts with personal experience, cooperative learning, divergent thinking, creative process

Time: 2–4 hours (can be done over several periods)

Materials: copy of The Earth Charter for each student, 100–150 blank file cards, access to creative art supplies such as costumes, musical instruments, paints, poster board and other art supplies

This activity involves students in identifying the many issues addressed by the 16 principles of The Earth Charter and gives opportunities to explore creatively the challenges involved in acknowledging and balancing this diverse array of human and ecological concerns. The activity requires at least two hours and is best carried out over three or four class periods. The creative process will be enhanced by having students who enjoy drama, drawing, music, writing and other creative arts to share leadership in ways that encourage everyone's artistic potential.

Procedure:
Note: Steps 1–7 take about 40 minutes.
1. Explain to students that they will be working collaboratively in small, diverse groups to develop a creative presentation or "balancing act" that explores the challenges of balancing human needs with the needs of all the other living beings in our Earth community.

2. Read the last paragraph of the preamble to The Earth Charter with your students. This paragraph, in the section titled "Universal Responsibility," prepares us to "affirm the following interdependent principles for a sustainable way of life as a common standard by which the conduct of all individuals, organizations, businesses, governments, and transnational institutions is to be guided and assessed."

3. Have students divide into 16 groups of two or three students each. Since much of The Earth Charter is focused on exploring the magnificent diversity of cultures and life forms, encourage students to work with partners from different backgrounds.

4. Give each pair or triad one of the 16 Earth Charter principles to read. Instruct them to search for as many noun phrases as they can find and write the number of the principle and each these phrases in large print on file cards. For example, students studying Principle 8 ("Advance the study of ecological sustainability ....") would select at least a few of the following noun phrases: ecological sustainability, open exchange, knowledge, sustainability, developing nations, traditional knowledge, spiritual wisdom, cultures, environmental protection, human well-being, information, human health, genetic information, public domain. (These are 14 of the more than 100 global priorities identified by the thousands of people who helped write The Earth Charter.)

5. Have the students lay the file cards face up over a large area on the ground or gym floor, and then form a circle around the cards. Spread out the cards, leaving enough space for students to walk among them without stepping on them.

6. Instruct students to take a round-trip walk through the file cards, first to get an overview of the topics and issues, and then to pick up one or two cards they feel connected to or attracted to. Once they have selected their cards, they return to their place in the circle.

7. Have the students form new groups with one or two different partners. Instruct them to take turns reading out one of their cards and sharing the personal or local connections they have with that global issue. They can also take turns recording these connections. For example, a student who selects a card that says "Principle 7: Renewable Energy Sources" might say, *"I use gas in my car and oil in my house, but these fossil fuels won't last forever"* or *"Sugar gives me energy,"* or *"I love being out in the sun."* There are no wrong answers.

Note: Steps 8 to 9 take at least 90 minutes and can be split into one period for preparing and a second period for presenting.

8. Have the students keep the cards they have chosen and form new (but still diverse) groups of about 6–8 students with at least one self-identified artistic leader in each group. One way to do this is to have students put their names on color-coded sticky notes according to what subjects they enjoy the most (red for art or drama, green for science, blue for physical education,

yellow for reading/writing, etc.) and then form multi-colored groups.

9. Explain that the challenge for each group is to develop a creative presentation that includes and balances all of the issues that the members of their group are concerned about (the issues on the cards they have picked up), and then to present their "balancing acts" to the rest of the class. They can use drama, art, music, poetry or any other creative way of balancing the issues. Give students plenty of time to share their personal connections to The Earth Charter issues with the rest of the group. Trust that the groups will come up with many creative ideas on their own. When we have facilitated this activity, we have seen poetry, art, skits and many other creative presentations emerge. For example, one group created a mural showing their issues as an interconnected web, explaining that if one string of the web is broken, everyone else feels the impact.

Creating an Earth Charter globe

Key concepts: visualization of The Earth Charter principles

Skills: reading comprehension, visualizing abstract concepts, cooperative learning, divergent thinking, creative process

Time: 2–4 hours (can be done over several periods)

Materials: copy of The Earth Charter for each student, 20 sheets of Bristol board or cardboard approximately 55 cm (22") square, scissors, paint, pastels, newspapers, nature magazines and other art supplies

It takes only a few periods to create a globe that your class can display and use to educate the rest of the school about The Earth Charter. Some teachers will recognize that the pattern for making this globe is an enlarged version of a common pattern for making tree ornaments out of Christmas cards. To get a clear idea of what you and your students will be creating, see the instructions and pictures of the globe made at the 2003 Youth Explore The Earth Charter conference. Go to <http://members.shaw.ca/earthcharter/> and follow the "Youth Explore The Earth Charter" link.

Preparation: Cut 20 circular panels 55 cm (22") in diameter from Bristol board or cardboard.

Procedure:

1. Divide the class into four groups and assign each group one of the four sections of The Earth Charter: Respect and Care for the Environment; Ecological Integrity; Social and Economic Justice; and Democracy, Nonviolence, and Peace. Make sure that each group has a few students who enjoy reading, a few students who enjoy visual arts, and a few students who are passionate about that section of The Earth Charter.

2. Explain that the goal is to cooperate in creating a globe that shows the students' personal and local connections with The Earth Charter. Each group is responsible for working together to create five circular panels: one panel that illustrates the main theme of their section of The Earth Charter, and four panels that illustrate the four principles within that section. The panels should vividly communicate what the themes and principles mean to them as global citizens, as well as what actions they can take locally to implement the principles. Students may collect items from nature and use any of the available art supplies to draw images or symbols, write down important phrases, make a collage, or find other ways of translating the words of The Earth Charter into visual images. Give students two or three class periods to discuss and research the issues and to create their panels.

3. After the groups have completed their panels, but before constructing the globe, have them present and explain their panels to the rest of the class. One idea

is to display the panels as in an art gallery. Using the jigsaw approach, have students tour the "gallery" in groups of four, each student in the group representing one of the four sections of The Earth Charter. Students then can guide each other through the visionary world you have all created together. You may also want to facilitate a class discussion about connections between The Earth Charter panels and students' own lives.

4. To transform the 20 circular panels into an Earth Charter globe, begin by making a template for an equilateral triangle, the three points of which extend to the edge of the circle. (A teacher or student who knows about geometry can help with this.)

5. Trace the template on the back of each circle, and fold along the traced lines to form triangles with three side flaps, as shown.

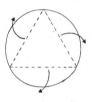

6. Arrange five of the panels as if they were the triangular pieces of a pie, with the artwork and flaps facing up, as shown. Then staple (or tape or glue) them together along two sides to form a large dome. Arrange and staple another five panels to form a second dome.

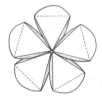

7. Staple together the remaining ten panels into one long horizontal band, as shown. If you think of the long strip as the equator, and the two domes as the North Pole and the South Pole, it is fairly easy to put the globe together. Hang your globe in a central location in your school and use it to educate other students about The Earth Charter.

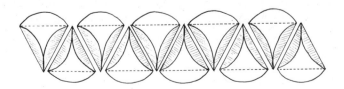

The Way Forward
Earth Charter meditation

Key concepts: reflecting on "The Way Forward" final section of The Earth Charter

Skills: meditation, visualization, connecting with nature

Time: 40 minutes including debriefing

Materials: copy of The Earth Charter and a piece of high quality 8.5" by 11" paper for each student, felt pens

This walking meditation[4] is a reflective activity that provides opportunities for students to develop intellectual, emotional and spiritual connections with the last section of The Earth Charter.

Procedure:

1. Have students take turns reading "The Way Forward" aloud, one sentence at a time, and then hand out felt pens and paper and have students print the sentence they read on the paper. Here are a few examples:

> *Live with reverence for the mystery of being, gratitude for the gift of life, and humility regarding the human place in nature.*
>
> *Life involves tensions between important values.*
>
> *We must find ways to harmonize diversity with unity.*
>
> *The arts, sciences, religions, educational institutions, media, businesses, non-governmental organizations, and governments are all called to offer creative leadership.*

2. Post the quotations along a route through a place of great natural beauty such as a trail through a forest.

3. Gather students at the beginning of the route and send them one at a time for a silent walk along the trail. Encourage them to take time to stop and read each quotation, and then tune in to what the living beings in this ecological community have to tell them before moving on to the next quotation. You and your students may want to debrief through art, writing or discussions in pairs or small groups; or you may wish to use this as a private meditation on individual actions we can take to implement the principles and values of The Earth Charter.

In the words of one of our students, "The Earth Charter is the world I want to live in." In the words of The Earth Charter, "Let ours be a time remembered for the awakening of a new reverence for life, the firm resolve to achieve sustainability, the quickening of the struggle for justice and peace, and the joyful celebration of life."

Linda Hill is the author of Connecting Kids: Exploring Diversity Together *(New Society Publishers, 2001), mentor to The Earth Charter Youth Initiative and coordinator of Inclusive Leadership Adventures, a non-profit peace education project that guides participants in exploring and celebrating diversity. She lives in Duncan, British Columbia.*

Notes

1. For several adaptations of The Earth Charter for younger audiences, see <www.earthcharter.org>. Click on "Resources" and then on "3.1 Primary and Secondary School."

2. The Move Forward Challenge was adapted by Michael Slaby, coordinator of the international Earth Charter Youth Initiative, from an improvisational theater exercise.

3. I learned Equality Tag from a summer camp counsellor who adapted it from Joanna Macy's Systems Game found in *Coming Back to Life: Practices to Reconnect Our Lives, Our World* by Joanna Macy and Molly Young Brown, New Society Publishers, 1998.

4. The Earth Charter Meditation was adapted from "The Trail of Beauty" activity in Joseph Cornell's *With Beauty Before Me: An Inspirational Guide for Nature Walks*, Dawn Publications, 2000. Cornell's many books are filled with ideas for connecting students to other living beings that can easily be adapted to guide students to explore The Earth Charter. See <www.sharingnature.com>.

References

Cornell, Joseph. *Journey to the Heart of Nature.* Dawn Publications, 1994.

Cornell, Joseph. *With Beauty Before Me: An Inspirational Guide for Nature Walks.* Dawn Publications, 2000.

Earth Charter Commission. "The Earth Charter: Values and Principles for a Sustainable Future," San Jose, Costa Rica: Earth Charter International Secretariat, 2000, available as a four-page pamphlet online at <www.earthcharter.org>. Click on "About Us."

Macy, Joanna and Molly Young Brown. *Coming Back to Life: Practices to Reconnect Our Lives, Our World.* New Society Publishers, 1998.

Resources

At The Earth Charter Initiative website <www.earthcharter.org>, one can freely download and print copies of The Earth Charter in English as well as 31 other languages. The Resources section has an extensive collection of educational resources. Among the most useful background documents are the 45-page *Earth Charter Handbook* and the 100-page *Earth Charter: A Study Book Of Reflection For Action* by Elizabeth Ferraro and Joe Holland. Among the many educational resources is Brendan Mackey's five-page *Earth Charter Curriculum Stimulus Material*, which suggests activities for five subject areas. *Good Practices in Education for Sustainable Development Using The Earth Charter* outlines Charter-inspired projects around the world. In addition to these documents, the website has educational ideas and outlines for several entire courses submitted by educators from around the globe.

Walking into Wonder

Through observation walks, students discover the extraordinary in the ordinary and develop personal connections to the world around them

Photographs by John Sherk

by Cynthia Macleod

Subject areas: ethics, science, language arts, art

Key concepts: observation walks, natural systems, human impact, transportation, free writing, active observation, journaling, artifacts

Skills: observation, working in groups, drawing, writing, making presentations

Location: classroom and outdoors

Time: 2 hours per walk (30 minutes pre-walking, 1 hour walking, 30 minutes post-walk discussion or journaling)

Materials: journals, sketchpads, digital cameras or video recorder (optional)

Every day I walk twenty minutes to school along the streets of Brooklyn. Day after day, I walk on the same sidewalks and cross the same streets. Often, I find myself lost in my own thoughts — usually going over my lesson plans for the day or making "to do" lists. Sometimes I am in a rush and catch myself practically jogging. But most days I try to set aside this time to attend to the details of my surroundings. Every day the walk differs from the one the day before — a handful more leaves are off the chestnut tree; someone has lost a gray glove on the ground; a small house sparrow enjoys a pothole full of rainwater. When I begin to see these signs, I know that I have left off my usual rush and have entered the realm of observant walking. Each new detail makes the familiar trip more and more like an adventure. I look at everyday sights with fresh eyes, my senses sharpen, and I begin to absorb my surroundings. In this way, my daily walk helps me to make contact with my environment and the delicate and miraculous systems that exist within and around it.

Why teach observant walking?

Walking is an environmentally friendly mode of transportation for many. Yet observant walking is not the kind of walking that most of us usually do, and it may be an entirely new experience for some of our students. Learning to walk with awareness can open us to a greater sense of connection with our surroundings and enable us to find joy in the specifics of our life settings. For our students, this personal connection to their immediate place can jump-start a lifetime of caring for the environment. By taking class time for observant walking, teachers can help students see the ordinary as extraordinary, to understand their connection to their environment and to think consciously about how they wish to relate with it.

Whether in an urban or a rural setting, there are many opportunities to integrate observation walks into a curriculum. Observation walks can be part of an environmental science class geared towards scientific observation; they can be part of a social studies unit looking at the history of a place; or, as I use them, they can be part of an environmental ethics curriculum, helping students explore questions about the relationship between humans and the Earth. Observation exercises are useful as an introduction to a course, as a precursor to readings or as a weekly assignment. Although the activities described here work best with students aged 13 and up, they can be modified for younger students by focusing on discussion instead of reading and writing and by emphasizing group work. Walks can be assigned to students individually as homework or they can be undertaken all together or in small groups during class time.

Pre-walking

Observation walks, to be most effective, should be preceded by what I term "pre-walking." This stage of the activity encompasses readings and discussions about how to walk as an active observer. I have found it easiest to begin by eliciting students' own experiences of times when they have been particularly aware of their environment. Often this will have been when they were traveling, had just moved to a new place or were about to leave someplace they love. Sometimes students will remember special places close to home, such as a tree in which they built a tree house or a park where they spent time with their family. Ask students, in pairs or small groups, to think of such special places in their lives and then to share with the class what they remember about these places. Did the water in the pool they loved seem bluer than any blue they had seen? Were the stars brighter the night before they left than in any sky they had ever seen? What was different or special about this place that made their surroundings stand out?

An in-depth conversation about the significance of special places to students can help them to recognize why observation is important and to realize that they already unwittingly record information about

the places where they go. Another tack is to discuss journeys, long and short, and how students have been influenced by the journeys they have taken. Another is to discuss the five senses and how each sense observes in a different way. Readings, particularly pieces about the local area, can also be a rich aspect of pre-walking.

Free walking

Somewhat analogous to free-writing exercises, free walking is a great way to introduce students to the idea of walking as a learning tool. Students walk freely for a defined period of time, five to ten minutes, in an area that is familiar to them or in a place they consider peaceful. I ask students to let their attention wander during free walks and see what jumps out at them. A free-walking exercise can be neatly followed by a focused free-writing exercise. Students can write continuously, without pausing, about what they noticed while they walked and what thoughts or memories these observations stirred in their minds.

Focused walks

I use a variety of walks for different purposes. All of the following walks share the need for careful attention to the surroundings, and each gives tools to help students heighten their sensitivity to a specific aspect of their environment. Students can a take a series of focused walks along the same route and then compare and discuss the different modes at the end of the series. They can take the same walk during different seasons and note the changes over time. In each case, students can discuss their observations or keep a walking journal in which they record observations and sensations.

Theme walk

For a theme walk, plan a route that will enable the class to make a variety of observations on a particular theme (e.g., water). Before leaving the classroom, have students brainstorm questions to be answered on the walk. Questions for a water walk, for example, might include the following: In what different ways are people observed using water? Is there evidence of water being wasted or polluted? How could water be used more efficiently and without polluting it? If your walk takes you to a river or lake, consider: How does the look, smell or feel of the water change at different points on the walk? What might cause these changes? In a science course, the walk could include taking water samples and measuring properties such as pH and temperature.

Perspective walk

Perspective walks focus on having students see familiar places in new ways. For example, walk to a high place with a view, such as a hill or high building near the school; walk down a street that is parallel to the one that students usually walk; or have students use magnifying glasses to observe commonplace objects along their way home from school. Have students list or sketch ten things they see that they have never observed before in the familiar area. They might also use digital cameras to capture different perspectives. As a follow-up activity, students could make a visual presentation of what they saw and how they saw it.

Human impact walk

Walk in an area where the impact of human activity is clearly visible, such as an industrial area, urban area, shopping mall, or well-used trail in the woods or mountains.

Ask students to imagine what the place might be like if people had never been there. Is it evident that people have respected this place? If not, what kinds of objects might be there if humans always had respected this place? What objects are there due to humans? How might the area have looked 50 years ago? 100? 200? How might we reduce our impact on the area now or restore features that have been lost? Students can complete writing or drawing exercises imagining what the area looked like in the past and envisioning what it might look like in another 100 years if the human impact continues. You can introduce or follow up a human-impact walk with readings, old maps and drawings related to the history of the area.

Sensory walk

On a sensory walk, have students initially focus only on what they see; next, on what they hear (they can work in pairs with one student closing his or her eyes and being led by the other); then on what they feel; and, finally, on what they smell. It is helpful for any of the walks, but particularly this one, for students to go at a slower pace than they are used to, or to return to the same place again and again in different seasons or

weather. Encourage students to be as quiet as possible in order to focus on their senses.

Alternatively, walks can be focused on a particular sense. For example, an entire walk may focus on listening for both sounds and silence. Students can bring instruments and try to make sounds in harmony with or in contrast to the sounds of a place.

Systems walk

During a systems walk, students can try to identify parts of a given system in the area in which they walk. These can be natural systems (e.g., the water cycle, food webs) or human-built systems (e.g., transportation, sanitation). What are the different parts of the system? How do the parts connect? How could the system be improved? If students are looking at a natural system, how do people affect this system? What evidence is there of these effects? If students are looking at a human-built system, what can they observe of the impact of the system on the environment? What alternatives to the current system can they imagine?

Wildlife walk

Have the students take a walk focusing on wildlife and signs of wildlife. Encourage them to look for nests, hives, insect galls, tracks and scat, and to see if they can observe animals in places where they might not usually be seen, such as underground, on pond beds or in tree cavities. Ask students to think about the relationships between different species. How do they compete with or support each other's livelihood? In what ways are the animals particularly well adapted to the area? What might be the impact of human presence on the populations, diversity and behavior of the wildlife?

Mapping walk

Have students walk with the intention of later making a map of the area showing only its natural features. In a familiar urban area, this is a great exercise for getting students to think about the landscape in a new way. Encourage students to be specific, such as by writing "a young spruce tree" instead of "a tree," and making detailed sketches so that each natural feature can be differentiated on the maps. Ask them to look beyond vegetation and to note such features as where land slopes and in what direction, where there is water, or where there are rocks and of what type. Back in the classroom, ask pairs or groups of students to combine their maps. If the groups have walked different routes, they can then switch maps and each try to follow the other group's map to a specified destination.

Post-walking

After a walk, allow time for writing or class discussion to help students process their experiences. Encourage them to make connections between the very concrete observations they have made that day and much wider environmental issues. Questions to ask students include: What would be the result if everyone in the world copied an observed behavior such as littering or planting native shrubs? Was anything that you observed different from what you do in your own lives? What could you do to change something you saw (e.g., a system or a specific place) for the better? What steps would you need to take and what help would you need in order to make the change? The walks can be the impetus for student-led environmental projects (e.g., a trash pickup at a place discovered on a walk) and for challenging students to reduce their impact, including by walking more!

Another exercise is to list all the different observations made during the walk and have students discuss or write about the connections between them. Sketching can also be a powerful part of processing. If the class is scientific in nature, students can be asked to sketch plants or animals that they have observed closely or are studying currently. Later, students can research the species and come to understand how it fits into larger themes the class is studying. Whether students have taken observation walks on their own or as a class, post-walking adds another element to the exercise and gives room for students to process their experiences and connect with the context of the curriculum.

Artifact study

Another assignment that works well either after observation walks or on its own is an artifact study. Have students select objects from their daily lives or objects found on an observation walk to present as artifacts of modern life. The objects can be mentally "collected" using sketches, photographs and descriptions or, if appropriate (e.g., in the case of artifacts from home), brought into the classroom. Have the class brainstorm on the following questions: What would these objects show future archeologists about how people in the early 21st century relate to the natural world? What categories could these artifacts fall into? If the students have collected the artifacts on an observation walk, what might someone who hadn't been on the walk think about the area based on seeing the artifacts?

Have students develop categories for the artifacts that help explain the human-nature relationships they demonstrate. For example, articles of clothing might show people to be consumers of nature, while CDs of ocean sounds might show nature as a source of relaxation for humans, and discarded batteries might show people as destroyers of nature or ignorant of their effects upon it. Direct students to think about how these different relationships might affect both people and nature over time. In what different ways could we be relating to our environment and what kind of artifacts do students imagine these relationships might create? Are there specific inventions that might help people to relate to nature in positive ways? Have students write down or sketch these ideas and share them with the class after the walk.

Developing observation skills through walking experiences, recording what is noticed and studying everyday objects as artifacts can ultimately help students to attend more carefully to the world around them. Through this attentiveness, students often begin to question for themselves the rights and wrongs of our behavior toward our environment. Yes, sometimes students giggle at the idea of walking super-slowly or frown at the thought of a walk in soft rain. Yet, in my experience, a picture begins to emerge in the discussions and journal entries that follow, showing that students' surroundings have become somehow new, and that this newness has brought forth a deeper level of inquiry.

Cynthia Macleod, *former Chair of the Religion and Ethics Department at Brooklyn Friends School, is a writer and a consultant with Fitzgerald Analytics, Inc.*

Resources

Cronon, William, ed. *Uncommon Ground: Rethinking the Human Place in Nature.* W.W. Norton & Company, 1996. The essays in this collection are helpful in conceptualizing the artifact assignment and possible types of categories.

Leslie, Clare Walker and Charles Roth. *Keeping a Nature Journal: Discover a Whole New Way of Seeing the World Around You.* Storey Publishing, 2000. A step-by-step guide to nature journals with ideas on how to assess journals and use sketching.

Peterson, David and H. Emerson Blake. *Writing Naturally: A Down to Earth Guide to Nature Writing.* Johnson Books, 2001. Excellent essays and exercises to hone nature-writing skills.

Snyder, Gary. *Turtle Island.* New Directions Publishing, 1974. A literary example of what can come from looking at familiar places in unaccustomed ways; useful for class discussions and reading assignments before or after walking exercises.

Sobel, David. *Place-Based Education: Connecting Classrooms & Communities.* The Orion Society, Nature Literacy Series 4, 2004. An excellent introduction to place-based educational theory and practice as well as descriptions of teachers who incorporate the relationships between school, community and environment into their teaching

Thoreau, Henry David. *Walking.* Harper San Francisco, 1994. Very useful for pre-walking; an excellent literary introduction to the possibilities of walking observantly.

Building Green

Creating environmentally friendly trade programs in vocational-technical schools

Chuck Spitz

by Jennifer Wolf

Subject areas: residential building trade instruction

Key concepts: sustainability; green building; environmentally friendly design, materials and practices; energy efficiency, resource conservation, indoor air quality

Skills: hands-on skills in the use of environmentally friendly alternatives to traditional building materials and methods

Location: classroom and project site

Time: flexible, depending on instructor resources and administrative and budget constraints

Materials: Internet access, sample materials for demonstration

In many high schools, environmental education is well integrated into science, social studies and other subject areas. But what about in vocational-technical high schools, where the primary emphasis is the development of practical knowledge and marketable skills? The answer, at least in my home state

of Massachusetts, is that while many vocational-technical students are acquiring basic environmental literacy in their general coursework, environmental education is virtually nonexistent in the building trade programs beyond dealing with occupational safety and health regulations.

Environmental education specific to trade programs is an area ripe for exploration for one simple but compelling reason: trade program students are literally the builders of the future. Eric Hart, director of Bear Mountain Ecoschool, a Missouri organization that promotes "green" building practices, believes that "raising awareness of environmental and sustainability issues among building contractors and among kids who are going into the building trades is sorely needed .... Building contractors and most carpenters don't realize how much of an impact they can have on making healthier environments for people to live in."[1]

Despite the lack of environmental education in training programs, awareness is growing within the building industry that environmental issues affect the builder's bottom line. The depletion of many natural resources that go into building products, and the rising price of petroleum and petroleum-based products, in particular, are increasing the cost of conventional

Left: The energy lab at Birmingham Seaholm High School in Birmingham, Michigan, generates its own energy with solar, wind and geothermal systems. Right: Students in a building trades program at La Follette High School in Madison, Wisconsin, install oriented strand board over I-joists that use less material than standard beams.

building materials and techniques. Restrictions on the use of diminishing landfill space and regulations for handling and disposing of hazardous materials also have a direct impact on costs. Growing consumer awareness is having an impact as well. As public concern for the environment increases, so does the demand for "green" products, extending even to the homes people buy. Homebuyers are discovering that green-built houses are safer, quieter and more comfortable to live in, have a higher resale value and offer substantial long-term savings in operation and maintenance over conventionally built homes.

As the construction industry heads in a greener direction, it will benefit from a cadre of workers who are well-prepared for the new kind of green building that the future will demand. But teachers and administrators whose task it is to produce technically proficient tradespeople may be reluctant to alter curricula without tangible evidence that environmental education can be smoothly dovetailed into it. While the trade shop is not the most appropriate place for extensive exploration of environmental concepts (nor is there time, in any case), trades programs provide excellent hands-on opportunities to reinforce students' basic environmental literacy. In the following example, a typical curriculum in residential construction is used to show how environmental topics and "green building" practices can be incorporated easily into trades programs, without detracting from their primary emphasis on the development of practical skills. With minor adaptation, the principles and methods can be used in the other trades or in design and technology or building courses in any high school.

A greener curriculum in residential construction

Programs in residential construction are often divided into units that correspond to a semester-long building project. A typical program sequence is as follows:

- introduction to residential construction
- foundations (concrete, wood and special applications) and forming (footings, foundation and edge forms)
- interior framing (floors, sills, walls, ceiling, roofs)
- blocks and bricks
- exterior framing (cornices, gables, windows, doors, walls)
- interior finishing (insulation, drywall, doors and trim, cabinets, floors)

Environmentally friendly design, materials and practices can be incorporated into each of these units. If the class project is to construct a house, teachers and students have a unique opportuntity to make the entire project a green building.

Introduction to residential construction

The introductory unit provides an overview of the typical residential construction process and includes such topics as design, types of materials, mechanical and electrical systems, and site management. The green building concept can be introduced in this unit through discussion of the three major environmental issues related to house construction: energy efficiency, resource conservation and indoor air quality. These issues run throughout the project and, literally, throughout the house.

Energy efficiency: The biggest environmental impacts of a house are the air pollution and greenhouse gas emissions generated by the burning of fossil fuels to produce the energy needed to build the house and to operate it over its lifetime. Reducing a house's energy needs by 30 percent reduces carbon dioxide emissions by about 15,400 kilograms over 30 years. Energy efficiency makes economic sense as well: as petroleum reserves continue to decline, the cost of heating will surely continue to rise.

Resource conservation: The construction of an average house generates up to five tons of waste in the form of wood, metals, paper, plastic and cardboard. Resource conservation in green building means reducing the amount of construction waste, reusing materials, recycling on site and using building materials that have recycled content. In the design phase, it means planning for household recycling, which is already mandatory in many communities.

Indoor air quality: Indoor air pollution is a significant problem in houses, especially in new ones, because of off-gassing, or the emission of harmful chemicals from construction materials. Particle board used for cabinets, shelves, counters and furniture can contain formaldehyde, as can carpets and carpet padding. Adhesives and paints and other finishes can contain harmful volatile organic compounds (VOCs). The by-products of the combustion of oil or natural gas in the furnace and stove can be harmful as well. A green-built home will be made with low-toxicity or non-toxic materials and have appropriate ventilation.

Discussion points/activities:
• Compare the overall cost of reusing an existing building with the cost of building an entirely new structure. The cost savings in reuse could be substantial.

• In planning a new structure, provide an overview of structural design elements and mechanical systems from an environmental perspective.

• Discuss operating energy and embodied energy. When we think of energy efficiency, we often think only of operating energy, such as the energy needed to heat or cool a house. Embodied energy is all the other energy consumed in the life cycle of a building: energy used in harvesting resources, manufacturing products, transporting materials, building, and recycling or removing of structures. Many energy-efficient houses require less operating energy, even over several decades, than it took to build the house. Have students compare the embodied energy of materials made with recycled content with the embodied energy of new materials.

• Estimate the cost of the class building project using a standard cost-information reference such as the *Dodge Repair and Remodel Cost Book*, but cross-referencing costs with *The GreenSpec Guide*[2] or a similar "green" building materials guide.

• In designing the house, consider ways to make it eco-friendly. For example, identify opportunities to capture solar energy, both passively and actively; to incorporate materials that are reused, recycled, sustainably harvested or otherwise resource-efficient; and to use eco-friendly finishes.

• Talk about land use planning, site management and landscape elements from an environmental standpoint.

• Invite an architect to talk about eco-friendly design. Visit an eco-house or other "green" building.

• Refer to a book on design, such as *A Place In the Sun*[3] about the Real Goods Solar Living Center, or any of dozens of books on eco-friendly design.

• Refer to other student eco-building projects, such as Project EFFECT, an eco-building project undertaken by a group of Pennsylvania high school students.[4]

• Before the class building project begins, initiate a job site waste reduction and recycling program. Students can rotate responsibility for monitoring compliance and sorting recyclable materials. Have students investigate how they can reuse or sell the recyclable materials they generate during the project. (Local yellow pages list industrial and community recycling centers.)

Foundations and forming

A unit on concrete foundations provides an opportunity to discuss the huge amounts of energy used and pollution generated in the production of Portland cement, the principal bonding component of concrete. Fly ash (waste from coal-fired power plants) can be substituted for one-quarter of the cement in concrete, thereby lessening the overall environmental impact while making use of a "trash" material. In addition, some of the concrete in footings can be displaced by durable, non-biodegradable "trash" that typically ends up in landfills (like those old cassette players and obsolete computers), and concrete reinforcement bars can be manufactured from recycled steel. Use photos from job sites where these techniques have been employed to illustrate their application.

A unit on foundations also presents an opportunity to instruct in the use of non-petroleum form-releasing agents, such as those made from a vegetable base. Let students experiment with both.

Student-built electric bike.

Dennis Carter

Interior framing

For wood framing, introduce the concept of sustainable harvesting and the certification programs of the Forest Stewardship Council, such as The Rainforest Alliance's SmartWood program.[5] Visit a lumberyard, and have students investigate where and how the lumber was harvested (easily found through a Web search). Discuss lumber products from urban salvage and recycled sources. Ask how scrap lumber can be reused on the building project. Discuss and demonstrate engineered wood products such as glue-laminated beams, joists, columns and arches, all of which use less wood but are as strong or stonger than similar all-wood products. For steel framing, investigate sources of steel studs, joists and girders made from various combinations of pre- and post-consumer recycled steel.

Blocks and bricks

In a discussion of masonry, mention brick manufactured from reprocessed oil-contaminated soil, and concrete block that has been aerated and insulated. This type of block, sometimes made with the addition of fly ash, is very lightweight, has an excellent insulation value, and can be used for load-bearing walls and worked with standard hand tools. Use this brick and block in the class building project.

Exterior framing

Roofs: Discuss and demonstrate organic roofing felt made from asphalt, recycled paper, and sawdust chips or recycled wood pulp. Discuss and display the various alternatives in roofing materials, such as fiber-cement (can resemble and be worked like wood, clay or slate), cast concrete, metal (steel or aluminum made from industrial remelt), polymer, clay, slate and wood. Also discuss gutters, leaders and drains made from recycled plastic or cast iron.

Exterior walls and trims: Discuss and demonstrate alternatives to plywood for structural sheathing, such as oriented strandboard or OSB (made from strands of fast-growing, tree-farmed woods bound with resins that do not offgas) or exterior fiberglass-faced gypsum (can be made from recycled glass and recycled gypsum). Also discuss structural panels, such as Agriboard, which is made of OSB and strawboard (waste wheat straw mixed with a resin that does not contain formaldehyde), has good insulative value and typically saves on framing and labor.

For exterior finishing, discuss and demonstrate fiber cement products for siding, fascia and trim, available from several different manufacturers. Fiber cement is made from cement, sand and cellulose fibers cured with pressurized steam. It is generally given a "green designation" because of its exceptionally long life and low maintenance requirements.

Windows: Compare the insulation values and maintenance requirementsof wood, vinyl and composite window frames, and of single- and double-paned windows. Use cutaway samples to demonstrate these.

Exterior doors: Investigate energy-saving choices for exterior doors, such as fiberglass doors with plastic exteriors, and steel doors with cores of polystyrene blown in with pentane, an insulation-blowing agent that does not deplete atmospheric ozone. When a wood product is needed, consider doors made from molded wood fibers bonded with heat and pressure.

Interior finishing

Insulation: In addition to the standard types of fiberglass insulation, discuss and demonstrate options for sprayed, board and loose-fill insulation, such as loose-fill cellulose made from recycled newsprint, permalite board made from a combination of perlite and recycled cellulose binders, and fiberglass batt made from recycled glass.

Interior panels: Discuss and demonstrate a variety of interior wall panels, such as drywall made from recycled gypsum and other recycled fibers, or Gridcore (made of recycled corrugated cardboard), Medite (made from recovered and recycled softwood, without formaldehyde — also good for cabinets, furniture, fixtures and moldings) and strawboard (made of waste wheat straw mixed with a resin that does not contain formaldehyde).

Finishes, sealants and adhesives: When dealing with interior surfaces, discuss the environmental implications of paints, stains, varnishes and sealants used to protect surfaces for long-term durability. In their conventional forms, all of these products contain solvents, stabilizers, toxic metals and volatile organic compounds, such as xylene, epoxy, toluene and ketones. Introduce water-based and plant-based paints and finishes as low-odor, low-toxicity alternatives.

Throughout the building

Throughout the building, there will be opportunities to introduce low-toxic adhesives (solvent-free), caulks (hole and insulation fillers made from cork, damar resin, citrus terpene, coconut oil and natural latex), joint compounds, fasteners (nails made from scrap steel, for example) and shims (made from recycled plastic).

Interior doors and cabinets: A number of doors for interior use are made from molded wood fiber that has the texture and workability of real wood. The use of molded wood fiber does not further deplete already devastated Pacific Rim forests as does the use of doors made from Luan mahogany. For cabinets, there are eco-friendly pre-fabs that feature formaldehyde-free medium-density fiberboard (MDF) and low-toxic finishes. Cabinet doors can be crafted from solid or veneered certified sustainably harvested wood or from laminate. Photographs or product samples from vendors could be used to illustrate/demonstrate what is available.

Counters and floors: For countertops, there are natural and engineered stone surfaces as well as surprisingly beautiful, workable and durable cast concrete products. There are also decorative surface materials made from blends of recycled paper products, biobased resins and colors, which look like stone but have the workability

Students installing salvaged paving stones in a homebuilding project.

David Smith

of wood. Countertops are also made now from durable and formaldahyde-free bamboo laminates.

Eco-friendly options in flooring include hardwood from recycled or sustainably harvested sources, bamboo, linoleum, cork flooring and natural fiber carpeting, as well as rubber and low-toxic laminate. Most commercially available carpeting is now made from petroleum, a nonrenewable resource. It is treated with a host of toxic chemicals to make it resistant to fire, mold and stains. Like paints and solvents, it can cause serious short- and long-term health problems through off-gassing, and it presents a problem in disposal at the end of its life. Introduce natural-fiber alternatives such as wool, cotton and hemp.

From theory to real world solutions

Ultimately, in a trade-specific curriculum, there is nothing so effective in building students' awareness and interest as the demonstration and application of the alternative materials themselves. Students should have as many opportunities as possible to handle the materials and to observe and practice the building techniques involved in using them. Manufacturers anxious to promote the knowledge and use of their products may be willing to come to the shop or building site to demonstrate product uses and to instruct in specific applications and construction techniques.

Today's vocational-technical students are literally the builders of the future. Incorporating environmental education into trade workshops and building projects puts the concepts, designs and materials of environmental sustainability — the real world solutions to real environmental problems — directly into their hands.

Jennifer Wolf writes about sustainable home building and remodeling and owns The Boomerville Press, a Web-based publishing enterprise in Athens, Georgia.

Notes

1. Eric Hart, personal correspondence, October 27, 1999.

2. Alex Wilson and Mark Piepkorn, eds., *Green Building Products: The GreenSpec Guide to Residential Building Materials*, New Society Publishers, 2005. (See Resources for more information.)

3. John Schaeffer et al., *A Place In the Sun: The Evolution of the Real Goods Solar Living Center*, Chelsea Green Publishing, 1997. (See Resources for more information.)

4. Project EFFECT (Environmentally Friendly Facility Exploring Conservation Technologies), <http://library.thinkquest.org/6076/New%20 Pages/PEIntro.html>. (See Resources for more information.)

5. For information about the Rainforest Alliance's SmartWood certification, visit <www.rainforest-alliance.org/programs/forestry/smartwood/>.

References

Commonwealth of Massachusetts. *History and Social Science Curriculum Framework*. Massachusetts Department of Education, 1997.

Disinger, John F. "Environment in the K–12 Curriculum: An Overview," in Wilke, Richard J., ed. *Environmental Education: Teacher Resource Handbook: A Practical Guide for K–12 Environmental Educators*. Corwin Press, 1997.

Volk, Trudi L. "Integration and Curriculum Design" in Wilke, Richard J., ed. *Environmental Education: Teacher Resource Handbook" A Practical Guide for K-12 Environmental Educators*. Corwin Press, 1997.

Resources

Print and audio-visual

Building With Awareness: The Construction of a Hybrid Home, Ted Owens, 162 minutes. Syncronos Design, 2005 [DVD]. A how-to film with plenty of hands-on demonstrations of the design and construction of a straw bale house, including rubble trench foundations, post and beam framing, adobe walls and earth plasters, roof framing and insulation, rainwater cisterns, photovoltaic electrical systems, wiring for straw bale and adobe, and more. Available at <www.buildingwithawareness.com>.

Environmental Building News. A monthly newsletter on environmental building design and construction, published by Building Green, 122 Birge Street, Suite 30, Brattleboro, VT 05301. Subscription information: <www. buildinggreen.com/ecommerce/ebn.cfm>.

Schaeffer, John, et al. *A Place In the Sun: The Evolution of the Real Goods Solar Living Center*. Chelsea Green Publishing, 1997. An outstanding case study of a major green building project, with photos, architectural drawings and information indexed for accessibility.

Wilson, Alex and Mark Piepkorn, eds. *Green Building Products: The Green-Spec Guide to Residential Building Materials*. New Society Publishers, 2005. Contains over 1,400 descriptive listings of green products, grouped by function, for every phase of residential construction, along with advice on what to look for in green products.

Websites

<http://library.thinkquest.org/6076/New%20Pages/PEIntro.html> Project EFFECT (Environmentally Friendly Facility Exploring Conservation Technologies). Students at Souderton Area High School near Philadelphia, Pennsylvania, helped to design, finance and build an eco-home in their community. Their website tells how they used the experience as a learning and teaching tool. This is an exemplary case study.

<www.ncat.org/greentree/welcome.html> Green Tree: Decisions for Environmental Buildings. This website of the National Center for Appropriate Technology features a decision-making process that helps students evaluate a range of resource-efficient materials for use in particular projects and see examples of their application.

<www.nahbrc.org> National Association of Home Builders Research Center, Green Building Program. Online resources to help homebuilders understand the rapidly expanding green building market, including a downloadable set of "Green Home Building Guidelines" at <www.nahbrc. org/greenguidelines/theguidelines.html>.

<www.energystar.gov> Energy Star. The US Environmental Protection Agency's Energy Star Qualified New Homes program certifies new and remodeled homes that meet stringent energy-efficiency criteria. Teachers might consider Energy Star certification for their class building project.

<www.rmi.org> Rocky Mountain Institute. The "Buildings and Land" webpage has links to information on green building issues specific to the single-family houses, including resource-efficient house construction, environmentally friendly building materials, indoor air quality and recycling.

<www.usgbc.org> U.S. Green Building Council. A coalition of more than 800 organizations from across the building industry and developers of the LEED Green Building Rating System. The website gives access to articles, case studies, guidelines and initiatives, and discusses the benefits of green building and the importance of green building certification.

Ancestral Arts

In collecting and preparing their own earthy materials, students gain an appreciation of traditional art techniques and an admiration for the people who developed them

Photographs by Elizabeth Lorentzen

by Elizabeth Lorentzen

Subject areas: visual arts, social studies, physics, chemistry

Key concepts: clay properties, origins, and potential, Native American pottery traditions, function and aesthetics of pottery, environmental ecology, sustainability

Skills: identification of natural clay sites, clay preparation, hand-built (coil) pottery technique, pottery firing techniques, observation

Location: outdoors

Time: 1 class period to dig clay, 2 class periods to sift clay and grind oyster shells, 3–4 class periods to build coil pots, 18- to 20-hour period to fire pots

Materials: natural clay, shovels, oyster shells, 12" x 18" boards, water, 5-gallon buckets, concrete bricks, old window screens, dust pan, brush, colander or piece of window screen to sift ground oyster shells

iven: Clay does not begin life in a plastic bag. So how to impress this upon my beginning pottery students? Beginning at the beginning seemed the only way to go.

In the beginning, there were no boxes of 48 crayons, no neatly bagged slabs of clay, no machine-spun skeins of yarn in a multitude of colors. There was only the overwhelming need of the human spirit to communicate its inner workings, the raw materials the Earth could provide, and human ingenuity. An introduction to the historic origins of this human ingenuity, of media and technique, can give students a greater understanding of the context in which the arts arose and of their relationship to both the Earth and their human inventors. Beyond understanding media and technique, students can learn to appreciate the natural gifts from the Earth, and the need to respect and use these gifts wisely. Popovi Da, son of renowned potter Maria Martinez, expressed it this way: "We work in harmony with nature; we do not take more materials than we need." I have undertaken this approach with several high school art classes, but it was the challenge of teaching a pottery class for the first time that started me on my journey.

In our area, the earliest known inhabitants were the Oneotas, a group of hunter-gatherers occupying our river valley circa 950–1550 AD. They made shell-tempered pottery that has been found locally as recently as last summer. To promote an understanding of the pottery-making process from beginning to end, we undertook to make pottery in the manner of the Oneotas. (It is suggested that readers research the pottery methods employed by indigenous people in their own area to make the experience more pertinent to their own location and resources.)

Clay pots are filled with sawdust in preparation for firing.

Our town's park system includes a hill from which clay was dug and fired in brick kilns during the 1870s. With the blessing and permission of the park commission, we dug clay from this location, packing it in five-gallon pails, which we brought back to the art room. *(Grain of Truth #1: Digging one's own clay is not as easy as getting it out of a plastic bag.)*

To prepare the clay for use, sifting was necessary to remove stones, roots and other foreign objects. We used old window screens for this purpose, catching the sifted clay on large sheets of plastic placed underneath the screens.

Clay fired over an open fire is exposed to rapid temperature changes, and so requires tempering — that is, "opening" or strengthening it with a substance such as sand or grog (fired clay ground to a powder) to prevent breakage. The tempering agent also makes clay easier to handle. The Oneotas used clam shells for this purpose. Since clams were scarce, we obtained oyster shells from the local agricultural feed store, which were then ground up by students. Lacking the Oneotas' quern and grinding stone, this process required the use of large glacial stones and various 20th-century implements of destruction — that is, concrete bricks and sledge hammers. This step also required strong constitutions and experimentation, but the students developed innovative techniques of their own. Standing on a concrete brick and moving it back and forth over the oyster shells with the feet was one method; steady dropping of the broad side of a sledge hammer was another. The shells were sifted and reground until reduced to coarse powder. This took a long time. *(Grain of Truth #2: The Oneotas were patient and strong.)*

Before beginning the construction of our pots, we visited the archaeology department of the local college where students were introduced to original Oneota pots and pot sherds. The form and decoration of Oneota pottery was discussed, as well as the building and firing processes as deduced from archaeological evidence. Back in our own classroom, we viewed the video *Maria*, in which Maria Martinez, a Native American from the southwestern United States, demonstrates the steps in producing traditional coil-built pots. She also explains how pottery making links her to the land and the traditions of her ancestors, an integral part of the process for her.

Materials for Making Clay Pots

To mix the quantity of clay needed for individual pots (enough to form a ball of clay 6–8" in diameter), we started with three cups of sifted clay. To this, we added one cup of ground oyster shells and a small amount of water (starting with a half cup), and kneaded them in. More water or dry clay was added to adjust the clay to a workable plasticity. Since we were working in a classroom setting with time constraints, we added a tablespoon of bentonite or epsom salts to the clay to improve plasticity and hasten the aging process. For firing 30 pots, we used 18 garbage bags full of sawdust. As this is an inexact science, these quantities are meant to serve only as a guide.

Using the coil-building method, students produced pots reminiscent of the Oneotas' in form and decoration. In the manner of Maria Martinez, the students placed a mound of dry clay on a board, poured a small quantity of water in the middle of it and worked the two substances together, adding more water as necessary to make a workable clay. Oyster shells were then kneaded into the clay and the clay was placed in a plastic bag overnight before coil-building began.

The native clay was not always cooperative. The students found it to be less plastic than the commercial-grade clay and made as many as three separate attempts before producing a successful pot. *(Grain of Truth #3: The Oneotas were skilled artisans.)*

Upon completion, the pots were set outside our classroom door to dry in the sun. Archaeological evidence has indicated that the Oneotas used an open bonfire to fire their pottery so we followed their example: we chose and covered a site for firing our pots and obtained a burning permit from the city.

As the pots became ready to fire, we monitored the weather and the wind velocity. Finally, a clear, cloudless day with no wind arrived. Pots were filled with sawdust obtained from a foray to our local lumberyard and carried to the firing site next to our school's pond. A bed of wood shavings and sawdust was laid down, the pots placed in concentric circles with space left between each pot, more sawdust mounded over the top and some oak firewood placed on top of this mound. This arrangement allowed for the slow, steady intensification of heat needed to fire the pottery and prevent breakage. Water was drawn from the pond in five-gallon buckets and the area around the firing site was wet down to prevent the fire from spreading. A student whose family participates in rendezvous and re-enactments of colonial America started the fire for us with flint and fiber. Although it was a later method of fire-starting than that used by the Oneotas, it was an education for those of us who had not seen it done before.

The fire burned rapidly through dried grasses used as tinder, igniting the sawdust, which in turn ignited the oak firewood. More sawdust was added until the oak was burning steadily, and finally the fire became a smoldering heap and was allowed to burn down to

More Arts from the Earth: Painting and Weaving

An historical approach is an exciting way to explore traditional arts. In creating their own tools and collecting dyestuff and other raw materials from nature, students gain a greater understanding of the context in which the arts arose and a new admiration of their human inventors.

Neolithic Painting: As part of the introduction to painting class, we study the Neolithic cave painters and "walk their walk" by making paint brushes fashioned from deer tail hair inserted into hollowed-out sticks that are sharpened at the other end to produce a stylus point for finer lines. Hair from a deer's body is hollow, a characteristic that allows the hair to trap air for insulation, but makes for a stiff, unyielding and unsuitable brush head. The tail hair is not hollow, so it makes a pliable, cohesive brush. Pigments are obtained from earth compounds and minerals: kaolin, a fine white clay produces white; iron oxide, a reddish-brown; copper carbonate gives a soft green; ground charcoal is used for black; and yellow ochre produces a yellow tan. Using a shaved stick "palette knife," we mix pigments with melted lard or vegetable oil to produce the paint in the manner of the first painters. Symbols chosen by the students to represent their connection to nature are then rendered on flat limestone or other suitable rocks using the brushes and pigments they have prepared.

Weaving Navajo Blankets: As part of a fibers class, students personally meet and learn about the Navajo Churro sheep, which produce wool that is later picked, combed and spun into yarn. We adjourn to the countryside ditches and fields, gardens, and our own cultivated "dyestuff" garden outside the art room door (a useful tool for introducing some botany into the art curriculum) to gather dyestuff for natural dyes. These are then simmered on the stove in the home economics room and the liquid used to dye yarn, both our own handspun and other machine spun yarn. A study of Navajo chief blankets ensues and the students design and weave on handmade tapestry looms their own interpretation of a Navajo chief blanket using some of the natural dyed yarn the class has produced, their own handspun Navajo Churro and other yarns of their choosing.

ash. Students and teacher monitored the fire regularly throughout the day and as it smoldered through the night. Total firing time was about 18–20 hours.

The pots emerged hardened and blackened by the fire. They were allowed to cool, brushed off, and washed to remove any remaining debris from the surface. The firing site was flooded with more water drawn from the pond to ensure that the fire was completely out.

Although some 20th-century adaptations were necessary, my students' understanding of the whole process, the interaction between potter, clay and the Earth from which it comes, was strengthened. In the three years since we began, much has been learned through trial and error because we lacked a master potter who would pass on the gift of experience to us as apprentices. We have gained great respect for those first potters who discovered the versatility of clay and molded this gift from the Earth to their own uses. *(Grain of Truth #4: Henceforth, ancient pottery will be regarded with great awe and respect for the craftsmanship, inventiveness and plain hard work its production required!)*

With the advent of the computer, emphasis in visual arts education is shifting away from the more traditional arts and towards those that can be accomplished with such new technologies. The need to educate students in their use cannot be denied. But we ignore the roots from which we have come at our peril. We need to strengthen our understanding of the relationship between the Earth and the human spirit, and to cultivate respect for the Earth's gifts and regard for the ingenuity of past times. The result, for our students, will be a more balanced view with which to approach the challenges of the 21st century.

Elizabeth Lorentzen is an art instructor at Decorah High School in Decorah, Iowa.

Resources

Pottery

Educational VideoNetwork. *Maria! Indian Pottery of San Ildefonso.* 27-minute video detailing the process from digging clay to coil-building pottery to firing. Educational VideoNetwork, Huntsville, TX.

Spivey, Richard. *Maria.* Northland Publishing, 1979.

"Using Natural Clays," *Ceramic Monthly,* June-August 1994, p. 100.

Natural Dyeing

Van Stralen, Trudy. *Indigo, Madder and Marigold: A Portfolio of Colors from Natural Dye.* Interweave Press, 1993.

Rock Art

La Pierre, Yvette. *Native American Rock Art: Messages from the Past.* Thomasson-Grant Publishing, 1994.

GIS in the Classroom

Marsha Alibrandi

by Marsha Alibrandi

Subject areas: environmental science, technology, geography

Key concepts: integration into curricula of geographic information systems (GIS) and global positioning systems (GPS)

Skills: gathering data, constructing databases, integrating GIS and GPS

Location: field work and classroom, computer labs

Materials: GPS/GIS equipment and software, local or municipal GIS agencies

 call comes in to a 911 emergency dispatcher. The distraught caller is on a cell phone and is unfamiliar with the neighborhood. The dispatcher asks, "What can you see from where you're standing?"

"A drugstore, a hydrant, a bus stop, I don't know ... buildings! Come quick! Somebody's hurt!"

The dispatcher consults a computerized map of the city, locates three combinations of hydrants and bus stops, and then finds a drugstore in one of those locations. She searches the board for the nearest response vehicle, and orders, "Possible accident victim on Maple and East 12th!"

The computerized maps used by the dispatcher are part of a system known as a Geographic Information System (GIS). GIS is a small acronym for a powerful set of tools that will likely be used as extensively in the future as word processing is today. The power of GIS to coordinate geographic information is already demonstrated to us daily by Internet tools such as Mapquest and Google Earth, and by television weather maps showing satellite images, political borders, temperature, and precipitation and wind isolines. Traditional printed maps are built in layers represented by different colors. For example, on a topographic quadrangle map, land contours are shown in brown, water in blue, vegetation in green, and the built environment in black, red or purple. The advantage of a GIS map is that it can correlate many more layers of information and can do so in seconds, in adjustable zoom-in and zoom-out scales. Some GIS programs can vary the angle at which a map or graphic is represented, providing both standard bird's-eye views as well as more oblique views, and others can rotate and transform images in other ways.

Much of the power of GIS lies in its mathematical capability of representing data graphically. While GIS is most widely known for linking information to maps, it can also relate information from several databases, or perform several functions on a single set of data. Thus GIS can link a number of technologies, such as spreadsheet, chart and graphics software; word processing; digital photography; and even digital video (an example being video clips of weather patterns). Because of its complexity, GIS is not a simple software package; it is, however, a tool that integrates information from many disciplines and provides real applications for research and data-gathering by students and communities.

The development of GIS coincides with and facilitates many new studies in biogeography. For instance, in tracking migratory birds and other species, the United States Fish and Wildlife Service collates information from sightings by local groups across the continent. This information is entered into GIS databases, and the databases are then integrated to create maps that show migratory corridors, overlapping ranges of species and potential interference from human development. These multilayered displays are invaluable tools in land-protection efforts, such as creating migration buffer zones of optimal size and location. Satellite images and aerial photographs also can be integrated into GIS to produce maps that can be used in environmental assessment and monitoring. For example, groups monitoring the health of local ponds and lakes take readings of turbidity and chlorophyll; these readings are then matched to satellite photos to determine with greater accuracy the conditions represented by the colors picked up by satellite sensors. Fine-tuned in this way, satellite-photo information can be plotted into GIS maps that show water quality and indicate problem areas. Such information can be entered as separate layers over successive time periods to reveal cumulative effects. Similarly, GIS maps can be created to show patterns of vegetation and the impact of human land use as well as natural events. The possibilities for environmental applications are endless.

GIS in the green classroom

So what does GIS have to do with green classrooms? Where would these maps have relevance for environmental studies? Students of environmental science teacher Randy Raymond of Cass Technical School in Detroit used GIS maps of the municipal water distribution infrastructure to conduct an environmental survey of lead pipe for the city. They discovered traces of lead in water-quality test data, and located the sources by comparing the address to the underground pipeline maps. Raymond has also used GIS in the Rouge River Water Quality Monitoring Project, in which students map the locations of brown trout, a species that has been reintroduced to the watershed. In another regional watershed study, students in Kathryn Keranen's classes at Thomas Jefferson High School in Fairfax, Virginia, gathered and mapped water-quality information as part of a study of siltation in the local watershed.

John Nicolucci and Rex Taylor at Crescent School in Willowdale, Ontario, developed a Geographics course based on the GIS software MapInfo. Together with former students who went on to become professionals in GIS technology, Nicolucci and Taylor wrote a workbook of GIS activities for Grades 9 to 12 titled *MapInfo Geography Student Workbook and Teacher's Guide*. The workbook leads students from simple to more complex GIS applications. In early exercises, for instance, they find their home addresses and plan a route for getting from one place to another within their city. Later they are introduced to thematic mapping skills: they might call up a world map and use shading to highlight countries with high populations, or query the changes in population over time. In one activity, students must select a site for a landfill by evaluating layers of data on hydrology, population density and distance from urban centers, along with information on leakage and engineering problems. GIS facilitates the coordination of these variables in a modeling format and allows students to make queries or set limits and parameters that establish criteria for potential sites.[1]

The GLOBE Program, an early application of student-gathered data, has integrated GIS to a greater degree. Students gather and submit local environmental data and generate GIS displays of the data <www.globe.gov>. GIS training for teachers has grown in recent years, one important resource being the Environmental Systems Research Institute's GIS in Education Community at <http://edcommunity.esri.com/apps/calendar>.

Generating interest is the easiest part of integrating GIS into the classroom. Popular among scavenger-hunt enthusiasts, for instance, is the Global Position-

Marsha Alibrandi

ing System (GPS) game of "Geo-caching." Participants hide (or "cache") various items at specific points of latitude/longitude, and finders must photograph them with the requisite coordinates displayed on their GPS screens. Another project along this line is the Degree Confluence Project, in which thousands of participants globally are "ground truthing," or recording what they find at the intersections of whole-numbered points of latitude and longitude (e.g., 44°N 117°W). The surrounding area is photographed along with the GPS reading, which must show the exact degrees (e.g., N44.00.00 and W117.00.00). Thousands of these confluences of latitude and longitude have been documented at the project's immense website, where they are archived by country, coordinates and visitors' names.

Resources for GIS

Incorporating GIS technology into curricula is not simple, but it has become easier with new resources. The Environmental Systems Research Institute (ESRI), which provides schools with low-cost software to promote the use and development of GIS courses and applications. Another product from ESRI leads students into GIS with step-by-step activities for world geography. *Mapping Our World* is a great primer that includes a one-year license for ArcView or Arc-GIS software for educational purposes. The lessons, designed to be completed in one or two class periods of 45 minutes, are tested and essentially foolproof. Authors Malone, Parker and Voigt offer several training opportunities in the United States and elsewhere and are among a group of educators offering online

certificates in GIS though Eastern Michigan University.

For teachers, obtaining data can be one of the most challenging aspects of using GIS in the classroom. GIS data layers are generated by compiling thousands of bits of information, work that is often done by government agencies. Therefore, the quest for data should begin with a local government agency. Most state and provincial GIS offices have directories of the data layers available. In GIS circles, it is customary to swap data, and many municipal, county, state, provincial and regional planning agencies have mounted GIS maps on the Internet (see the GeoCommunity GIS Data Depot at <http://data.geocomm.com/> and the United Nations Food and Agriculture GISFish site <http://www.fao.org/fishery/gisfish/index.jsp> for free GIS data).

One of the best opportunities to introduce GIS to a school community is by observing the annual GIS Day, when GIS professionals can be invited to make presentations to students, faculty and guidance counsellors. GIS Day is usually held on the Wednesday of Geographic Awareness Week (typically the third week of November). ESRI maintains a website to support local observances of GIS Day at <www.gisday.com>.

Even with data sources and such free software as ESRI's ArcExplorer and ArcVoyager, the plunge into GIS in the K–12 classroom can be challenging. Charlie Fitzpatrick, K–12 Education and Libraries coordinator at ESRI, finds that teachers who are familiar with software like PageMaker, PhotoShop and SimCity and with Internet sites such as Google Earth have an advantage in grasping the more sophisticated GIS capabilities and relational database applications. Richard Audet, a researcher of GIS use in K–12 settings, finds that, for teachers who have worked with GIS, year three seems to be that magic threshold when their own facility with the technology converges with a suitable application for it and things fall into place.

Benefits of GIS in the classroom

Given the level of difficulty, what are the benefits of using GIS in the classroom? First, by its very integrative nature, a geographic information system extends beyond the boundaries of a single discipline. The application of GIS to environmental studies is thus a hand-in-glove fit. As scientific research becomes increasingly specialized, there is greater need for a means of integrating knowledge in order to understand the dynamics and interrelationships of variables in complex natural systems. The ability to integrate data from many different disciplines into a graphic format literally gives new dimensions to environmental research. The interdisciplinary application of GIS is an especially exciting prospect for teachers. For example, a local project in which students collect information from interviews and historical photographs, calculate flood levels over time and map a floodplain scenario would cross all disciplines; and all of these components could be linked through GIS. Even digital videos can be integrated by linking them to areas of a town map.

Second, by posing spatial problems and manipulating data to address those problems, students develop problem-solving skills. Those familiar with GIS will have a clear advantage in post-secondary programs or careers in environmental science.

Third, as GIS becomes a standard tool of regional planners, opportunities arise for students to participate in studies of local environmental issues through mentorship and community-service arrangements. Because GIS can do so many things, those who can execute the technology are in high demand and generally welcome assistance from student apprentices who can gather or enter data.

Getting started

A visit to a municipal or regional planning agency will usually yield a first acquaintance with GIS. Since many GIS offices operate in conjunction with college or university partners, post-secondary programs in applied geography or urban/regional planning are also good places to begin.

Connecting with GIS professionals and educators is the best route toward implementing the technology in schools. Teacher teams that include a computer education specialist should approach regional GIS providers for technical advice on obtaining maps, data hardware and software. ESRI's ArcGIS Explorer download page <http://edcommunity.esri.com/software/agx/> is the best place to begin for free software and online support, but local GIS software will serve if your interest is in sharing local data layers. If the local software choice is ArcView or ArcGIS, then ESRI support will be helpful. If the local software isn't ArcView, don't worry, as the softwares can communicate with one another.

Projects in which students gather data and build databases linking their data with geographic locations are great first steps in applying the technology. In watershed projects, for example, water-quality sampling locations can be geo-coded with a GPS or located on an existing GIS map. The collected data can then be graphed over time or shown in relation to features of the surroundings at the sampling site and upstream or downstream to determine ecological patterns. Comparing historic and cadastral (tax parcel) maps of an area can help students develop the "layered" understanding required in thinking spatially about environmental problems. For example, the past uses of industrial sites such as mills and factories can be critically significant in investigating sources of environmental contamination, as in the infamous case described in John Harr's *A Civil Action*. Shoreline surveys and interviews with residents can help students begin to form a database of historic and current land uses.

The merging of geospatial technologies and the Internet has advanced public understanding of geospatial technologies and put more geospatial information in the hands of citizens. The steady rise of geospatial applications over the past decade shows no apparent slowdown. In fact, geospatial applications are becoming as ubiquitous as the cell phone — they are now even built into cell phones, and are on more automobile dashboards than ever before. Teachers can look forward to greater utility and application of these technologies in the coming decades — and new ways of putting learning on the map!

Marsha Alibrandi taught Social Studies at Cape Cod Regional Technical High School for 15 years and is currently a geography and social studies teacher-educator at Fairfield University in Connecticut.

Note

1. Many of the school projects mentioned in this article are described in greater detail in Alibrandi, Marsha, *GIS in the Classroom: Using Geographic Information Systems in Social Studies and Environmental Science*, Heinemann, 2003.

Resources
Print

Alibrandi, Marsha. *GIS in the Classroom: Using Geographic Information Systems in Social Studies and Environmental Science.* Heinemann, 2003.

Malone, L., A. Palmer and C. Voigt. *Mapping our World: GIS Lessons for Educators.* ESRI, 2002.

Websites

<http://confluence.org> Degree Confluence Project

<list.terc.edu/mailman/listinfo/edgis> EDGIS. A listserv for those interested in the educational applications of GIS.

<www.esri.com/industries/k-12> ESRI "GIS for Schools."

<www.gisday.com> GIS Day. A day of demonstrations and promotion of GIS, held during Geography Awareness Week in November.

<http://blogs.esri.com/Info/blogs/gisedcom/> GIS Education Community blog.

<http://edcommunity.esri.com/apps/calendar/> Clearinghouse for GIS training opportunities, learning activities for students, new materials and programs.

Voices of the Land:
A Course in Environmental Literature

by Emma Wood Rous

Subject areas: language arts interdisciplinary courses

Key concepts: nature writing and literature, sense of place, observation, point of view, nature journals, historical views of land, impacts and actions

Skills: reading and writing in all genres, values clarification, observation and interpretation, higher order interdisciplinary thinking

Location: classroom and in field

Time: options for a one-year or semester course as well as individual units

Materials: nature literature in class sets and individual texts, excerpted readings, journals (see suggested readings)

Emma Wood Rous

In adolescence, we define our identity, independence and values; and values, as much as scientific data, determine our treatment of nature. An ecological perspective argues for an interdisciplinary approach to learning. For these reasons, environmental studies are increasingly extending beyond the science classroom. The special power of literature to engage and inspire us makes language arts an ideal context for raising students' awareness of environmental issues.

Twenty years ago, I started teaching environmental literature as a high school language arts course. "Literature and the Land" has all of the usual "English" elements: interpreting good literature, honing writing skills in a variety of genres, research projects and oral presentations. It has unexpected elements, too, such as mountain hikes and plant transects. The curriculum is shaped by two themes that recur in nature writing and

are appropriate to adolescents' emerging sense of self and social responsibility: the importance of a sense of place and the influence of point of view on our treatment of the Earth.

Introductory reading and writing

The semester course described here is designed for groups of mixed ability and offers a wide range of readings for a whole class, small groups or individuals. Many texts are excerpted (see sidebar) and can be used for a short unit as well as for a full semester or year. To foster attachment to place, teachers may seek out the literature, art and history of their own area and, where appropriate, the excellent "Stories from Where We Live" collections, covering 13 North American bioregions.[1]

I open with a story chosen for readability and its exploration of the course themes of place and point of view — often Borden Deal's short story "Antaeus."[2] The main character, T.J., uprooted from his southern farm, persuades his new urban friends to build a roof garden. Like the mythical wrestler Antaeus who loses strength when not in contact with the Earth, T.J. loses his sense of place when separated from his home. Students note the conflicting views of the characters: T.J. wants to plant vegetables, his friends want a lawn, and the building owners care only about damage to their property. Who should decide how land is used? Is ownership the highest value? When the boys are forced to destroy their garden, T.J. sets out for the south and home. Another good introductory story is Sarah Orne Jewett's "A White Heron," in which an ornithologist-collector tries to tempt a young girl to betray her love of beauty and wild things and show him a heron's nesting place.[3]

After the opening reading, students write "land autobiographies" describing places that have influenced who they are. In *Writing Toward Home*, Georgia Heard suggests writing about our "querencia," the place where we feel most at home, the place that gives us strength.[4] Students may describe ordinary, everyday places as well as special places they have visited, perhaps on a trip. The writing should be rich in evocative sensory description and make clear the significance of the place to the writer. Students can write about one place only, but, to avoid superficial treatment, no more than four or five. Allowing time for drafting, conferencing and rewriting, the assignment takes about two weeks. I complete the assignment along with students, and we share our final pieces in small groups. In the ensuing discussion, students explore what natural places mean to us: they define our sense of "home," offer diversity and beauty, and may be either comfortably familiar or an escape from the familiar.

Nature journals

The "land autobiography" serves as a good introduction to a semester-long land journal project because it demonstrates the importance of developing a personal relationship with a particular area. As David Orr writes in *Earth in Mind*, "I do not know whether it is possible to love the planet or not, but I do know that it is possible to love the places we can see, touch, smell and experience. And I believe that rootedness in a place is the most important and least recognized need of the human soul."[5] More effective than statistics and doomsday predictions, an attachment to a special place fosters a desire to protect that place ... as well as others. As one student wrote, "This spot of land is more than just a place to me; it is a piece of me." Land journals help students become land stewards.

Students choose a local natural area and make weekly journal entries consisting of written observations and reflections, drawings, collections, photographs, research, history, soil tests, plant surveys, poems, stories and so on. Their sites are labeled on a topographic map in the classroom. They may make one long entry or several shorter ones each week. Some write their entries while they are on the site, some at home after a visit. I ask for about 700 words a week, or an equivalent effort in drawing, research or poetry. As I read the entries, I use sticky notes to pose questions, compliment effective passages or share my own experiences. I do not edit, but list spelling words on the notes. Students complete self-evaluations each quarter, using the class goals for the land journals (see sidebar). I grade journals twice each quarter, giving students a progress report as well as

Bev Conway

Land Journal Goals

- To increase awareness and powers of observation of the natural world, including seeing changes over time
- To apply a variety of points of view in looking at land, including poetic, historic, scientific, personal, artistic and political
- To see land as an integrated, ecological whole
- To learn a variety of journal-keeping styles and to discover and develop a personal voice
- To develop a personal relationship with, and a sense of caring for, a piece of land
- To have a weekly "time out" from routine activity

a final grade, and base grades on consistency, quality of effort and attention to the goals.

Students are free to choose the focus of their entries, but I model approaches with in-class writings and may offer an optional "prompt" such as telling a story, writing a letter or taking the perspective of a Native American or a first European settler. I suggest things to try in journals, such as the following:

- Look closely, pay attention, use your senses.

- Look from different points of view: close up, wide angle, inside out, personify.

- Change your sense of scale.

- Ask a big question that's hard to answer.

- Find a mystery.

- Look for patterns.

- Look for contrasts, edges, transitions, light and dark.

- Look for changes over time.

- Create a symbol or metaphor.

- Use imagination or memory.

- Describe the same thing in 13 different ways (as in the poem "Thirteen Ways of Looking at a Blackbird" by Wallace Stevens.[6])

- Draw as well as write; combine drawing and writing with maps, labeling, etc.

- Write in different genres: personal narrative, poetry, fiction, letter, stream of consciousness, lists, sensory description.

An opening unit on perception helps students sharpen their observational skills and begin to experience seeing the world from different points of view. Using the "Seeing" chapter from Annie Dillard's *Pilgrim at Tinker Creek*[7] as a core reading, we look at how context, expertise and expectations influence what we "see." Blindfold walks, drawing and sensory writing (smell or touch "mystery" bags; listening, looking and tasting exercises) all help us pay closer attention and deepen our delight and connection with the natural world. We look at optical illusions, hidden pictures and holograms to make the analogous point that the world and environmental issues can be seen from different points of view, that not everything is immediately obvious. Is a forest a habitat or a commodity? Does a highway project represent a safety issue, a historic preservation issue or an environmental impact issue? Students explore how needs, interests, personality and experiences affect our view of the world and, in turn, our treatment of it.

Course readings offer students models of nature journal styles and illustrate a range of views of the natural world. An 18th-century journal kept for 25 years by Englishman Gilbert White[8] chronicles daily events in his garden: the temperature, the arrival or departure of birds, seasonal changes. It is an objective collection of data without personal reflection or lyrical description, but it builds sensitivity to natural rhythms. John Muir's field journals were written on his extended foot travels in the southeastern United States, the Sierras and the glacier country of the northwest coast. His style combines scientific observation of rock formations and glacial action with highly subjective exuberance and poetic description of his surroundings. Thoreau is an observant naturalist, but we read him mainly for his poetic use of metaphor and philosophical explorations. Bernd Heinrich, a contemporary scientist, artist, photographer and observer of ravens and the northern forest, combines many approaches to create a "renaissance" journal, a flexible and inclusive style many students find appealing. In *Ceremonial Time*, Jon Mitchell's explorations of the square mile around his Massachusetts home lead him to a spiritual connection with the first people to inhabit that land.[9] Clare Walker Leslie keeps a naturalist's sketchbook of field drawings with written annotations.[10] One of Hannah Hinchman's sketchbook techniques is to record an exploratory walk by means of an illustrated map.[11] These nature journalists are introduced to illustrate journaling perspectives ranging from poetic, literary and artistic to scientific and historical, as well as for their contribution to American literature and conservationism.

I inform students that my own journal keeping evolved from trip chronicles to periodic observations of my daily surroundings. As a result, I stopped looking for the extraordinary in faraway places and learned to appreciate the extraordinary in my own "backyard." Inspired by Hannah Hinchman's "illuminated journals," I recently made a rule that every page of my journal should include something visual. Drawing makes me look at things differently and more carefully — I see shape and texture, light and shadow, shades of color. Looking for things to draw (or collect, map or photograph) makes me more alert to visual opportunities and discoveries. It also produces a much more engaging journal! Sharing my personal growth with journals inspires students to explore and further develop their own styles.

Students experiment with different formats in their journals and reflect on how various styles enrich their ways of looking at the world. They learn about themselves as observers, storytellers, historians, poets, fantasy writers, researchers, visual artists and scientists. As they learn to see from different points of view, they are building their connection to their land and deepening their sense of place.

Nature literature

Readings in the "Literature and the Land" course are organized in units that explore appreciation of place and the role of point of view. We study world mythology and the "golden age" archetype, frontier views of North America, Romanticism, the beginnings of the conservation movement and modern environmental issues. We read Aldo Leopold, Willa Cather, Barbara Kingsolver, Edward Abbey, Barry Lopez, John McPhee, Shakespeare (*The Tempest*), Terry Tempest Williams, Loren Eiseley and Mary Oliver among others (see suggested readings). While nature writing is traditionally nonfiction, fiction and poetry also have their place in our study.

Emma Wood Rous

The question of how point of view affects treatment of land is the essential question of our assigned readings, starting chronologically with world creation stories. How do people treat land if they personify and deify it? ... if they are taught to "have dominion over" it, or to "till and keep it" (Genesis I:28 and II:15)? What treatment would students expect from North American settlers who saw rich and bountiful forests, fields and seas (George Percy, John Smith); a pleasurable garden (Robert Beverly); a stepping stone to heaven (Samuel Sewall); or a "waste and howling wilderness" (Michael Wigglesworth)? Students read myths, legends and journal excerpts as well as view the PBS television *Land of the Eagle* segment "The Great Encounter" for varied views of land, especially the "new" land of North America. In some years, we also read fiction and nonfiction about the settlement of the American West (Lewis and Clark, Sanford, Bird, Pruitt Steward, Austin, Cather, Cooper, Rolvaag, Steinbeck, Stegner, Doig, Wister, Guthrie, Twain).

Europeans' fascination with the natural abundance they found in North America led quickly to exploiting those resources. We study the Romantic and Transcendentalists' reaction to the abuse of nature with readings by Wordsworth, Emerson and Thoreau. As students read excerpts from *Walden*, they choose passages they like, don't understand or don't agree with for class discussion. A series of appealing children's books by D. B. Johnson helps make Thoreau's ideas accessible (e.g., *Henry Hikes To Fitchburg*[12]). Students write

about a chosen aphorism, discussing its meaning and relationship to the rest of Thoreau's philosophy, and expressing their own opinion. We discuss Thoreau's statement that "a man is rich in proportion to the number of things which he can afford to let alone," debate how much is enough, and list what we consider essential to life and what is a luxury. When students challenge Thoreau's emphasis on simplicity, I introduce the concept of an environmental footprint and the North American rate of consumption (20–30 percent of the world's total resources are consumed in the United States). To help students appreciate contemporary efforts to minimize our impact on the Earth, we watch films about Helen and Scott Nearing (*Living the Good Life*[13]) and Vicki Robbin and Joe Dominguez (*Less Is More*[14]) and read excerpts from E.F. Schumacher's *Small Is Beautiful*. When we finish reading *Walden*, students write a final paper entitled "Where I Want to Live and What I Want to Live For" in which they consider goals for family, education, life style and career, and urban versus suburban or country living. Some students adhere to goals of material wealth; others express a sense of social responsibility. Because these papers are personal, students are motivated to write them — and I look forward to reading them.

Impacts and actions

The relationship between individual interests and resulting impacts on nature can be found repeatedly in American history and literature, and in current environmental controversies. Edward Abbey's *Desert Solitaire* and John McPhee's *Encounters with the*

(continued on page 196)

Suggested Nature Readings

Excerpts

The following passages and chapters from selected works provide samples of a wide range of nature writing.

Pilgrim at Tinker Creek by Annie Dillard: chapter 2, "Seeing" (skipping from the Donald E. Carr quote to the von Senden account of newly sighted patients).

The Immense Journey by Loren Eiseley: "The Flow of the River" and "The Secret of Life."

"Nature" (essay) by Ralph Waldo Emerson in *Essays and Poems by Ralph Waldo Emerson*: the "transparent eyeball" passage.

Walden by Henry David Thoreau: Introduction, much of "Economy," all of "Where I Lived, and What I Lived For," short descriptions of the ponds, all of the conclusion.

Small Is Beautiful by E. F. Schumacher: chapter 5, "Technology with a Human Face."

Going to Extremes by Joe McGinniss: chapters 1–5 ("The Ferry," "The Road," "Anchorage," "The First Day North" and "Prudhoe Bay"); chapter 8 ("The Village," on indigenous people caught between tradition and the contemporary world); chapter 10 ("Crescent Lake," contrasts with Thoreau's sojourn at Walden Pond); chapter 14 ("Kahiltna Glacier," motivations for homesteading, then leaving, the wilderness); chapter 16 ("Anchorage," arguments for and against oil drilling); chapters 17, 18 ("Bettles" and "The Brooks Range," McGinniss' wilderness experience).

Don Coyote by Dayton O. Hyde: chapters 1–5, 13, 14, 15, 27–30 (skip stories of Hyde's youth and raising coyote pups).

Desert Solitaire by Edward Abbey: Introduction, chapters 1–3, four pages on killing a rabbit in chapter 4, "Polemic" (for park management philosophy), "Rocks" (for fun!), first half and last page of "Down the River," "Dead Man at Grandview Point," "Bedrock and Paradox."

Exploration of the Colorado River and Its Canyons by John Wesley Powell, introduction by Wallace Stegner: entries for August 2–6, 13, 15–17, 24, 26–31 and September 1.

Encounters With the Archdruid by John McPhee: "The River," on a Lake Powell and Colorado River trip with Floyd Dominy (Bureau of Reclamation) and David Brower (Friends of the Earth).

Journals of Lewis and Clark by Meriwether Lewis and William Clark (edited by Bernard DeVoto): entries for July 17–18, 1805; July 18–20 and August 11, 1806.

Roughing It by Mark Twain: excerpt on Lake Tahoe.

The Solace of Open Spaces by Gretel Ehrlich: preface and first chapter.

A Choice of Heroes by Michael Gerzon: "The Frontiersman, Images of the Earth."

My First Summer in the Sierra by John Muir: short passages from "Mt. Hoffman and Lake Tenaya," "A Strange Experience," "The Mono Trail," "Bloody Canon and Mono Lake," "The Yosemite" and "The Tuolumne Camp." (I use descriptions of meadows, clouds, peaks and falls that match my own slides of Yosemite.)

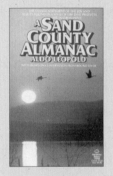

A Sand County Almanac by Aldo Leopold: Part IV, "The Land Ethic," "Thinking Like a Mountain" and a few descriptive passages from the monthly Almanac.

Entire works

The following full-length titles are used as whole-class assignments (usually three in a semester). Many other titles are offered for student-choice reading assignments.

My Antonia by Willa Cather
Into the Wild by Jon Krakauer
Never Cry Wolf by Farley Mowat
Animal Dreams by Barbara Kingsolver
The Rediscovery of North America by Barry Lopez
Giants in the Earth by O.E. Rolvaag
The Tempest by William Shakespeare

Additional books to consider

Collapse: How Societies Choose to Fail or Succeed by Jared Diamond
Ordinary Wolves (fiction) by Seth Kantner
The Golden Spruce by John Vaillant
Reading the Landscape of America by May Theilgaard Watts

Archdruid explore the conflicting goals of developers and preservationists. Loggers versus old growth forest preservation (Vaillant), ranchers versus wolf re-introduction (Lopez, Mowat, Hyde), oil drillers versus wilderness preservation (McPhee, McGinniss), dam builders versus free-flowing rivers (Powell, Abbey, McPhee, Reisner), local builders versus open space advocates — students read literature, research news and reference materials, and interview local advocates, trying to arrive at their own conclusions and develop their own environmental philosophies. Readings may lead to forums and debates, to position papers, or to action projects such as pamphlets, informational posters, cleanup days, recycling programs or water monitoring.

Even within the environmental movement, students discover a range of beliefs, from the strict preservationist views of John Muir (the land is God's sacred gift and should be left alone) and Aldo Leopold's ecologist's view (land has rights and should be used only to the extent that it can maintain its natural balance), to Gifford Pinchot's conservationism (resources should be managed to control waste and conserve for future generations). They also read the views of pro-developer, property rights advocates such as James Watt and Gayle Norton. Students arrange these land-use philosophies on a continuum from greatest impact on land to least, and then place themselves on the continuum and explain and support their choice.

Keeping land journals and reading literature by people who love their chosen homelands — T.T. Williams on Great Salt Lake, Barbara Kingsolver on the Southwest, Edward Abbey on the rimrock country, Janisse Ray on southern pine forests, Thoreau on Walden Pond — deepen students' appreciation of their own natural surroundings. In his journal, a student says, "When I write about the land and use words to describe it, I'm seeing the land differently and really observing it. So, because I'm so attached to this land now, I want it to be preserved the way it is forever." We nurture and protect what we care for — be it person or land.

Reading historical views of the natural world and how these conflicting views, often selfish and destructive, still influence our relationship with the environment, students come to understand the need for a new vision. As Abbey writes, "We have to learn to look at the world through different eyes .... We must work with our perceptions to change our perspective and create a reality in which we can respect the Earth."

Educators succeed when students see that protecting the rights of land is as important as protecting human rights because we are all part of the same community of life. We can hope for the future when students take responsibility on a personal and social level for preserving this unity.

Emma Wood Rous

Emma Wood Rous *developed and taught the Literature and the Land course at Oyster River High School in Durham, New Hampshire. She is the author of* Literature and the Land: Reading and Writing for Environmental Literacy, 7–12 *(Portsmouth, NH: Heinemann/Boynton Cook, 2000).*

Notes

1. *Stories from Where We Live* series, Sara St. Antoine, ed., Milkweed Editions, 2000.

2. Borden Deal, "Antaeus," in *Short Stories: Characters in Conflict*, John Warriner, ed., Holt, Rinehart & Winston, 1981.

3. Sarah Orne Jewett, "A White Heron," in *A White Heron and Other Stories*, Dover Publications, 1999.

4. Georgia Heard, *Writing Toward Home: Tales and Lessons to Find Your Way*, Heinemann, 1995.

5. David Orr, *Earth in Mind: On Education, Environment, and the Human Prospect*, Island Press, 2004.

6. Wallace Stevens, "Thirteen Ways of Looking at a Blackbird" in *Wallace Stevens: The Collected Poems*, Vintage Books, 1982.

7. Annie Dillard, *Pilgrim at Tinker Creek*, HarperPerennial, 1998.

8. Gilbert White, *The Natural History and Antiquities of Selborne, in the County of Southampton* (1789), Oxford University Press Oxford, 1993.

9. Jon Mitchell, *Ceremonial Time*, Addison-Wesley, 1997.

10. Clare Walker Leslie, *Keeping a Nature Journal*, Storey Books, 2003.

11. Hannah Hinchmann, *A Trail Through Leaves*, Norton, 1997.

12. D. B. Johnson, *Henry Hikes To Fitchburg*, Houghton Mifflin, 2000.

13. *Living the Good Life with Helen and Scott Nearing*, John Hoskyns-Abrahall (director), Bullfrog Films, 1977.

14. *Less Is More*, Ken Ellis (producer), Green Means series, KQED Public Broadcasting, San Francisco, 1993.

Social Justice and Language Arts

Illustrations by Tom Goldsmith

by Christopher Greenslate

Subject area: language arts

Key concepts: connecting language arts to current global challenges, literature, poetry, non-fiction, writing

Location: indoors or outdoors

Time: continuously (whenever you can)

Materials: appropriate text, article or poem; writing materials; computer

High school can be a time of extreme complexity and anxiety for many of the students who traverse our halls and campuses. It is a time when teens are navigating relationships with friends and family, worrying about appearances and grades, coming to terms with their changing bodies, learning to drive and in some cases getting that first paying job. However, it is also the time when young people are developing a moral compass, falling in love with new ideas, overtly challenging perceptions, and in many instances shirking the status quo for a new brand of lifestyle and identity. At this point in their lives, teens are truly starting to think for themselves and to expand their radius of inquiry beyond home and school to social and environmental issues in the wider world.

Educators who wish to teach about these larger issues often find themselves on the philosophical and political fringe, and may even ask themselves whether they are taking advantage of students by introducing ideas that in some way validate their own world view. However, clean water and air, human rights, animal protection, and problems of world hunger, racism, sexism and homophobia are not partisan issues. These are the concerns of our era and will not find resolution unless our youth are educated and empowered toward that end. If we avoid these topics in high school in the belief that our students will be introduced to them in college or later in life, we are being naïve and irresponsible. It's because we aren't teaching our youth about these issues that we continue to see racism, sexism, speciesism and alarming rates of environmental destruction.

Of the various high school disciplines, it is the language arts curriculum that typically extends itself most readily to these very real and serious subjects, and with good reason. Finding an author's purpose and discovering what comment on life an author is making are at the heart of studying literature, poetry, essays and speeches. This puts the language arts teacher in an excellent position to help students explore these issues. Whereas math and science teachers find themselves teaching about how things work in an objective environment, English teachers are constantly immersed in exploring the subjective ideas that are central to who we are and what we believe. This article looks at some of the many ways of extending issues of social justice into the language arts curriculum through literature, poetry, expository texts and writing.

Literature and social justice

In most areas, high schools have a set of texts for English classes that are pre-selected and placed in the curriculum by grade level. Whether these are textbooks that include a variety of selections or individual novels and plays, they offer literally an infinite number of possibilities for making connections to larger issues of social justice. While it is best to let students choose the books they'd like to read for class credit, and develop assignments that are flexible enough to accommodate that choice, by and large the majority of English classrooms will have books that all students will read together in a more structured environment. If you teach in a school that works hard at aligning curricula to state or provincial standards, the case can usually be made that the standards or skills are what is most important, not the books used to teach to those standards. So, for those who believe in student choice, standards-based education may be a blessing in disguise.

With such works as William Golding's *Lord of the Flies* there are a number of ways to connect to social justice issues. A primary theme, as well as the conflict in this work, is "civilization versus savagery." This theme explores the idea that we live by two competing impulses as human beings: the instinct to live by rules, act peacefully, follow moral commands and value the good of the group, against the instinct to gratify one's immediate desires, act violently to obtain supremacy over others and enforce one's will. First and foremost, a theme of this size poses such questions as: What does it mean to be civilized? How can we build a society that is fair and just for all? Are humans inherently evil? The boys on the island are at first peaceful and respectful, doing their very best to work together for a common goal: to survive and to be rescued. In the course of the novel, we watch this cooperation, respect and peace deteriorate to the point of murder. While reading this novel, I assign pre-selected groups (the boys in the novel didn't have choice about who was on the island) of four or five students to work through a number of steps and activities to try to determine whether they would survive outside the confines of civilization. First, they get to know each of their group members in depth by sharing answers to reflective questions such as the following.

What are you good at?
What are your weaknesses?
What makes someone a good person?
How do you react when someone is being aggressive?
Do you consider yourself a leader? Why or why not?
What makes you really mad?
How do you react when you have to take orders?
Do you work better by yourself or in groups? Explain.
What does community mean to you?
Do you believe that working together helps a group to survive? Explain.

Next, students decide what tasks and responsibilities must be undertaken on their island and who is going to do what. While I do give suggestions to groups who are struggling, it is a great learning experience for students to have to decide what they will need to do in order to survive. The responsibilities they commonly come up with include building shelters, finding food, finding fresh water, harvesting coconuts for milk, exploring the island to see what is there, keeping a signal fire going for rescue, writing a large message in the sand that would be visible to planes, making sure that people are working, maintaining community relations, facilitating meetings and organizing events.

LORD OF THE FLIES

About twice each week during our study of the novel, I give the students a problem that they have to solve in their "survivor" groups. Problems like the following are common.

1. It has been raining for two weeks and the storm is destroying your huts.

2. Someone in your group is stealing food while the others sleep.

3. The place that you decided would be the latrine is starting to smell and attracting bugs and other creatures.

4. You're harvesting food faster than it is growing. If you keep it up you will run out.

5. The signal fire is out of control and starting to burn parts of the island.

6. The water supply that you've been using has made two of you very sick.

7. You started fishing (or hunting) to survive, but you're finding that the animals are fewer in number and harder to find. You haven't found any animals in two days.

8. The weather has become so hot that you've left the beaches and can't come out of the forest without being severely burned or suffering from heat exhaustion.

I then have students use the library or Internet to find out how their problem is similar to current environmental problems or other challenges that humans are facing. Specifically, they have to look for ways in which these problems could be solved or may have been prevented. Groups then give presentations to the class about what they discovered and the solutions they have come up with.

While the foundation is being laid for a fundamental understanding of how communities cohere or dissolve and how human needs are directly connected to the environment, it is also possible to pick up on tangentially related issues. For example, early in the novel, the boys on the island forage for food from plants that grow around them, and it is a time of peace and cooperation. When they start hunting, the boys become violent, going beyond killing a pig for food to abusing it as well. This scene lends itself to discussion of the connection between animal abuse and human violence and to reading and discussing some of the many articles that have been written about this connection.[1]

Exploration of the perceived dichotomy between civilization and tribal life is also explored in such works as *Things Fall Apart* by Chinua Achebe and *Cry, the Beloved Country* by Alan Paton. Like *Lord of the Flies*, these novels present other issues that can be tapped as well, such as racism, poverty, violence and colonialism. The environment and human anthropocentrism are addressed in *Ishmael* by Daniel Quinn, in which commonly held ideas such as "the world was created for man" are discussed and debunked in favor of the idea that humans are part of nature and are dependent on the Earth in ways that we are aware of but carelessly continue to ignore. Quinn also debunks the belief by modern "civilized" societies that theirs is the only right way to live and that tribal societies should adhere to the same rules.

In addition to novels, there are many short stories that give voice to concepts and themes connected to social justice issues. Such stories as "A Sound of Thunder" by Ray Bradbury and "The Turtle" by John Steinbeck address issues of the environment explicitly. Whether or not these issues are explicit in a work (oftentimes they are not), our job as language arts teachers is to make the connections apparent to our students, or, better yet, ask them guiding questions so that they may find the links on their own.

Poetry and social justice

There is great opportunity and power in poetry. Poetry is the one place where we often see the natural world described in luscious detail and with a level of beauty that competes with the environment itself. Walt Whitman, Pablo Neruda and Octovio Paz are just a few examples of authors whose poems directly illuminate the beauty of the natural world. As with novels and stories, the themes, images and motifs in poems can be drawn out and connected to larger issues.

Poems that express a love of nature and sense of stewardship toward the natural world, such as

this one by Emily Dickinson, are great springboards into reflection on one's own feelings concerning the Earth and other species:

> If I can stop one heart from breaking,
> I shall not live in vain;
> If I can ease one life the aching,
> Or cool one pain,
> Or help one fainting robin
> Unto his nest again, I shall not live in vain.

Richard Wright's haikus are also good examples of the way one's life and feelings are connected to and expressed through elements of the natural world:

> I am nobody:
> A red sinking autumn sun
> Took my name away.

> In the falling snow
> A laughing boy holds out his palms
> Until they are white.

Students can extend their reading and writing of poetry beyond the classroom by publishing a book of their own poems, in which they speak out on issues of social justice or reflect on their personal connections to the natural world. This project could include a class discussion of environmentally friendly ways to reproduce the book: what type of paper to use, what "post-consumer content" is, how many books to print and so on. Students could sell the books to raise funds for a local community project or non-profit orga-

nization. If your administrators are open to it, they could also use sidewalk chalk to display their poetry across the campus, thereby piquing interest in both poetry and global concerns. In my classroom, each student chooses a poem (or a song with literary quality) to present to the class as a vehicle for teaching us about an issue and about a poetic device such as alliteration, allusion or onomatopoeia.

Expository articles and social justice

Reading expository articles is a great way for students to improve their reading skills as well as prepare for discussions of how issues raised in a work of literature are connected to the real world. For example, if your students are studying *Romeo and Juliet*, you may wish to have them read articles that discuss teen suicide, teen relationships, pressures on young people to preserve family traditions, or the challenges faced by gay and lesbian youth. If your class is reading Orwell's *1984*, you might consider having your students read selections from Noam Chomsky's book *Media Control: The Spectacular Achievements of Propaganda*. As noted earlier, articles about the link between animal abuse and violence could be used to explore that theme in *Lord of the Flies*.

Students may also select expository articles for sharing with the class. Once a theme or issue has been introduced in a poem or work of literature, ask students, "How does this theme connect to our lives or to the world today?" This requires them to think critically and make personal and real-world connections on their own. From there, students can search for articles and use the Socratic seminar method to raise questions and

initiate class discussion. In this way, expository articles not only complement the study of literature, but also provide a basis for explicit discussions of things happening in the world today.

Writing and social justice

Encouraging students to explore social justice issues through commonly taught modes of writing, such as research, evaluative, persuasive, autobiographical and reflective essays, is another way to engage them in deeper thinking about important global concerns. For example, if your class is reading *Frankenstein* by Mary Shelley, students could be assigned a research paper that explores a controversial topic related to scientific and technological "advancements," such as cloning, genetic modification and stem cell research. Similarly, in a study of Margaret Atwood's *The Handmaid's Tale*, students might research and explore such topics as women's suffrage, gender roles, reproductive health and its connection to women's issues, abortion rights and repressive governments.

Other modes of written expression, such as speeches and business letters, also afford opportunities to write about themes and issues studied in class. Students could write business letters to elected officials or to the heads of corporations and other organizations to express opinions or ask questions about controversial issues or perceived injustices. While teachers might share with students some examples of letters they've written, they can avoid manipulation by letting students choose what to write about and to whom. If students are struggling, ask them what issue is important to them and who they think could change that.

Literature, poetry, essays, letters and speeches are means by which humans communicate with each other about life-changing experiences, and they help us to see the world anew. A work of literature can validate a part of us we never knew existed, and a powerful speech can motivate us to make change. Poetry can bring new realities into being, and reading a well-developed research paper can change the way we eat or where we shop. Introducing students to these global concerns should not be a peripheral issue or afterthought in education; it should be the core of how and what we teach. If you teach English and choose to stay focused on the surface level of forms, themes and historical context, you are robbing your students of a chance to make their own education more meaningful. Every poem or work of literature can be connected to present-day social justice issues. Our job as educators is to find these connections, let students explore them, answer questions and provide support. If you do this, you will be amazed as you watch your students leap to new levels of engagement and meaningful learning.

Christopher Greenslate teaches English, Social Justice and Journalism at La Costa Canyon High School in Carlsbad, California. Teaching materials for these courses are posted at his website <www.cmgreenslate. com>.

Notes

1. See, for example, the resources concerning this connection at the websites of Teach Kind < www.teachkind.org> and the Humane Society of the United States <www.hsus.org>.

Designing a Green City

by Iori Miller and Susan Sheard

Subject areas: urban geography, environmental science, language arts, architecture

Key concepts: sustainability, energy conservation, alternative energy sources, water management, climate change, waste management, transportation systems, forest/wildlife management and protection

Skills: urban planning/design, research and analysis, innovative thinking, report writing, creating a bibliography, group work, presentation skills

Location: mostly indoors, but could incorporate field trips

Time: 10 to 20 hour-long periods

Materials: chart paper and markers; access to computers and library; class set of the novel *Ecotopia* by Ernest Callenbach, or other "eco-utopian" novel (optional); Green City Project Planning Sheets; Green City Project Assessment Sheets

T o many, the idea of urban environmentalism is an oxymoron. True, there is little of the natural environment in the asphalt-and-concrete jungles of most 21st-century cities. But as city dwellers become increasingly concerned about urban sprawl, air quality and waste management, there is a call to rethink how our cities fit into the natural environment. Considering that more than 50 percent of the human population now dwells in urban environments, it is becoming more and more important that we reconsider how cities are built and managed. This activity encourages students to envision what a sustainable city might look like. Their mission: to design and present a "Greentopia," a sustainable city of the not-so-distant future.

Illustrations by Tom Goldsmith

Before students can begin to design their green city, they will require background knowledge and inspiration. For this reason, the project is a good culminating activity for a unit on ecology and sustainable living. The students' preliminary studies should give them a foundation in basic principles of ecology and the ways in which our daily habits and choices as consumers affect the health of the environment, both locally and globally. Students should have opportunities to see (and smell) first-hand a sewage treatment plant and a landfill site, and to calculate their ecological footprint in order to realize that the weekly curbside garbage deposit is only a small part of the environmental impact of city dwellers. The knowledge and insight gained through such experiences will provide students with a rationale for envisioning a more sustainable city.

Introduction: Imagining a green city

One way to introduce the green city project is with a brainstorming session in which students explore possible solutions to urban environmental problems.

1. Divide the class into groups of four and provide each group with chart paper.

2. Have the groups divide their charts into four equal sections with the headings "Greenhouse gas emissions," "Toxic runoff," "Habitat loss" and "Traffic congestion" (or, as a class, generate your own four categories of urban environmental challenges). Allow the groups five to ten minutes to brainstorm and record the causes of these problems in urban settings. For example, under "Toxic runoff," students might list motor oil and salt on roads, fertilizers and herbicides on lawns, pet feces, gasoline spills at gas stations, and the paved surfaces that allow such toxins to flow directly into storm sewers during heavy rain. Ask the groups to share their lists with the class.

3. Give the groups another 10 to 15 minutes to generate and record solutions to the problems they have identified. Encourage them to include plausible solutions as well as solutions that may seem far-fetched, and to envision how their ideas could actually be applied in the real world. Also encourage them to think about

---

Green City Project Planning Sheet

Mission Statement: Your mission is to design a community that meets the basic needs of its human inhabitants while sustaining the health of the surrounding air, water and soil for all time, and leaving undisturbed those wilderness areas that are large enough to sustain complex ecosystems that include predators and ungulates (which require very large, unfragmented areas for survival).

1. Before you begin your research, brainstorm and record your ideas for the following key components of your city.
- Agriculture and food production
- Economy (i.e., how will people make money)
- Education
- Energy production and conservation
- Forest/wildlife management and protection within the city
- Housing
- Public spaces (i.e., the design and arrangement of streets, parks, squares, gardens)
- Transportation
- Waste management (including garbage and sewage)
- Water supply and treatment

2. Decide who will research each of the key components.

3. Research the key components for which you are responsible. Bring your findings to class and be

prepared to share them with your group. Keep a detailed and accurate list of all websites, books and other media you use while researching, as your group must submit a complete bibliography.

4. Prepare a written report. After your group members have shared their findings, discuss your ideas and add to them as a group. Decide on a name for your green city and write a report in which you describe how all of its key components will be designed. Justify your reasons for these designs with references to environmental principles and issues. Your report must be written clearly in your own words and must include a complete bibliography. You may write it together or assign different sections to different group members.

5. Prepare a presentation. In addition to writing a report, prepare to present your green city to the class in a compelling way. For example, in presenting your ideas, some members of your group could act as urban planners while others play the role of skeptical and questioning town councilors. Or you could be reporters, or a delegation of citizens making a presentation about your city to another community. In addition to thinking of creative ways to present your information to the class, you may wish to draw or create a model of your city.

---

ways in which several problems might be solved at once. For example, increasing the density of housing near workplaces or creating a fast and efficient public transportation system could reduce the use of personal vehicles, thereby reducing both greenhouse gas emissions and traffic congestion.

4. Once the groups have shared their ideas with the class, a lively discussion will likely follow. This session should lead students to the realization that in order to live sustainably we must rethink the basic components of urban infrastructure and design. One way to frame this is by introducing James Lovelock's Gaia theory, the idea of planet Earth as a living organism. Ask students to envision a city as an organism that interacts with its environment: it ingests food, water and other natural resources such as trees and minerals; it circulates people and materials; it inhales and exhales atmospheric gases; and it expels wastes.

5. Hand out the Green City Project Planning Sheet and discuss the assignment: to design a city in which the needs of humans are met without compromising the health of surrounding ecosystems, wildlife habitat, air, water and soil. The planning sheet provides students with a mission statement and a step-by-step procedure for designing and presenting their green city. (Teachers can decide how much research time will be given in class and how much research is to be completed independently.)

6. Hand out and review the Green City Project Assessment Sheet (or create your own assessment criteria). The assessment sheet outlines the requirements for the written report and oral presentation, and makes students aware at the outset that group members who participate actively will receive higher marks than those who are overly reliant on others.

Providing green city models

When presenting the project to the students, emphasize that the green city is in fact the city of the future. In designing their city, they will be joining the many visionaries already engaged in the groundbreaking work of developing "green" technology and design. It is easy to feel bogged down by the complexity of environmental problems, and, too often, alternatives to the status quo are dismissed as unrealistic. It is crucial that students see for themselves that green technologies and sustainable systems are not "pie in

---

Green City Project Assessment Sheet

Assessment Criteria for Written Report (50 marks)

Describe how all of the key components will be designed in your green city:	/10
Justify the reasons for your design with reference to environmental principles and issues:	/10
Explain your ideas clearly and in your own words:	/10
Proofread your work carefully to ensure correct spelling, grammar and punctuation:	/10
Include a complete, accurately written bibliography:	/10

Assessment Criteria for Presentation to the Class (20 marks)

The presentation is well organized; each member clearly understands and carries out his or her job:	/5
Your group's ideas are presented clearly and thoroughly:	/5
Your group uses pictures and/or a model effectively to help explain your ideas:	/5
Rather than just reading your report, your group presents its information in a compelling way that holds the audience's attention:	/5

Assessment Criteria for Individual Contribution to the Project (60 marks)

During group brainstorming and sharing sessions, you offered ideas and listened carefully to others' ideas:	/20
You researched the key components for which you were responsible and brought your findings to class with you:	/20
You helped to write the final written report, and you participated actively in the preparation for your group's presentation and in the presentation itself:	/20

Project total: _____ /50 + _____ /20 + _____ /60 = _____ /130 = _____ %

---

the sky," but actually work. The following activities will give students ideas for their projects and at the same time expose them to some of the many careers that would enable them to practice and promote an ethic of environmentalism.

• Visit sites where students can see wind turbines, solar panels, energy-saving devices and living systems for water filtration.

• Invite local "green" builders and representatives from companies that are developing sustainable technologies to visit the class to discuss new developments in materials, energy efficiency and alternative energy.

• Invite an urban planner to talk about alternative approaches to transportation and development that would enable cities to accommodate growing populations without adding to urban sprawl and traffic congestion.

• Have students read Ernest Callenbach's novel *Ecotopia* or another work that depicts a sustainable community. The main character of *Ecotopia* is a reporter on assignment to explore Ecotopia, a small country formed from three breakaway states (Washington, Oregon and northern California).

Ernest Callenbach's *Ecotopia*: Questions for Discussion

1. Create a table with three columns. As you read *Ecotopia*, use your table to compile three lists: "Obsolete Technology," "Current Technology" and "Futuristic Technology."

2. Create a table with two columns titled "Keep" and "Reject." As you read *Ecotopia*, list aspects of Ecotopia you will keep or reject when planning your green city.

3. Why do you think the author included the sex scenes? Do you think the book would be better or worse without them? Why? *(Note: To some readers, these scenes may seem gratuitous, included only as a "hook" to keep readers.)*

4. How would you describe the main character's attitude towards women? How does it compare with attitudes portrayed by male characters in today's media?

5. How do you feel about the way cultural differences are dealt with in the novel, particularly in the chapter "Race in Ecotopia: Apartheid or Equality?"

6. Do you think the ritual war games would be a necessary part of life in a society like the one portrayed in *Ecotopia*? Why or why not?

7. Would you describe *Ecotopia* as good literature? Why or why not?

8. Would you describe *Ecotopia* as a utopia or a dystopia? Explain your answer.

In his reports back to New York, he describes and comments on every aspect of Ecotopian life from housing and transportation to economics and education. The novel provides a detailed and accessible model of a sustainable society and presents many ideas that students can use as a basis for their research. (See discussion questions in sidebar.) A word of caution: Ecotopia contains language and references to sex that some may find objectionable, and the quality of writing is less than exemplary.

Green city research

An online search using the following categories and search words will enable your students to find up-to-date information on the most important topics related to green cities:

Economy: eco-economics, economic sustainability

Education: environmental learning, green education

Energy Production and Conservation: alternative energy, climate change and cities, energy efficiency, solar energy, wind energy

Housing: energy-efficient housing, green buildings, indoor air quality, LEED standard

Public Spaces: livable communities, new urbanism

Transportation: energy-efficient transportation, urban transportation

Waste Management: living systems, solar-aquatic wastewater treatment, urban waste reduction

Project outcomes

Most classes show a keen interest in the concept of a green city and respond in a variety of ways to the assignment. One group chose to pattern their project after Callenbach's book, making their "Metrotopia" the capital city of a country based on ecologically sound values. Another group decided that urban dwellers should live underground and travel to and fro on above-ground transit systems that snake beneath a canopy of undisturbed natural forests. Their argument was that much of the necessary light could be brought underground by means of mirrored tubes based on principles of fiber optics. Not surprisingly, some students have

followed the old sci-fi idea of cities existing beneath transparent glass domes. This allows for natural light while also capitalizing on the ability of a glass building to retain heat.

Instead of designing their city from scratch, some students have chosen to retrofit an existing city for a more benign co-existence with nature. Many borrow an interesting idea from Callenbach's book, which is that creeks long ago buried in storm sewers should be brought back to the surface to run freely. The one common realization that nearly all students arrive at in the planning process is that "small" works better than "big," even on the scale of cities. Perhaps it is just a coincidence, or perhaps it just makes sense. One student even suggested that large cities should consist of many cells, or a series of smaller cities, interspersed within an area of green space.

As an increasingly urban society, it is imperative that we find more sustainable ways of designing human habitats. The green city project challenges students to think critically about the status quo, but most importantly it exposes them to emerging environmental technologies and provides opportunities for them to explore how our cities can work with, rather than against, the natural environment.

Iori Miller teaches at Leaside High School in Toronto, Ontario. Susan Sheard teaches with the York Region Board of Education at Sibbald Point Outdoor Education Centre near Jackson's Point, Ontario.

Resources

Bellini, James. *High Tech Holocaust.* Sierra Club Books, 1989. Investigates the environmental and human health costs of industrial technologies.

Benford, Gregory. *Timescape.* Spectra, 1980, 1992 (fiction). Recognizing that the world is on the brink of ecological collapse, a scientist tries to send a warning back in time to those who could prevent the worst from happening.

Butler, Octavia E. *Parable of the Sower.* Time Warner Publishing, 1995 (fiction). Fleeing from disease, out-of-control pollution and fires in a future Los Angeles, an 18-year-old black protagonist heads north with others to found a new society and a faith called "Earthseed."

Klee, Gary A. *World Systems of Traditional Resource Management.* V.H. Winston and Sons, 1980. A survey of cultures whose traditional practices enabled them to live in balance with their ecosystems.

Robinson, Stanley, ed. *Future Primitive: The New Ecotopias.* Tor Books, 1994 (fiction). An anthology of short science fiction stories that depict societies living in harmony with nature; includes stories by Gary Snyder, Robinson Jeffers, Gene Wolfe, Ursula LeGuin and Robert Silverberg.

Schumacher, E.F. *Small is Beautiful: Economics as if People Mattered.* Harper and Row and Blond and Briggs Ltd., 1973.

Kathy LaBranche

Exemplary Models and Programs

❀ **Global Field Trip** by Rosemary Ganley

❀ **Tips for Successful Overseas Projects** by Alana Robb

❀ **The Earth Community School** by Frans C. Verhagen

❀ **Soy-powered Learning** by Gail Littlejohn

❀ **The Steveston Fish Hatchery** by Bob Carkner and Barry Barnes

❀ **The Living Machine at Darrow School** by Lisa Riker

Global Field Trip

Global studies through immersion travel

Photographs by Hal Bowen, Jamaican Self-Help

by Rosemary Ganley

All meaningful global education begins in the imagination of teachers, those practical visionaries who infuse their daily work with the attitude that everything is connected and has significance. These teachers believe that the ability to critique the way things are is a necessary mental skill, and their greatest joy is to see their students take action for social justice.

Inspired by this teaching philosophy, I began leading groups of secondary students and teachers on awareness visits to Jamaica in 1984. These "field trips with soul" — two-week visits that offer first-hand exposure to a developing country — became for me the most exciting and challenging component of the school year. More than 800 youth from my area have now experienced this "southern exposure," and many

have later plunged into social justice work at all levels, both at home in Canada and in international non-governmental organizations (NGOs).

The Jamaica experience

Each trip is tailored to the participating school or group of schools, and planned and implemented in partnership with Jamaican Self-Help, a 28-year-old NGO in Peterborough, Ontario. As teachers, our goals for the visits are to give students opportunities to meet the people of Jamaica, to make friendships with people working for social justice, to become more culturally sensitive and adaptable, to think critically about North American consumer culture, and to have an opportunity for personal reflection. A typical group includes 15 students from ages 15 to 18 and a couple of teachers from different disciplines. After extensive pre-trip

preparation, the groups travel to Jamaica, spending two weeks in the capital city of Kingston or in a nearby town.

Each weekday, participants perform voluntary service at inner-city centers or farms. The work placements are arranged beforehand, and the students go in pairs and small groups to projects that Jamaican Self-Help supports financially. They are well received and integrated into the work, whether that be tutoring children, assisting at a health clinic, distributing food to seniors or cutting coffee or nutmeg on farms. They travel in group vans or taxis or on public transport. Evenings are spent in discussion and learning activities, in cultural outings and in dialogue with guest speakers on many aspects of Jamaican life. Weekends include some island travel, focusing on botany or topography, on industries such as bauxite production, and on the negative and positive effects of tourism.

Each of our awareness trips operates on a non-profit, cost-recovery basis. In 2008, the cost for the student is $2,100, which includes air fare from Toronto, accommodation, two meals a day, ground transportation and incidentals. A convent or hostel in Kingston provides us with safe, clean, affordable accommodation.

During their stay in Jamaica, the young visitors have many opportunities to encounter the paradoxes of global forces and their effects on the lives of vast numbers of people. Jamaica is a semi-developed country with great disparity among economic classes; grinding urban poverty and high unemployment; unequal access to good education; health, gender and race struggles; and a rapidly increasing population. The country also has newly emerging environmental concerns such as deforestation, exclusive beach devel-

opment and harmful fishing practices. Drugs and guns underlie an alarmingly high violent crime rate. At the same time, the country is blessed with a vigorous democracy, an energetic citizenry, articulate leaders, a free press, many fine schools, and a vibrant cultural and sport life. For students, the trip is an intensive study of issues of race, wealth, poverty, gender, class, gender, the environment and economics.

In "solidarity mode," we compare each Jamaican dilemma with a similar and equally difficult Canadian problem. The pain and confusion that some youth feel at some points in this deliberate encounter with a world of deprivation are borne in a community of support and shared lament. Debriefings take place daily, experiences are shared in both small and large groups, feelings are expressed, silent reflection and writing is encouraged, and readings are suggested. There are, equally, experiences of beauty, of a landscape endowed abundantly with wood and water, and a rich, vibrant culture struggling with some success against the McWorld monoculture.

Returning home

Upon their return, the groups meet with facilitators at one-week, three-week and then six-month intervals and are given opportunities to continue to develop as a globally-minded people. It is our hope that the participants will gradually transform into people resolved to join with others to make positive changes, personally and politically. Jamaican Self-Help welcomes our students as volunteers in various capacities, and now has a Youth Wing. Many schools and community groups invite returned participants to give presentations about their experiences — one group of 15 young people

spoke to 65 interested groups within one month of their return. We make an effort to help the students move from personal anecdote to analysis of the situations in which they worked, and to suggest to their audiences both the seriousness of the plights they saw and the actions that globally-minded people can take alleviate them.

In 1996 and again in 2000, Jamaica Self-Help asked 200 past participants if their Jamaican experience affected the choices they had made since. Their answers included the following: "I have more interest in different cultures"; "I am majoring in international studies at university"; "I became a medical doctor and am going overseas"; "I organized a `Think Fast' at my school"; "I am more sensitive to those in need at home"; "I have never taken a 15-minute shower since Jamaica."

Working with an NGO

In organizing such trips, working with a development NGO is crucial. These organizations can provide contacts and assist with pre- and post-trip activities. In our case, we teachers work with the Education Committee of Jamaican Self-Help. The committee sets the policies for the trips, recruits and trains leaders, provides at least one facilitator for the whole process, monitors and evaluates the trips, and reports back to Jamaican Self-Help. The teachers, for their part, report back to the school administration, trustees and parents. All partners seem to benefit from the collaboration: the schools by having a reliable infrastructure and experienced leaders to foster their learning objectives, the NGO by attracting attention and potential new supporters, and the local partners by sharing their

lives and work with genuinely interested visitors.

While Jamaica is our destination, many schools now offer short-term, service-learning trips to other developing countries, such as Guatemala, Mexico, the Dominican Republic and Haiti. Such trips are producing slow, deep-rooted change in communities and schools as hundreds of returning young adults tell their stories. Having experienced a wider world and seen both the effects of impoverishment and the potential for creative solutions, they are moving into decision-making roles, seeking to change unjust and unsustainable policies that affect people in both developing and developed countries. Their work is increasingly hailed by educators, leaders, politicians, the media and citizens.

Although the North-South dynamic is ever changing and deeply complex, our goals have remained constant. We seek to enter, with our students, into a situation that will provide what Salvadoran theologian Jon Sobrino calls "a long, loving look at the real." The central challenge is to manage the tension inherent in such projects in pursuit of a large and noble aim: a more hospitable world.

Rosemary Ganley is a retired teacher who is active in Jamaican Self-Help in Peterborough, Ontario, and serves on the Canadian Board of Amnesty International.

Resource organizations

Across North America, hundreds of youth groups in schools and communities raise public awareness about development issues and fundraise for projects in developing countries. In the United States, the non-profit New Global Citizens profiles development projects around the world and provides local groups with the tools to support whichever project they have selected. Whether organizing trips to a developing country, raising funds for projects or educating the local community about development issues,

Tips for Successful Overseas Projects

by Alana Robb

The following are things to consider when organizing student trips to developing countries.

1. At least one of the trip leaders must have experience in the destination country. The leaders must be knowledgeable, feel comfortable and be able to keep their cool and not show confusion.

2. Ensure that students have preparation and orientation. They should learn about the history, geography, economy, education system and religion of the destination country, as well as cross-cultural communication and some language of the country. Orientation should include patterns of trade, why development in the country may have been arrested, the impact of debt, and why material advances are difficult. In spite of such preparation, students are still likely to encounter the unexpected, but they will be ready for the experience.

3. Ensure that you have reliable contacts in the destination country and a mechanism whereby students can link with students as equals.

4. In addition to fundraising to defray travel costs, every trip should involve fundraising for a specific development project in the destination country. Allow students to choose the project they would like to assist with, preferably something basic and concrete, such as the purchase of fencing, equipment, a well or a boat. Once in the country, visit the site of the project so that students can see how a small amount of money can make a big difference in village life. Fundraising is an excellent way to gain community support and raise community awareness.

5. Allow students to reflect on their experience. Build debriefing sessions into the program during the visit as well as after returning. Discussing findings and reflecting on daily experiences during the visit helps to alleviate stress and culture shock and makes students more sensitive to their new environment. One way of debriefing after the trip is to have students make presentations to their classmates and others in the community.

6. Take utmost care to avoid any negative impact on the host country. Numbers of overzealous teenagers, however well intentioned, sweeping through a tiny country could have a negative impact on the inhabitants, especially the youth. The end result could be an enriching experience for the students but feelings of envy and resentment on the part of the hosts. The indiscriminate handing out of treats and gifts to children is strongly discouraged, as it creates an expectation that could mar future visits.

Alana Robb has lived and worked in Africa and China and is the Manager of International Student Services at Saint Mary's University in Halifax, Nova Scotia. These tips for overseas projects were suggested by **Burris Devanney**, *founder of the Nova Scotia–Gambia Association and leader of many student trips to that small West African country.*

local development organizations will be essential allies in your endeavors. National umbrella organizations such as the Canadian Council for International Co-operation or InterAction in the United States can put you in touch with those nearest you.

Contacts:

Canadian Council for International Cooperation, Ottawa, (613) 241-7007, <www.ccic.ca>.

InterAction: American Council for Voluntary International Action, Washington, DC, (202) 667-8227, <www.interaction.org>.

New Global Citizens, Phoenix, (602) 263-0500, <www.newglobalcitizens.org>.

The Earth Community School:

A back-to-basics model of secondary education

EARTH COMMUNITY SCHOOL

Illustrations by Tom Goldsmith

by Frans C. Verhagen

One of the main characteristics of the 21st century is the emergence of a sustainability revolution. Its momentous importance and challenge was perhaps best expressed by William D. Ruckelshaus, the first administrator of the U.S. Environmental Protection Agency, when he asked:

Can we move nations and people in the direction of sustainability? Such a move would be a modification of society comparable in scale to only two other changes: the Agricultural Revolution of the late Neolithic, and the Industrial Revolution of the past two centuries. These revolutions were gradual, spontaneous, and largely unconscious. This one will have to be a fully conscious operation,

guided by the best foresight that science can provide. If we actually do it, the undertaking will be absolutely unique in humanity's stay on earth.[1]

Yet while this revolution is taking place, education continues to operate with little acknowledgment of its urgency, in what C.A. Bowers has termed a "culture of denial" of the ecological dimension.[2] We must ask: Where do we want our society to go and how do we organize our educational enterprise to make young people response-able and responsible to the social, economic and environmental goals of the sustainability revolution?

While teaching Earth Science to eighth graders in the New York City Public School System, I developed a practical ideal of "Earth-literate" secondary education called the Earth Community School (ECS) model. The model is based on the assumption of a need to shift from an anthropocentric to a biocentric mode of instruction and learning, and from traditional subject area curricula to an integrated curriculum that has sustainability as its organizing principle. Like all educational models, the Earth Community School model is a work in progress. The following is an outline of its goals, organizing principle and components, and some suggestions for its implementation.

The integrated goals of the Earth Community School model are:

- to contribute to societal goals of fostering sustainable, just and participatory communities and societies

- to help young people to develop Earth literacy, a perspective or set of values with which to respond to the major social and ecological challenges of the present and the future

- to help making the sustainability challenge the guiding principle of the curriculum

Organizing principle: contextual sustainability

The organizing principle of the ECS model is contextual sustainability, which is defined as ecological sustainability within the context of social justice and participatory decision-making. Contextual sustainability is a bridging concept that recognizes the reciprocal relationship between the ecological and social worlds, the environmental and peace movements, and human-human and human-Earth mediations. Its main elements are:

Ecological Sustainability: An ecologically sustainable society is one that lives within the boundaries of Earth's carrying capacity and acts to restore and protect the health and biodiversity of local and global ecosystems.

Social Justice: Social justice refers to equitable, fair or right relations, both personal and systemic, between humans. Gross poverty and gross affluence are major causes of ecological degradation; without social justice, ecological sustainability is impossible.

Participatory Decision-making: Neither ecological sustainability nor social justice will be realized if it is not owned by those who are affected. The Earth Community School model places great value on the wide and diverse participation of parents, students and the whole school community in charting the basic direction of the school and making associated decisions.

Components of the ECS model

The Earth Community School model's guiding principle of contextual sustainability can be applied to any level of education, but the following six components apply to the secondary level.

1. An integrated core curriculum that promotes Earth literacy

Earth literacy has two main characteristics: Earth awareness and Earth care.[3] Thus an Earth Community School's core curriculum reflects and is organized in respect to interconnected ecological and social challenges on the local and global levels (Earth awareness); and it leads the school community forward in developing the attitudes and skills to deal with those eco-social challenges (Earth care). A corollary of Earth literacy is that students would come to identify themselves as members, not masters or even stewards of the web of life. Young people must be helped to incorporate in their definition of self the concept of ecological self; this is most important for secondary school students, who are very much engaged in a search of who they are.[4]

In contrast to an interdisciplinary approach, where topics are divided among disciplines, in an integrated curriculum topics are analyzed into various themes or concepts and these themes translated into activities. Thus if the topic of air quality were chosen for a semester, activities would be developed for such themes as air pollution and monitoring. Some activities would include more social studies content, while others would favor science. Typically, arts, language and math would be used in any of them.

2. Eco-efficient school operations

An important part of the ECS model is the application of Earth literacy to school operations. Students, teachers, and administrative and custodial staff work together to develop procedures to ensure the efficient and frugal use of water, energy, paper and other resources. Making students more responsible for the physical environment of the school might even include, as is done in some Asian countries, cleaning classrooms and other areas of the school.

3. A vital mission statement and associated curriculum committee

An Earth Community School should have a mission statement that reflects and directs the curriculum, the operations and the life of the school. This statement of purpose must be owned by the school community as a whole, and this is possible only when it is the outcome of a well-planned process in which all stakeholders

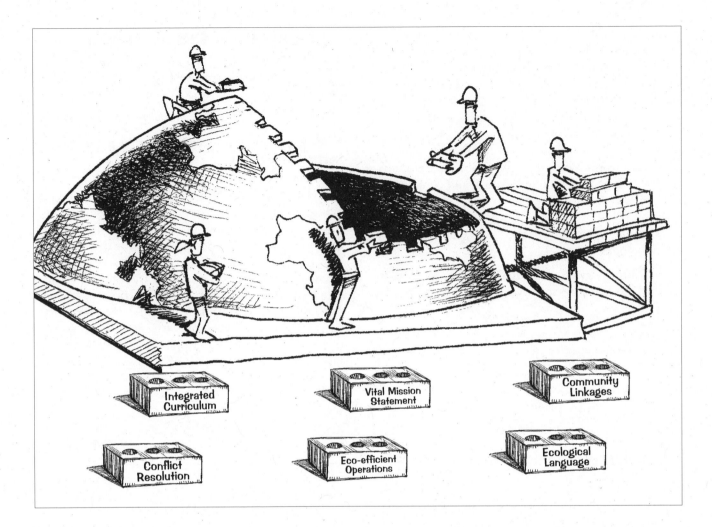

Integrated
Curriculum

Vital Mission
Statement

Community
Linkages

Conflict
Resolution

Eco-efficient
Operations

Ecological
Language

reach consensus on the basics and develop an esprit de corps. This process may take several years. The stronger the consensus on fundamentals, the faster the edifice of an Earth Community School can be built. The process of mission clarification, monitoring and development would be the responsibility of a school-wide curriculum committee.

4. Community linkage

Emphasizing the relationship between the school and the local community, Earth Community Schools engage in activities such as assisting those in need, participating in beautification projects, planting trees, and monitoring the quality of local water, soil and air. Such activities would be part of an effort to develop sustainable communities that reflect the integrated social and ecological values of the Earth Charter.

5. Creative conflict resolution

An ECS curriculum contains programs that deal with preventing violence and resolving conflict among humans, between humans and animals, and between humans and Earth.

6. Ecologically robust language

Language reflects and constructs our values, ideology and world views.[5] In an Earth Community School, students learn how language perpetuates the dominance of anthropocentric biases and are taught new grammatical and lexical strategies which make language the carrier of a biocentric world view.[6]

Implementation of the ECS model

Implementation of the Earth Community School model would ideally take place on three levels: teacher-classroom, school-parents-community, and district-state/province-federal. The more immediately promising is the school-parents-community level, particularly in jurisdictions where the emergence of the charter school movement is giving schools, parents and communities greater flexibility to experiment. The adoption of the model at the district-state/province-federal level will occur only if subsidiary levels exert pressure for such an educational strategy.

The implementation of the ECS model very much depends on the leadership of the principal or of a team composed of parents and staff. This school leadership team must be willing to engage in the challenging process of rethinking the ideological foundations of educational strategies, of initiating a process of faculty discussion towards the development of a vital mission statement, and of establishing a school curriculum committee that will safeguard, monitor and develop that mission statement. The following actions are suggested to teachers who want to contribute to the model's implementation at their secondary school.

1. Rethink and refine one's perspective in order to shift from environmental education that is anthropocentric to an Earth literacy that is biocentric, and uses Earth-friendly language.

2. Develop an introductory, perspective-building Earth literacy module that will tie the rest of the year together. Lesson plans could include titles such as "Valuing the Earth," "Befriending the Earth" and "Becoming an Earth-literate person." Work with teachers in other subject areas to make the Earth literacy module more universal.

3. Initiate a meaningful process for developing a mission statement.

4. Organize an Earth Assembly program, either for a whole grade or for the whole school that deals with a major environmental challenge, such as clean air or waste prevention.

5. Have students write reports on those assemblies or on Earth literacy topics as part of the school's literacy program, or have them become involved in environmental projects in the community with local private or public organizations.

6. Network with educators outside of the school and communicate your ECS experiences in magazines and union newsletters, at conferences, etc.

7. Be alert to the possibilities that present themselves both inside and outside the school during this time of flux in educational practice and theory. For instance, when giving feedback on curriculum frameworks or new programs, add the word "ecological" alongside terms such as social and economic.

8. Above all, persist, being convinced of the importance of the Earth Community approach both for people and for the planet.

Never before has humanity so urgently needed a perspective that sustains the Earth rather than works against her. Never before has there been such a need for knowledge of willingness to live in harmony with Earth's systems and all other life forms. The Earth Community School is an ultimate "back to basics" model, constituting a challenge for any educational system that earnestly intends to contribute to eco-social revitalization within the 21st century's emerging sustainability revolution.

Frans C. Verhagen is a sociologist who directs Sustainability Research and Education at Earth and Peace Education Associates International and teaches a course on Sustainable Communities at Pace University in New York City.

Notes

1. William D. Ruckelshaus, quoted by David R. Boyd, *Sustainability within a Generation: A New Vision for Canada*, The David Suzuki Foundation, 2004, p. v.

2. C.A. Bowers, *The Culture of Denial: Why the Environmental Movement Needs a Strategy for Reforming Universities and Public Schools*, State University of New York Press, 1997.

3. D. Orr, *Ecological Literacy: Education and the Transition to a Postmodern World*, State University of New York Press, 1992.

4. Mitchell Thomashow, *Ecological Identity: Becoming a Reflective Environmentalist*, MIT Press, 1995.

5. C. Schaeffner and A. Wenden, eds., *Language and Peace*, Dartmouth Press, 1999.

6. F. Verhagen, "Ecolinguistics: A Retrospective and Prospective," in *Festschrift Fill 2000*, B. Ketteman, H. Penze, eds., Stauffenburg Verlag, 2000; and G.M. Jacobs et al, *Linking Language and the Environment: Greening the ESL Classroom*, Pippin Publishing, 1998.

References

Beane, J. A. *Curriculum Integration: Designing the Core of a Democratic Education*. Teachers College Press, 1997.

Beyer, L. E. and M. W. Apple. *The Curriculum: Problems, Politics, and Possibilities*. State University of New York Press, 1998.

Edwards, A. R. *The Sustainability Revolution: Portrait of a Paradigm Shift*. New Society Publishers, 2005.

Hawken, P. *Blessed Unrest: How the Largest Social Movement in History is Restoring Grace, Justice and Beauty to the World*. Penguin Books, 2007.

Rasmussen, L. *Earth Community, Earth Ethics*. Maryknoll, 1996.

Wenden, A. *Education for a Culture of Social and Ecological Peace*. State University of New York Press, 2004. The contextual sustainability educational framework is fully described in this book, which also has chapters dealing with value clarification and development.

Soy-powered Learning

Students monitoring the soybean crop and extracting oil from hand-harvested beans.

Photographs by Joe Lindbloom

by Gail Littlejohn

For several years, biodiesel fueled the engines of learning at Oak Forest High School in Oak Forest, Illinois, when teachers of plant science, chemistry, physics and technology joined forces in an interdisciplinary research project on the use of soybean oil as an environment-friendly fuel.

When the first crop of soybeans was planted behind the school in 1999, Dawn Sasek's plant science students became hands-on agronomists in their own living laboratory, experimenting with seed varieties, fertilizers and cultivation methods to increase yields. Each fall, they harvested their crop by hand, dried the soybeans and then pressed them to extract their oil (the first press was designed and built in the school's industrial technology department). The raw soybean oil then went to the chemistry lab, where Laurel Dieskow's students synthesized and purified it into a methyl ester (biodiesel). In an effort to increase both the quantity and quality of the fuel, the students learned advanced procedures in chemical analysis, such as gas chromatography.

The proof, however, was in the propulsion. To test the fuel's performance, Joe Lindbloom's physics students, together with Bill Farley's industrial technology students and members of an after-school Energy Club, designed a unique hybrid diesel-electric system for a 1999 Volkswagen Beetle that was donated to the project. Testing the car on the school track gave opportunities for investigating such topics as fuel efficiency, power outputs, and the complex energy conversion components of hybrid systems.

The bean-to-Beetle project engaged science and technology students in a real-world application of their learning and revved up curricula in several subject areas. Industrial technology students modified the gas-powered rototiller used to plow the school's soybean field so that it would run on biodiesel. Biology students practiced field study techniques by gathering data on soybean growth and creating spreadsheets for analysis. Students interested in the economics of soybeans visited the Chicago Board of Trade and regularly "bought" and "sold" soybeans through a New York company that operates a mock commodities

Left: Batches of biodiesel separated by density. Right: Installing a hybrid diesel-electric engine in a donated Volkswagen Beetle.

exchange for students. Other students wrote articles for local newspapers, made presentations to community groups and helped in writing grant applications. A sister school developed a project involving GPS (global positioning system) mapping, which had students tracking rainfall and other variables that affect soybeans, an important crop in Illinois.

"We were like pioneers," says Joe Lindbloom, referring to this interdisciplinary project approach to learning. "The questions and problems were there, but the answers and solutions were open-ended .... It's the way education should be."

Gail Littlejohn is co-editor of Green Teacher *magazine in Toronto, Ontario. The Oak Forest High School biodiesel project ran for several years from 1999, and ended with the retirement of key teachers.*

Reference

Richard Mitchell, "Fuel Your Curriculum," *The Science Teacher*, November 2000, pp. 30-33.

The Steveston Fish Hatchery

Building and operating a fish hatchery links students to the fate of the world's fish stocks

Photographs by Steveston Secondary School

by Bob Carkner and Barry Barnes

For almost 20 years, a fish hatchery at Steveston Secondary School in Richmond, British Columbia, trained young biologists and contributed to the enhancement of salmon stocks on Canada's west coast. When it opened on March 1, 1988, the school's unique 25,000-egg salmon hatchery was lauded by the federal Fisheries and Oceans department as "the most complex school hatchery program in North America." By the time the school closed nearly 20 years later, the hatchery had exceeded everyone's expectations: 120,850 salmon fry had been released into local rivers; more than 400 students and hundreds of community members had volunteered their time in

hatchery operations; and dozens of groups had visited the hatchery each year to learn about the care, feeding, life cycle and habitat needs of salmon.

Many species of mammals, birds and fish rely on salmon as a major food source, and they are prized by both commercial and recreational fishers. Yet some salmon species have declined steeply in recent years due to a multitude of problems, including the destruction of stream habitat through urbanization, industrial pollution and careless logging practices, and conflict between the United States and Canada over appropriate fish catch quotas.

In 1983, as part of the Canada's Salmonid Enhancement Program, 1,000 coho salmon eggs were hatched in Steveston Secondary School's biology

Operations began each year with collecting eggs from chinook salmon caught in the Chilliwack River.

classrooms and released as fry into a North Vancouver creek. The following year, 1,500 eggs were hatched, and by 1985 enthusiasm for a full-scale facility was growing. Funded by the school board, a provincial lottery and various donors, the hatchery was built over a period of two years, with 95 percent of the work being done by Grade 11 and 12 construction students. The 10-meter by 30-meter building, adjacent to the school's science wing, was divided into two areas: one housed the water troughs in which the fry developed over a five- to six-month period; the other was a teaching lab for the many groups that used the hatchery. The facility operated entirely on a recirculating water system, a design feature necessitated by the fact that there were no freshwater streams in the area. Eighteen thousand liters of spring water were trucked in each fall to start the system, and for the next six months this water was continuously filtered, purified and recycled. The cost of building such a facility today is about $250,000, but with equipment and most labor donated, the school district's investment was limited to a $40,000 start-up grant.

The eggs that began each year's brood came from live chinook salmon that were caught in the Chilliwack River about 80 kilometers to the east and brought to the school in a tank trailer. In the final, spawning phase of their life cycle, the fish were netted from the tank and killed quickly with a blow to the head. The eggs were removed from the females, and the sperm squeezed from the males and mixed with the eggs. The eggs were then rinsed and placed in incubating trays, where they hatched at around six weeks. The newly hatched young, called alevins, retained a large yolk sac as an energy source, and as this was absorbed, they became free-swimming. At around 12 weeks, they

were transferred to troughs, where they grew until they were released at about 35 weeks.

The fish were released in the spring, usually mid-May, the time when young salmon "smolt," a process of hormonal and enzyme change that adapts them for the move from fresh water to the ocean. By waiting until this time, we ensured that the young fry would be in the stream for only a short time and not displace any naturally occurring fish species by competing for food. We released the fish about 50 kilometers from the school in a tributary of the Nicomekl River, a stream that historically had a good run of salmon but which, prior to restoration, had been degraded to the point that the run died out. Young salmon become imprinted on the smell of a stream in just a few days, and it is the sense of smell that leads them back to the same stream to spawn and die after four years in the ocean. On average, over 100 of each season's smolts eventually made their way back as adults, a return that is consistent with the percentage return of wild populations and was more than adequate for the size of the stream.

The day-to-day work of operating the hatchery was done entirely by student volunteers in the school's Hatchery Club. Each day during the start-up phase, and three times a week thereafter, the water was tested for pH, temperature, hardness, oxygen and ammonia. Daily maintenance took about one hour and included cleaning the tanks, filling the food dispensers and changing the foam sheets in the water filters. Students also weighed and measured the fish to ensure that they were developing within normal criteria. These observations helped to determine the overall fitness of the fish and how much food must be supplied.

In addition to running the hatchery, the students took field trips to facilities such as fish farms, fish

Left: The continuously circulating water in the hatchery was tested three times each week.
Right: Hatchery-raised salmon fry were transported to a stream for release.

processing plants, and federal and volunteer hatcheries. Visits to other hatcheries allowed them to validate that what they were doing was correct, and to compare techniques and get ideas for improving the running of the school hatchery. Through such visits, students also came to see themselves as equals in a network of fisheries experts, most of whom are adults who are paid for their work; and they often took on the role of teachers as they explained our recirculating water system.

To take advantage of the educational opportunities afforded by having an on-site hatchery, a Grade 11 Aquaculture course used the hatchery as a built-in laboratory. Students learned husbandry techniques and devised experiments, such as increasing the water flow and observing the effects on growth rate or fitness. Aquaculture students and Hatchery Club members were given priority admission to some related junior college programs, and some found careers in federal hatcheries.

The hatchery was visited annually by more than 30 community and school groups who learned about the life cycle and habitat of salmon and had an exciting feeding-time tour of the tanks. The hatchery was the coordination center for the distribution of eggs to local elementary schools that participated in the Salmonids in the Classroom Project. In addition, Steveston students produced display vials showing each of the first four stages of the life cycle — egg, eyed egg, alevin and fry. Specimens were preserved in formaldehyde in vials that were sealed with silicone

and made available to educators as lesson aids through the provincial teachers' federation.

On one level the story of the Steveston Salmon Hatchery was about salmon enhancement, but on another level it was about developing strategies and projects that helped our students and community more fully understand the environmental issues that are affecting the survival of species on this planet. While a project such as the Steveston Salmon Hatchery is an enormously ambitious undertaking, it is also affirmation of the great things that can be accomplished when a group of dedicated students, teachers and community members work together toward a worthwhile goal.

Bob Carker was the former principal of Steveston High School in Richmond, British Columbia, and is now retired. Barry Barnes was a biology teacher at the school and now teaches at the Faculty of Education at the University of British Columbia in Vancouver. Both were founding members and instrumental in the development of the hatchery.

Resources

The following agencies can offer advice and technical expertise on starting a school fish hatchery or other aquaculture project:

Canada: Contact the federal Department of Fisheries and Oceans or the provincial/territorial Ministry of Natural Resources.

United States: Contact the U.S. Fish & Wildlife Service or the state Department of Natural Resources or Sea Grant agency.

The Living Machine at Darrow School

At a rural high school in the Berkshire Mountains of New York, a glorious greenhouse full of tropical plants is treating wastewater and transforming the curriculum

Photographs by Lisa Riker

by Lisa Riker

At Darrow School in New Lebanon, New York, we are proud of what most people would never dream of talking about: our wastewater. Since 1998, our Living Machine — a series of beautiful plant-filled tanks housed in a greenhouse — has treated all of the wastewater from the dining hall, academic buildings and most of the dormitories in this co-educational boarding school of 140 people.

Before the Living Machine was installed, wastewater went into septic tanks and leach fields, but no one knew any longer how old these were or even where they were. By the early 1990s, we recognized that if we weren't already polluting our environment, we soon would be. In investigating new wastewater treatment solutions, the school administrators became interested in "green"

systems that would be more environmentally sustainable than traditional wastewater treatment methods. Ultimately, we decided to build a Living Machine designed by the environmental engineering company Living Machines, Inc. We had been impressed with their demonstration project in South Burlington, Vermont, a Living Machine that processes 80,000 gallons of wastewater per day. We were also pleased that we would have whatever technical support might be needed. More importantly, we were excited about the idea of a wastewater facility that does its job without chemicals and without polluting the environment around it.

A school makes a pretty dramatic statement when it puts a wastewater treatment plant in the middle of its campus. Not only does it represent a shift from the traditional idea that waste should be hidden, but it has

a distinct effect on the physical plant and on the way people think about what goes down the drain. A Living Machine is an aesthetically pleasing, conspicuous facility. There is no question that something important is happening inside a greenhouse that houses tanks full of glorious tropical plants. It just hums with life. It leads to questions about the environment and raises everyone's consciousness. No longer can anyone be shy about discussing waste, nor can anyone prefer to think that wastewater magically disappears.

Our Samson Environmental Center houses the Living Machine and a classroom space that is used for visiting groups and in-house presentations. The total price tag of US$1.2 million covered the construction and engineering costs, the new classroom space, and the entire collection system that feeds wastewater to the Living Machine from the buildings on campus. While this is large amount of money, a good portion of that expenditure would have been necessary even if we had replaced the traditional septic tank and leach field system. Furthermore, raising the funds was not as difficult as one might imagine, since a Living Machine is a unique and compelling project with a tangible end product that is very useful and educational. Being a private school, we drew upon the support of our alumni, who donated most of the money raised for the project; but we also received grants from foundations whose evaluators were impressed by the Living Machine's educational and outreach possibilities. We

host a great many visits by elementary school children, high school science classes, college students and interested parties from other communities. As a result, many of our students have become experts in ecological wastewater treatment.

Engineers from Living Machines, Inc. were at the school during the start-up of the system and stayed until they were assured that we could handle the daily monitoring and operation. They made quarterly return visits during the first year of operation and have since provided technical support over the phone. Because it is a wastewater treatment plant, we were required by the state to have certified operators on site. Our Physical Plant Director and I obtained certification as Class 1 WWTP (wastewater treatment plant) operators. However, I am happy to say that most of what I learned in my wastewater treatment courses does not apply to our work with the Living Machine. Most of my interaction with it is hands-off: I generally walk once a day through the greenhouse just to make sure that everything looks, sounds and smells (or rather doesn't smell!) as it should. Students help me by monitoring the dissolved oxygen in the tanks, keeping track of daily flow, and feeding the fish that live in our display pond at the end of our Living Machine. Rather than being merely data gatherers, the students are the true eyes and ears of the facility, and they become so knowledgeable about the system that they often know when something isn't quite right. It

Inside the Living Machine

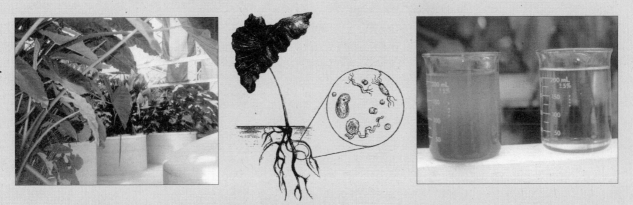

Left: Open aerobic tanks inside the Living Machine create a humming oasis of tropical plants. Center: Microbes thrive and propagate on the surfaces of submerged plant roots, feasting on passing nutrients. Right: Wastewater before and after treatment.

At Darrow School, wastewater begins its journey through the Living Machine at an underground tank outside the greenhouse. Somewhat like a septic tank, it is an anaerobic (without oxygen) environment where solids settle and armies of anaerobic bacteria begin to break down the organic material. The wastewater is then pumped into the greenhouse to a closed, partially aerated tank. Here, smelly gases are vented through a carbon filter, which absorbs odors, and aerobic bacteria begin to take over the work of digesting the waste. Next, it's onto a series of five open, aerated tanks filled with plants, snails and a multitude of waste-eating microorganisms. As the water circulates in the tanks, billions of microbes clinging to plant roots make their living by digesting organic material

that swirls past. In the process, they transform organic molecules into essential plant nutrients that are taken up by the plants.

The second-to-last stop is a clarifier, which separates any remaining solids and recycles them back to the anaerobic tank to begin the process all over again. Treated wastewater flows on to a "polisher" where plants, bacteria and filters work together to remove any organic material that remains. The finished water is not pure enough to drink, but it is clean enough for flushing toilets, watering gardens or dispersing into underground beds. The wastewater's journey takes about four days, from the time it flushes down a toilet in the dormitory to when it emerges as clean water at the end of the Living Machine.

provides them with an opportunity to take ownership of a process that is critical to our lives on this site.

The Living Machine has also become a vibrant science laboratory. For example, it provides the perfect segue into systems thinking for ninth grade students studying environmental science. They design their own "Biosphere," learn basic water-quality tests for monitoring the Living Machine, and use daily flow data to learn how to represent data graphically. There is a wonderful food chain in the system, complete with bacteria, rotifers and stalked ciliates for the Biology students to study during a unit on microorganisms. The tropical plants have great cells to study and are a good resource for the study of photosynthesis. Both the Biology and Chemistry classes study nutrient cycling. Our Stream Ecology class spends the semester studying a local stream and performing water-quality tests. They then transfer that knowledge to the Living

Machine and compare it to a riparian system. The Botany and Botanical Drawing class has a plethora of species to choose from and has worked on a field guide for the plants in the Living Machine.

Integrating environmental sustainability into our curriculum has been a gradual yet deliberate process, with much work done through in-house faculty education. When the system was first built ten years ago, we debated whether treating our wastewater would or would not make us an "environmental" school. Three years later, the faculty entered into an impassioned discussion of the definition of environmental sustainability and how our curriculum would live up to our ideas. It was exciting that, as a faculty, we were actually arguing about the use of such terms as "carrying capacity" and "natural ecosystems." We had come so far in a few short years!

Beyond science, our Political Economy students

Darrow students give tours of the system and monitor water quality and flow rates.

learn about different types of governments, market systems, supply and demand — the usual topics that one would expect to find in such a course. In addition, we tackle the subject of environmental economics and the idea of putting a price tag on ecological services. Ultimately, the students develop their own set of environmental sustainability indicators. Another course we are excited about is Environmental Ethics, which all seniors must take. In our never-ending quest to prepare our students for college and life, we require them to give a formal presentation at the end of the course and we open the presentations up to the wider community.

While we have made much progress toward becoming environmentally sustainable, we do not want anyone to think that we are finished. We must still remove bio-solids from a settling tank and dispose of them offsite. While we could have closed this loop by treating them in a reed bed, this would have added to the initial cost

of the system and we were not sure we could afford it at the time. More recently, in partnership with the New York State Energy Research and Development Authority, we installed a two-kilowatt photovoltaic array on the roof of the environmental center classroom to offset the energy use of the Living Machine. While we still face many challenges, the Living Machine has put us on the road to modeling environmental sustainability through our curricular and living decisions.

Lisa Riker is the former Director of the Samson Environmental Center (SEC) at Darrow School in New Lebanon, New York. She is currently the Chair of both the Science and Mathematics departments at The Hewitt School in New York City.

For more information about Darrow School, contact Craig Westcott, Director of the Samson Environmental Center, (518) 794-6000. For more information about Living Machines, contact Worrell Water Technologies in Charlottesville, Virginia, at (434) 973–6365, <www.livingmachines.com>.

Index

A

Acid-base titration, 68
Airlifts and pumps, 71, 84, 87
Air quality
    and driving, 150-153
    monitoring, 58-63
Algae
    excessive growth, 50
    identifying, 49-50
Ammonia, 89
Aquaponics, 89
Aquarium, set-up, 70-74
Aquatic
    ecosystems, 46-52, 77,
        82-90, 91-94
    habitat, 47-48
    life, 41-42, 46
ArcView and ArcGIS, 189
Argument analysis, 19-21
Art, pottery, 183-186
Artifact study, 176
Audit, resource and waste, 44,
    104-108
Automobile emissions, 79, 151

B

Bill of Rights, activity, 115-116
Biochemical oxygen demand,
    81, 89
Biodiesel
    making, 139-140, 141-145,
        216-217
    teaching about, 139-140
Biodiversity, 77, 83, 89
Bio-indicators, 58-63
Biological monitoring, 58-63
Biomimicry, 33, 40-41
Bioremediation, 41, 83, 89
Breathing walls, 41
Buildings, green, 177-181

Business education
    partnerships, 36-39

C

Carbon cycle, 64, 65
Carbon dioxide flux, 64-69
Cars, eco-tips, 150-153
Catalytic converter, 151
Cells, living system, 87
Change, managing, 4-5
Chemical Handling (course),
    37
Chemistry, small-scale, 146-149
Clay, pottery making, 183-186
Community
    involvement, 29-30, 36-39
    mapping, 156-160
    observation walks, 173-176
Conservation
    in building construction,
        179
    of water resources, 46-52
Construction, green homes,
    177-181
Consumer awareness, 127-132
Controversial issues, 18-21,
    194, 196, 197
Convergence, 11-12
Cooperative
    education, 36-39
    poem, 168
Creative problem solving, 10-17
Critical thinking, 18-21
Cultural sites, mapping, 156-160

D

Data sources, GIS, 189
Debates
    industrial hemp, 133-138
    lake management, 51-52
Degree Confluence Project, 189

Demystification strategy, 19-21
Design
    ecological, 41-42
    of green cities, 202-206
Disability, 161-164
Dissolved oxygen, 81, 89
Divergence, 12-14
Driving, green tips, 150-153
Duck banding, 55

E

Earth Charter, 165-172
Earth Community School,
    212-215
Ecological
    design, 41-42
    economics, 96-102
    footprint, 103-107, 194
Economics, 96-102, 114-117
Ecosystems
    characteristics of, 23
    classroom models, 42, 82-90
Ecotopia, 205
Electrolysis, 148
Emissions
    vehicle, 79, 151
    nitrogen, 76
Employment, 36-39
Energy
    audit, 44, 104, 106, 107
    conservation, 179
Engine idling, 151-152
English literature, 191-196,
    197-201
Environmental
    assessment, 38, 117-119,
        123, 188
    building design, 177-181
    industries program, 36-39
    literature, 191-196
    projects, creating, 12-17

Equality Tag, 167-169
Eutrophication, 47-52
Expository writing, 200
Externalities, economic, 99

F

Fair trade, 129
False analogies, 20
Fertilizers, 76-79
Field study
    skills, 28-31
    special education, 162-165
Filters, aquarium, 71
Fish
    curriculum links, 73-74
    school hatchery, 218-220
    selecting for aquarium, 72-73
Flux, carbon dioxide, 64-69
Freshwater aquarium, 70-74
Fuel
    biodiesel, 139-140, 141-145
    fossil, 76-77
Future thinking, 2-9, 43,
    110-113

G

Games
    Equality Tag, 167-169
    Land Game, The, 116-117
    Planet Transit, 121-126
Garbage audit, 104-108
Gas collection, 148
Genuine Progress Indicator, 100
Geo-caching, 189
Geographic information systems,
    187-190
Globe, Earth Charter, 170-171
Green
    buildings, 177-181, 205
    cities, 202-206
    driving, 150-153
    maps, 156-160
Greenhouse effect, 65

Green Map System, 156-160
Gross Domestic Product, 97,
    99-100

H

Habitat
    of lakes, 47
    schoolyard, 44
Hatchery, fish, 218-220
Hemp debate, 133-138
How Green Is Your School?,
    106
Human rights, 114-120
Human-scale education, 31-35

I

Iceberg model, 6
Indicator species, 59-61
Indigenous arts, 183-186
Indoor
    air quality, 179
    climate regulation, 41
Industrial hemp, 132-138
Industries
    construction, 177-178
    co-op education program,
        36-39
    and environment, 121-126
Inquiry, interdisciplinary
    projects, 25-27
Integrated learning, 22-27,
    28-30, 31-35, 56, 213
Integrated Studies in Systems,
    22-27
Interviewing, 29
Invasive species, 47
Issues, controversial, 18-21

J

Jamaican Self-Help, 208
Journals, nature, 191-193

L

Laboratory
    co-op education course, 37
    small-scale chemistry,
        146-149
Ladder of influence, 7
Lake management, 46-52
Land Game, The, 116-117
Land journals, 192-193
Language arts, 191-196,
    197-201
Lichens, as bio-indicators,
    58-63
Life cycle analysis, product, 98,
    117-120
Literature
    environmental, 191-196
    and social justice, 197-201
Living Machine, 221-224
Living systems, 40-44, 82-90
Lord of the Flies, 198-199

M

Manufacturing Challenge
    (activity), 101
Mapping
    GIS, 187-188
    Green Maps, 156-160
    walks, 175
Maquiladoras, 129
Marijuana, 135
Materials, green building,
    179-181
Mechanistic thinking, 8
Meditation, Earth Charter, 172
Mental models and worldviews,
    3, 6, 7, 43
Microbes, in soil, 65
Microscale science, 146-149
Models
    Earth Community School,
        213-214
    Ecosystem, 42, 82-90
    Green City, 202-206

Monitoring
   air quality, 58-63
   CO_2 flux from soil, 64-67
   protocols, 61
   water quality, 48-49, 92-93

N

Native American arts, 183-186
Nature writing, 191-196
Nitrates, in lakes, 49-51
Nitrifying bacteria, 83
Nitrogen
   fixation, 75
   pollution, 75-81
Non-governmental
   organizations, 210
Nutrients, excess, 48-51, 77, 79

O

Oak, Joke, Croak exercise, 7
Observation skills, 173-176, 190
Oral history, 29
Osborn, Alex, 10
Outdoor skills, 28-30
Overseas projects, tips, 211
Oxidation, in soil, 65
Oxygen demand, 81, 89

P

Paradigms, 6, 7, 43
Phosphate, excess, 48-51, 89
Phytoremediation, 82-90
Planet Transit game, 121-126
Poetry, 168, 199-200
Pond project, problem solving,
   11
Poster, product life-cycle analysis,
   119
Pottery making, 183-186
Problem solving, 10-17, 29-30
Product life cycles, 98, 114-120
Public education, 55-56
Publishing, by students, 29, 200

R

Rafts, in river monitoring,
   91-93
Residential construction,
   177-181
Respiration, soil, 64-69
Rights, human, 114-110
Rivers, monitoring, 91-94
RiverWatch program, 91-94
Role play
   Debate About Hemp,
      133-138
   Lake Management Debate,
      51-52

S

Salmon hatchery, 218-220
Science, small-scale, 147-149
Scientific protocols, 61
Sensory walks, 175
Small School, The, 31-35
Social impact assessment, 38
Social justice, 114-120,127-131
   and literature, 197-201
Soil respiration, 64-69
Soybeans, 216-217
Special education, 161-164
Survey, green school, 106
Sustainability, 2-9, 43, 213
Systems thinking, 7-8, 22-27, 43

T

Tag, Equality, 168-169
Tamarack program, 28-30
Tanks, aquarium, 71
Thumb wrestling exercise, 7
Titration, 68, 142
Trade and environment,
   114-120, 127-131
Trades, environmental
   co-op education, 36-39
   green construction, 177-181
Transesterification, 139, 142
Travel, global, 208-211

U

Urban design, 202-206

V

Vegetable oil, biodiesel from,
   141-145
Vehicles, green driving tips,
   150-153
Visioning, 4-5, 8-9, 110-113

W

Walks, observation, 173-176
Waste
   audit, 104-109
   management, 103-109, 163
Wastewater treatment, 41, 52,
   89, 93, 221-224
Watch Where You Step activity,
   8
Water
   management, 46-52
   monitoring and testing,
      48-49, 92-93
   purification, 41, 82-90,
      221-24
Water use conflicts, 51-52
Watersheds
   characteristics of, 46
   models of, 163
Weaving, 185
Web of Life activity, 163
Well plates, 147-148
Wetland education, 53-57
Wildlife walks, 175
Word association exercise, 6
Work placements, 39
Worldviews, 3
Writing, 29, 192-193, 201